Tax Sovereignty in the BEPS Era

Series on International Taxation

VOLUME 60

Series Editors

Prof. Ruth Mason, University of Virginia School of Law
Prof. Dr Ekkehart Reimer, University of Heidelberg

Introduction & Contents

The Series on International Taxation deals with a wide variety of topics in the global tax arena. The authors include many of the field's leading experts as well as talented newcomers. Their expert views and incisive commentary has proven highly useful to practitioners and academics alike.

Objective

The volumes published in this series are aimed at offering high-quality analytical information and practical solutions for international tax practitioners.

Readership

Practitioners, academics and policy makers in international tax law.

Frequency of Publication

2-3 new volumes published each year.

The titles published in this series are listed at the end of this volume.

Tax Sovereignty in the BEPS Era

Edited by

Sergio André Rocha
Allison Christians

Published by:
Kluwer Law International B.V.
PO Box 316
2400 AH Alphen aan den Rijn
The Netherlands
Website: www.wolterskluwerlr.com

Sold and distributed in North, Central and South America by:
Wolters Kluwer Legal & Regulatory U.S.
7201 McKinney Circle
Frederick, MD 21704
United States of America
Email: customer.service@wolterskluwer.com

Sold and distributed in all other countries by:
Quadrant
Rockwood House
Haywards Heath
West Sussex
RH16 3DH
United Kingdom
Email: international-customerservice@wolterskluwer.com

MIX
FSC® C103993

Printed on acid-free paper.

ISBN 978-90-411-6707-1

e-Book: ISBN 978-90-411-6708-8
web-PDF: ISBN 978-90-411-8832-8

© 2017 Kluwer Law International BV, The Netherlands

All rights reserved. No part of this publication may be reproduced, stored in a retrieval system, or transmitted in any form or by any means, electronic, mechanical, photocopying, recording, or otherwise, without written permission from the publisher.

Permission to use this content must be obtained from the copyright owner. Please apply to: Permissions Department, Wolters Kluwer Legal & Regulatory U.S., 76 Ninth Avenue, 7th Floor, New York, NY 10011-5201, USA. Website: www.wolterskluwerlr.com

Printed in the United Kingdom.

Editors

Sergio André Rocha is a tenured professor of tax and finance law at the Rio de Janeiro State University. He holds a master's degree and a PhD in Law, and a Post-Doctorate ("Livre-Docente") in Tax Law from the University of São Paulo. Sergio André started his professional career in 1998 at the audit and consulting firm Arthur Andersen. In 2010, he became a tax partner at EY, serving as a tax advisory partner, a tax policy and controversy partner, and an international tax partner. In June 2016, founded Sergio André Rocha Advocacia & Consultoria Tributária. His work is focused mainly in international taxation and cross-border transactions, corporate restructuring, and direct taxation. Sergio André is the Vice-President of the Brazilian Society of Tax Law ("SBDT"), serving as a Director of the Brazilian IFA Branch ("ABDF"), and a Council Member at the Brazilian Institute of Tax Law ("IBDT").

Allison Christians is the H. Heward Stikeman Chair in the Law of Taxation at the McGill University Faculty of Law where she teaches and writes on national, comparative, and international tax law and policy. She focuses especially on the relationship between taxation and economic development; the role of government and non-government institutions and actors in the creation of tax policy norms; and the intersection of taxation and human rights. She has written numerous scholarly articles, essays, and book chapters, as well as editorials, columns, and articles in professional journals, addressing a broad array of topics, and has been named one of the "Global Tax 50" most influential individuals in international taxation. Recent research focuses on the role of activists in reforming disclosure rules for multinational companies; evolving international norms of tax cooperation and competition; the relationship between tax and trade; and evolving conceptions of taxpayer rights. Professor Christians also engages on topics of tax law and policy via social media with her Tax, Society, and Culture blog and on twitter @taxpolblog.

Contributors

Reuven S. Avi-Yonah the Irwin I. Cohn Professor of Law and director of the International Tax LLM Program, specializes in corporate and international taxation. He has served as a consultant to the US Department of the Treasury and the Organisation for Economic Co-operation and Development (OECD) on tax competition, and is a member of the steering group for OECD's International Network for Tax Research. He is also a trustee of the American Tax Policy Institute, a member of the American Law Institute, a fellow of the American Bar Foundation and the American College of Tax Counsel, and an international research fellow at Oxford University's Centre for Business Taxation. In addition to prior teaching appointments at Harvard University (Law) and Boston College (History), he practiced law with Milbank, Tweed, Hadley & McCloy in New York; with Wachtell, Lipton, Rosen & Katz in New York; and with Ropes & Gray in Boston. After receiving his BA, summa cum laude, from Hebrew University, he earned three additional degrees from Harvard University: an AM in history, a PhD in History, and a JD, magna cum laude, from Harvard Law School. He has published more than 150 books and articles, including Advanced Introduction to International Tax (Elgar, 2015), Global Perspectives on Income Taxation Law (Oxford University Press, 2011), and International Tax as International Law (Cambridge University Press, 2007).

Aleksandra Bal is a manager of the Current Awareness and Tables (CAT) Knowledge Group at International Bureau for Fiscal Documentation (IBFD) in Amsterdam. She is also the Managing Editor of the IBFD flagship journal Bulletin for International Taxation. She holds a PhD degree (International Tax Law) from Leiden University and two master's degrees from Maastricht University (LLM International and European Tax Law and MSc Fiscal Economics). Prior to joining IBFD, Ms Bal worked as a tax consultant for Big4 companies in Germany, specializing in VAT. She publishes regularly on a wide variety of tax topics.

Tomas Balco is currently working as Head of International Tax Division/General State Counsel at Ministry of Finance of Slovak Republic, where he is responsible for the areas of Tax Treaties negotiation, application and interpretation as well as Transfer Pricing

Contributors

and EU Taxation matters. He also represents Slovakia at the OECD expert groups, EU Council and EU Commission Expert Working Groups and United Nations Committee of Experts. Tomas was also in charge of the Tax Policy Aspects of Slovak Presidency in the EU Council (SK PRES 2016). He has more than sixteen years of practical experience in international taxation both private and public sectors, having worked in different countries and continents. Tomas is involved as faculty member and teaches in academic programs at different Universities and Institutes including University of Lausanne (MASIT Program), University of Pretoria (African Tax Institute), IBDT in Sao Paulo (Brazil).

Yariv Brauner is a Professor of Law, University of Florida Levin College of Law. Brauner joined the Florida faculty in 2006, after teaching at NYU, Northwestern and ASU. He has been a Visiting Professor or a guest speaker in various universities in the US and abroad. He is an author of articles published in professional journals and law reviews, and a co-author of US International Taxation – Cases and Materials (with Reuven S. Avi-Yonah and Diane M. Ring), now in its 3rd. ed. He taught multiple courses in the fields of Taxation, Corporate Taxation, International Taxation, International Trade Law, and the Law of Multinational Corporations.

Ricardo André Galendi Júnior received his LLB from the University of São Paulo. He is currently a master's candidate at the University of São Paulo and an associate at Lacaz Martins, Pereira Neto, Gurevich & Schoueri Advogados.

Tracy A. Kaye Professor of Law and Eric Byrne Research Fellow, specializes in US federal income, international, European Union, and comparative tax law. During 2014, she was the Fulbright Senior Research Scholar at the University of Luxembourg where she examined the implications of automatic exchange of information. As the PwC Visiting Professor at the Vienna University of Economics and Business in 2012, her research resulted in an article entitled Innovations in the War on Tax Evasion that explored the impact of the Foreign Account Tax Compliance Act. After her visit as a scholar at the Max Planck Institute for Intellectual Property, Competition and Tax Law, her research was selected for the Third Annual Comparative Law Work-in-Progress Workshop at the University of Michigan Law School. Professor Kaye is known internationally for her comparative work on tax avoidance, tax discrimination, and tax incentives. Kaye is currently the Chair of the Academia Committee of the International Fiscal Association. She is also the Director of Seton Hall Law School's Dean Acheson Legal Stage Program, sponsored by the Court of Justice of the European Union and the American Embassy in Luxembourg to promote understanding of European Union Law among American lawyers. In spring 2002, she was a Fulbright Senior Scholar at the Albert-Ludwigs-Universitat in Freiburg, Germany. She is also an Associate Member of the European Association of Tax Law Professors. Prior to beginning her academic career at Seton Hall Law School, Kaye studied law and taxation at the Universities of Georgetown, DePaul and Illinois. She earned a BS in Accountancy, magna cum laude, at the University of Illinois; an MS in Taxation at DePaul University; and her JD, cum laude, at the Georgetown University Law Center. She worked as a tax legislative advisor for a US Senator, who was a member of the Senate Finance Committee, and practiced with Arthur Young & Co. in Chicago, Boston, and Washington, DC. She was selected as a Fellow of the American College of Tax Counsel and serves as the Regent for the Third Circuit on the Board of Regents.

Natalia Quiñones is a partner with Quiñones Cruz in Bogota, Colombia. She is a member of the DeSTaT research project on Development, Sustainability, Tax and Transparency, led by Oslo University and funded by the Norwegian Research Council. She teaches international taxation at Universidad de los Andes and Universidad del Rosario in Bogota, and is a PhD Candidate at the University of Amsterdam (UVA).

Ramon Tomazela Santos Master of Laws (LLM) in international taxation at the Vienna University of Economics and Business ("Wirtschaftsuniversität Wien" – WU) in Austria. Master of Laws in tax law at the University of São Paulo (USP). Member of the Academic Committee of the international tax law postgraduate program of the Brazilian Institute of Tax Law (IBDT). Visiting professor in postgraduate courses in Brazil.

Luís Eduardo Schoueri is a Full Professor of Tax Law at the University of São Paulo Law School ("USP"), the Vice-President of the Brazilian Institute of Tax Law ("IBDT") and a founding partner at Lacaz Martins, Pereira Neto, Gurevich & Schoueri Advogados. He obtained his master's degree in Law at the University of Munich and his doctor's and free professor's degree at the University of São Paulo. Since 2013, he is a Professor at the "Tax Law Summer School" (Pontifícia Universidade Católica Portuguesa, Portugal), at the LLM in International Tax Law, Amsterdam Center for Tax Law (University of Amsterdam, The Netherlands) and at the LLM in International Tax Law (Vienna University of Economics and Business, Austria). Professor Schoueri has also lectured as a Visiting Professor at the Université Catholique de Louvain, Belgium (2012), the Université Paris 1 Pantheon-Sorbonne, France (2010–2011) and the University of Florida, United States (2007). In 2013, he was Professor at the "The Greit Lisbon Summer Course on European Tax Law," University of Lisbon, Portugal. He was also the Hauser Global Professor of Law for the 2016 Spring Semester at the New York University ("NYU"). For 2017–2018, he is Professor in Residence at IBFD. Besides several articles published in Brazil and abroad, Professor Schoueri has authored various books on tax law, including Direito Tributário ("Tax Law," 7th ed., 2017), Preços de Transferência no Direito Tributário Brasileiro ("Transfer Pricing in Brazilian Tax Law," 3rd ed., 2013), Ágio em Reorganizações Societárias ("Goodwill in corporate reorganizations," 2012) and Normas Tributárias Indutoras e Intervenção Econômica ("Tax norms with inducing effect and economic intervention", 2005).

Romero J.S. Tavares is an international tax attorney and tax policy consultant based in Vienna, Austria, with a career spanning twenty-four years. He is a Lecturer and a Researcher (PhD/DIBT) in the Global Tax Policy Center and in the Global Transfer Pricing Center at Wirtschaftsuniversität Wien, where he was on an "academic sabbatical" from 2014 through 2016. Romero was the lead international tax partner at Deloitte in São Paulo in 2001–2004 and worked with Deloitte in the US (Detroit, Michigan) from

Contributors

1996 through 2001. Through 2014, he was a senior tax partner at EY in Brazil, where he held numerous leadership roles in areas such as corporate tax advisory, tax policy, and tax controversy. Since 2014, Romero has relocated to Vienna with his family, and serves as International Tax Policy Advisor to Brazil's Confederação Nacional da Indústria (CNI). In this role, he represented Brazilian Industry at the BIAC-OECD and in the BEPS debate. While on his academic sabbatical in Vienna, Romero has also worked part-time as Vice-President of Supply Chain Design, Tax & Trade for a large US-Singapore multinational conglomerate. He is now an independent practitioner serving a select portfolio of multinational enterprises and countries, also "Of Counsel" to Deloitte Wirtschaftsprüfungs GmbH in Vienna, and also serving as an International Tax Policy Advisor to the World Bank Group. Early in his career, Romero has served as a law clerk to a Federal Prosecutor Office in Brazil. Romero is a tax scholar with thirty-three articles, papers, and book chapters published; he holds a law degree from the Catholic University of Recife, Brazil, a Master's Degree in international business from the University of Detroit, and he attended numerous postgraduate programs in the areas of US and international tax law, international economics, and leadership, at top universities such as INSEAD, Leiden, and Harvard Law School.

Guillermo O. Teijeiro graduated LLB from La Plata University, Argentina, and obtained an LLM degree from Harvard University. He was trained as foreign associate with the international tax group of Caplin & Drysdale, and later spent a year at Harvard Law School as Visiting Scholar, under the sponsorship of the International Tax Program and the Harvard Tax Fund. Mr. Teijeiro has been a member of the Board of the City of Buenos Aires Bar Association, as well as of the Board of the Argentine IFA Branch, in five different biannual periods (he is currently President for the period 2017–2018). A former plenary member of IFA Permanent scientific Committee (2006–2014), Mr. Teijeiro is currently a member of IFA General Council, and Vice President of IFA LatAm, Regional Committee. Mr. Teijeiro has authored and co-authored several tax articles and books published, *inter alia*, by Bloomberg BNA, Law & Business Inc., Tax Analysts, Euromoney, The Economist, Thomson Reuters, Lexis-Nexis, Kluwer, Global Legal Group, Chambers Publishing, TaxMan, Marcial Pons, ICDT, IPDT, Depalma, La Ley, Astrea, Abaco, Abeledo Perrot, and Ediciones Contabilidad Moderna. He has been speaker on tax matters at IBA, ABA, UIA, IFA and IFA Latin America congresses. He has lectured extensively on corporate and international tax law, in law, economics and business graduate schools, as well as business chambers and professional organizations. Mr. Teijeiro teaches International Taxation at the Master Program in Taxation, Argentine Catholic University, Buenos Aires, as well as CIDTI Program, Austral University, Buenos Aires. He is a member of the Advisory Board of the Master Program in Taxation of Universidad Torcuato Di Tella, Buenos Aires.

Haiyan Xu is a full professor and SJD supervisor of civil & commercial law in the Law School, University of International Business and Economics Beijing, China, and a SJD candidate of International Tax law as well in Michigan Law School since 2014. In 1999, after Haiyan obtained her PhD degree from Graduate School of Chinese Academy of

Social Sciences, her research focused on property law, contract, secured transactions and consumer's protection law. She published more than sixty articles and books in these fields. She submitted a research report on the indirect agency system to the Commission of Legal Affairs, the Standing Committee of National People's Congress (NPC) in 1998, and successfully advised the legislature to introduce American law on unnamed agency and undisclosed agency into Chinese Contract Law of 1999 in Article 402 and Article 403. In 2000, she was invited to join the panel for drafting Chinese Civil Code by Professor Liang Huixing, the former member of the Committee of Law, NPC. Haiyan was responsible for drafting the chapter of Agency Law. "The Legal Study on the Condominium Management" won the second place in the Eleventh Best Research Reports (2010), and "The New Category of Civil Rights in the Food Safety Law" won the first Place for the academic paper (2011). Research on the Legal System of the Trust Transferability of the Right of Land Contractual Management in the Process of New Urbanization was selected as the Key project of National Social Science Foundation (4AFX017) in 2014. Haiyan began to pursue her SJD degree of International Tax Law, supervised by Prof. Reuven S. Avi-Yonah, in Michigan Law School since 2014. The cowriting paper Evaluating BEPS: A Reconsideration of the Benefits Principle and Proposal for UN Oversight was published in Harvard Business Law Review, Vol. 6, No. 2, Summer 2016. Additionally, Haiyan was a visiting scholar at the University of Amsterdam Law School (1998), the University of Wisconsin Law School (2008–2009), the University of Michigan Law School (2011–2012). She was a member of the Working Group I (MSMEs), United Nations Commission on International Trade Law, at the recommendation of the Ministry Commerce in China in 2014. Haiyan is the Vice President of Beijing Venture Capital Law Society, a council member of Chinese Consumers Protection Law Society, and an adjunct professor at Huaqiao University since 2004.

Xeniya Yeroshenko is a PhD candidate at the University of Ferrara, Italy. Her PhD research focuses on comparison of the EU treaties with the fundamental treaty on creation of Eurasian Economic Union (EAEU) and studies of the relevant EU experience on selected issues in the sphere of tax harmonization for potential further implementation in the EAEU region.

Summary of Contents

Editors	v
Contributors	vii
Preface	xxiii

PART I
The Essential Paradox of Tax Sovereignty — 1

CHAPTER 1
BEPS and the Power to Tax
Allison Christians — 3

CHAPTER 2
Tax Sovereignty and Digital Economy in Post-BEPS Times
Ramon Tomazela Santos & Sergio André Rocha — 29

CHAPTER 3
Justification and Implementation of the International Allocation of Taxing Rights: Can We Take One Thing at a Time?
Luís Eduardo Schoueri & Ricardo André Galendi Júnior — 47

CHAPTER 4
An Essay on BEPS, Sovereignty, and Taxation
Yariv Brauner — 73

PART II
Challenge to the Foundational Principles of Source and Residence — 95

Summary of Contents

CHAPTER 5
Evaluating BEPS
Reuven S. Avi-Yonah & Haiyan Xu — 97

CHAPTER 6
Jurisdictional Excesses in BEPS' Times: National Appropriation of an Enhanced Global Tax Basis
Guillermo O. Teijeiro — 125

CHAPTER 7
Taxing the Consumption of Digital Goods
Aleksandra Bal — 143

PART III
Acceptance and Implementation of Consensus by Differently-Situated States — 163

CHAPTER 8
The Birth of a New International Tax Framework and the Role of Developing Countries
Natalia Quiñones — 165

CHAPTER 9
The Other Side of BEPS: "Imperial Taxation" and "International Tax Imperialism"
Sergio André Rocha — 179

CHAPTER 10
Country-by-Country Over-Reporting? National Sovereignty, International Tax Transparency, and the Inclusive Framework on BEPS
Romero J.S. Tavares — 201

CHAPTER 11
How Are We Doing with BEPS Recommendations in the EU?
Tomas Balco & Xeniya Yeroshenko — 243

CHAPTER 12
U.S. Tax Sovereignty and the BEPS Project
Tracy A. Kaye — 279

Index — 293

Table of Contents

Editors	v
Contributors	vii
Preface	xxiii

PART I
The Essential Paradox of Tax Sovereignty — 1

CHAPTER 1
BEPS and the Power to Tax
Allison Christians — 3

§1.01	Introduction		3
§1.02	Defining the Power to Tax, 1920s-Style		6
	[A]	A Set of Framing Questions	6
	[B]	A Set of First Principles	8
	[C]	A Set of Second-Best Principles	11
§1.03	Defining the Power to Tax, 2010s Style		14
	[A]	A Set of Framing Questions	15
	[B]	A Set of First Principles	16
	[C]	Are We at Second-Best Principles Yet?	18
§1.04	What We Have, and Have Not, Learned		19
	[A]	Using Power to Compel Assistance	20
	[B]	Refraining from Tax as an Exercise of Power	23
	[C]	The Power to Destroy	25
§1.05	Conclusion		27

Table of Contents

CHAPTER 2
Tax Sovereignty and Digital Economy in Post-BEPS Times
Ramon Tomazela Santos & Sergio André Rocha 29

§2.01	Introduction		29
§2.02	Sovereignty and the Jurisdiction to Tax in International Law		30
	[A]	Jurisdiction to Prescribe	31
	[B]	Jurisdiction to Enforce	33
§2.03	Jurisdiction to Tax as Customary Law		34
§2.04	Expansion of Tax Jurisdiction		37
§2.05	Substantive Jurisdiction and the Digital Economy		37
	[A]	The Problem of Lack of Nexus: Residence Taxation and Source Taxation	38
	[B]	Digital Permanent Establishment	38
	[C]	Withholding Income Tax on Digital Transactions: Collecting Agents	40
	[D]	The Introduction of a "Bit Tax" on Digital Transactions	42
	[E]	Interim Conclusions on Substantive Jurisdiction	42
§2.06	Enforcement Jurisdiction and the Digital Economy		44
	[A]	Interim Conclusions on Enforcement Jurisdiction	45
§2.07	Conclusions		46

CHAPTER 3
Justification and Implementation of the International Allocation of Taxing Rights: Can We Take One Thing at a Time?
Luís Eduardo Schoueri & Ricardo André Galendi Júnior 47

§3.01	Introduction			47
§3.02	Three Waves of Justification of Residence Taxation in the International Tax Debate			48
	[A]	Economic Allegiance and the Framing of Double Tax Treaties		50
	[B]	Neutrality and the Apogee of Bilateralism		52
		[1]	The Rise of Neutrality: CEN and CIN as Welfare Benchmarks	53
		[2]	Drowning in the Alphabet Soup: CEN, CIN, CON, and Tax Inversions in the U.S.	55
	[C]	Cooperating for Value Creation		58
§3.03	Sovereignty and Inter-nations Equity			63
	[A]	Information Exchange in the Brazilian Context		66
	[B]	The Challenges of the Digital Economy		69
§3.04	Conclusion			71

Table of Contents

CHAPTER 4
An Essay on BEPS, Sovereignty, and Taxation
Yariv Brauner 73

§4.01 Introduction 73
§4.02 Sovereignty 76
§4.03 The International Tax Regime 78
§4.04 BEPS and the Sovereignty Claim 82
    [A] BEPS Action 2 (Neutralize the Effects of Hybrid Mismatch Arrangements) 82
    [B] Action 13 (Guidance on Transfer Pricing Documentation and Country-by-Country Reporting) 86
    [C] Action 14 (Making Dispute Resolution Mechanisms More Effective) 88
    [D] Action 15 (Developing a Multilateral Instrument to Modify Bilateral Tax Treaties) 89
    [E] Post BEPS EU Action 90
§4.05 Conclusion 92

PART II
Challenge to the Foundational Principles of Source and Residence 95

CHAPTER 5
Evaluating BEPS
Reuven S. Avi-Yonah & Haiyan Xu 97

§5.01 Introduction: The Financial Crisis and Inequality 97
§5.02 The Limits of the BEPS Project 100
    [A] New Shoes on the Old Road: An Old Approach for the New Destination 101
    [B] The Survival and Continuity of Notional and Illusionary Independent Entity Principle and Arm's Length Principle 102
    [C] The Survival and Continuity of the Problematic Benefit Principle 104
    [D] Limited Inclusiveness and Multilateralism 105
    [E] The limits of Action 1 106
    [F] The limits of Action 2 107
    [G] The limits of Action 3 108
    [H] The Limits of Action 4 108
    [I] The Limits of Action 5 110
    [J] The Limits of Action 6 111
    [K] The Limits of Action 7 112
    [L] The Limits of Actions 8–10 113
    [M] The Limits of Action 11 115
    [N] The Limits of Action 12 116

Table of Contents

	[O]	The Limits of Action 13	116
	[P]	The Limits of Action 14	117
	[Q]	The Limits of Action 15	118
§5.03	Reconsidering the International Tax Regime: A Multilateral Solution		118
	[A]	Neutrality	119
	[B]	Competitiveness	119
	[C]	Corporate Expatriations	120
	[D]	Can the Proposal Be Adopted?	120
§5.04	Conclusion		124

CHAPTER 6
Jurisdictional Excesses in BEPS' Times: National Appropriation of an Enhanced Global Tax Basis
Guillermo O. Teijeiro 125

§6.01	Full Inclusion CFC Rules under Brazilian Tax Law: Absence of Minimal Personal Connection	125
§6.02	Indirect Taxation of Capital Gains: Absence of a Minimal Economic Connection: *Vodafone* and *Sanofi Pasteur* Cases	130
§6.03	The Sixth Method of Transfer Pricing: A Latin American Experiment Attributing Additional Notional Income to Commodity Exporters	132
§6.04	The Case of the Digital Economy under BEPS Action 1: Extraterritoriality of Special Withholding or Equalization Levies	135
§6.05	Final Comments	138

CHAPTER 7
Taxing the Consumption of Digital Goods
Aleksandra Bal 143

§7.01	Introduction		143
§7.02	Legal Framework		145
	[A]	European Union	145
	[B]	Australia	148
	[C]	New Zealand	149
§7.03	The Concept of Digital Goods		150
	[A]	Introductory Remarks	150
	[B]	General Definition	150
	[C]	Definition for Indirect Tax Purposes	152
§7.04	Design Issues and Sovereignty		155
	[A]	Concept of Sovereignty	155
	[B]	Intra-jurisdictional Reach	156
	[C]	Tax Collection	159
§7.05	Summary		161

Table of Contents

PART III
Acceptance and Implementation of Consensus by Differently-Situated States 163

CHAPTER 8
The Birth of a New International Tax Framework and the Role of
Developing Countries
Natalia Quiñones 165

§8.01 Why Developing Countries Are Fundamental to the Functioning of
the New Framework 167
§8.02 Current Involvement in the International Tax Architecture:
Substantive or Formal Multilateralism 170
§8.03 Dispute Resolution and Sovereignty in a Post-BEPS World 172
§8.04 Conclusions 174
References 175

CHAPTER 9
The Other Side of BEPS: "Imperial Taxation" and "International Tax
Imperialism"
Sergio André Rocha 179

§9.01 Introduction 179
§9.02 Development of "Imperial Taxation" in the Post-BEPS World 184
§9.03 "International Tax Regime" and "International Tax Imperialism" 188
§9.04 BEPS and "International Tax Imperialism" 190
  [A] Arbitration 190
  [B] Transfer Pricing 192
  [C] Hybrid Mismatches 193
  [D] Digital Economy 194
  [E] Improper Use of Tax Treaties 194
§9.05 In the Defense of a "Developing Countries' International Tax
Regime" 196
§9.06 Tax Sovereignty in Post-BEPS Times 198
§9.07 Final Remarks 200

CHAPTER 10
Country-by-Country Over-Reporting? National Sovereignty, International
Tax Transparency, and the Inclusive Framework on BEPS
Romero J.S. Tavares 201

§10.01 Introduction 201
§10.02 The Pre-BEPS Tax Transparency Game: Competition or Reform? 205
  [A] Defining Tax Transparency 205
  [B] Tax Transparency and Tax Competition: Harm as a Matter of
    Law 207
  [C] Tax Transparency and the General Public 213

xix

Table of Contents

§10.03		Project BEPS, the Global Forum and Transfer Pricing	219
	[A]	Redundancies in Tax Transparency Initiatives	219
	[B]	Tax Transparency and Transfer Pricing Post-BEPS: Enforcement or Policy Debate?	223
	[C]	Tax Transparency and Transfer Pricing Enforcement Post-BEPS: Use of Master Files and Foreign UTP Disclosures	225
§10.04		CBCR and the Post-BEPS World of Transfer Pricing: Winners, Losers and Gamblers	228
§10.05		Social Responsibility in Tax Activism	234
§10.06		Where Do Developing Countries Fit In?	237
§10.07		Conclusion	240

CHAPTER 11
How Are We Doing with BEPS Recommendations in the EU?
Tomas Balco & Xeniya Yeroshenko 243

§11.01		Introduction	243
§11.02		Overview of the BEPS Action Plans as Addressed by the EU	248
	[A]	Action 1 Addressing the Tax Challenges of the Digital Economy	248
		[1] Direct Taxes: Lack of Action	248
		[2] Indirect Taxes: Single Registration Point Implemented and VAT Package Expected	250
	[B]	Actions 2, 3 and 4: Focus on Domestic Law Provisions and Adoption of ATAD	252
		[1] Action 2: 'Somewhat' Neutralising the Effect of Hybrid Mismatch Arrangement Within the EU	253
		[2] Action 3: Did Somebody Say There Was a Need for Designing 'Effective CFC Rules'?	254
		[3] Action 4: Limitation of Interest Deductibility or Shall We Call it Interest Deferral Rule?	256
		[4] Other Measures Introduced by ATAD Directive	258
		[a] Exit Tax	258
		[b] General Anti-avoidance Rule	259
		[c] Switch-Over Clause	260
	[C]	Action 5 Countering Harmful Tax Practices	261
		[1] Code of Conduct: Agreement on Patent Box – Modified Nexus	261
		[2] DAC 3: Automatic Exchange of Rulings	263
	[D]	Actions 6 and 7	264
	[E]	Actions 8–10: Aligning Transfer Pricing Outcomes with Value Creation in the EU?	266
	[F]	Action 11: Measuring and Monitoring BEPS in the EU?	267
	[G]	Action 12: Possible Mandatory Disclosure Rules	267
	[H]	Action 13: Revising Requirements Fort Transfer Pricing Documentation	268

	[I]	Action 14: Dispute Resolution – Enhancing the Current Arbitration Mechanism in the EU?	270
	[J]	Action 15: Multilateral Instrument (MLI)	271
§11.03	Other EU BEPS Issues: Progress and Developments		271
	[A]	Changes to Parent Subsidiary Directive	271
	[B]	Changes to Interest Royalty Directive: Pending	273
	[C]	Other: Code of Conduct Activities	274
	[D]	Common EU Blacklist: Is That Feasible?	274
	[E]	Access to Beneficial Ownership Information	276
§11.04	Summary and Conclusions		276

CHAPTER 12
U.S. Tax Sovereignty and the BEPS Project
Tracy A. Kaye 279

§12.01	Introduction		279
§12.02	OECD BEPS Project		280
	[A]	Action 6: Preventing the Granting of Treaty Benefits in Inappropriate Circumstances	282
	[B]	Action 13: Transfer Pricing Documentation and Country-by-Country Reporting	283
§12.03	U.S. Response to the BEPS Project		284
	[A]	CbC Reporting	286
	[B]	Treaty Abuse Limitations	288
§12.04	Conclusion		291

Index 293

Preface

The idea for this book arose during the IFA Congress in Basel (2015). The editors are respectively the general reporters for Subject 1: "Assessing BEPS: Origins, Standards, and Responses" (Professor Allison Christians, writing together with Professor Stephen Shay), and Subject 2: "The Future of Transfer Pricing" (Professor Sergio André Rocha) of the IFA 2017 Congress in Rio de Janeiro. After a meeting discussing the Rio Congress in Basel, the editors were discussing the implications of financial account regulation from a tax sovereignty perspective. That conversation gave birth to this book.

The power of a country to freely design its tax system is generally understood to be an integral feature of sovereignty. However, globalization and income mobility have increased the impacts of a country's decision on other countries. Now, more frequently than not, one country's exercise of sovereignty overlaps, interferes with, or even impedes that of another.

In this context, tax sovereignty is sometimes pointed out as cause of some of the most dire problems of the twenty-first century. The idea of sovereignty suggests that countries are independent actors in a global market, freely competing with each other for business and investment opportunities. On the other hand, tax competition is at the center of situations that create base erosion and profit shifting opportunities, which in some cases are viewed as harmful to tax sovereignty.

While the notion of unlimited tax sovereignty has created problems, in the absence of a formal international central power, any reaction against a country's legitimate action carries the potential to violate such country's sovereignty. Sovereignty accordingly becomes an impediment to designing a principled allocation of taxing rights across countries, and a typical "risk-society" problem that is embedded in ambivalence and complexity.

Moreover, in a world in which countries' relative influence and power are unequal, an attempt of a country – or a group of countries – to establish standards that others will follow comes close to the notion of an illegitimate intervention on a nations' power of self-determination.

Concern with this state of affairs is the main driver of this book. The authors' contributions deal with different facets of a single topic: How tax sovereignty is shaped in a post-BEPS world. The book unfolds in three parts.

Preface

The first, *The Essential Paradox of Tax Sovereignty*, features four chapters. In Chapter 1, Allison Christians introduces the topic by demonstrating how BEPS arose from the paradox of tax sovereignty and analyzing why multilateral cooperation and soft law consensus became the preferred solutions to a loss of autonomy over national tax policy. The chapter concludes that without meaningful multilateralism in the development of global tax norms, the paradox of tax sovereignty will necessarily continue and worsen, preventing resolution of identified problems for the foreseeable future. Ramon Tomazela Santos & Sergio André Rocha pick up this thread in Chapter 2, where they demonstrate that BEPS addresses the symptoms, but not the problems, of the sovereignty paradox. In their view, the central defining problem of this paradox is an ill-defined jurisdiction concept. The chapter demonstrates why tax policymakers need to change the conventional wisdom on sovereignty in order to incorporate new nexus connections due to the changing nature of trade and commerce.

In Chapter 3, Luís Eduardo Schoueri & Ricardo André Galendi Júnior further the inquiry by providing a detailed analysis of the interaction of contemporary cooperation efforts with the sovereignty of states in light of historical claims in economic allegiance, economic neutrality and now cooperation against abusive behavior. Yariv Brauner rounds out this first part in Chapter 4, which establishes the evolution of the concept of tax sovereignty. The chapter proposes an instrumental role for sovereignty in the process of improving cooperation and coordination of tax policies among productive (non-tax haven) countries, to balance claims and serve as a safeguard against political (in this case international) chaos. Brauner concludes that such a change to the business of international tax law would ensure at least an opportunity for all participants to succeed on their own terms.

Part Two of the book, *Challenge to the Foundational Principles of Source and Residence*, takes an in depth look at why residence and source continue to be the two essential building blocks of tax sovereignty and the backbone of the international tax system, surviving BEPS but still subject to multiple challenges in theory and practice. In Chapter 5, Reuven Avi-Yonah and Haiyan Xu argue that BEPS simply cannot succeed in solving the sovereignty paradox because BEPS follows the flawed theory of the benefits principle in assigning the jurisdiction to tax. Avi-Yonah and Xu therefore make a compelling argument that for the international tax regime to flourish in the face of sovereign and autonomous states, countries must commit to full residence-based taxation of active income with a foreign tax credit granted for source-based taxation.

In Chapter 6, Guillermo O. Tejeiro continues the analysis of the fundamental jurisdictional building blocks, demonstrating that by resorting to legal fictions within BEPS and beyond it, states are attempting to enlarge the scope of their personal or economic nexus, or to grasp taxable events and bases beyond their proper reach under well-settled international law rules and principles. Aleksandra Bal furthers the discussion in Chapter 7, with an analysis of how digital commerce has upended traditional notions of source and residence. Bal advocates the consumer's usual residence as a good approximation of the place of actual consumption and therefore the best-justified place of taxation.

Part Three of the book, *Acceptance and Implementation of Consensus by Differently-Situated States*, considers tax sovereignty after BEPS from a range of

Preface

perspectives. Chapters 8 through 10 focus on perspectives from lower income or developing countries, while Chapters 11 and 12 review the landscape from the perspective of Europe and the United States, respectively. Accordingly, in Chapter 8, Natalia Quinones explores how developing countries might take advantage of the new international tax architecture, developed for purposes of coordinating the BEPS action plans, to ensure that their voices are truly shaping the standards. She argues that the knowledge gap between developing and developed is getting narrower instead of wider, with major negative impacts expected for the international tax order.

Sergio André Rocha continues this discussion in Chapter 9, with a proposal: instead of simply accepting the BEPS Project's recommendations and their reliance on historical decisions about what constitutes a country's "fair share of tax", developing countries should join in the formation of a "Developing Countries" International Tax Regime to focus discourse on the rightful limits of states' taxing powers. Furthering the theme of autonomous priority-setting, Romero J.S. Tavares focuses in on a key part of the BEPS consensus in Chapter 10, exploring whether implementing the CBCR country by country reporting standard, without a deeper transfer pricing reform, should be viewed as a priority in every country. He further questions whether this particular initiative, even if important, is worthy of mobilization of the scarce resources of developing countries. Tavares concludes with an incisive review of the role of the inclusive framework in prioritizing some needs over others.

Tomas Balco & Xeniya Yeroshenko then consider BEPS implementation from the very different perspective of the EU in Chapter 11. The chapter demonstrates that even, within the EU, BEPS implementation is not straightforward, as the interests of member states sometimes conflict and the basic notion of tax sovereignty remains fundamental even while tax coordination and harmonization across the EU expands. However, the authors note that the progress made in the last several years on key cooperation norms, which was largely inspired by BEPS, has been unprecedented. Finally, Tracey Kaye provides a capstone to the book in Chapter 12, where she makes the convincing case that although some in the United States saw the BEPS Project as a threat to US tax sovereignty, this project was in fact necessary in order for the United States to effectively wield its tax sovereignty. Kaye's chapter thus ends the book with a clear picture of the ongoing paradox of tax sovereignty in the world after BEPS.

The editors would like to take this opportunity to thank the authors for their efforts. We would also like to thank Kluwer, in the person of Simon Bellamy, for all his patience and support.

Sergio André Rocha
Allison Christians
Rio de Janeiro State University
McGill University Faculty of Law

PART I   The Essential Paradox of Tax Sovereignty

CHAPTER 1
BEPS and the Power to Tax

Allison Christians

§1.01 INTRODUCTION

Governments throughout the world are using their taxing powers in a war of all against all in which everyone – or nearly everyone – is losing the power to exercise unilateral control over tax policy. The problem, which is felt locally, nationally, and regionally in the form of ongoing fiscal and budgetary pressures, is most clearly visible from an historical and international perspective. But seen is not solved. To solve the problem and rescue societies from engineering the path to their collective fiscal destruction requires an abrupt departure from history: namely, developing institutions and processes for a comprehensive and globally inclusive multilateral tax regime.

To date, national lawmakers (along with many scholars and policy observers) have decried and avoided the deliberate creation of any such regime.[1] Yet past decisions to prevent comprehensive multilateralism have led precisely to the conditions that require it for the power to tax to be restored going forward. This chapter demonstrates how and why these conditions have evolved and concludes that multilateralism is inescapable because it has become a necessary precondition for exercising

---

1. *See*, e.g., Yariv Brauner, *An International Tax Regime in Crystallization*, 56 TAX L. REV. 259 (2003); Vito Tanzi, *Is There a Need for a World Tax Organization?*, in Assaf Razin and Efraim Sadka, eds., THE ECONOMICS OF GLOBALIZATION: POLICY PERSPECTIVES FROM PUBLIC ECONOMICS (1999); Stephanie Soong Johnston, U.N. Rejects Global Tax Body, Strengthens Existing Tax Expert Committee, 2015 WTD 136-2 (July 16, 2015) ("during the conference, U.N. Member States were considering upgrading the U.N.'s tax committee to an intergovernmental commission, which would have changed the balance of power between world organizations involved in the development of international tax rules. Many developing countries and civil society organizations pushed hard for the global tax body, but many developed countries, including the U.S., opposed the idea.").

the power to tax.[2] To regain effective autonomy in tax policymaking, governments will have to end their deep-seated resistance to multilateralism on grounds of sovereign entitlement. This will require lawmakers to muster the political will to accept that a multilateral tax regime is necessary, justified, and possible, and start designing the requisite institutions and processes.

Unfortunately, there are few reasons for optimism, judging from long- and deeply held resistance to multilateralism in taxation. As many scholars of tax history are aware, the fragile consensus that currently impedes the power to tax emerged from an imperfect framework created about a century ago by four distinguished economists assigned to the task by the League of Nations.[3] Setting their minds to thinking about how to divide the world's income tax base among nation-states, the economists built a technical rule-based framework upon an optimistic theory of cooperative convergence of sovereign equals, each trusted to act responsibly out of a sense of nationalistic self-preservation.[4] Contemporary tax trends demonstrate that this convergence theory has failed. In place of cooperation and convergence, the international tax system is characterized by opportunistic self-dealing, and ruthless competition.[5] A major outcome has been an observable decline in the will of nations to exercise the power to tax income – most especially corporate and capital income – on a global scale.[6]

---

2. At least, in terms of taxing income and capital. Other forms of taxation, such as poll, excise, or payroll taxes, may be less dependent on global cooperation among states. However, these forms of taxation have often been rejected as appropriate in comparison to income taxation for various economic and normative policy reasons. For a seminal discussion, *see* Boris I. Bittker, *A "Comprehensive Tax Base" as a Goal of Income Tax Reform*, 80 Harv. L. Rev. 925 (1967).
3. Gijsbert W. J. Bruins, Luigi Einaudi, Edwin R. A. Seligman, and Sir Josiah Stamp, Report on Double Taxation, April 5, 1923 (hereinafter, "1923 Report"); *see* Reuven Avi-Yonah, *The Structure of International Taxation: A Proposal for Simplification*, 74 Tex. L. Rev. 1301, 1306 (1996) (demonstrating how these principles formed the foundations for contemporary international tax consensus, and referring to the current international tax regime as a "miracle," albeit a "flawed" one); Steven Dean, *The Incomplete Market for Global Tax Information*, 49 Bost. Coll. L.R. 605, 644–649 (2008), 639 ("It would be difficult to overstate the significance of the work of the committees and experts ... that formed the basis for ... today's very successful international tax regime."); Allison Christians, *Networks, Norms, and National Tax Policy*, 9 Wash. U. Glob. Stud. L. Rev. 1 (2010) (outlining the policy trajectory for global tax consensus from the 1920s to the present).
4. 1923 Report at 51 ("Looking forward to the future, the influence of example by others and the spirit encouraged by the operations of the League of Nations indicate the possibility of a development away from localised ideas and from the earlier stages of economic thought ...").
5. *See* Allison Christians, *Putting the Reign Back in Sovereign*, 40 Pepp. L. Rev. 1373 (2013) (arguing that recent trends suggest that as the stakes rise in international tax competition, nations become more mercenary toward each other, going so far as to bind themselves to mutually beneficial cooperative arrangements and then "engage in everyday acts of sabotage ... in order to advance their own interests at the expense of others.").
6. *See, e.g.*, Reuven S. Avi-Yonah, *Globalization, Tax Competition, and the Fiscal Crisis of the Welfare State*, 113 Harv. L. Rev. 1573, 1604 (2000); Allison Christians, *Drawing the Boundaries of Tax Justice*, in Kim Brooks, ed., Quest for Tax Reform: The Carter Commission 50 Years Later (Carswell, 2013) 53. The personal income tax is threatened by weakness in the corporate income tax because the latter acts as a backstop to the former. In the simplest case, if there is no corporate tax, individuals will hold assets and income in private corporations, investing and reinvesting their savings without tax unless and until they choose to disinvest by paying themselves dividends or selling the shares; more complex schemes would use corporations to transfer assets and income to future generations free of estate or gift taxes. The potential for indefinite and

Chapter 1: BEPS and the Power to Tax §1.01

Likely at least in part, in response to the public reactions to this trend, some governments are now making efforts to defend their ability to wield the power to tax. The most visible evidence of their commitment is in a current initiative being undertaken by the Organisation for Economic Cooperation and Development (OECD) on "base erosion and profit shifting," or BEPS, which concerns itself mainly with corporate income taxation.[7] However, the OECD's approach to solving the BEPS problem is also primarily rules-based, replicating the flawed approach taken by the League of Nations before it.

Fundamentally, the power to tax cannot be restored simply by changing technical rules. Instead, restoring the power to tax requires addressing the very nature of the pluralistic, internationally networked tax policymaking system that both defines and constrains autonomy in tax policymaking. This system has, for the entirety of its existence, been characterized by structural exclusivity in terms of its actors, institutions, processes, and substance.[8] It has involved distinguished experts working through epistemic networks of politically powerful nations to write complex technical rules for global adoption. But neither the combined expertise of the actors nor the substance of the technical rules they devised could prevent the power to tax from destroying itself. Instead, the past built the present: a world of rampant, race-to-the bottom, anti-cooperative tax strategizing by taxpayers and lawmakers alike that has, to varying degrees, undermined the autonomy of nations to exercise the power to tax.

Accordingly, this chapter explains the paradox of the power to tax by looking backward, to past processes and past decisions, and comparing them to the contemporary reworking of the power in the BEPS process. Part I examines how governments conceptualized and exercised their competing tax powers through the League of Nations. Part II analyzes the contemporary rewrite currently being undertaken at the OECD. Part III examines what nations have, and have not, learned about the power to tax, and what lawmakers will need to learn in order to preserve their power. The chapter concludes with an examination of the kinds of institutions and processes needed for a comprehensive and globally inclusive multilateral regime to restore the power to tax.

---

potentially permanent tax deferral would replicate the current status quo for U.S.-based multinationals, which accumulate large amounts of cash "offshore" for this purpose. *See*, e.g., U.S., Offshore Profit Shifting and the U.S. Tax Code – Part 2 (Apple Inc.): Hearing Before the Permanent Subcommittee on Investigations of the Committee on Homeland Security and Governmental Affairs, 113th Cong (2013) (Sen. John McCain) at 8 (noting Apple's cash reserves of USD 145 billion and stating that Apple could choose to subject itself to U.S. taxes if it repatriated its offshore funds by, for example, paying inter-company dividends). As of December 27, 2014, Apple's cash reserves had grown to nearly USD 178 billion. *See* Apple, "Form 10-Q For the Fiscal Quarter Ended December 27, 2014" (online: investor.apple.com) http://investor.apple.com/secfiling.cfm?filingid=1193125-15-23697&cik=320193 at 32. The problem of hoarding in a private corporation can be addressed with anti-deferral rules that force corporations to disgorge profits deemed unnecessary for the business, but these regimes involve extensive monitoring of private transactions that put tremendous enforcement pressure on tax agencies.

7. OECD, Addressing Base Erosion and Profit Shifting (2013), at http://dx.doi.org/10.1787/978926 4192744-en (hereinafter, Report on BEPS).
8. For a discussion of the pertinent institutions and processes that make up this system, *see* Christians *supra* note 3.

§1.02 DEFINING THE POWER TO TAX, 1920S-STYLE

In 1921, the Financial Committee of the League of Nations took it upon itself to study the problem of sharing the global tax base by dividing the primary power to tax among competing jurisdictions.[9] They did so because as nations concurrently adopted modern income taxation as a preferred means of revenue-raising, multiple jurisdictions began making competing claims over the same income. The resulting double taxation was considered a collective action problem: a clear threat to national economic interests that might only be solved by global cooperation. The Committee appointed four economists to study the problem: Gijsbert W. J. Bruins of the Commercial University, Rotterdam (Netherlands; Luigi Einaudi of Turin University (Italy); Edwin R. A. Seligman of Columbia University (United States (U.S.)); and Sir Josiah Stamp of London University (United Kingdom (U.K.)).

The Financial Committee gave the distinguished group a set of framing questions. In response, they sought to articulate a set of principles that could serve as a guide for national lawmakers. The principles appeared as a Report on Double Taxation, submitted to the Committee in 1923.[10] The 1923 Report demonstrates fairly clearly that the economists found principles but no consensus on a single proposition for allocating taxing powers. Instead, they settled on drawing up a second-best framework for considering the immediate problem, and working toward the first-best solution, a multilateral treaty, as an ongoing project. The second-best framework is the origin of the BEPS problem as the OECD articulates it today.

[A] A Set of Framing Questions

Articulating what questions matter and who ought to answer them are significant decisions.[11] In framing a particular set of questions and assigning it to the four economists, the Finance Committee indelibly framed the study of international taxation as a technical matter in search of a scientifically derived solution.[12] This is

---

9. The question of how this particular committee came to take on the responsibility forms a part of the narrative surrounding the emergence of the League's, and ultimately the OECD's, grip on international tax policy, and the enduring role for business leaders in all formal policymaking efforts ever since. See Christians supra note 3.
10. See discussion supra note 3.
11. See, e.g., David Kennedy, *Challenging Expert Rule: The Politics of Global Governance*, 27 SYDNEY L.R. 5 (2005) ("background norms and institutions are more important in global governance than we have thought ... the vocabularies, expertise, and sensibility of the professionals who manage these background norms and institutions are central elements in global governance. ... [E]xpert work might be reinterpreted and contested in political terms, despite the ubiquity of the conviction among international legal experts that their expert work is not political."); Martti Koskenniemi, *Global Governance and Public International Law* 37 KRITISCHE JUSTIZ 241 (2004) ("Globalization invokes not government, but governance, a spontaneous process, pushed by private interests and actors in a thoroughly pragmatic process, accountable to no-one."); *see also* Christine Schwöbel, *Whither the Private in Global Governance?* 10 INT'L J. CONST.L. 1106 (2012).
12. In some respects, the League of Nations sought to, and did, supplant the International Chamber of Commerce, which was formulating its own agenda for international taxation at the same time. *See* What is ICC?, http://www.iccwbo.org/id93/index.html (explaining that the ICC adopted an

consistent with the constitutive mandate of the League itself: to enable "technical experts" to solve problems where diplomacy and bureaucracy had failed.[13] The League was expected to afford "authoritative channels for the use of scientific and expert knowledge in the interest not of any one power, but of the solution of the problems themselves."[14] International tax experts continue to adhere to this perspective, regularly convening in "high-level scientific committees" to study international tax issues in "scientific programmes."[15]

The list of questions indicates why the League might have chosen economists as the appropriate source of expertise. The questions covered the economic consequences of double taxation and asked whether any general principles could be formulated for a multilateral agreement that would divide the global income tax base, or whether nations should instead agree amongst themselves, and in either case, what principles could guide them in this quest. These questions are framed in economic terms, the choice of legal institution or instrument to follow from the "correct" economic answer. Once developed, the reader is led to conclude that the League would simply put the necessary political machinery in motion to implement the scientifically derived recommendations, and the problems would be neatly solved.

Both are fanciful propositions. Far from being a technical or scientific matter, the questions asked implicate not just economics but also politics, culture, society, institutions, diplomacy, and above all, power.[16] Moreover, the economists repeatedly acknowledged that economics could not answer the questions they were asked to solve.[17] Power was the key to dividing the global income tax base then, as it is today.

---

initial resolution that the taxing jurisdiction should turn on the nature of the tax, with distinctions being made between "super" and "normal" taxes. Exceptions were made for particular kinds of income, including that from international shipping (as to which residence-based taxation was to be preserved) and that from sales of manufactured goods (to be apportioned under formula). However, the U.S. rejected this approach, in favor of a system that would favor the source jurisdiction, as its credit system did. The ICC ultimately came to a consensus in 1923, when it issued a new resolution on jurisdictional primacy.)

13. Christians, *supra* note 3.
14. J.T. Shotwell, *First Pages from the History of the League of Nations, in* THE LEAGUE OF NATIONS STARTS: AN OUTLINE BY ITS ORGANISERS 46, 50 (1920).
15. *See, e.g.*, 68th Congress of the International Fiscal Association, 12–17 October 2014, Mumbai, India, available at http://www.globalfinance.mu/images/pdf/IFA%20Sponsorship%20Brochure.pdf (stating that the International Fiscal Association (IFA) seeks to study and advance international and comparative fiscal law and the financial and economic aspects of taxation, and that it does so "through its Annual Congresses and the scientific publications relating thereto as well as through scientific research. Although the operations of the IFA are essentially scientific in character, the subjects selected take account of current fiscal developments and changes in local legislation.").
16. *See* Michael Livingston, *Reinventing Tax Scholarship: Lawyers, Economists, and the Role of the Legal Academy*, 83 COR. L. REV. 365 (1998); Diane Ring, *Who is Making International Tax Policy: International Organizations as Power Players in a High Stakes World*, 33 FORD. INT'L L.J. 649 (2010). The economists acknowledged this reality. *See, e.g.*, 1923 Report at 22 (doubting whether governments would agree to solutions that, even if correct as a matter of economic principle, would appear to be against national self-interest.).
17. 1923 Report at 36 ("the multiplicity of the claims of origin... constitute a serious embarrassment in considering the fractional rights of each particular share and to that extent weakens the claims of origin"); at 38 ("It is well-nigh impossible to ascribe the real economic origin [of the returns to commercial credit] to either country"); at 39 ("To allocate the exact proportion of economic

The League of Nations selected the four economists for their individual reputations, coupled with the political power of their home nations, as well as their own power within those nations. Bruins was a monetary expert from the Netherlands who later served as both League of Nations commissioner and technical advisor to Austria.[18] Einaudi ultimately became the President of Italy.[19] Edwin R. A. Seligman was a dominant figure in U.S. public finance and economics.[20] Sir Josiah Stamp was a leading British economist and tax expert who ultimately directed the Bank of England.[21]

There is perhaps little mystery to these choices. The U.S. and Britain, equals in terms of international diplomatic power, were deadlocked over the issue of which country should cede its right to tax; the Netherlands and Italy key international players with aligned agendas.[22] Now almost one hundred years later, three of these countries – the U.S., the U.K., and the Netherlands – continue to be key players in international tax norm creation despite also being three of the most major beneficiaries of the architecture they created and have diligently maintained in the interim. In 1921, the experts were expected to bring about a neutral, objective, even scientific solution to the articulated problem of double taxation. Instead, they devised principles for building consensus around a range of possible allocations, each of which was essentially arbitrary, and none of which could possibly be acceptable to all governments.[23]

[B] A Set of First Principles

The economists laid out a framework for dividing the tax base by trying to articulate a nation's jurisdiction to tax as a function of what they termed "economic allegiance." This was a reasoned and deliberate move away from the citizen/state relationship traditionally understood to confer jurisdiction as explained and justified by social contract theory that is important to remember given today's environment of increasing labor mobility.[24]

The focus on economic allegiance arose from the sense that the tax base, as a product of economic activity, ought to be divided not on the basis of a taxpayer's

---

allegiance to origin or domicile in each particular category is well-nigh impossible. Such an attempt would savour too much of the arbitrary.").
18. Gianni Toniolo, CENTRAL BANK COOPERATION AT THE BANK FOR INTERNATIONAL SETTLEMENTS, 1930–1973, at 93 (2005).
19. Einaudi, Luigi, in COLUMBIA ENCYCLOPEDIA 876 (6th ed. 2000); Einaudi, Luigi, in BRITANNICA CONCISE ENCYCLOPEDIA (2006), available at http://www.britannica.com/EBchecked/topic/1813 10/Luigi-Einaudi.
20. Seligman, in Lyman Abbott et al., 10 NATIONAL CYCLOPAEDIA OF AMERICAN BIOGRAPHY 49 (James T. White & Company 1899).
21. J. Harry Jones, JOSIAH STAMP PUBLIC SERVANT (1964).
22. See, e.g., H. David Rosenbloom & Stanley I. Langbein, United States Tax Treaty Policy: An Overview, 19 COLUM. J. TRANSNAT'L L. 359, 361 (1981).
23. 1923 Report at 39 ("where any two countries desire to [a particular] allocation, they would do well to be guided, ideally at least, by the above analysis … a certain rough justice can be attained.").
24. 1923 Report at 18 ("The older theory of taxation was the exchange theory, which was related directly to the philosophical basis of society in the 'social contract,' according to which the reason and measure of taxation are in accordance with the principles of an exchange as between the government and the individual.").

political or social connections to a country, but by economic interaction with and within it. As the economists put it, "In the modern age of the international migration of persons as well as of capital, political allegiance no longer forms an adequate test of individual fiscal obligation. It is fast breaking down in practice, and it is clearly insufficient in theory."[25]

Making the case against dividing taxes based on political allegiance, the economists argued that an economic interaction with a jurisdiction could be determined by considering four factors. These were the physical location of an object to be taxed, especially an asset that produces income ("*situs*"); the enforceability of rights, for example with respect to an income-producing asset ("*enforceability*"); the jurisdiction of normal residence by the subject of the tax ("*residence*"); and, the "*origin*" of the income to be taxed ("*source*").[26] The group ultimately condensed the four factors to two main categories of tax jurisdiction analysis that characterize international tax discourse today, namely, source and residence. The two other elements – *situs* and enforceability – were subsumed in this exercise as generally less relevant or dispositive, or susceptible to facile manipulation (e.g., storing a stock certificate in a lock box would eviscerate any formalistic *situs* rule).[27]

Despite confronting double taxation as a likely scenario, the economists correctly predicted that source countries would shy away from imposing source taxation on non-residents, while residence countries would need information from the source country in order to impose residence-based income taxation.[28] The economists explained that source countries would avoid source taxation because it would either drive investment away to lower-tax source jurisdictions, or force the jurisdiction to offer higher returns to compensate for the tax.[29] Whether or not this is empirically verifiable, especially if a residence state is somewhere waiting to impose a tax in the event the source state does not, the economists' prediction that source countries would refrain from taxing many items of income at source turned out to be prescient.[30]

However, refraining from taxation does not mean that a nation prefers another country to tax the income in its stead; perhaps the opposite is true. A nation that seeks

---

25. 1923 Report at 19.
26. *Id.* at 22–26.
27. Today's "patent box" evokes the same observation. *See*, e.g., Andrew Goodall, BEPS: *UK Patent Box Under Scrutiny*, Accounting Web, September 18, 2014, at http://www.accountingweb.co.uk/article/beps-uk-patent-box-under-scrutiny/564220.
28. This suggests that non-taxation was a predictable result from the very beginning of international taxation theory, and that comprehensive information exchange would be key to residence-based taxation. Perhaps that is why at least one early U.S. treaty had an automatic information exchange provision. Convention Respecting Double Taxation, U.S.-Swed., March 23, 1939, 54 Stat. 1759. For a discussion, *see* Dean, *supra* note 3 at 644–649.
29. 1923 Report at 8 ("It is a truism of public finance that a tax on consumption is not only a burden on those who consume but a barrier to those who no longer consume because they are dissuaded from consumption through the rise of the price of the commodity in question due to the tax. So the burden and the barrier, in the case of double taxation, are striking instances of this general doctrine.").
30. *See* Vito Tanzi, *Globalization, Technological Developments, and the Work of Fiscal Termites*, 26 Brook. J. Int'l L. 1261, 1274 (2001) ("The sixth fiscal termite is the growing inability or, often, unwillingness by countries to tax, especially with high rates, financial capital and incomes derived by individuals with highly tradable skills.").

to attract capital by offering tax incentives may well view the investor's home country's residual tax as an extra-territorial intrusion on domestic policy objectives.[31] Moreover, when nations are not in reciprocal economic positions (with roughly equal imports and exports of capital vis a vis other jurisdictions), they cannot expect to pick up in residence taxation what they give up in source taxation.[32] Asking (or forcing) countries that are effectively unable to tax at source to direct resources toward helping residence countries do so instead creates an inevitable clash of interests.[33]

The efficacy and meaning of source and residence, not to mention the economic allegiance doctrine itself, continue to bedevil tax policy theorists, even as the categories have enjoyed more or less universal acceptance.[34] But what is perhaps most enduring about the economists' proposed way of thinking about the global income tax base is their ready admission that in many cases – perhaps a majority of cases – the idea of origin would simply confound economic analysis. To the economists, it was all too clear that assigning origin would be scientifically impossible: many types of income would have several places of origin, and the whole would be fundamentally indivisible into parts.[35] There were too many variables, and too much interdependence among them, to extract a precise origin for each portion of a dollar of income earned in a global economy. The economists concluded that the division of the global income tax base would be a question of political feasibility, and not science.[36]

This is the reality that the OECD confronts in its BEPS project. The problems for states in taxing today – even around such phenomena as electronic commerce,

---

31. This type of conflict has been attributed to the lack of a tax treaty between Brazil and the U.S., for example, and is the source of much debate regarding the concept of "tax sparing," under which residence countries refrain from imposing residual taxes in order to give effect to certain source country tax incentives. For discussion, *see* Allison Christians, *Tax Treaties for Investment and Aid to Sub-Saharan Africa: A Case Study*, 71 BROOK. L. REV. 639 (2005); Kim Brooks, *Tax Sparing: A Needed Incentive for Foreign Investment in Low Income Countries or an Unnecessary Revenue Sacrifice*, 34 QUEEN'S L. J. 505 (2009).
32. Many countries are effectively unable to tax at source because their need for greater volumes of foreign investment overrides their need for tax revenue from foreign investment. *See, e.g.*, Adam Rosenzweig, *Why Are There Tax Havens?* 52 WM & M. L. R. 923 (2010). Many or perhaps most of these countries have little opportunity to tax on a residence basis because they lack outward investment: very few of the world's largest multinational companies are headquartered outside the OECD. *See* PWC, *Global Top 100 Companies by Market Capitalisation*, March 31, 2014 update, at http://www.pwc.com/gx/en/audit-services/capital-market/publications/assets/document/pwc-global-top-100-march-update.pdf.
33. *See* Dean *supra* note 3.
34. Reuven Avi-Yonah has gone so far as to claim that the source and residence classification scheme rises to the level of customary law owing to its widespread acceptance. *See* Reuven Avi-Yonah, INTERNATIONAL TAX AS INTERNATIONAL LAW (2007).
35. *See supra* note 17.
36. 1923 Report at 49–50 (discussing what debtor and creditor countries would be expected to accept, and concluding that "At the present stage of our considerations ... we do not see any other form of compromise which is likely to reconcile the conflicting interests and to have any prospect of success upon three points: (1) to reconcile the widely opposed interests of debtor and creditor exchequers; (2) to admit those ideas which, though widely accepted in many countries, are, in our view, in relation to income tax, to a considerable extent economically undeveloped in so far as they ascribe undue importance to origin taxation; and, lastly, (3) to conform to what is, in the experience of fiscal administrations, practically possible in dealing, in such a complex world, with the income of individual persons.").

intellectual property, hybrid financial instruments, and hybrid entities – are not in material respects that much different than those encountered in 1921, even if they loom vastly larger in scope and importance. In retrospect, it is not too hard to see why things went wrong. We can blame the utter incoherence of thinking about income as if it were something over which nation-states could possibly assert sole or even dominant ownership rights in a world that is characterized by economic interdependence. Economic interdependence is not a matter of nature or science, but instead it is a matter of power, institutions, and political decision-making. So too, must income taxation be.

[C] A Set of Second-Best Principles

In hindsight, the economists might have discarded *situs* and enforceability too quickly in favor of source and residence, given the obvious complications of the income division problem. Perhaps trying to measure more variables would have made the job easier.[37] The economists' examples are illustrative in this regard. For instance, they posit the difficulty of assigning a single origin to a stream of income that is earned by a vessel "ply[ing] navigable waters which traverse different countries," using docks and appurtenances along the way that materially contributed to profitable operations, depending as well on the good management and "business sagacity" of the captain and the owner, wherever they may be at a given time.[38] Unstated though equally relevant, the vessels would have also benefited from the existence of a multiplicity of private legal protections and financial instruments accepted across legal systems, to assure that commercial intentions would be respected.

It was obvious to the economists, and it is still obvious today, that a dollar earned in the global economy is the product not of the effort of one person or group of persons – and not of one nation or of a handful of nations – but rather of the entirety of the global economic community. It relied then, as it does now, on the enforcement of rights,[39] the ability to exchange currency,[40] the existence of uniform weights and

---

37. This could be especially true today, as economic measurement tools become increasingly sophisticated and economists are starting to return to some basic theories to see if modern economics can prevail where traditional economics did not. See, e.g., Matthew Weinzierl, *Revisiting the Classical View of Benefit-Based Taxation*, working paper, March 2014, available at http://www.law.nyu.edu/sites/default/files/upload_documents/Matthew%20Weinzierl.pdf.
38. 1923 Report at 24; 33–34.
39. Courts in various jurisdictions and forums have acknowledged and protected various corporate rights including the right to sue, to freedom of expression, freedom of assembly, compensation for non-pecuniary harm, privacy, and equal treatment under the law. See Troy & N.C. Gold Mining Co. v. Snow Lumber Co., 173 N.C. 593, 92 S.E. 494 (1917) (affirming a foreign corporation's right to sue in a local court); *Singer v. Canada*, Communication No. 455/1991, UN Doc CCPR/C/51/D/455/1991 (1994) (protecting corporate right to freedom of expression); *Autronic AG v. Switzerland* A 178 (1990) (same); (1990) 12 EHRR 485 (same); *A and H v. Austria*, App No. 9905/82 7 Eur HR Rep 137 (1985) (protecting corporate right to freedom of assembly); *Comingersoll SA v. Portugal* 2000-IV 355 (protecting corporate right to compensation for non-pecuniary harm); *Société Colas Est and Others v. France* 2002-III 421 (protecting corporate right to privacy); *Santa Clara County v. Southern Pacific Railroad*, 118 US 394 (1886) (protecting corporate right to equal treatment).
40. For a discussion, see A. L. Calvet, *A Synthesis of Foreign Direct Investment Theories and Theories of the Multinational Firm*, 12 J. INT'L BUS. STUDIES 43 (1981).

measures standards,[41] contract and property protections,[42] the ability to assess creditworthiness and impose accountability on all those involved in trading across borders,[43] the ability of individuals to exchange their labor for compensation in multiple nations,[44] the physical, financial, and legal infrastructure built in multiple nations,[45] and on and on.[46] The greater economic interdependence achieved through regional and global trade and finance agreements, the less possible it is to use economic principles to explain or justify any primary, let alone sole, claim of right to the global income tax base.

Just as U.S President Obama, famously calling on American companies to respond to their communities by paying tax, claimed "If you've got a business, you didn't build that,"[47] so the four economists in 1921 can be heard to make the same pitch to the nations of the world. This principle accords with the idea that income is a creature not of human industry alone but of the collective efforts, through generations, within the institution of the nation-state and beyond it, through pluralistic international orders.

In a seminal work on taxation and philosophy, philosophers Liam Murphy and Thomas Nagel observed a similar phenomenon in the context of the relationship between the individual and the products of labor.[48] Their goal was to debunk the "myth of ownership" – that is, what they viewed as a form of everyday, or unreflective, libertarianism that compels individuals to make moral claims over pre-tax income without taking into consideration the vital contributions made by the state to such income.[49] So too governments, themselves, may be embracing a myth of ownership in respect of the global income tax base. Devising a way of thinking differently about

---

41. See Bureau Internationale des Poids et Mesures, The Role and Objectives of the BIPM, at http://www.bipm.org/en/about-us/role.html.
42. See, e.g., *Oakdale Mfg. Co. v. Garst*, 18 R.I. 484, 28 Atl. 973 (1894) (affirming the right of foreign corporations to the enforcement of local contracts); *Cumberland Tel. & Tel. Co. v. Louisville Home Tel. Co.*, 114 Ky. 892, 72 S.W.4 (1903) (affirming the right of foreign corporations to protection of local property and other interests).
43. See generally David K. Eiteman, Arthur I. Stonehill and Michael H. Moffett, MULTINATIONAL BUSINESS FINANCE, 13th ed. (Prenctice Hall, 2012).
44. See, e.g., Farhad Noorbakhsh and Alberto Paloni, *Human Capital and FDI Inflows to Developing Countries: New Empirical Evidence*, 29 WORLD DEVEL. 1593 (2001); Chien-Hsun Chen, *Regional Determinants of Foreign Direct Investment in Mainland China*, 23 J. ECON. STUDIES 18 (1996); Maurice Kugler and Hillel Rapoport, *International Labor and Capital Flows: Complements or Substitutes?*, 94 ECON. LETTERS 155 (2007); Nigel Driffield and Karl Taylor, *FDI and the Labour Market: A Review of the Evidence and Policy Implications*, 16 OXF. REV. ECON. POL'Y 90 3 (2000).
45. See, e.g., Steven Globerman and Daniel Shapiro, *Governance Infrastructure and US Foreign Direct Investment*, 34 J. INT'L BUS. STUDIES 19 (2003); Christian Bellak, Markus Leibrecht and Jože P. Damijan, *Infrastructure Endowment and Corporate Income Taxes as Determinants of Foreign Direct Investment in Central and Eastern European Countries*, 32 WORLD ECON. 32, 267 (2009).
46. See, e.g., Bruce A. Blonigen, *A Review of the Empirical Literature on FDI Determinants*, 33 ATL. ECON. J. 383 (2005); Marie M.Stack, Geetha Ravishankar and Eric J. Pentecost, *FDI Performance: A Stochastic Frontier Analysis of Location and Variance Determinants*, 47 APPLIED ECON. 3229 (2015).
47. President Obama Campaign Rally in Roanoke, July 13, 2012, available at http://www.c-span.org/video/?307056-2/president-obama-campaign-rally-roanoke.
48. See Thomas Nagel and Liam Murphy, THE MYTH OF OWNERSHIP: TAXES AND JUSTICE (2002).
49. Id.

income, and the rights and obligations of various nations to it and to each other, may be the only way to find a plausible solution for the long term.

For the economists rationalizing a primary jurisdiction for vessels traversing multiple nations, the second-best answer was a reversion to formalism. Source being indivisible, *situs* easily manipulated, and residence inconclusive, the economists turned to legal enforceability to point to the place of registry as the best plausible answer for the sea-going vessel. Of course, registry is simply a form of assigning nationality in the case of a vessel. Acknowledging that this returned them to political allegiance, which they had already discarded as normatively irrelevant to the question, the economists noted that this occurred because of the "economic implications" of such nationality in the context of a vessel.[50]

The economists may have intended to imply that nationality gave the vessel a legal life and existence and protected its ability to earn an income and create a profit, thus creating some allegiance that could be drawn upon to make a conclusion about the jurisdiction to tax.[51] The consequences of a decision like this, favoring certainty over accuracy–"wrong, but done" – are easily predictable. A formalistic registry rule, just like any other formalistic nationality rule, creates a global market for legal tax avoidance among governments and taxpayers.[52]

This example translates very easily to the modern "footloose" multinational corporation, whose ability to play everywhere and pay nowhere has become a constant theme in media and popular culture.[53] The income of every multinational is fundamentally the product of enforceability – of rights,[54] of legal existence,[55] and even of fictional accounts of activity undertaken, such as setting prices between members of an affiliated group.[56] Yet overly formalistic rules still prevail, including those around

---

50. 1923 Report at 34.
51. The theory that the corporation, as a creature of the state, explains or justifies its governance as a matter of law has been described as "highly nonfunctional dogma" and a "quasi-theology," yet this theoretical link has been used to formulate a benefits theory explaining the jurisdiction to tax corporations. Compare Elvin R. Latty, *Pseudo-Foreign Corporations*, 65 YALE L.J. 137, 139 (1955) with Avi-Yonah *supra* note 34 and Christians *supra* note 6; *see also* Steven A. Dean, *More Cooperation, Less Uniformity: Tax Deharmonization and the Future of the International Tax Regime*, 84 TUL. L. REV. 125, 144 n.79 (2009) (explaining "the Lockean notion that governments earn the right to collect tax revenues by providing the services that make the creation of the underlying income possible"); J. Clifton Fleming, Jr., Robert J. Peroni & Stephen E. Shay, *Fairness in International Taxation: The Ability-To-Pay Case for Taxing Worldwide Income*, 5 FLA. TAX REV. 299, 307 (2001) (explaining benefits theory in international taxation more generally).
52. Formalistic rules are simplifying, which can be a valuable tax policy goal, but they can also defeat competing tax policy goals, especially in the context of regulating complex economic activity. *See*, e.g., Steven Dean, *Attractive Complexity: Tax Deregulation, the Check-the-Box Election and the Future of Tax Simplification*, 34 HOFSTRA L. REV. 405 (2005); Samuel L. Donaldson, *The Easy Case Against Tax Simplification*, 22 VA. TAX REV. 645 (2003).
53. *See*, e.g., Edward D. Kleinbard, *Stateless Income*, 11 FLA. TAX REV. 699 (2011).
54. *See supra* note 39.
55. The corporation does not exist but for the operation of law within a state as well as the recognition among states of such laws. *See Demarest v. Flack*, 128 N.Y. 205, 28 N.E. 645 (1891); *see also* Latty *supra* note 51.
56. A central feature of the current international tax regime is the consensus that multinational firms are obliged to calculate their tax liability on a country-by-country basis by setting inter-company prices according to a fictional account that treats each entity of the group as if it were unrelated to the others, known as the arm's length transfer pricing method. This consensus is reflected in

corporate residence and legal ownership of assets. Governments and multinationals respond accordingly.[57]

Nations have autonomous powers to create and enforce the existence of corporations and their rights, and they exercise them. Other nations have powers to respect or ignore those decisions, and they, on the whole, respect them. The result of this consensus is visible in the extremely low global tax rates enjoyed by immensely profitable corporations.[58] Many observers appropriately respond with the question: is this the result of incapacity, or lack of will? As the consensus is unwritten, it is not always clear whether the under-taxation of multinational companies arises because nations as a group cannot, or alternatively will not, exert their power to tax.[59] The pressure to act has become so great over the past few years that governments appear to feel compelled to take corrective action.[60] This is where the OECD, as the self-described leader in formulating global tax policy, comes in.[61]

§1.03 DEFINING THE POWER TO TAX, 2010s STYLE

An assumption driving popular consternation around the under-taxation of multinationals is that some of these corporations are household names, which makes them seem to "belong" to one nation or another. Apple, Google, Amazon, GE, Starbucks, and so on are quintessentially American companies that seem intuitively to belong, and

---

the OECD model tax treaty upon which the vast majority of the world's tax treaties are based, as well as in the domestic laws of most OECD member nations and many non-OECD member nations. *See* Comm. On Fiscal Affairs, OECD, MODEL TAX CONVENTION ON INCOME AND ON CAPITAL (2012) [hereinafter OECD Model Treaty]; OECD Report on BEPS at 42; 26 USC 482 (U.S. rule requiring arm's length transfer pricing); ITA s. 247 (Canadian rule); *see also* Hugh J. Ault and Brian J. Arnold, COMPARATIVE INCOME TAXATION: A STRUCTURAL ANALYSIS (2d Ed., Aspen, 2004) (discussing similarity of rules across countries).

57. *See* Rosenzweig, *supra* note 32; *see also* Diane M. Ring, *One Nation Among Many: Policy Implications of Cross-Border Tax Arbitrage*, 44 B.C. L. REV. 79 (2002).
58. *See*, e.g., U.S. DEP'T OF TREASURY, *Treasury Releases Business Taxation and Global Competitiveness Background Paper* 36 (July 24, 2007), *available at* http://www.treasury.gov/press-center/press-releases/Documents/07230%20r.pdf ("Since 1980, the U.S. has gone from a high corporate tax-rate country to a low-rate country (following the Tax Reform Act of 1986) and, based on some measures, back again to a high-rate country today because other countries recently have reduced their corporate tax rates ... The evolution of OECD tax rates over the past two decades suggests that [corporate income tax] rate setting is an interactive game subject to the pressures of international competition.").
59. Allison Christians, *Avoidance, Evasion, and Taxpayer Morality*, 44 WASH. U.J.L. & POL'Y 39 (2014) (discussing the public outcry over multinational "tax dodging"); Kimberly A. Clausing, *Multinational Firm Tax Avoidance and Tax Policy*, 62 Nat'l Tax J.703 (2009) (examining "the relationship between the inherently global behavior of multinational firms and the corporate tax policies of national governments"); Rosanne Altshuler and Harry Grubert, *The Three Parties in the Race to the Bottom: Host Governments, Home Governments and Multinational Companies* 7 FLA TAX REV. 137 (2005).
60. *See*, e.g., Montano Cabezas, *Tax Transparency and the Marketplace: A Pathway to State Sustainability*, 10 MCGILL INT'L J. SUST. DEV. L.&POL'Y 179 (2014) (describing events that led the OECD to embark on the BEPS initiative).
61. Comm. on Fiscal Affairs, OECD, OECD's CURRENT TAX AGENDA, (2012), *available at* http://www.oecd.org/ctp/OECDCurrentTaxAgenda2012.pdf.

therefore owe allegiance, to the U.S.[62] But in appealing to this vision, politicians and civil society activists return to nationality and political allegiance as the basis for making tax claims – a rhetorical choice that has legal consequences in a world of formal nationality rules. Returning to nationality ignores the four economists' warnings about the fundamental absurdity of assigning tax power on the basis of political categories, even if it is in line with their ultimate concession to the economic impossibility of division on other grounds. We see here a reversal of course in the OECDs articulation of BEPS, but we can equally predict that national allegiance will not determine the course of corporate income taxation. Instead, that course will be forged solely by lawmakers in the world's most economically powerful states.

[A]   A Set of Framing Questions

Like the League of Nations before it, the OECD began its latest quest for global tax reform by observing that international taxation is a technical problem that requires an objective solution, to be formulated by committees of experts.[63] Observing that "[b]ase erosion constitutes a serious risk to tax revenues, tax sovereignty and tax fairness for OECD member countries and non-members alike," the OECD posits that this is essentially a problem of domestic rules not keeping up with a changing and increasingly economically integrated business environment.[64] In this environment, income is based increasingly on intellectual property, as well as technological and communication innovation.[65]

---

62. *See, e.g.*, Offshore Profit Shifting and the U.S. Tax Code – Part 2 (Apple Inc.): Hearing Before the Permanent Subcommittee on Investigations of the Committee on Homeland Security and Governmental Affairs, 113th Cong (2013) (Statement of Carl Levin); *see also Top American corporate tax avoiders*, FORTUNE (July 7, 2014), at http://fortune.com/2014/07/07/top-tax-avoiders/ ("The S&P 500 stock index supposedly includes the largest public American companies. It turns out that 28 of them are incorporated in places like Ireland and Switzerland to avoid high U.S. tax rates. These companies sure seem American—except when it comes to paying taxes.").
63. Indeed, the OECD nods to the 1923 Report while effectively distancing itself from it. *See* Report on BEPS at 5 ("Domestic and international rules to address double taxation, many of which originated with principles developed by the League of Nations in the 1920s, aim at addressing [jurisdictional] overlaps so as to minimize trade distortions and impediments to sustainable economic growth); at 35–36 ("developments brought about by the digital economy are putting increasing pressure on [the 1923 Report's] well-established principles and in particular on the concept of permanent establishment").
64. *See, e.g.*, Erik Cederwell, Making Sense of Profit Shifting: Pascal Saint-Amans, May 22, 2015, at http://taxfoundation.org/blog/making-sense-profit-shifting-pascal-saint-amans (quoting Mr. Saint-Amans, that "The international common principles drawn from national experiences to share tax jurisdiction have not kept pace with the changing business environment. ... The current national tax rules are not coordinated, so there are gaps and frictions among different countries' tax systems which are not dealt with by bilateral treaties or in the design of national tax rules. Sophisticated multinational enterprises (MNEs) can take advantage of these technically legal tax asymmetries. They are often aided by some governments willing to engage in harmful tax practices, which can be addressed with greater transparency and economic substance requirements.").
65. *See generally* Arthur J. Cockfield, *The Rise of the OECD as Informal "World Tax Organization" Through National Responses to E-commerce Tax Challenges*, 8 YALE J.L. & TECH. 136 (2006); *see also* OECD, *OECD/G20 Base Erosion and Profit Shifting Project: Addressing the Tax Challenges of*

Stage set, the OECD undertakes its own framing of the questions to be asked, albeit by implication rather than direct query.[66] Noting that some multinational companies are engaged in increasingly aggressive tax strategies, and that countries are facing "massive revenue losses," the OECD in effect asks: do "the current rules [of international taxation] ensure a fair allocation of taxing rights on business profits, especially where the profits from such transactions go untaxed anywhere?"[67]

While the League of Nations covered the economic consequences of double taxation, the OECD is also focused on the problem of non-taxation owing to "gaps" in the international tax system. The OECD seems to be trying to find the right balance between the two poles of double taxation and complete non-taxation.[68] At base, however, the OECD asks the exact same questions as the League of Nations did before it, namely: is there any principled way to share the power to tax by dividing the global income tax base, and if so, (how) will nations implement it?

[B] A Set of First Principles

To answer this question, the Report on BEPS offered its own set of key principles that underlie the taxation of cross-border activities. These include the jurisdiction to tax, transfer pricing, leverage and anti-avoidance.[69] At its core, however, the first principle

---

the Digital Economy, September 16, 2014, at http://www.oecd.org/ctp/addressing-the-tax-challenges-of-the-digital-economy-9789264218789-en.htm; Tom Bergin, *Special Report: How Big Tech Stays Offline on Tax*, Reuters (July 23, 2013), available at http://www.reuters.com/article/2013/07/23/us-taxbigtech-idUSBRE96M08W20130723.

66. The OECD uses passive-voice construction to excess in its reports, which often obfuscates its intent and meaning. For example, the OECD notes several times that "questions are being raised," that "work has been launched," and that "proposals have been tabled." Presumably, these are the questions, work items, and proposals that the OECD members, themselves, are asking, working on, and proposing, and want their committees to address. Using the passive voice reflects the OECD's desire to aggregate its members' political preferences into a single, and effectively anonymous, institutional position, and thereby to create soft law norms that will allow governments to act within the domestic sphere where they might otherwise face resistance. See Christians, *supra* note 3.
67. OECD Report on BEPS at 7 (noting that "These issues were already flagged by tax commissioners at the 2006 meeting of the Forum on Tax Administration in Seoul and different instruments have been developed to better analyse and react to aggressive tax planning schemes which result in massive revenue losses"). The use of the term "fair here" is telling in that ultimately, the OECD does not engage on the question of fairness, as discussed *infra*.
68. OECD Report on BEPS at 9 ("Furthermore unilateral and uncoordinated actions by governments responding in isolation could result in the risk of double—and possibly multiple—taxation for business. This would have a negative impact on investment, and thus on growth and employment globally. In this context, the major challenge is not only to identify appropriate responses, but also the mechanisms to implement them in a streamlined manner, in spite of the well-known existing legal constraints, such as the existence of more than 3000 bilateral tax treaties. It is therefore essential that countries consider innovative approaches to implement comprehensive solutions.").
69. This approach may represent a concerted effort to avoid engaging in a discussion about what justice or fairness might require. I have argued that the manner in which the topic is treated in OECD debates and reports and at conferences of international tax experts is a fundamental barrier to any project that concerns itself with articulating normative principles for taxation. See Christians, *supra* note 59; Christians *supra* note 70; *see also* Allison Christians, *Fair Taxation as a Basic Human Right*, 9 INT'L. R. CONST. 211 (2009).

is what drives the BEPS project. What the OECD is doing with all its restatement of principles, whether intentionally or not, is attempting to solve the jurisdictional problem – that is, the essential power to tax. This problem ran through all of the League of Nations' work on double taxation, and it has run through all of the OECD's cooperative work to date.[70]

Perhaps surprisingly, then, the Report on BEPS does little to actually establish principles for explaining the power to tax in order to solve the jurisdiction conundrum. Instead, it simply restates consensus positions as if they were principles. The OECD states that "the right to tax is traditionally based on a factor that determines connection to a jurisdiction,"[71] just as the four economists observed in their time.[72] But then the OECD observes that the "[j]urisdiction to tax is exercised on an entity by entity basis, not on a group-wide basis, subject to the exception of the availability of domestic group consolidation regimes."[73] Of course, this is not an immutable fact of nature but a political choice. There are clear and ready alternatives, including look-through rules for affiliated groups, which many countries have but under-use, or a multilaterally agreed apportionment formula, which the OECD is reluctant to discuss as a viable alternative.[74]

The OECD demonstrates that the problem posed by the under-or non-taxation of multinationals is political. The Report on BEPS explains that the politics are evident in the influence of multinationals over governments. The evidence of that influence: the intricate and expansive network of international institutions and process created to solve double taxation problems, and the complete lack thereof at all to solve its opposite.[75] The Report on BEPS does not explain that the influence of certain governments over others is also a crucial element of the politics of international taxation.[76] The evidence of this influence is that a "rich countries club" still frames all of the global tax policy questions and decides who will answer them.

---

70. See Diane Ring, *Democracy, Sovereignty and Tax Competition: The Role of Tax Sovereignty in Shaping Tax Cooperation*, 9 FLA. TAX R. 555 (2009); Allison Christians, *Sovereignty Taxation and Social Contract*, 18 MINN. J.INT'L L. 99 (2009).
71. OECD Report on BEPS at 33.
72. 1923 Report at 18.
73. OECD Report on BEPS at 42.
74. See, e.g., McClure and Weiner, *Deciding Whether the European Union Should Adopt Formula Apportionment of Company Income*, in Cnossen, ed., TAXING CAPITAL INCOME IN THE EUROPEAN UNION (2000) at 243–292; Michael J. McIntyre, *The Use of Combined Reporting by Nation-States*, in Arnold, Sasseville and Zolt, eds., THE TAXATION OF BUSINESS PROFIT UNDER TAX TREATIES (2003) at 245–298); Reuven Avi-Yonah and Kimberly Clausing, *Reforming Corporate Taxation in a Global Economy: A Proposal to Adopt Formulary Apportionment*, TNT 13 June 2007 at 114.
75. OECD Report on BEPS at 34 ("Corporations have urged bilateral and multilateral co-operation among countries to address differences in tax rules that result in double taxation, while simultaneously exploiting difference that result in double non-taxation.")
76. For instances, in a response to an OECD questionnaire on country-level responses to the BEPS initiative, India stated that "the approach of expecting developing countries to implement all the decisions made by the developed countries appears to be somewhat patronising and should be avoided. Steps must be taken to involve the developing countries in all decisions that are made." See India Response to OECD Questionnaire (undated), *available at* http://www.un.org/esa/ffd/wp-content/uploads/2014/10/ta-BEPS-CommentsIndia.pdf.

Perhaps the most problematic of the restatement of conventions and assumptions as principles lies in the re-assertion of the residence rule as if it could answer the jurisdiction problem. Thus, the OECD states that "[u]nder the rules of tax treaties, liability to a country's tax first depends on whether or not the taxpayer that derives the relevant income is a resident of that country."[77] The Report states that "[a] number of theoretical arguments can be used to argue that income should generally be taxed exclusively in the State of residence," cites the 1923 Report for debunking this principle, and then implies that we need to return to residence owing to "developments brought about by the digital economy."[78]

The OECD's inclination to turn again to residence looks very much like the economists' concession to enforceability as a last resort for the vessel whose source of income could not be disaggregated with any confidence.[79] The Report on BEPS notes that "Nowadays it is possible to be heavily involved in the economic life of another country, e.g., by doing business with customers located in that country via the internet, without having a taxable presence therein (such as substantial physical presence or a dependent agent)."[80] In their time, the four economists noted that "In not a few instances, the real brains of the management may be found at a distance" to the location of an income-producing enterprise.[81] Both circle around to a solution that rests in assigning the jurisdiction to tax to a single nation based on a determination of nationality, in defiance of the economic reality they ostensibly set out to use as their guide to a principled answer.

[C] Are We at Second-Best Principles Yet?

It is facile to conclude that if the corporation, or a part of it, belongs in some legal sense to one nation, naturally their income must also belong to that nation. The account anthropomorphizes the corporation and each of its corporate parts as single, independent persons, citizens of nation-states and therefore subject in every respect to the authority of the relevant governments.[82] As such, the multinational is drawn into an imagined national social contract, where belonging begets obligation to other group members. Failing to pay stated tax rates, exploiting the nation for financial advantages, leaving the nation to gain other advantages: all are easily portrayed as an obvious betrayal of this contract.[83]

---

77. Report on BEPS at 34.
78. Report on BEPS at 35.
79. See supra text at note 50.
80. Report on BEPS at 7, 35, and 49.
81. 1923 Report at 30.
82. See generally Marvin T. Brown, Corporate Identity and Citizenship, in BUSINESS AND CORPORATE INTEGRITY: SUSTAINING ORGANIZATIONAL COMPLIANCE, ETHICS, AND TRUST 14 (2014).
83. See, e.g., Congressional Record, Volume 151-Part 18: October 27, 2005 to November 7, 2005, pp 24008–24009, H.R.4571 – Lawsuit Abuse Reduction Act of 2004 (Statement of Sheila Jackson-Lee discussing a bill that defined a "Benedict Arnold Corporations" as one that "in bad faith, takes advantage of loopholes in our tax code to establish bank accounts or ship jobs abroad for the main purpose of tax avoidance...these corporations are 'Benedict Arnolds' because they

The account of corporation as citizen belonging to a society becomes incoherent as soon as we try to imagine the multinational corporation as a multinational citizen. The multinational is not a citizen, confined by immigration policies, by family obligations, or by human needs. As the BEPS initiative clearly demonstrates, it can freely pick and choose nationality for itself. It can freely multiply and choose nationalities for each of its members. It can choose to have no nationality for itself, or for any of its affiliates. It can change its nationality at whim.

If a corporation is a person, the multinational corporation is a fractionalized, fickle, and shifting one, which has children and marries them together, then kills them off and assumes their personality at will. Many nations might make claims over it, whether in part or as a whole. But multinationals equally use the system of belonging to their advantage, by strategically aligning with nations that make belonging attractive by detaching it from social obligations.[84]

Since in this context belonging is incoherent, the exercise of dividing income on its basis becomes a theater of the absurd. The income of a multinational is the product of an infinite amount of internal and external variables, from legal property and contract protections and constraints on labor mobility, to global financial and currency markets, to management structure and daily decision-making. Yet this globally created income tax base must belong to someone, and that someone must belong to some society. Nation states want to make claims of right over some portion of the global pool of corporate income.[85] Despite its inherent illogic, making claims of right over the multinational corporations that earn the income has long been an accepted way to do so.

§1.04 WHAT WE HAVE, AND HAVE NOT, LEARNED

In 1963, economist Nicholas Kaldor famously asked whether poor countries would ever "learn to tax."[86] He might have done better to direct his inquiry toward the wealthy nations of the world. Learning to tax is not about acquiring knowledge. Making a claim of right over the global income tax base is, very simply, a matter of power rather than principle. We may wish that nations were guided by normative principles, and we may try to find evidence that normative principles have guided behavior in the past, but this is a challenging task. Dividing the global tax base has always been a power struggle amongst nations.[87] To be sure, powerful nations have chosen to exercise their power to control taxation through economic, rather than military force. In practice, this has meant that richer countries have set up systems and

---

have given up their American citizenship; however, they still conduct a substantial amount of their business in the United States and enjoy tax deductions on domestic corporations.").
84. *See* Julie Roin, *Taxation Without Coordination*, 31 J. LEGAL STUD. S61 (2002).
85. They do not necessarily or only want to do so for purposes of taking some of it through taxation: negotiated expansion is an often overlooked, yet primary, goal of exercising the power to tax.
86. Nicolas Kaldor, *Will Underdeveloped Countries Learn to Tax?*, 41 FOREIGN AFFAIRS 410 (1963).
87. For a discussion, *see* Allison Christians, *Global Trends and Constraints on Tax Policy in the Least Developed Countries*, 42 U.B.C. L. REV. 239 (2010).

rules to benefit themselves.[88] This is a constraint on policymaking that we must expect will continue.

Accordingly, some countries have learned that they have the power to effect immediate change in the international tax status quo. Others do not have that power, no matter what they may learn about international taxation.[89] In reviewing the 1923 Report for purposes of explaining the U.S. position on international tax treaties in the early 1980s, Professors David Rosenbloom and Stanley Langbein rejected unilateral measures as "almost inevitably ineffectual."[90] The events of the past several years suggest that unilateralism can be a highly effective strategy for powerful nations. But the outcome of these events make a strong case for working ever harder toward multilateralism.[91]

Unilateralism in taxation is not always or necessarily ineffective; rather, it can be asymmetrically effective, which results in a transfer among nations of the burdens and benefits of the power to tax. The ongoing global effort by the U.S. to achieve its goals with respect to tax evasion by U.S. persons is illustrative in this regard, especially when juxtaposed against its approach to the problem of tax avoidance by multinational companies.

[A]   Using Power to Compel Assistance

The U.S. adopted a new counter-tax evasion initiative in 2010. Known as the Foreign Account Tax Compliance Act (FATCA), the express purpose of the law was to end tax

---

88. See Christians *supra* note 3.
89. See, e.g., Action Aid, *The BEPS process: failing to deliver for developing countries*, September 2014, at http://www.francophonie.org/IMG/pdf/beps_16th_sept_2014_actionaid.pdf ("despite attempts to provide space for developing countries' needs, the current international tax system is still dominated by the outcomes of negotiations between OECD member states – the world's richest countries.").
90. Rosenbloom & Langbein *supra* note 22.
91. The OECD states that multilateralism is preferred because "it may be difficult for any single country, acting alone, to fully address the issue." Report on BEPS at 8. The OECD worries that unilateral and uncoordinated reforms could lead the world back to double taxation, which would negatively impact economic growth and employment. For this reason, the OECD urges that it is "essential that countries consider innovative approaches to implement comprehensive solutions." *Id.* The OECD's vision of multilateralism is not comprehensive, however. It is instead club-based. The fact that this format has led to results makes it attractive to its members compared to the alternatives, but this offers no consolation to those systemically excluded from its decision-making and disadvantaged by the decisions themselves. See, e.g., Cockfield *supra* note 65 at 186–187 ("In a world where governments jealously protect their tax sovereignty, the OECD reform process, which emphasizes multilateral deliberation and consensus-building through 'soft institutions,' may be the best available option for the development of international tax policy that promotes international welfare while permitting nations to continue to pass tax laws in their perceived national self-interest."); Soong-Johnston *supra* note (quoting a commentator in response to the failure to expand the UN's role in tax policy as a counterweight to the OECD that 'This is not only a tragic day for the world's developing countries, who will now have to accept that global tax standards will get decided in a closed room where they are not welcome,' said Tove Maria Ryding, policy and advocacy manager on tax justice at the European Network on Debt and Development. 'It was a painful moment to see the developed countries celebrating the fact that nothing will change and everything will remain the same.'").

evasion by individual U.S. taxpayers.[92] The mechanism involves requiring extensive financial reporting by all non-U.S. financial institutions in the world, on pain of penalty in the form of super-withholding taxes on U.S.-source income, including gross-basis receipts from asset sales.[93] The administrative burden in fulfilling the reporting requirements falls mainly outside the US, on non-U.S. financial institutions and on other governments that must comply with U.S. demands or face economic sanctions and effective lockout from the global financial system.[94]

FATCA makes plain two lessons that nations have learned about international taxation, both of which deliver disheartening blows to the cause of global tax justice. First, FATCA demonstrates that powerful nations can create systems and institutions that benefit themselves at the expense of less powerful nations.[95] By leveraging U.S. control over the global financial system, FATCA forces the populations and governments of poorer countries to direct precious tax administration and regulatory compliance resources toward the enforcement of the U.S. tax system over their own.[96] This is a costly diversion of administrative resources to benefit the world's richest nation. It also results in the breakdown of multilateralism in tax information exchange, and with it the prospects for personal income taxation by poor countries over the long term.

In using threat of sanctions to force other countries to deliver information, the U.S. eliminated any pretense of bargaining with other nations as equals in international society. After FATCA, information will flow from all countries to the U.S., but information will only flow in the opposite direction if and to the extent the U.S.

---

92. FATCA was enacted as part of the Hiring Incentives to Restore Employment Act §§ 501–531, Pub. L. No. 111–147, 124 Stat. 71 (2010) *available at* http://www.gpo.gov/fdsys/pkg/PLAW-111publ147/pdf/PLAW-111publ147.pdf.
93. *See* 26 U.S.C. 1471 et seq.
94. This has prompted calls from tax justice activists for reciprocal information exchange that responds to the fact that "active tax havens are in rich countries, and many developing countries would need to sacrifice scarce resources to set up the arrangements to collect the information to be exchanged." TJN responds to new OECD report on automatic information exchange, February 13, 2014, at http://www.taxjustice.net/2014/02/13/press-release-tjn-responds-new-oecd-report-automatic-information-exchange/.
95. This is by no means a new lesson, and there are many examples in international taxation from which to choose, but FATCA provides a particularly stark example in juxtaposition with BEPS. For other salient examples, *see*, e.g., Miranda Stewart, *Global Trajectories of Tax Reform: The Discourse of Tax Reform in Developing and Transition Countries*, 44 HARV. INT'L L.J. 139 (2003) (outlining the tax policy constraints effected by international financial institutions); J.C. Sharman, HAVENS IN A STORM: THE STRUGGLE FOR GLOBAL TAX REGULATION (2006) (outlining how the U.S. effectively dismantled the OECD's initiative to counter-tax havens in the late 1990s).
96. Foreign financial institutions face two options under FATCA (unless their home governments commit to enforcing FATCA universally); fail to comply and bear the cost of the possible sanctions, should the U.S. follow through on its threat, or bear the costs to comply with FATCA in order to ensure their continued access to the global financial markets. Financial institutions that choose the latter will pass their compliance costs to all of their customers and clients, whether they are U.S. persons or not. Foreign governments, compelled to sign bilateral side agreements with the U.S. in order to lessen the burden on their major financial institutions, take on the cost of U.S. tax administration and enforcement themselves by agreeing to act as intermediary and forcing all of their financial institutions to comply with FATCA rather than choose not to comply and face the possible consequences.

unilaterally chooses to reciprocate, which it will do on its own terms.[97] As capital also continues to flow from poor to rich countries more generally, the continuing information asymmetry will effectively prevent residence-based taxation by poorer countries.[98] This is particularly damaging to less developed countries, which are the most fiscally vulnerable to both tax competition and tax evasion.[99] For nations battling tax evasion that is facilitated by the U.S. itself, as well as other rich countries, asymmetrical information exchange poses a grave offense to global tax justice.

The second lesson flows from the first: FATCA is a reminder that a government's choice to refrain from acting is a similarly effective policy constraint tool that powerful nations deploy at will. Few countries in the world stand in similar economic position to the U.S. To the extent that source-based withholding such as that threatened under FATCA ultimately burdens the jurisdiction that imposes it, the decision to levy a sanction in order to achieve tax policy ends represents a certain fearlessness (or recklessness, depending on one's perspective). U.S. lawmakers prominently displayed this fearlessness in forcing global acceptance of technical rules designed to shore up the part of its tax base that these lawmakers want to be seen to protect, namely, personal income.[100]

But the power to compel assistance from other countries is also the power to prevent other countries from exercising their own policy preferences. That the U.S.

---

97. In its wholly unilateral design, FATCA was not written to stop global tax evasion, but only that undertaken by U.S. residents and those deemed resident by virtue of their citizenship or immigration status in the U.S. The U.S. perversely positions itself to remain a tax haven for non-U.S. persons to evade the tax laws of their own home countries. For a discussion, *see* Christians, *supra* note 5. The OECD has responded to FATCA by revisiting the multilateral information exchange initiatives it tried to advance in connection with the harmful tax practices, this time in the form of a "Common Reporting Standard," or CRS. The CRS would institute a fully reciprocal information exchange regime, but it would do so through cooperation rather than economic sanction. The CRS also differs from FATCA in that it imagines information exchange on the basis of the taxpayer's residence and not her citizenship or legal immigration status, as the U.S. system does. Tax justice advocates have criticized the CRS framework for imposing the burdens of information sharing disproportionately to the harms suffered from tax evasion. *See* Tax Justice Network *supra* note 94. Whether the U.S. will sign up to the CRS or continue to go its own way with FATCA remains to be seen.
98. *See, e.g., Illicit Financial Flows from Developing Countries: 2001–2010: Overview*, GLOBAL FIN. INTEGRITY, http://iff.gfintegrity.org/iff2012/2012report.html ("The developing world lost US$859 billion in illicit outflows in 2010, an increase of 11% over 2009. The capital outflows stem from crime, corruption, tax evasion, and other illicit activity.").
99. *See, e.g.*, Roy W. Bahl and Richard M. Bird, *Tax Policy in Developing Countries: Looking Back—And Forward*, 62 NAT'L TAX J. 279 (2008) (examining the pressures created by tax competition on less developed countries, and noting that the failure to raise revenues leads to "suboptimal" spending on infrastructure which retards public policy goals including industrial development).
100. However, the subsequent decision to engage other countries in agreements to accept FATCA, and to delay any implementation of withholding pending such agreements, appears to have been taken specifically to avoid having to follow through on the threatened withholding tax, for fear of capital flight. *See, e.g.*, Niels Jensen, *How to Kill the Scapegoat: Addressing Offshore Tax Evasion with a Special View to Switzerland*, 63 VAND. L. REV. 1823, 1851 (2010) ("FATCA might also have an adverse effect on foreign investment in the United States. The U.S. economy has come to rely on foreign capital and holds over $2 trillion of foreign assets. Exposing income from invested foreign capital to the looming threat of a thirty percent withholding tax may deter investors and lead to significant capital flight.").

holds this power and is willing to use it is evidenced in its approach toward the OECD's initiative, which would impact U.S. autonomy over taxation by imposing external constraints designed by other OECD members. The U.S. reaction to the BEPS initiative demonstrates that refraining from tax also represents an exercise of the taxing power, and that this type of power exertion can have potent results.

[B] Refraining from Tax as an Exercise of Power

The U.S. has not used its power to respond to threats to the corporate income tax base in the same manner as it has responded to threats to the personal income tax base. On the contrary, the message from U.S. lawmakers on BEPS has been caution, restraint, and patience pending thorough multilateral consensus.[101] For example, Robert Stack, who serves as U.S. Deputy Assistant Secretary for International Tax Affairs, has consistently praised FATCA for demonstrating the strength of U.S. leadership on tax policy, "rapidly becoming the global standard in the effort to curtail offshore tax evasion."[102] However, in regards to the BEPS initiative, Mr. Stack called for the U.S. to delay any action until all nations come to a unified consensus on a principled approach that is not "governed by self-interest."[103] Mr. Stack's expressed concern is that India, China, and other countries want to "recalibrate the global paradigm that has been in place since the 1920s."

Mr. Stack has not offered his insights into why governing in self-interest was appropriate for the U.S. to do in the context of personal taxation under FATCA, but would not be appropriate for other countries to do in the context of corporate taxation under BEPS. Nor has he opined what he means by "recalibration" and why it should be avoided as a topic of discussion and action. Finally, he has not addressed why refusing to discuss these emerging concerns should be seen as anything other than a self-interested strategy to achieve national goals regardless of the normative implications.

In contrast to Robert Stack's position, various international tax reform plans provide a clear picture of the power the U.S. could hold to unilaterally counter the BEPS problem, if it so chose. For instance, the comprehensive tax reform plan introduced by Senator Max Baucus in 2013[104] – as well as variations of that plan proposed by the Obama administration in 2015[105] and by various tax policy observers over the

---

101. *See* Jim Fuller and David Forst, *US Inbound: the US Position on BEPS*, 24 INT'L TAX R. 59 (2013).
102. Robert Stack, *Myth vs. FATCA: The Truth About Treasury's Effort To Combat Offshore Tax Evasion*, September 20, 2013, at http://www.treasury.gov/connect/blog/pages/myth-vs-fatca.aspx.
103. *See* Fuller and Forst *supra* note 101.
104. Senate Finance Committee International Business Tax Reform Discussion Draft in Legislative Language (November 19, 2013) [hereinafter, Baucus Plan Option Y]. *See also* Max Baucus, *Summary of Staff Discussion Draft: International Business Tax Reform* (November 19, 2013); Joint Committee on Taxation, *Technical Explanation of the Senate Committee on Finance Chairman's Staff Discussion Draft of Provisions to Reform International Business Taxation*, JCX-15-13 (November 19, 2013).
105. Dept. of the Treasury, *General Explanations of the Administration's Fiscal Year 2016 Revenue Proposals*, February 2015, *available at* http://www.treasury.gov/resource-center/tax-policy/Documents/General-Explanations-FY2016.pdf (featuring a call for a 19% minimum corporate

years[106] – suggested that the U.S. could comprehensively eliminate footloose capital by asserting its jurisdictional claim over more of the foreign income of US-controlled foreign subsidiaries.[107] In brief, the Baucus plan would disgorge lightly taxed foreign income of US-based multinational groups by imputing dividends to the U.S. Parent company on all incomes earned overseas (rather than only certain forms of passive income as the current system addresses), and impose a minimum residual tax on all corporate income, thus reducing some advantages offered by low or zero tax rate jurisdictions.[108]

As in the case of the threatened sanctions under FATCA, this course of action would also require a certain level of fearlessness on the part of the U.S. It would leverage the nation's global economic might to achieve tax policy ends. The same risk posed by imposing penalties in the form of gross-basis withholding under FATCA applies to the taxation of multinational groups on the basis of the statutory residence of the ultimate parent or headquarters company. If the Baucus plan or some variation were adopted, U.S. multinationals would face a global minimum tax rate that other countries do not currently impose on their resident multinationals.[109]

Accordingly, if Mr. Stack is correct that the U.S. appropriately serves as a global leader on tax policy, other residence countries might be expected to ultimately follow the U.S. lead. They might do so by enacting more comprehensive, taxation of multinational companies with headquarters formed or doing business in their jurisdictions. However, it seems very unlikely that the U.S. will pursue this route, or, for that matter, other similar options such as imputation of worldwide income to U.S. parent companies of multinational groups.[110] It is as likely that the U.S. will forego comprehensive international tax reform, thereby furthering the opportunities and incentives that lead to BEPS.

---

tax on U.S.-headquartered firms plus a one-time 14% tax on previously untaxed foreign earnings of U.S.-headquartered firms).
106. *See, e.g.*, Robert J. Peroni, J. Clifton Fleming, Jr. and Stephen Shay, *Getting Serious about Curtailing Deferral of U.S. Tax on Foreign Source Income*, 52 S.M.U. L. REV. 455 (1999).
107. *See* discussion in Allison Christians, *What the Baucus Plan Reveals About Tax Competition*, 71 TAX NOTES INT'L 1113 (December 23, 2013).
108. Baucus Plan Option Y. The precedent is the existing subpart F regime, which is currently limited to passive income as a matter of legislative choice. 26 U.S.C. §§951 et seq. Option Y would impose a tax at the parent level (i.e., by imputation of subsidiary income to the parent) on all "low-taxed income" earned by foreign subsidiaries of U.S.-headquartered companies. Low-taxed income refers to active income that is subject to a foreign tax rate that is less than 80% of the maximum U.S. corporate statutory rate (currently 35%). Income subject to the tax would be eligible for foreign tax credits and the income inclusion would be "coupled with a full exemption for foreign earnings upon repatriation."
109. For a discussion, *see* Samuel C. Thompson, *Logic Says No to Options Y, Z, and C, but Yes to Imputation*, 143 TAX NOTES 579 (May 5, 2014).
110. Imputing worldwide income to the parent company (with foreign tax credits and later tax-free repatriation) has been promoted by Thompson *supra* note 109, as well as by other tax policy observers and lawmakers over the years. *See, e.g.*, Edward D. Kleinbard, *Stateless Income's Challenge to Tax Policy, Part 2*, 68 TAX NOTES INT'L 671 (November 12, 2012); J. Clifton Fleming Jr., Robert J. Peroni and Stephen E. Shay, *Perspectives on the Worldwide vs. Territorial Tax Debate*, 57 TAX NOTES INT'L 75 (January 4, 2010); Bipartisan Tax Fairness and Simplification Act, S. 3018, February 23, 2010 (introduced by Ron Wyden and Judd Gregg).

Chapter 1: BEPS and the Power to Tax §1.04[C]

The contrast between building a comprehensive, globally enforced rule for individual taxpayers and simply refusing to do so for corporate taxpayers is not about a lack of power but a lack of political will, as it always has been. A natural conclusion is that to date, U.S. lawmakers have not seen a greater good in stopping globally facilitated tax avoidance by US-based corporations, as they have in stopping globally facilitated tax evasion by U.S. individuals. This may be because grassroots groups calling for tax reform in the name of justice have not been as vocal in the U.S. tax policy debate as they have in Europe.[111] The OECD acknowledges that its current work on BEPS arises due to the pressures brought to bear on it by nongovernmental organizations. Whether that pressure will suffice to compel the organization to develop lasting solutions depends heavily on the respective powers that can be wielded by the various stakeholders – politicians, business owners, tax activists, and other members of civil society.

[C] The Power to Destroy

Chief Justice John Marshall, in an oft-quoted declaration, stated that "the power to tax involves the power to destroy."[112] Less often quoted is the remainder of his observation, which resonates throughout the ages:

> that the power to destroy may defeat and render useless the power to create; that there is a plain repugnance in conferring on one government a power to control the constitutional measures of another, which other, with respect to those very measures, is declared to be supreme over that which exerts the control, are propositions not to be denied.[113]

The Chief Justice was concerned about sharing of power among the federal and state governments of the US. But his words are equally descriptive of the process by which a state exercising its power to engage in tax competition destroys the power of another state to exercise its power to tax, and it can be seen equally in tax competition among the several states as well as among nation-states.[114] The contrast between the U.S. approaches to FATCA and BEPS are demonstrative of this power. In the case of

---

111. *See* generally Allison Christians, *Tax Activism and the Global Movement for Development through Transparency*, in TAX, LAW AND DEVELOPMENT, Miranda Stewart & Yariv Brauner, eds. (Edward Elgar, 2013) 288–315.
112. *McCulloch v. Maryland*, 17 US 316 (1819).
113. *Id.*
114. Many examples exist of state-level tax competition within the U.S., as they do in sub-state regions of other countries. For instance, tax incentives designed to attract favored industries including manufacturing and film production are common. For an overview of the phenomenon, *see* Ronald B. Davies, *State Tax Competition for Foreign Direct Investment: A Winnable War?*, 67 J. INT'L ECON. 498 (2005); *see also* Lars P. Feld, *Income Tax Competition at the State and Local Level in Switzerland*, 31 REG. SCIENCE & URBAN ECON. 181 (2001); Michael J. Keen and Christos Kotsogiannis, *Tax Competition in Federations and the Welfare Consequences of Decentralization*, 56 J. URBAN ECON. 397 (2004); for a discussion of film tax incentives in particular, *see* Alexander Malyshev, *Financing Film through Aggressive Tax Incentives: A Losing Proposition for the States*, 19 MEDIA L. & POL'Y 229 (2009–2010); Adrian H. McDonald, *Down the Rabbit Hole: The Madness of State Film Incentives as a "Solution" to Runaway Production*, 14 U. PA. J. BUS. L. 85 (2011–2012).

both action and omission, the U.S. approach demonstrates that unilateralism results in richer and more powerful nations achieving their goals, while effectively preventing poorer or less powerful nations from doing the same. This is what makes tax competition seem fundamentally anti-competitive, in an echo of the kinds of industrial policy that led countries to adopt regional and global trade agreements.[115]

Rosenbloom and Langbein suggested that "[t]he early work of the League revealed the justification for bilateral approaches," on the theory that "[m]ultilateral agreement is difficult when countries are in different legal or economic circumstances."[116] That is no less true today than it was one hundred years ago, but we can now lament what might have been had countries insisted on multilateralism and universal participation in decision-making before agreeing to any given set of principles. Power politics and bilateralism in international tax achieved a certain scope and form of global convergence, but the multiple fronts being fought on tax evasion and avoidance demonstrate that the convergence is based on weak principles and strong powers.

Fundamentally, returning to the first principles without critically inspecting the process by which the new rules will be articulated is a categorical repeat of past mistakes. One hundred years of tinkering by the same group of countries, within the same exclusive epistemic community, spans the distance between the League of Nations' 1923 Report and the OECD's current project on BEPS. If anything has been demonstrated in that century of thought, it is that tax cooperation cannot be imposed from without but rather it necessitates full participation in decision-making by all affected parties as a precondition.

It was not enough for four economists from four key countries to write out the rules of international tax coordination in 1923; it will not be enough for a group of experts from a still exclusive group of countries to revise those rules today. Rebuilding the power to tax requires building lasting cooperation in the international tax system, which in turn will require confronting and systemically changing entrenched traditions

---

115. The potential for tax competition to be anti-competitive is the impetus for investigations by the European Commission into EU Member State tax practices for possible violations of the antitrust provisions of the Treaty for the Functioning of the European Union. Consolidated Version of the Treaty on the Functioning of the European Union, 2008 O.J. C 115/47, [hereinafter TFEU]. Historically, the EU Commission tended to refrain from reviewing tax measures under the TFEU because direct taxation was regarded as a sovereign prerogative of Member States. See, e.g., Claire Micheau, State Aid and Taxation in EU Law in RESEARCH HANDBOOK ON EUROPEAN STATE AID LAW 194 (Edward Elgar, Cheltenham, U.K.: 2011). This view shifted in the mid- to late 1990s under the direction of then-Competition Commissioner Mario Monti, and, under the direction of current Competition Commissioner Margrethe Vesteger, the issue has recently regained international prominence by focusing on tax breaks enjoyed by certain highly recognized multinational companies. Current European Commission investigations into possible violations of the TFEU include Ireland, the Netherlands, Luxembourg, and Belgium. See European Commission, State aid: Commission investigates transfer pricing arrangements on corporate taxation of Apple (Ireland) Starbucks (Netherlands) and Fiat Finance and Trade (Luxembourg), June 11, 2014, at http://europa.eu/rapid/press-release_IP-14-663_en.htm; European Commission, State aid: Commission opens in-depth investigation into the Belgian excess profit ruling system, February 3, 2015, at http://europa.eu/rapid/press-release_IP-15-4080_en.htm.
116. Rosenbloom & Langbein supra note 22.

of exclusivity and privilege. That is a difficult and controversial exercise that will yield no easy answers. But finally learning how to tax may well depend on undertaking it.

§1.05 CONCLUSION

Individuals, nations, and international institutions have long asked themselves how the power to tax ought to be exercised, by whom, and under what circumstances. The question has always been answered loosely with principles but primarily with power. The principles and power, translated into law over time, built the architecture of the international tax system. To date this architecture has been burdened by fundamental flaws that have proven very challenging to overcome. To find a way forward, we must re-examine the blueprint, as well as the architects, and not simply accept past consensus positions as if they were appropriate principles. Looking back will not reveal long-lost or secret solutions to today's problems of international taxation, but it may move us closer to understanding what principles still need to be developed, and what flaws corrected, in order to change course.

Multilateralism in taxation is difficult because countries are in different economic positions, but this is precisely why getting to a principled solution requires a laborious processes involving broad participation and enduring contestation. Unilateralism and bilateralism have tried and failed for a century to facilitate national taxing powers in a manner that is equitable, or efficient, or administrable. The contemporary result is growing distrust in tax governance and skepticism about the underlying motivations of tax policymakers. Avoiding multilateralism by continuing to constrain debate and control consensus prolongs this status quo and puts the power to tax with autonomy at risk throughout the world.

Despite the inevitable appeal of unilateralism, the case for multilateralism appears to be radically improving, suggesting that principles matter in the long run. Cynically, this may be because it is diplomatically expedient to at least appear to act with principle in the international community of states. Less cynically, developing strong principles has the potential to shake up a consensus that is producing harmful results for many, to the benefit of a few. Whichever is true, nations have devoted at least some of their resources to try to get the principles for dividing the global income tax base right over the years. If there is any conclusion to be drawn as the latest wave of international reform unfolds, perhaps it is that ceding ground to experts from the world's richest countries only demonstrates how political taxation really is, and ceding ground to unilateralism only demonstrates how critical it is to keep working toward multilateralism.

CHAPTER 2

Tax Sovereignty and Digital Economy in Post-BEPS Times

Ramon Tomazela Santos & Sergio André Rocha

§2.01 INTRODUCTION

The extensive development of the Internet and other technologies for distance communication in the twentieth century have made it possible for companies to reach customers all over the world. Information technology has opened possibilities not only for adopting new business models but also for selling products and services in a digital form.[1]

Generally speaking, e-commerce comprises electronic sales of: (i) traditional tangible products, such as books, computers, office supplies, electronic equipment, and clothing and accessories; (ii) consumer services, such as travel services, airline flights, automobile rentals, hotel accommodations, and online financial services; (iii) digital products, such as e-books, e-newsletters, photos, videos, music, software, online databases, and computer games; and (iv) customer information and advertising products, among others.[2]

This chapter does not intend to suggest solutions to tax problems e-commerce creates. Rather it seeks to highlight the challenges imposed by digital transactions on the traditional concept of tax sovereignty – especially due to the need to adapt international tax regimes to a new economic reality.

The chapter first discusses the development of the principle of territoriality and the recognition of tax jurisdiction as customary in international law. Then, it addresses the expansion of tax jurisdiction due to the development of e-commerce and new

---

1. Pernilla Rendahl, *Cross-Border Consumption Taxation of Digital Supplies* (Amsterdam: IBFD, 2009), p. 1 (introduction, IBDT online books).
2. Brian J. Arnold and Michael J. McIntyre, *International Tax Primer*, 2nd Edition (The Hague: Kluwer Law, 2002), p. 150.

business models thereby demonstrating the current process of reconfiguring the concept of tax sovereignty. Finally, the chapter will focus on a new facet of tax sovereignty in a globalized world in which the consumer market stands out as the main connecting factor for the taxation of income derived from e-commerce.

§2.02 SOVEREIGNTY AND THE JURISDICTION TO TAX IN INTERNATIONAL LAW

The sovereignty of states was duly recognized following the Peace of Westphalia in 1648, which ushered in modern public international law.

Territorial space was the starting point to limiting the power of sovereign states within the international community, incorporating the ideals of equality, parity, and uniformity among nations. The principle of national sovereignty, which now governs international relations, implies exclusivity in the exercise of the state's powers and the obligation of non-interference by other sovereign states. Thus, sovereign states have the right to regulate autonomously their legal systems, as well as their international legal relations, without external interferences.

The concept of territoriality relates to the ascension of sovereign states as independent political communities in the realm of international relations.

Over time, the concept of sovereignty has resulted in an intense appeal to the principle of territoriality in its classic meaning, according to which a sovereign state's power to tax should be restricted to the perimeter of its territory. Thus, in a traditional sense, tax sovereignty meant the full and exclusive exercise of taxing rights of a state within its borders.[3] However, the concept of sovereignty has been undergoing a process of slow and gradual change to face emerging challenges of the modern world.

Indeed, during the twentieth century, the growing interaction between sovereign states in the international sphere forced the adaptation of the concept of sovereignty. The traditional territorial confinement that until then had limited the exercise of taxing rights was replaced using connecting factors as a criterion to legitimize international taxation. This expansion of tax sovereignty occurred during the post-war period during which the need for reconstruction of countries involved in armed conflicts increased the voracity of tax administrations in collecting tax revenues. Thus, the power to tax started to reach for facts or legal transactions that maintained a tie with the state through connecting factors.

Nowadays – in the absence of a multilateral body with the authority to impose or even harmonize tax policy decisions across countries,[4] at least outside the boundaries of the European Union – tax sovereignty stands out as the main component of international tax regimes, limiting legislative acts and enforcement capabilities of sovereign states.

---

3. Rifat Azam, "The Political Feasibility of a Global E-Commerce Tax." University of Memphis Law Review, Volume 43, No. 3, (2013), p. 13.
4. Tsilly Dagan, "Dilemmas of Tax Policy in a Globalized World" (2011), p. 7. Available at: http://ssrn.com/abstract=1957945.

[A] Jurisdiction to Prescribe

The jurisdiction to prescribe (material territoriality) restricts the power of the state to include, in the abstract description of a triggering event, an economic substrate that has no tie with its territory. Thus, the jurisdiction to prescribe needs a connecting factor to link the triggering event with the relevant state.[5] This connecting factor can be subjective or objective,[6] provided that it incorporates an effective tie between the triggering event and the state that intends to tax it.[7]

The connecting factors extend the geographic scope of tax rules using material or personnel links that precipitates a tax obligation in a territory. Legislators select elements of social reality linked to the jurisdiction of the state to create a valid and enforceable legal provision.

The principle of territoriality is directly related to the exercise of tax sovereignty. As with any other law or act enacted by public authorities, tax rules are instruments for the exercise of state sovereignty. Thus, facts described in the abstract scope of legal provisions should maintain close links with the respective state, within the sphere of its jurisdiction.

In the exercise of its legislative activity, a sovereign state has the freedom to choose the connecting factors that it considers relevant to the exercise of its taxing rights. In fact, the very possibility of defining concepts such as residence or nationality, under domestic law provisions, already gives certain leeway to national legislators.

However, this freedom to choose the relevant connecting factors cannot overflow the boundaries of the power of the state, which is embedded and enshrined in its legal order. Thus, the technical process of choosing connecting factors, which selects the international facts or situations to be covered by domestic tax provisions, must maintain a reasonable connection to the jurisdiction of the sovereign state concerned, under the penalty of breaching customary international law. The examination of the degree of linking between the economic substrate and the sovereign state should be conducted on a case-by-case basis. For example, it is not reasonable to tax the worldwide income of non-resident tourists, but it seems legitimate to tax income expended in their acts of consumption within the country.

The connecting factor selected by a state should also reflect *economic allegiance*. A mere formal link with the country is not strong enough to justify the exercise of its tax jurisdiction. For example, the famous *"Report on Double Taxation"* prepared by the four economists (Edwin Seligman, Josiah Stamp, Gijsbert Bruins, and Luigi Einaudi) in 1923 concluded that the mere relation of citizenship could not be considered a

---

5. Luís Eduardo Schoueri, "Princípios no Direito Tributário Internacional: Territorialidade, Fonte e Universalidade." *Princípios e Limites da Tributação*, ed. Roberto Ferraz (São Paulo: Quartier Latin, 2005), pp. 336–337.
6. Claudio Sacchetto, "The Evolution of the Principle of Territoriality and the Crisis of Taxation of Global Income in the Country of Residence." *Rivista Di Diritto Tributario Internazionale*. Volume 2 (2001), p. 59.
7. Heleno Torres, *Pluritributação Internacional sobre as Rendas das Empresas*, 2nd edition (São Paulo: Revista dos Tribunais, 2001), p. 69.

sufficient tie to impose income tax on non-residents. Instead, a permanent or habitual residence within the country was required for the exercise of taxing rights.[8-9]

This position seems to be based on the idea that the connecting factor required to assert jurisdiction to tax income must be linked with the territory where the production factors (i.e., labor, capital, or both combined) are located. From this point of view, mere political allegiance, such as citizenship, would be an insufficient basis for asserting tax jurisdiction with regard to income tax, since political links neither produce the income nor preserve the capital. Thus, an economic attachment would be required.[10]

Although this idea may be convincing from an economic perspective, experience suggests that political allegiance may also be used as a connecting factor. A good example of this is the United States, which adopts nationality as connecting factor to justify a citizenship-based taxation of the worldwide income earned by its citizens, even when they live permanently abroad. In brief, the United States argues that holding an American passport or a green card is such a privilege that it entitles the levy of income tax, since an American citizen may enjoy the protection of the U.S. Government wherever needed.[11] From an economic perspective, the United States could charge a periodical stamp duty on the passport as a contribution to finance U.S. public services.[12] From a public international law perspective, there is nothing to prevent the levy of income tax.[13]

Tax sovereignty ascribes great power to states in defining the geographic scope of their tax laws, but it finds limits in international law. The exercise of the right to tax by a state to obtain tax revenues for the development of its core activities finds certain limits in international law, particularly in the requirement for connecting factors.

In spite of all concepts discussed above, some authors argue that the jurisdiction to prescribe is unlimited, so that tax law provisions can include facts and people anywhere in the world, regardless of the existence of an objective link with the state.[14] These authors argue that states only must respect the jurisdiction to enforce, since tax inspection is limited to their territory. The underlying idea guiding these authors lies in the fact that, in defining the geographic scope of domestic tax laws, national legislators

---

8. *Report on Double Taxation Submitted to the Fiscal Committee Economic and Financial Commission Report by Experts on Double Taxation Documents*, E.F.S 73.F.19 (April 5, 1923).
9. Giedre Lideikyte-Huber, "Taxation without Representation: The Case of Resident Non-Citizens," Bulletin for International Taxation, Volume 69, No. 10 (Amsterdam: IBFD), p. 573.
10. Eric C.C.M. Kemmeren, *Principle of Origin in Tax Conventions – A Rethinking of Models* (Dongen: Pijnenburg Vormgevers/Kemmeren: 2001), p. 21.
11. Reuven Avi-Yonah, *International Tax as International Law – An Analysis of the International Tax Regime* (New York: Cambridge. University Press, 2007), pp. 22–23.
12. Eric C.C.M. Kemmeren, *Principle of Origin in Tax Conventions – A Rethinking of Models* (Dongen: Pijnenburg Vormgevers/Kemmeren, 2001), pp. 28–29.
13. Reuven Avi-Yonah, *International Tax as International Law – An Analysis of the International Tax Regime* (New York: Cambridge. University Press, 2007), p. 22.
14. Gerd Willi Rothmann, "Tributação Internacional sem Sujeito Passivo: uma Nova Modalidade do Imposto de Renda sobre Ganhos de Capital?," *Grandes Questões Atuais do Direito Tributário*. 13º Volume (São Paulo: Dialética, 2006), pp. 108–109; Gilberto Castro Moreira Junior, *Bitributação Internacional e Elementos de Conexão* (São Paulo: Aduaneiras, 2003), pp. 36 e 37; Betina Treiger Grupenmacher, *Tratados Internacionais em Matéria Tributária e Ordem Interna* (São Paulo: Dialética, 1999), pp. 43–53.

do not violate the independence of another sovereign state, such as in the practice of coercive acts abroad.

This understanding is based on the classic comprehension of sovereignty as an absolute freedom of exercising taxing rights, capable of overlapping with other legal systems, in the absence of limits imposed by international law. Thus, the free exercise of taxing rights is considered as an essential attribute of sovereignty, which grants to states the right to adopt a tax policy that best suits their interests. However, this historical heritage of the concept of sovereignty, which was developed from the political resistance of states against the acceptance of external limits to their jurisdiction, must be transcended. Tax sovereignty cannot be exercised in an absolute, arbitrary, and unlimited manner, under penalty of becoming a form of tyranny,[15] based on pure physical power (i.e., *"the law of the fiscal jungle"*).[16]

Therefore, to avoid arbitrariness in the exercise of taxing rights, a connecting factor with the state concerned is required from an international law perspective. Such connecting factors, which reveal the existence of a sufficient relationship with the state, may be based on domicile, residence, citizenship, place of effective management, place of incorporation, situation of land, source of income, or source of payment, etc.

[B]   Jurisdiction to Enforce

The jurisdiction to enforce (formal territoriality) concerns the effectiveness of tax laws since a sovereign state cannot execute coercive acts outside the limits of its territory thereby infringing on the sovereignty of other independent nations. Thus, the jurisdiction to enforce does not concern the design of the tax law in itself (jurisdiction to prescribe), but the activities related to tax collection.[17] It is important to be aware that, for those authors who believe that public international law does not limit the jurisdiction to prescribe, a state's tax jurisdiction is restricted only by its enforcement competence.

Under the existing framework of international taxation, the principle of national tax sovereignty implies that tax authorities of a country can only practice acts necessary to enforce tax obligations within their own jurisdictions. Thus, tax authorities of a country cannot execute acts of authority in another sovereign state such as inspection and collection of taxes owed by virtue of its own domestic laws. As the binding force of the acts of authority is limited to the territory, enforcement actions and the collection of taxes in other jurisdictions violate the sovereignty of other states. Therefore, the practice of acts of authority in a foreign country is repudiated by public

---

15. Benvenuto Griziotti, *Principios de política, derecho y ciência de la hacienda*. Tr. Enrique R. Mata (Madrid: Editorial Réus, 1935), p. 16.
16. Rutsel Silvestre J. Martha, *The Jurisdiction to Tax in International Law, Theory and Practice of Legislative Fiscal Jurisdiction* (Netherlands: Kluwer Law International, 1989), p. 19.
17. Gerd Willi Rothmann, "Tributação Internacional sem Sujeito Passivo: uma Nova Modalidade do Imposto de Renda sobre Ganhos de Capital?," *Grandes Questões Atuais do Direito Tributário*. 13° Volume (São Paulo: Dialética, 2006), pp. 108–109.

international law since it is considered as a form of invasion or an affront to national sovereignty.[18]

However, the lack of enforceability of tax obligations outside the limits of the territory of the competent state is related to the effectiveness of tax law, which guides the geographical application of tax rules. It does not interfere in the role of the material territoriality in delimiting the abstract scope of tax laws (i.e., jurisdiction to prescribe).

As can be seen, the jurisdiction to enforce is not concerned with the discussion about how to select a proper connecting factor to justify the exercise of taxing rights by a sovereign state. It focuses on the enforcement and collection of taxes, preferably at the lowest possible cost. There is an international consensus that withholding income tax ("WHT") is an effective enforcement method that allows the taxation of income derived by non-residents, without the imposition of extra-territorial measures.

The problem is that even WHT levied at source, along with the imposition of tax liability on the collecting agent (financial institutions or intermediaries), seems to be inefficient in taxing e-commerce transactions, as will be shown in section §2.05[C] below.

§2.03 JURISDICTION TO TAX AS CUSTOMARY LAW

In general, the principle of material territoriality can be considered as customary law, which is mandatory and binding from an international law perspective.[19] In general, it is well established that customary law, in the condition as source of public international law, is composed of two elements. The *material element* exists in the general and constant use in social practice, while the *psychological element* concerns the widespread conviction of its obligatory character (*"opinio iuris vel necessitatis"*).[20]

In this context, the fact that countries repeatedly meet the requirement of a connecting factor to create their tax laws confirms the existence of international customary law, as the *"opinio iuris"* among sovereign states is proved by induction, based on the analysis of a consistent and reiterated practice sufficiently proven. This understanding was reached by the International Court of Justice in the case *"Délimitation de la fronteire maritime dans la région du golfe du Maine,"* between Canada and the United States, in 1984.[21]

Another important element, in addition to the consistent and reiterated practice of sovereign states, relies on the analysis of decisions rendered by tax courts. It is important to verify whether either the *material territoriality* or the *connecting factors*

---

18. Eduardo Jobim, "A troca de informações no direito tributário internacional e seus influxos nos direitos fundamentais dos contribuintes." *Revista Tributária e de Finanças Públicas* n. 72, ed. Dejalma de Campos (São Paulo: Revista dos Tribunais, 2007), p. 227.
19. Luís Eduardo Schoueri, "Princípios no Direito Tributário Internacional: Territorialidade, Fonte e Universalidade." *Princípios e Limites da Tributação*, ed. Roberto Ferraz (São Paulo: Quartier Latin, 2005), p. 337.
20. Thiago Carvalho Borges, *Curso de Direito Internacional Público e Direito Comunitário* (São Paulo: Atlas, 2011), p. 82.
21. Hildebrando Accioly et al., *Manual de Direito Internacional Público*. 20th Edition (São Paulo: Saraiva, 2012), pp. 138–139.

Chapter 2: Tax Sovereignty and Digital Economy in Post-BEPS Times §2.03

are invoked by judges as international customary law. This is because a widespread social practice will be legally regarded as customary law when contemplated in decisions of national or international courts, which appropriate the content of the reiterated practice.[22]

In this sense, it is worth mentioning the emblematic decision rendered by the International Court of Justice in the Lotus case, which dealt with the collision of vessels on the high seas. This decision confirmed the need for reasonable link between the factual matter and the sovereign state to determine the abstract scope of legal rules, as well as to justify them before the international community. (In the Lotus case, a ship carrying the flag of a state was considered as an extension of its territory, and thus subject to its jurisdiction when on the high seas.) According to this precedent, the exercise of jurisdiction outside the territory requires a genuine link between the sovereign state and the person or object inserted into domestic legal provisions for its legitimacy in international law.[23]

Another illustrative judgment is the Vodafone case, which involves the collection of income tax allegedly owed on an indirect sale of an equity interest in a telecommunication company domiciled in India (Hutchison Essar Limited "HEL").[24] When examining the case at trial, the Indian Supreme Court held that the concept of *"tax presence"* must be interpreted in the context of the transaction subject to income tax, in order to bind the non-resident taxpayer to the tax jurisdiction of India. The Court considered that, to check whether there is a reasonable link with Indian jurisdiction, the tax authorities should observe the legal nature of the transaction, regardless of the indirect transfer of rights and benefits to the country. Based on these assumptions, the Court decided that the transaction had no effective causal link with the underlying assets of the company in India.[25] For this reason, Vodafone International Holdings BV could not be obliged to withhold income tax on the capital gain obtained by Hutchison Telecommunications International Limited.

Given this background, a relationship between tax jurisdiction and the ability to pay principle can be established. It is a common understanding that the ability to pay principle requires a direct correlation between the tax obligation and the economic substrate selected by legislators. That is why compliance with the ability to pay

---

22. José Souto Maior Borges, *Curso de Direito Comunitário*. 2nd Edition (São Paulo: Saraiva, 2009), p. 157.
23. Rutsel Silvestre J Martha, *The Jurisdiction to Tax in International Law, Theory and Practice of Legislative Fiscal Jurisdiction* (Netherlands: Kluwer Law International, 1989), p. 7.
24. Nishith Desai and Mahesh Humar, "The Vodafone Saga – An Analysis of the Indian Supreme Court's Decision," Bulletin for International Taxation (Amsterdam: IBFD, 2012), p. 368.
25. See the following passage: *"Moreover, tax presence has to be viewed in the context of the transaction that is subjected to tax and not with reference to an entirely unrelated matter. The investment made by Vodafone Group companies in Bharti did not make all entities of that Group subject to the Indian Income Tax Act, 1961 and the jurisdiction of the tax authorities. Tax presence must be construed in the context, and in a manner that brings the non-resident assessee under the jurisdiction of the Indian tax authorities. (...) That transaction has no nexus with the underlying assets in India. In order to establish a nexus, the legal nature of the transaction has to be examined and not the indirect transfer of rights and entitlements in India."*

principle in determining the scope of tax laws is a key element in preserving the rationale of a tax system. The jurisdiction to tax, by requiring that the economic substrate is bound to the state by a connecting factor may be seen both as *customary law* and as a *general principle of law recognized by civilized nations*. As Article 38 of the Statute of the International Court of Justice requires countries to comply with the general principles of law recognized by civilized nations, it clearly limits the freedom of national legislators in designing their tax systems.[26]

It is true that, in times of economic crisis, sovereign states often resort to the geographical expansion of the scope of their tax laws to obtain revenues required to protect their domestic economy. This is done mainly to restrain the increase in unemployment rates, fluctuations in the balance of payments, and the accumulation of international debts, among other negative impacts.[27] However, the violation of international customary law in times of economic crisis does not preclude the recognition of external limits on the tax sovereignty of states in addition to those provided for in international tax treaties.

The truth is that the old proverb is quite correct: *"Necessity knows no law."* When faced with insurmountable financial difficulties, sovereign states try to increase tax revenues at any cost, legally or illegally. Regarding international relations, these sovereign states violate not only the principles and practices governing public international law, but also tax treaty provisions introduced through international treaties.

For example, in the recent case of Argentina, many barriers and obstacles were created to the importation of products from Brazil in breach of the Treaty of Asunción, which set up the Southern Cone Common Market (MERCOSUR).[28] Brazil is also an interesting example, since its federal government is often accused of adopting peculiar interpretations to circumvent tax treaties obligations. This was one of the main reasons behind the termination of the tax treaty signed with Germany in 2005. More recently, Finland has also threatened to terminate its tax treaty with Brazil if it continued to tax the remuneration derived from technical services in Article 21 ("other income").

The examples above show that countries may violate both international tax treaties and customary law. Therefore, any breach of customary international law should not be an obstacle to its recognition as a source of public international law, as even formal international rules are subject to direct violation by sovereign states.

To sum up: on the one hand, countries are free to design their own domestic tax rules as long as a proper connecting factor between their jurisdiction and the taxable event exists. On the other hand, countries must not enforce their domestic tax rules outside their own territory.

---

26. Luís Eduardo Schoueri, "Princípios no Direito Tributário Internacional: Territorialidade, Fonte e Universalidade," *Princípios e Limites da Tributação*, ed. Roberto Ferraz (São Paulo: Quartier Latin, 2005), pp. 334–337.
27. Hermes Marcelo Huck, Foreword. *In:* Daniel Gatschnigg Cardoso, *Limites da Tributação do Comércio Internacional e Desenvolvimento Econômico* (São Paulo: Quartier Latin, 2010).
28. Ives Gandra da Silva Martins, "Responsabilidade do Fisco nos Lançamentos Tributários em que resta Vencido." *Revista Dialética de Direito Tributário* n. 223 (São Paulo: Dialética, 2014), p. 111.

§2.04 EXPANSION OF TAX JURISDICTION

Over time, new social phenomena generated by new technologies – such as global integration, tax competition, financial crisis, e-commerce, and technological advances – have triggered states to seek to expand the geographic scope of their domestic tax laws, with the aim of increasing tax revenues. To achieve this goal, sovereign states have softened the connection factors between taxable events and their internal legal order. This has had a significant impact on the traditional idea of economic allegiance.

This process of reconfiguring material territoriality and tax jurisdiction can be seen as a natural consequence of the changes in social reality and in the global community. This requires a more fluid definition of the geographic scope of legal provisions to adapt tax rules to modern society. That is precisely why indirect and modest connecting factors have been used by certain states to increase their tax revenues.

Currently, the jurisdiction to tax is going through a new revolution. Traditional connecting factors are being softened during a time of combating base erosion and profit shifting (BEPS) strategies being explored by multinational enterprises. One example of this new scenario is the tax on diverted profits introduced by the United Kingdom in 2015, which does not require a taxable presence within the U.K.'s territory.

The following sections of this chapter intend to show that new facets of the material territoriality should be explored to develop new foundations for exercising tax jurisdiction in a globalized world, marked by the development of e-commerce. The following comments will show that the Organisation for Economic Co-operation and Development's (OECD's) BEPS Project deals with the symptoms, not the causes of BEPS. Thus, the BEPS Project seems to be a short-term and temporary solution: since the problems' causes are not removed, the symptoms will simply reappear.

§2.05 SUBSTANTIVE JURISDICTION AND THE DIGITAL ECONOMY

As widely known, e-commerce is a global and highly mobile phenomenon. It enables businesses to exploit both the notion of tax sovereignty and the differences in national tax laws to mitigate their global tax liability.[29]

As geographical boundaries become irrelevant in certain activities carried out in the digital economy – mainly regarding commercial transactions conducted wholly or partly using the Internet – it is easy to move the location of a business to a different jurisdiction just by transferring electronic files to a new server.

In the Action 1 Report, the OECD recognizes that the digital economy is not at the margins of some real or physical economy. Rather, the whole economy is becoming digital, at least to a certain extent. Consequently, it is accepted that the digital economy raises policy and design issues across the international and domestic tax systems.

---

29. Jinyan Li, "E-Commerce Tax Policy in Australia, Canada and the United States," University of New South Wales Law Journal Forum, Volume 6, No. 2, (2000), pp. 314–315.

The following sections present a framework for analyzing the main problems faced by international tax regimes due to the development of e-commerce,

[A] The Problem of Lack of Nexus: Residence Taxation and Source Taxation

One of the main challenges of the digital economy, as pointed out by the OECD in Action 1 of the BEPS Project, deals with *"the ability of a company to have a significant digital presence in the economy of another country without being liable to taxation due to the lack of nexus under current international rules."*[30] Thus, e-commerce challenges current international tax regimes, which divide tax jurisdiction on cross border income between the source state and the residence state and set methods to alleviate double taxation through bilateral tax treaties based on the OECD and the UN Model Tax Conventions.[31]

The problem is that the current international tax regime was developed in an era in which the technological advances that exist today were unthinkable.[32] Tax rules were designed for brick and mortar businesses, long before the technological advances of the information age.

In this scenario, Action 1 of the OECD BEPS initiative attempts to redefine the parameters for allocating taxing rights between the source state and the residence state with regard to transactions effected in the digital economy. This will depart from the concept of physical presence as a prerequisite for the taxation of business profits.[33]

To reach this goal, the final report of the Action 1 of the OECD BEPS initiative sets out a number of alternatives for the taxation of income generated within the digital economy. The common ground among the different proposals is specifically the need to assign to the state in which the consumer market is located the right to tax the profits derived by non-residents by means of transactions carried out in the digital economy.

[B] Digital Permanent Establishment

As widely known, Action 1 of the OECD BEPS Project proposed the creation of a new concept of permanent establishment (PE) to determine the digital presence of a non-resident taxpayer that provides products and services electronically. The core of the discussion here goes beyond the long-running question of whether the existence of a website and server in a country – without the presence of employees and other physical assets – is sufficient to create a PE.

---

30. OECD, "Addressing the Tax Challenges of the Digital Economy," OECD/G20 Base Erosion and Profit Shifting Project, Action 1: 2015 Final Report (Paris: OECD, 2015), p. 16.
31. Rifat Azam, "The Political Feasibility of a Global E-Commerce Tax," University of Memphis Law Review, Volume 43, No. 3, (2013), pp. 7–8.
32. Jinyan Li, "E-Commerce Tax Policy in Australia, Canada and the United States," University of New South Wales Law Journal Forum, Volume 6, No. 2, (2000), p. 313.
33. Daniel W. Blum, "Permanent Establishments and Action 1 on the Digital Economy of the OECD Base Erosion and Profit Shifting Initiative – The Nexus Criterion Redefined?," Bulletin for International Taxation, Volume 69, No. 6/7, sec. 3 (Amsterdam: IBFD, 2015), Journals IBFD.

In this regard, the proposal presented by the OECD in BEPS Action 1 involves amending the concept of a PE and creating parameters to assess the scope of digital presence. As many economic activities are carried out exclusively in the digital environment, the OECD proposes to establish parameters to measure the digital presence of non-resident companies in the source state – for example, the volume of data collected, the turnover resulting from sales to local customers, and the number of electronic contracts concluded with customers and users in a specific jurisdiction.

The OECD mentions that a set of criteria may be chosen to address the significant presence in physical and digital activities. Based on this, new parameters should be established for allocating taxing rights to the source state, such as: (i) customer relationships for periods exceeding six months combining with given physical presence in the state in question; (ii) the sale of products or services over the Internet or other electronic devices, combined with the use of local infrastructure for delivery, payment, or other activities; and (iii) the sale of products or services to customers in the source state, involving the systematic collection of data and information.

The digital PE concept constitutes a milestone in terms of international taxation. Fundamentally, it serves as relevant criteria in allocating taxing rights over business profits of enterprises operating in cross-border situations. In general, absent a PE in the source state, the taxing right over business profits is allocated to the state of residence of the enterprise. Thus, the digital PE concept represents a minimum threshold to link the income of a non-resident enterprise to the state in which its business activity is effectively carried out.[34]

Procedures to measure the digital presence of a non-resident company also raise important questions – not only because of the need to establish objective, reasonable, and non-arbitrary criteria, but also due to the difficulty in monitoring and quantifying the degree of the virtual presence. Thus, the establishment of reasonable and non-arbitrary proxies for where economic activities take place is a challenge in itself.

Another consideration is the interaction of the concept of a virtual PE with distributive rules in the OECD Model, other than Article 7 (Business profits). For instance, the characterization of a PE in the source state may produce consequences in the application Articles 6 (Immovable property), 10 (Dividends), 11 (Interest), 12 (Royalties), 13 (Capital gains), 15 (Income from employment), 21 (Other income), 22 (Capital), and 24 (Non-discrimination). In practice, e-commerce blurs income categories and allows the manipulation of the source of income. For these reasons, taxpayers can either avoid source taxation or categorize the payment in the most favorable income category.

The greatest difficulty in this area, however, lies in the attribution of profits to a virtual PE. This would involve the simultaneous application of two fictions: (1) the fictitious characterization of a virtual PE; and (2) the fictitious independence of a PE for the purposes of profit allocation.

---

34. Giorgio Beretta, "New Rules on the Attribution of Profits to Permanent Establishments," Bulletin for International Taxation, Volume 70, No. 6 (Amsterdam: IBFD, 2016), pp. 322–323.

The BEPS Project does not present a serious analysis of the attribution of profits to PEs in the digital economy.[35] Basically, according to the Authorized OECD Approach (AOA), the attribution of profits to a PE must be based on the assets used, the functions performed and the risks assumed on the basis of the fiction that the head office and the PE are independent legal entities. The difficulty is how to undertake a functional analysis of a PE that only exists in the virtual world – without assuming risks, performing functions, or using the assets to develop concrete activities in the source state. The only alternative would be the adoption of simplified parameters or rebuttable presumptions. But from a practical standpoint, it would be very difficult to enforce a tax law based on a concept of a virtual PE. The regulatory difficulties related to the control of Internet content demonstrate that the effectiveness of laws directed to the virtual environment is minimal. This could encourage countries to adopt alternative solutions to resolve the issues arising from e-commerce. This is what happened in the United Kingdom with the introduction of the DPT.

Despite the suggestions presented by the OECD, the fact is that the progress experienced recently with regard to technology and information has provided significant challenges to traditional business models. Thus, the verification of a physical or virtual presence seems to be an obsolete criterion for the purposes of allocating tax jurisdiction.

[C] Withholding Income Tax on Digital Transactions: Collecting Agents

Another alternative suggested by the OECD consists of the levy of WHT on payments made by customers to purchase products or services offered by companies abroad through digital transactions. To enforce this tax measure, financial institutions would act as collecting agents and be required to withhold the tax from the payments and transfer the amounts to the states concerned.

The first problem with this alternative is that it aims at taxing income earned by a non-resident company, regardless of the effective characterization of a PE in its jurisdiction.

Although this problem may be solved through changes in the OECD and UN Model Conventions – and the amendment of more than 3,000 bilateral tax treaties by a multilateral instrument – it must be recognized that, in the current setting, this WHT on digital transactions is incompatible with tax treaties.

As widely known, Article 7(1) of tax treaties establish that profits arising from the exercise of a business activity should be taxed exclusively in the residence state. The only exceptions to this general rule rely on the economic activity performed in the source state being undertaken by way of a PE, as well as on the income being classified under specific distributive rules, which establish a specific allocation of the right to tax.

The definition of PE set out in Article 5 of the OECD Model is one of the key concepts in tax treaties for the allocation of taxing rights related to business activities.

---

35. Yariv Brauner, "BEPS: An Interim Evaluation," World Tax Journal, Volume 6, No. 1 (Amsterdam: IBFD, 2014), pp. 17.

It serves as criteria to legitimize the attribution of the taxing rights since it indicates a substantial degree of presence in the economic life of the source state. Therefore, in the current international tax regime – which was not conceived to protect the tax base of capital importing countries – the concept of PE justifies the taxation of a foreign person on profits attributable to the business activity developed in the consumer market in the same way as a domestic person.

Article 5 of the OECD MC deals with three different types of PEs: (1) a general PE; (2) a construction PE; and (3) a dependent agent PE. Each of these definitions of a PE requires the presence of certain elements for its characterization, such as, *inter alia*: (1) a territorial link evidenced by a fixed place of business; (2) a time threshold that indicates the level of permanence; and (3) the authority to conclude contracts in the name of the enterprise. Article 5(4) of the OECD Model also contains a list of preparatory or auxiliary activities that are to be treated as exceptions to the general definition of a PE even when a fixed place of business is characterized.

Thus, the simple adoption of a business model that either avoids the characterization of a PE or exploits the exemptions for preparatory or auxiliary activities cannot be overruled by the introduction of a WHT on digital transactions, except when the current tax treaty network is adapted for the inclusion of a saving clause allowing such taxation.

The WHT approach would only make sense if it is recognized that a nexus-based approach has failed since the allocation of taxing rights based on actual physical presence no longer makes sense in the digital economy. The difficulties faced by the agency PE and service PE concepts are indicative of the problems in establishing the even more innovative concept of digital PE.[36] Accordingly, this notion should be dropped.

A second problem stems from the fact that electronic cash (bitcoin) has gained strong popularity as a payment method used for e-commerce transactions. As electronic cash can be freely circulated among individuals and businesses without involving a financial institution after initial purchases, it may be very difficult to enforce a WHT on digital transactions.[37]

Indeed, the enforcement of this tax measure depends on the collection of the WHT by third parties such as financial institutions and other intermediaries. However, this is not completely feasible for online transactions paid with electronic cash.

In theory, the exchange of electronic cash for traditional currency is a transaction that can be identified and taxed by tax authorities. Nevertheless, the taxpayer may use electronic cash to carry out several transactions through the Internet, without having to convert it into actual money. This is possible because virtual currencies operate anonymously, without the identification of the parties of each transaction. At the same

---

36. Yariv Brauner and Andrés Baez, "Withholding Taxes in the Service of BEPS Action 1: Address the Tax Challenges of the Digital Economy" (2015), p. 6. Available at: http://ssrn.com/abstract=2586202.
37. Jinyan Li, "E-Commerce Tax Policy in Australia, Canada and the United States, University of New South," Wales Law Journal Forum, Volume 6, No. 2, (2000), p. 327.

time, they can serve as a proper unit of account to measure the value of digital goods and services.[38]

Anonymity is one of the main threats to tax compliance, because tax obligations cannot be enforced without identifying the taxpayer. Digital currency takes advantage of the current tax system since it is traded online via a peer-to-peer network with anonymous transactions and no intermediaries involved.[39] Lacking third-party intervention, the idea of imposing a WHT on digital transactions may not capture many sales of goods and services carried out on the Internet with electronic cash.

In this regard, it would be necessary to create an official electronic currency, controlled by the central bank, in order to replace existing bitcoins. Although this alternative is considered technically feasible, several regulatory issues may hinder its implementation in practice, such as exchange control and currency rates, among others.[40]

[D]   The Introduction of a "Bit Tax" on Digital Transactions

The OECD also mentions the introduction of a "bit tax" on digital transactions as a possible solution. This alternative would involve the introduction of a new tax, whose taxable base would be based on the number of bytes used by the website, along with some elements to permit the progressive taxation of the economic results (e.g., turnover or gross revenue). The "bit tax" is a new tax levied specifically the data stream flowing over the Internet, rather than on the transaction or on the income derived from it.[41]

[E]   Interim Conclusions on Substantive Jurisdiction

Given the analysis of the proposals presented above, it is fair to say that consumer market is a new type of connecting factor selected to legitimize substantive tax jurisdiction in BEPS times. All proposals presented by the OECD have in common the idea of assigning tax jurisdiction to the state in which the consumer market is located. This clearly represents an evolution of the traditional approach in which only human activity could generate income. The jurisdiction in which the consumer market was located had the right to impose consumption taxes. However, the mere exploitation of the consumer market was considered insufficient to justify the levy of an income tax. For this reason, a physical presence in the source state was required to comply with the benefit principle, according to which the right to tax should be attributed to the state

---

38. Aleksandra Bal, "Taxing Virtual Currency: Challenges and Solutions," Intertax, Volume 43, No. 5 (Alphen aan de Rijn: Kluwer Law International: 2015), pp. 380–394.
39. Aleksandra Bal, "Taxing Virtual Currency: Challenges and Solutions," Intertax, Volume 43, No. 5 (Alphen aan de Rijn: Kluwer Law International: 2015), p. 380.
40. Manuel Lucas Durán, "La eliminación del dinero en efectivo y su substitución por divisa electrónica como vía más eficaz para combatir el fraude y la elusión fiscales," *Instituto de Estudios Fiscales* (Madrid 2016), pp. 1–28.
41. Marie Lamensch, *European Value Added Tax in the Digital Era: A Critical Analysis and Proposals for Reform*, sec. 1.3.3. (Amsterdam: IBFD 2015), Online Books IBFD.

which provides public benefits to individuals or companies (i.e., public spending should be borne by the individuals or companies that benefit from public infrastructure and services).

The figure 2.1 below exemplifies the instances of taxation:

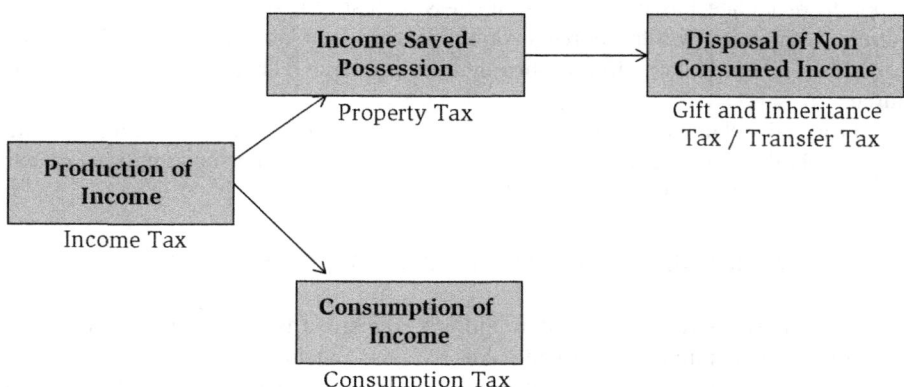

Therefore, the consumer market in itself was considered a proper connecting factor for the levy of Value Added Tax (VAT) on the international commerce of goods and services.

Nonetheless, under the auspices of the BEPS Project, the exploitation of the consumer market returned to the international agenda as a proper connecting factor to assert tax jurisdiction related to income tax. The underlying idea is that the consumer market is an important element in the generation of the income, given that the same business effort can produce different results depending on the consumer market involved.

The concept that the consumer market should become a new connecting factor with respect to tax jurisdiction has already been advanced in the tax literature by Michael Devereux and Rita de la Feria in an academic proposal for a *"destination-based corporate income tax."* According to these authors, countries should be entitled to tax income derived from sales made to their residents since the governments where consumers reside provide services that are complementary to the residents' consumption.[42] In this view, the origin of the income is connected with the customer's location. Proposals for a *"destination-based corporate income tax"* claim that, in a globalized economy, it is necessary to choose new connecting factors to assert tax jurisdiction, such as the customer's location, which is surely a less mobile element.[43]

---

42. Michael Devereux and Rita de la Faria, "Designing and Implementing a Destination-Based Corporate Tax," WP 14/07 (Oxford University Centre for Business Taxation: 2014), p. 12.
43. Luca Cerioni, "The New 'Google Tax': The 'Beginning of the End' for Tax Residence as a Connecting Factor for Tax Jurisdiction?," European Taxation, Volume 55, No. 5 (Amsterdam: IBFD, 2015), p. 186.

Putting aside all the criticisms that bear no relation to the tax sovereignty issue,[44] the consumer market seems to be as legitimate as any other connecting factor. From the perspective of economic allegiance and the benefit principle, it is fair to say that the taxpayer has benefited from the physical, legal, and economic infrastructure provided by the country in which the customer base is located. Moreover, the concept of corporate residence has become meaningless to justify residence-based taxation of Internet companies, while source taxation is based on an elusive criterion since economists are unanimous in that income does not have a single economic origin or source.

Proposals related to the implementation of a *"destination-based corporate income tax"* may challenge the actual difference between income tax and consumption tax, but this issue goes far beyond the issue related to tax sovereignty.

§2.06 ENFORCEMENT JURISDICTION AND THE DIGITAL ECONOMY

As discussed above, the jurisdiction to enforce concerns the effectiveness of tax laws since a sovereign state cannot execute coercive acts outside the limits of its territory thereby infringing on the sovereignty of other independent nations. Thus, the jurisdiction to enforce is not related to the abstract scope of domestic tax laws. Rather, it deals with activities concerning tax administration and tax collection.

Enforcement jurisdiction involves both practical and legal considerations. A sovereign state does not have the authority to compel foreign persons to collect taxes. Thus, the underlying problem that the digital economy raises for the corporate income tax is similar to problem that it raises for consumption taxes since both issues are connected with the practical difficulties of enforcing taxes when taxpayers are physically absent.[45] Non-resident businesses may have high level of interaction with a customer base located in a country through remote access devices without maintaining any physical asset in that jurisdiction.

It follows that the main challenge for a global policy towards the taxation of e-commerce transactions may be related the enforcement jurisdiction. That is because the enforcement of tax liabilities of non-resident companies that do not have any assets within a country is extremely difficult This is the case in spite of the growing trend towards the exchange of information and international assistance in tax collection among countries.

An additional issue of the digital economy deals with the disconnection between substantive and enforcement jurisdiction. This may happen because, in some of the alternatives proposed by the OECD, the compliance burden will have to be largely shifted onto third parties because it is difficult to have a complete overview of the

---

44. *See* Wei Cui, "A Critical Review of Proposals for Destination-Based Cash-Flow Corporate Taxation as an International Tax Reform Option," *Working Paper* (Oxford University Centre for Business Taxation: 2015).
45. Walter Hellerstein, "Jurisdiction to Tax in the Digital Economy: Permanent and Other Establishments," Bulletin for International Taxation, Volume 68, No. 6/7, (Amsterdam: IBFD, 2014), sec. 5, Journals IBFD.

details of the transaction. The main advantage of these measures is the reduction of administrative costs of tax administration since the company that provides digital goods or services is not required to comply with tax obligations in the customer's jurisdiction.

The question that arises is how to enforce a tax owed by a company which only conducts online transactions without any physical presence.

One alternative would be the use of available technologies to block or interfere with the company's virtual presence in a country if it fails to comply with its tax obligations.[46] Thus, the country would use technologies to restrict future sales to clients located within its territory as long as the non-resident company is a defaulting taxpayer.

However, for certain countries, the use of indirect coercive measures by the t administration is not allowed. For example, the Brazilian Supreme Federal Court, in the judgment of Extraordinary Appeal No. 666.405, decided that tax administration has legal means to make the collection of tax credits against the taxpayer, observing the due process of the law and the right to a full defense. As a consequence, tax authorities could not use indirect coercive measures to enforce their tax claims. This is a very sensitive issue when it comes to tax enforcement in the digital economy.

Moreover, e-commerce has an incredible potential for inhibiting tax audits, because tax authorities have no proper means to locate and access records kept electronically, when these files are not voluntarily disclosed by the taxpayer. In addition, the location of the records can easily be moved to different jurisdictions, thereby avoiding a comprehensive view of the sales and revenues obtained the taxpayer with online activities and e-commerce. The contents of the records may also be easily altered or encrypted, which makes tax audits of Internet companies less reliable.[47]

Due to the enforcement constraints mentioned above, successful taxation of e-commerce transactions depends mainly on securing voluntary taxpayer compliance. Thus, the best way to impose income tax on e-commerce transactions is by improving voluntary compliance. This may require several measures, ranging from the design of more rational domestic tax rules to an enhanced relationship between tax administrations and taxpayers.

[A] Interim Conclusions on Enforcement Jurisdiction

Unfortunately, meaningful information on the degree of tax compliance in the digital economy is not yet available. The design of effective tax rules to capture the income derived from e-commerce transactions will require significant legislative changes in all relevant countries, in compliance with both substantive jurisdiction and enforcement

---

46. Walter Hellerstein, "Jurisdiction to Tax in the Digital Economy: Permanent and Other Establishments," Bulletin for International Taxation, Volume 68, No. 6/7, (Amsterdam: IBFD, 2014), sec 3.2.2., Journals IBFD.
47. Jinyan Li, "E-Commerce Tax Policy in Australia, Canada and the United States," University of New South Wales Law Journal Forum, Volume 6, No. 2, (2000), p. 326.

jurisdiction. Therefore, to improve voluntary compliance in the digital economy, countries should adopt well-designed tax rules that: (i) reject arbitrary criteria; (ii) solve the problem of double or multiple taxation; (iii) reduce compliance costs; (iv) target tax avoidance behavior; and (v) counter the widespread perception of noncompliance in the digital economy.

Unfortunately, only the future will tell whether corporate income tax in its current form will survive the challenges raised by the digital economy.

§2.07 CONCLUSIONS

The challenges raised by the digital economy have started a process of reconfiguring tax jurisdiction – which requires a more fluid definition of the geographic scope of legal provisions – to adapt tax rules to modern society.

In the past, the mere exploitation of the consumer market was considered insufficient to justify the levy of an income tax. On the contrary, only the jurisdiction in which the consumer market was located had the right to impose consumption taxes.

However, this concept of tax jurisdiction was connected with the origins of the international tax framework, where brick and mortar businesses dominated the economy. It was long before the current advances in the digital economy. Nowadays, the main proposals for taxing income derived from digital transactions attribute tax jurisdiction to the state where the consumer market is located. Thus, the exploitation of the consumer market has returned to the international agenda to be a proper connecting factor to assert tax jurisdiction related to income tax.

On the one hand, from a substantive jurisdiction perspective, the consumer market seems to be a legitimate connecting factor for the taxation of the digital economy. Countries should be entitled to tax income derived from sales made to their residents. Moreover, the concept of corporate residence has become meaningless, while source taxation is based on an elusive criterion since the income does not have a single economic source.

On the other hand, from an enforcement jurisdiction perspective, it is extremely difficult to enforce tax liabilities of non-resident companies that do not have any assets within the country. This is the case in spite of the growing trend towards the exchange of information and international assistance in tax collection among countries. In addition, in several countries, in view of constitutional principles such as the due process of law, tax authorities cannot use indirect coercive measures to enforce their tax claims. For this reason, successful taxation of e-commerce transactions depends crucially on securing voluntary taxpayer compliance.

Therefore, countries should be very careful in designing tax rules to capture the income derived from e-commerce transactions. Voluntary compliance is essential in the digital economy. This requires well-designed tax rules in compliance with both substantive jurisdiction and enforcement jurisdiction.

CHAPTER 3
Justification and Implementation of the International Allocation of Taxing Rights: Can We Take One Thing at a Time?

Luís Eduardo Schoueri & Ricardo André Galendi Júnior

§3.01 INTRODUCTION

In international taxation, it is impossible to segregate the debate on abusive behavior from the debate on the allocation of taxing rights. The Base Erosion and Profit Shifting (BEPS) Project is intended to kick this fact into the long grass and has been so far very successful in doing so.

The Action Plan announces that its "actions are not directly aimed at changing the existing international standards on the allocation of taxing rights on cross-border income."[1] The statement is rather subtle. At the same time, it asserts the commitment of the BEPS Project with privileging the current allocation of taxing rights, but acknowledges that the actions may affect it, even if, allegedly, they are not aimed at doing so. Changes in the allocation of taxing rights are thus treated as a collateral consequence of making taxpayers pay their fair share. The determination of the State to which such fair share will be paid is considered as a natural outcome of taxpayer compliance, demanding no further debate. The message is clear: make taxpayers pay their "fair share," and whatever arises from their compliance with the tax rules will be fair.

---

1. OCDE (2013), Action Plan on Base Erosion and Profit Shifting, OECD Publishing, p. 11, available at http://dx.doi.org/10.1787/9789264202719-en, access on July 22, 2016.

Curiously enough, when one recalls the effervescence of public opinion with respect to tax avoidance,[2] when international media and several NGOs discussed whether the "fair share" was being paid, public's astonishment could be summarized on the fact that multinationals present in one jurisdiction were not paying taxes therein. This is more than merely pleading a "fair share" payment: there is also the idea that if a company acts within a market, then the latter should get taxes related therewith. In other words, the original movement towards the BEPS Project was motivated by the fact that, in the current regime, having access to the market is not sufficient to be liable to tax in the State of the market. The logic is very simple: people want the coffee company to be taxed where the coffee is drunk. Otherwise, they threaten not to drink the coffee.

It is doubtful whether merely making the company pay its fair share somewhere would make the coffee any less distasteful. Indeed, knowing that the company is paying taxes nowhere may make the consumer angry. However, announcing that the company is still not paying taxes in her/his State, but has started paying a huge amount of taxes somewhere else in another continent, would hardly bring any relief to her/his feelings of injustice.

The present chapter aims at analyzing how the BEPS Project has managed to divert the debate from such a central point as the allocation of taxing rights. For this purpose, in section §3.02, a historical evolution of the prevalent normative arguments in international taxation is proposed. The authors pose that economic allegiance, economic neutrality, and now cooperation against abusive behavior have all been used as grounds to justify the preference for allocating tax jurisdiction to the State of residence, being the inconsistencies of such approaches often ignored. In section §3.03, the interaction of the current cooperative trend with the sovereignty of States is analyzed.

§3.02 THREE WAVES OF JUSTIFICATION OF RESIDENCE TAXATION IN THE INTERNATIONAL TAX DEBATE

In one of his many outstanding articles, Professor Reuven Avi-Yonah has suggested that the history of U.S. international taxation could be divided into four periods: the "Age of Benefits (1918-1960)"; the "Age of Neutrality (1961-1980)"; the "Age of Competition (1981-1997)"; and the "Age of Cooperation (1998-)."[3] His division is based on the prevalent theoretical principle under which legislative enactments were debated in each one of the ages of U.S. international taxation.

---

2. For a comprehensive study on the role of NGOs and other "tax activists" in the current international tax debate, see A. Christians, "Tax activists and the global movement for development through transparency," in Y. Brauner and M. Stewart (ed.) *Tax, Law and Development* (Edward Elgar Publishing, Massachusetts, 2013), pp. 288-315.
3. R. S. Avi-Yonah. "All of a Piece of Throughout: the four ages of U.S. international taxation," 25 *Virginia Tax Review* 313 (2005).

In the present section, the authors pose that these ages and their respective underlying principles correspond in a great extent to the evolution of the prevalent normative argument in international tax debates as a whole. Except for the Age of Competition,[4] each one of Avi-Yonah's ages brings a justification for the dominant allocation of tax jurisdiction, and a main compelling reason for States to adhere to the proposed system.

In the first wave of justification, in which the overall allocation of taxing rights was constructed, it was argued that States should adhere to a certain view of economic allegiance, because it would be a fair way to avoid the pervasive effects of juridical double taxation. In the second wave, during which the bilateral treaties network was expanded, it was suggested that States should adhere to a certain view of neutrality, because it would increase "efficiency" and "global welfare." Finally, in the third and current wave, in which a multilateral treaty is proposed, States are expected to adhere to certain terms of a proposed cooperation, in order to combat abusive behavior, namely the so-called "base erosion and profit shifting." The first two justifications are undoubtedly flawed, as widely acknowledged by contemporaneous scholarship, and there is no reason to conclude that the third wave is any less inconsistent.

Even though each of these three waves presents different reasoning and justifications, they were all developed to endorse a certain view on international taxation regarding the allocation of taxing rights, which has never substantially changed. Indeed, the BEPS Project, the most ambitious outcome of the third wave, follows the very same traditional interpretation of the first wave, being "hampered by the focus on residence jurisdiction for passive income and source jurisdictions for active income."[5]

The conclusion regarding the focus of the BEPS Project on residence taxation is neither new nor innovative. Among several other contributions, an incisive statement is made by Yariv Brauner, who denounced the prevalence of the "interests of the stronger economies" in the current allocation of taxing rights, which has been evolutionarily formed, without a clear global leadership. The "typical manifestation of this increasing dominance" would be the inescapable "trend toward more residence-based taxation at the expense of source taxation, as promoted by the OECD."[6]

However, it is essential to stress the importance of the discourse focused on "cooperation," "abusive behavior" and allocation of tax jurisdiction in line with "value creation" for the current debate. Like economic allegiance and neutrality before them, these keywords are central to contemporaneous international tax discussions and have diverted attention from topics in which inter-nations equity should be evaluated.

---

4. Even though competitiveness is a strong normative argument from the perspective of the domestic tax system, it does not correspond to the purpose of international relations, where the focus is on reaching an agreement between multiple parties. For the purposes of the present chapter, the "Age of Competition" is considered as the dawn of the Age of Neutrality, as it will be described below.
5. R. Avi-Yonah and H. Xu, Global Taxation After the Crisis: why BEPS and MAATM are inadequate responses, and what can be done about, *University of Michigan Public Law & Legal Theory Research Paper* (2016) No. 494, p. 5.
6. Y. Brauner. "What the BEPS," 16 *Florida Tax Review* 2 (2014), p. 63.

[A] Economic Allegiance and the Framing of Double Tax Treaties

The formative period of the overall allocation of taxing rights coincides with the first relevant initiatives of the U.S. international tax policy.[7] Both were influenced by (or at least justified under) the notion of economic allegiance, as means to allocate the taxation of an item of income to a given State. In this first wave, it was argued that States should adhere to a certain view of economic allegiance, because it would be a fair way to avoid the pervasive effects of double taxation.

The origins of the economic allegiance are often attributed to Von Schanz, according to whom anyone who has a connection with a certain State should also contribute to the costs of financing it. As narrated by Hongler and Pistone, based on such perception, "Von Schanz reached the conclusion that taxing powers should be retained by three quarters with the country of source and only the remaining part with the state of domicile."[8]

However, the main players of international taxation during the 1920s held a different interpretation of the theory. When investigating the economic allegiance between origin and domicile, the so-called Four Economists concluded that, ideally, all corporeal wealth, including immovables and tangible movables, except for money, jewelry, furniture, etc., should be allocated predominantly or wholly to the place of origin, whereas all intangible wealth, except for mortgages, should be assigned to the domicile or residence.[9] They recognized that the exact allocation would be "well-nigh impossible" and "savour too much of the arbitrary," but suggested that "a certain rough justice" could be reached by allocating all the categories of the first division to the place of origin and all of the second to the place of domicile. According to this logic, "[w]hat each country would lose in the one case it would roughly gain in the other, and there would be the great additional advantage of comparative simplicity."[10]

The report further recognizes that, with respect to the allocation of taxing rights, "it is not possible on the grounds of pure economic theory to indicate what proportions should actually be adopted," insinuating the limitations of the economic allegiance.[11] Hence, it suggests that "the proportion presenting a true compromise for country A and the rest of the world may be adopted which is inappropriate for the relations of country B to the rest of the world."[12]

Even considering such limitations, the conclusion of the report is that the reciprocal exemption of the non-resident would be the "most desirable method of avoiding the evils of double taxation" and should be adopted "wherever countries feel

---

7. R.S. Avi-Yonah. "All of a Piece of Throughout: the four ages of U.S. international taxation," 25 *Virginia Tax Review* 313 (2005), p. 318.
8. P. Hongler; P. Pistone. "Blueprints for a New PE Nexus to Tax Business Income in the Era of the Digital Economy," *IBFD White Papers*, Amsterdam, IBFD, 2015, p. 20.
9. Report on Double Taxation submitted to the Financial Committee By Professors Bruins, Einaudi, Seligman And Sir Josiah Stamp (Document E.F.S.73.F.19.; April 5, 1923), in 4 *Legislative History of United States Tax Conventions* 1962 (hereinafter "the Four Economists Report"), p. 4043.
10. *Id.*, Ibid.
11. The Four Economists Report, p. 4050.
12. *Id.*, *ibid.*

in a position to do so."[13] It regards that in cases where such method would be "repugnant," countries should make the best arrangement they could by allocating taxing powers via conventions. It also foresees that with the industrialization of developing countries, the distinction between debtor and creditor countries would become more tenuous and the principle of residence more widely understood.[14]

As summarized by Avi-Yonah, the importance of the Four Economists Report cannot be neglected: it was "the first work by representatives of capital exporting and importing countries to lay out the fundamental compromise underlying the treaty network," namely that "active (business) income should be taxable primarily at source, while passive (investment) income should be taxable primarily at residence."[15]

Another important contributor of the formation of the currently established allocation of taxing rights was Mitchell Carroll, who bears the title of the "principal mover behind the main limitation on source taxation in the League models, namely the permanent establishment."[16] This author managed to consolidate the understanding that, absent a permanent establishment, benefits conferred by the source State would not be sufficient to justify taxation,[17] also ignoring the relevance of demand for the creation of value.

As seen, the Four Economists were aware of the limitations of the economic allegiance analysis they proposed, and were very straight-forward with respect to its limitations. The debate has significantly evolved since them. Unlike the Four Economists proposal, contemporaneous scholarship have stressed the importance of the market for the creation of value. Kirchhoff notes that taxes provide means for the maintenance of the State. He argues that to the extent that the State is distanced by constitutional strength from the economic activity, by granting the individual power over economic goods, the State can only be financed through participation in the private economic wealth. Under this conception, taxes would be the State's participation in the economic success of individuals.[18] In Kirchhoff's theory, if an individual derives income, this is due both to her/his personal effort and to the existence of the market: it would be a waste of effort if there was not a market where one could act. Thus, the justification (and cause) of taxation lies in the fact that the State is financed through its participation in the individual success of private agents.[19] One notes, in this theory, that the author has a clear vision of the State as a representative of the

---

13. The Four Economists Report, p. 4055.
14. Id., ibid.
15. R. S. Avi-Yonah. "All of a Piece of Throughout: the four ages of U.S. international taxation," 25 Virginia Tax Review 313 (2005), p. 322.
16. R. S. Avi-Yonah. "All of a Piece of Throughout: the four ages of U.S. international taxation," 25 Virginia Tax Review 313 (2005), p. 323.
17. M. B. Carroll, "International Tax Law: Benefits for American Investors and Enterprises Abroad," 2 International Law 692 (1968), p. 701.
18. See P. Kirchhof, Die verfassungsrechtliche Rechtfertigung der Steuer, in Steuern im Verfassungsstaat: Symposium zu Ehren von Klaus Vogel aus Anlaß seines Geburtstags, Paul Kirchhof et al., München, Beck, pp. 27–63 (32).
19. See P. Kirchhof, Die verfassungsrechtliche Rechtfertigung der Steuer, in Steuern im Verfassungsstaat: Symposium zu Ehren von Klaus Vogel aus Anlaß seines Geburtstags, Paul Kirchhof et al., München, Beck, pp. 27–63 (37 and 44).

community, being the tax the portion which the individual pays the community, for offering the conditions of his enrichment.

[B] Neutrality and the Apogee of Bilateralism

From the 1960s on, any and every major discussion on international tax policy in the U.S. would be carried out under the neutrality paradigm, which led Reuven Avi-Yonah to speak of an "Age of Neutrality" in the U.S. international tax policy. In this wave, prevalent during the period of expansion of the bilateral tax treaty network, it was suggested that States should adhere to a certain view on neutrality, because it would increase "efficiency" and "global welfare."

Economic efficiency is the main idea behind neutrality.[20] Even though economic efficiency is mostly a matter of economics, the adequate comprehension of economic debates is often central for lawyers,[21] especially for tax lawyers, if they intend to understand the facts ruled by tax law. In international tax discussions, it is common to refer both to Capital Export Neutrality ("CEN") and Capital Import Neutrality ("CIN"), being the former usually addressed as an optimal measure for global welfare. Both the classification and the option for CEN instead of CIN as an efficiency standard have first appeared in a work from Peggy Musgrave, in 1963, under the title *The Taxation of Foreign Investment Income*.

Whilst the importance of Musgrave's contribution is uncontroversial, one may consider that, even before the systematization of the theory, its main underlying concepts were already taken into account for the purpose of tax reforms.[22] The grounds of such theory were inherited by generations of tax and public finance scholars, being for decades the dominant normative argument in political debates, mostly due to the strong influence of Stanley Surrey.[23] Indeed, even though Brazil signed a tax treaty with the U.S. in 1967, the treaty was later rejected by the U.S. Congress. The main argument against it was the existence of a tax sparing clause in the signed convention, against which there was a strong rejection in Congress, attributable to the position expressed by Stanley Surrey on the issue when the treaty with Pakistan was refused.[24] The position of the U.S. Congress on tax sparing has not changed since then.[25]

Another factor that contributed to such enthronization was the relatively reduced participation of lawyers in international tax debates in the U.S., mostly carried out

---

20. *See* L. E. Schoueri. *Direito Tributário*, (4th ed., São Paulo, Saraiva, 2014), p. 46.
21. *See* K. Vogel, "World-wide vs. Source Taxation of Income – A Review and Reevaluation of Arguments," *in* S; Mclure; Musgrave et al, *Influence of Tax Differentials on International Competitiveness* (Amsterdam Kluwer, 1989), pp. 117–166 (137).
22. For its historical importance in the U.S., *see* R. S. Avi-Yonah. "All of a Piece of Throughout: the four ages of U.S. international taxation," 25 *Virginia Tax Review* 313 (2005), pp. 313–318.
23. *See* R. S. Avi-Yonah. "All of a Piece of Throughout: the four ages of U.S. international taxation," 25 *Virginia Tax Review* 313 (2005), pp. 324–330.
24. *See* L. E. Schoueri, Contribuição à História dos Acordos de Bitributação: a Experiência Brasileira, 22 *Revista Direito Tributário Atual* (2008), pp. 267–287.
25. *See* L. E. Schoueri, "Tax sparing: a reconsideration of the reconsideration," *in* Y. Brauner and M. Stewart (ed.) *Tax, Law and Development* (Edward Elgar Publishing, Massachusetts, 2013), pp. 106–126.

under the argument of maximization of global welfare, and ignoring fairness, equity, and distributional concerns.[26]

[1] The Rise of Neutrality: CEN and CIN as Welfare Benchmarks

CEN refers to the decision of an agent to invest her/his country or in a third State. A tax system compliant with the CEN paradigm would be that in which the investor pays taxes at the same rate over income, irrespective of the location of the investment.[27] CEN is ultimately concerned with the decision of an agent to invest in the country or abroad.[28]

There are basically two ways of achieving CEN, either: (i) all countries tax the income of their residents in an universal basis, granting unlimited credit in relation to taxes paid in other countries (even if foreign taxes were higher than local ones); or (ii) all States harmonize their tax bases and tax rates.[29] As investors are always able to invest in their own country, CEN will be accomplished if income derived from investments made abroad is subject to the same tax burden as income sourced in the State.[30]

Tax rates differ substantially among countries and it has become generally accepted that the residence country has the right to tax at its own rate foreign investments made by its residents. The consequence is that it is up to the State to decide whether to implement CEN or not, by crediting taxes paid abroad. Worldwide basis taxation plus the adoption of the full credit method in domestic legislation would thus ensure CEN. Ideally, a system coherent with CEN would neither allow the deferral of taxation by the State of residence, nor impose any limit to credits concerning taxes paid abroad. The authors are not aware of the existence of a State admitting unlimited credit.

The economic concern with CEN is that, in case it is not followed, it is likely that assets will be located in the country where they will produce a greater return after taxation, and not in the country where they are more productive.[31] The underlying idea is that, if income earned is taxed at the same rate irrespective of the jurisdiction where the investment is made, enterprises will invest where their profits before taxation are

---

26. See K. Vogel, "World-wide vs. Source Taxation of Income – A Review and Reevaluation of Arguments," *in* S; Mclure; Musgrave et al, *Influence of Tax Differentials on International Competitiveness* (Amsterdam Kluwer, 1989), pp. 117-166 (118).
27. See M. S. Knoll, "The connection between competitiveness and international taxation," 65 *Tax Law Review* (2012), p. 363.
28. See M. Kane. "Ownership Neutrality, Ownership Distortions, and International Tax Welfare Benchmarks," 26 *Virginia Tax Review* (2006), p. 55.
29. See M. S. Knoll, "The connection between competitiveness and international taxation," 65 *Tax Law Review* (2012), p. 363; F. Shaheen. "International Tax Neutrality: Revisited," 74 *Tax Law Review* (2011), p. 131.
30. See J. Hines Jr. "Reconsidering the taxation of Foreign Income," 62 *Tax Law Review* (2009), p. 272.
31. See R. S. Avi-Yonah. "Globalization, Tax Competition, and the Fiscal Crisis of the Welfare State," 113 *Harvard Law Review* 7 (2000), pp. 1573-1676 (1605).

higher.[32] Hence, considering that efficiency requires that economic agents make decisions irrespective of tax concerns, sponsors of CEN conclude that it promotes global welfare.

This is the traditional argument that has led economists to contend residence taxation as the optimal measure in international tax. Worldwide basis taxation assumes that, absent source taxation, the residence State will ensure CEN is kept.[33]

Some questionable assumptions are taken for granted by those who contend CEN as the optimal paradigm from a global welfare perspective. The first is that the State of residence will have incentives to increase tax revenues from taxation of profits of its companies. This premise does not take into consideration the efficiency costs from increasing tax collection from any source without further policy considerations. The CEN argument takes residence as something stable, which will not oscillate due to more advantageous alternatives, as the transference of residence to other jurisdictions.[34]

Second, it is assumed that the other States do not adopt tax policies of capital exporting countries. The choice of CEN as the optimal model assumes that States will ignore the reciprocal influences of tax policies among countries. As a consequence, the case for CEN is made without further consideration of how States actually behave. An ideal conduct is defended, without considering what in fact happens. CEN is sustained as a mechanism to increase efficiency, even though the actual behavior of States does not allow the alleged efficiency to be achieved at all.

Third, CEN supposes an ideal scenario where there are no other relevant economic distortions, such as other taxes[35] or substantial infrastructure differences among countries.[36] However, it should be considered that, in fact, national tax systems always include other taxes, which may justify reduced rates for incomes taxes. Also, ignoring differences in infrastructure amounts to incentivize companies to invest in developed countries. If there is a relation between tax burden and quality of public services, then developed countries tax income at higher rates, but also offer better public goods. In a scenario where CEN is privileged, the investor will only choose to invest in a developing country if her/his profits are high enough to overcome the differences of provision of public goods.[37]

Furthermore, CEN has never been truly implemented. If States believed that capital export should be neutral, then they should not only tax the positive difference

---

32. See J. Hines Jr. "Reconsidering the taxation of Foreign Income," 62 *Tax Law Review* (2009), p. 272.
33. See R. S. Avi-Yonah. "Globalization, Tax Competition, and the Fiscal Crisis of the Welfare State," 113 *Harvard Law Review* 7 (2000), pp. 1573–1676 (1605).
34. See J. Hines Jr. "Reconsidering the taxation of Foreign Income," 62 *Tax Law Review* (2009), p. 272.
35. See R. S. Avi-Yonah. "Globalization, Tax Competition, and the Fiscal Crisis of the Welfare State," 113 *Harvard Law Review* 7 (2000), pp. 1573–1676 (1609).
36. L. E. Schoueri. "Tax sparing: a reconsideration of the reconsideration," *in* Y. Brauner, M. Stewart. *Tax, Law and Development* (Edward Elgar Publishing, Massachusetts, 2013), pp. 119–120.
37. L. E. Schoueri. "Tax sparing: a reconsideration of the reconsideration," *in* Y. Brauner, M. Stewart. *Tax, Law and Development* (Edward Elgar Publishing, Massachusetts, 2013), p. 120.

in relation to taxes paid abroad, but also reimburse companies for the negative difference, which never seems to have happened.[38]

Affirming CEN as a welfare benchmark is to ignore the role of tax competition in tax policy design and to assume that all States are at similar levels of development and have made similar choices with respect to the role of the public sector, being thus able to provide similar public goods. Also, the argument lacks sincerity, since deferral and non-reimbursement of taxes have always been obstacles to the concreteness of the neutrality dream.

The normative argument against CEN was initially developed under the defense of CIN, which requires that income derived in a State is taxed at the same rate, irrespective of being derived by a resident or by a non-resident.[39] In order to preserve CIN, the investment shall be taxed at the same rate, regardless of the jurisdiction where the investor is a resident. CIN is essentially concerned with the decision to finance an investment with funds from the country or from abroad.[40]

In 1980, Thomas Horst published a seminal article[41] in which he argued that, while worldwide basis taxation would not distort the allocation of assets, territorial basis taxation would neutralize savings and investment behavior among countries. The author's conclusion is that, if all countries adopted territorial taxation, CIN would be achieved as savings neutrality, i.e., the system would not distort the decision of the investors from different State to spend or save. The critique made to CEN, in the sense that it would solely restrict international investments, cannot be reproduced with regard to CIN.[42] CIN is mostly about savings neutrality.

Horst also sustained that, since tax rates vary from country to country, it would be impossible to simultaneously achieve both CEN and CIN.[43] Avi-Yonah argues that, even though Horst was correct in 1980, his conclusion does not remain, since the convergence of tax rates would be currently feasible.[44]

[2]   Drowning in the Alphabet Soup: CEN, CIN, CON, and Tax Inversions in the U.S.

Even though CIN and CEN are intensively discussed in current international tax debates, the increasing of tax competition among countries has made these paradigms

---

38. L. E. Schoueri. "Tax sparing: a reconsideration of the reconsideration," *in* Y. Brauner, M. Stewart. *Tax, Law and Development* (Edward Elgar Publishing, Massachusetts, 2013), p. 120.
39. *See* R. S. Avi-Yonah. "Globalization, Tax Competition, and the Fiscal Crisis of the Welfare State," 113 *Harvard Law Review* 7 (2000), pp. 1573–1676 (1605).
40. *See* M. Kane. "Ownership Neutrality, Ownership Distortions, and International Tax Welfare Benchmarks," 26 *Virginia Tax Review* (2006), p. 55.
41. *See* T. Horst. "A note on the optimal taxation of international investment income," 94 *The Quarterly Journal of Economics* 4 (1980), pp. 793–798.
42. *See* L. E. Schoueri. "Princípios no Direito Tributário Internacional: territorialidade, fonte e universalidade." In: R. Ferraz (org.). *Princípios e limites da tributação*, (São Paulo, Quartier Latin, 2005), p. 362.
43. *See* T. Horst. "A note on the optimal taxation of international investment income," 94 *The Quarterly Journal of Economics* 4 (1980), pp. 793–798.
44. *See* R. S. Avi-Yonah. "Is it Time to Coordinate Corporate Tax Rates? A Note on Horst," *Public Law and Legal Theory Research Paper* Series, Paper No. 382 (2014), p. 1.

less relevant.[45] The perception that tax competition influences domestic legislation and the behavior of taxpayers added complexity to the debate and made the argument in favor of international tax neutrality even more flawed. If, from a domestic policy perspective it makes sense to speak of an "Age of Competition," from the point of view of the overall international tax debates, this age is nothing more than the dawn of theoretical belief on capital exporting neutrality as a welfare benchmark.

Tax competition takes place when States seek to attract investments and potentially increase their tax revenues, by means of reduced taxation over commercial activities.[46] Tax competition is a form of regulatory competition.[47] The tax policy of a State may affect migration, investments, and tax planning. While low taxation is seen as investment and employment-inducing, high tax rates are considered to incentivize the opposite consequences.[48]

The first use of the expression "capital ownership neutrality" ("CON") is attributed to Devereux, who coined the expression to refer to a tax system which is neutral in relation to the property of capitals.[49] Desai and Hines Jr., in articles on tax neutrality,[50] developed the thesis that the effects of international tax policy over welfare should be measured considering not only the location of the investments, but also its property. According to this analysis, tax policy should take into account not only the jurisdiction where capital is saved or invested, but also the jurisdiction where the effective owner of such capital is located.

These authors reject the conclusion according to which an investment is equally productive irrespective of who are its owners. CON would be relevant to efficiency, because property is relevant to efficiency, which would be ignored by Musgrave's model.[51] Claiming to have overcome Musgrave's model with respect to global welfare, the authors even qualify as "older wisdom" the defense of CEN.[52] Indeed, the new theory has gained momentum and recent scholarship on the issue has at least considered CON when addressing tax neutrality.[53]

---

45. *See* R. A. Galendi Jr., "Fundamentos da Tributação de Lucros no Exterior: entre competitividade e harmonização, 33 *Direito Tributário Atual* (2015), pp. 389–412.
46. *See* J. Roin. "Competition and Evasion: Another Perspective on International Tax Competition," 89 *The Georgetown Law Journal* (2000), p. 545.
47. *See* M. S. Knoll, "The connection between competitiveness and international taxation," 65 *Tax Law Review* (2012), p. 355.
48. *See* M. S. Knoll, "The connection between competitiveness and international taxation," 65 *Tax Law Review* (2012), p. 365.
49. *See* M. Devereux. "Capital Export Neutrality, Capital Import Neutrality, Capital Ownership Neutrality and all that," *Institute for Fiscal Studies*, Working Paper No. 2 (1990).
50. The most important articles are: M. Desai; J. Hines Jr. "Evaluating International Tax Reform," 56 *National Tax Journal* (2003), pp. 487–502; M. Desai; J. Hines Jr. "Old Rules and New Realities: Corporate Tax Policy in a Global Setting," 62 *National Tax Journal* (2004), pp. 937–960.
51. *See* J. Hines Jr. "Reconsidering the taxation of Foreign Income," 62 *Tax Law Review* (2009), p. 275.
52. *See* J. Hines Jr. "Reconsidering the taxation of Foreign Income," 62 *Tax Law Review* (2009), p. 270.
53. *See*, e.g., M. Graetz and A. Warren Jr. "Income Tax Discrimination: Still Stuck in the Labyrinth of Impossibility," 121 *The Yale Law Journal* (2012), pp. 1118-1167; *See* M. Kane. "Ownership Neutrality, Ownership Distortions, and International Tax Welfare Benchmarks," 26 *Virginia Tax Review* (2006), passim; M. S. Knoll, "The connection between competitiveness and international taxation," 65 *Tax Law Review* (2012), passim.

Chapter 3: The International Allocation of Taxing Rights §3.02[B]

CON is defined as an attribution of tax systems which keep incentives to the efficient property of assets.[54] A tax system compliant with CON is a system in which companies, irrespective of where they are located, compete on equal-footing for the acquisition of assets, in the sense that taxes do not affect their capacity of acquiring assets.[55]

There would be two main advantages of the CON paradigm when compared to Musgrave's model. The first one would be that the new formulation would consider the impact of economic distortions from other taxes. Second, CON would be able to incorporate the reactions of other States to changes in the taxation in the State of residence. The property of capital would be directly influenced by the tax policies of each State and such effects, if adequately measured, would have the potential to revert the Musgrave's conclusions regarding welfare.[56] In other words, CON would take the effects of tax competition over tax systems into account, being able to contemplate this element in the measurement of global welfare.[57]

CON demands that all countries tax similarly income derived by their residents abroad. If all States tax foreign income in a worldwide basis, using the credit method to avoid double taxation, CON will be privileged. In this case, there will be no tax incentive for the reallocation of assets among investors subject to different jurisdictions. The same would occur if all countries exempt their residents' foreign income. In such case, the applicable regime would be the same for all investors, and competition among potential buyers of assets would incentivize that they are held by the most productive owners.

The authors sustain that CON would be privileged either if all countries taxed income on a worldwide basis (CEN), or if they taxed income on a territorial basis (CIN). CON would also be contemplated if there was uniform adoption of any policy comprised in the gap between CIN and CEN, to which tax policies usually converge.[58]

The advent of CON was a clear academic response to the increasing of tax inversions in the U.S. As most jurisdictions migrated to territorial taxation of business profits, by means of participation exemptions,[59] along with other measures to attract investments and expand the activities of local companies abroad, the U.S. insisted on the CEN reasoning, in order to maintain the taxation of profits upon repatriation. This

---

54. See J. Hines Jr. "Reconsidering the taxation of Foreign Income," 62 *Tax Law Review* (2009), p. 275.
55. M. S. Knoll, "The connection between competitiveness and international taxation," 65 *Tax Law Review* (2012), p. 368.
56. See J. Hines Jr. "Reconsidering the taxation of Foreign Income," 62 *Tax Law Review* (2009), p. 271.
57. For a position considering national welfare instead of global welfare, see D. Shaviro, "Rethinking foreign tax creditability," *National Tax Journal*, vol. 63, 2010, pp. 709–722.
58. See J. Hines Jr. "Reconsidering the taxation of Foreign Income," 62 *Tax Law Review* (2009), p. 276.
59. J. Englisch. "Fiscal cohesion in the taxation of cross-border dividends (part one)," *European Taxation* (2004), p. 323. C. Romano. "Holding companies regimes in Europe: a comparative survey," *European Taxation* (1999), pp. 256–269.

led to major tax inversions of U.S.-based multinational enterprises,[60] in transactions involving billions of dollars and eroding the U.S. tax base. Ironically, such *tax* inversions are clearly tax driven, despite the strong commitment of the U.S. with neutrality.

[C] Cooperating for Value Creation

Wisely conceiving that "[p]eriodization becomes more and more difficult as one approaches the present," Avi-Yonah suggests that, in the U.S. tax policy "a new period began with the decision of the Clinton Administration to cooperate with the OECD's harmful tax competition initiative from 1998 onward." Focused on concerted action, the "Age of Cooperation" would promise "a way out from the need to balance U.S. international tax policy goals with competitiveness considerations."[61]

Competition in the market incentivizes companies to reduce their prices and increase the quality of their products and services. The belief that consumers are benefited by the healthy competition between companies lies at the very core of liberal capitalism. For this reason, States have intensively combated behaviors and structures that harm competition in the market, by means of strong antitrust legislation.[62]

However, globalization has also increased the competition among States, which have also been affected by the mobility of capital.[63] While companies compete essentially for consumers, States compete for productive resources (such as investments and qualified labor), for intangible capital and tax revenues. Among other attributes, the tax system is a relevant instrument available to States in their competition with the others.[64]

The consensus concerning the benefits of a free market for consumers is not reproduced with regard to State competition. Public finance debates bring two contrasting positions,[65] whose first arguments where developed in the context of discussions regarding the U.S. federalism.[66]

Following the Organisation for Economic Co-operation and Development's (OECD's) 1998 Harmful Tax Competition Report,[67] Avi-Yonah sees an age marked "by

---

60. The most comprehensive list of inversions we are aware is credited to Professor Mihir Desai, including approximately 75 inverted companies. See C. Hwang. "The New Corporate Migration: Tax Diversion through Inversion," 80 *Brooklyn Law Review* 3 (2015), pp. 807–856.
61. R. S. Avi-Yonah. "All of a Piece of Throughout: the four ages of U.S. international taxation," 25 *Virginia Tax Review* 313 (2005), p. 334.
62. See R. A. Galendi Jr., Fundamentos da Tributação de Lucros no Exterior: entre competitividade e harmonização, 33 *Direito Tributário Atual* (2015), pp. 389–412.
63. See L. E. Schoueri. Globalização, investimentos e tributação: desafios da concorrência internacional ao sistema tributário brasileiro, 113 *Revista Brasileira de Comércio Exterior* (2012), pp. 6–13.
64. E. Toder. "International Competitiveness: Who Competes against Whom, and for What?," 65 *Tax Law Review* (2012), p. 509.
65. See W. Oates and R. Schwab. "Economic Competition Among Jurisdictions: efficiency enhancing or distortion inducing?," 35 *Journal of Public Economics* (1988), pp. 333–354.
66. See ACIR (Advisory Commission on Intergovernmental Relations), *Regional Growth: interstate tax competition*, (Washington: Comission Report, 1981).
67. Cf. OECD. *Harmful tax competition*, Paris: OECD, 1998.

a different response to globalization than unilateral competition."⁶⁸ Cooperation is seen as a way out from competition: in a cooperative scenario tax policy objectives of a State are no longer subject to competitive pressures and the State is finally free to tax as it pleases.

According to Charles Tiebout, competition would make States more efficient and sensible to the needs and desires of their citizens.⁶⁹ Scholars who see the State as a (leviathanic) revenue maximizer organism share this perception.⁷⁰ For these authors, competition among jurisdictions would be a powerful formula to combat undesired expansionist tendencies of the public sector over the private sector.⁷¹ In this view, competition would have the welfare-generating function of disciplining the public sector, which is in a constant movement towards expansion.⁷² Stigler has argued that competition would not present obstacles, but opportunities for communities to choose the type and scale of the functions of the Government they desire. In Tiebout's model, competition among a relatively high number of jurisdictions, each offering a different combination between taxation and public expenses, along with free flow of citizens, would be capable of granting efficiency gains, thus maximizing social welfare.⁷³

For other scholars, however, jurisdiction competition would be a form of distorting public choice.⁷⁴ Accordingly, when seeking to attract industries and jobs, States would restrict taxation of companies to levels which are below the necessary for the provision of public services.⁷⁵ In 1980, the perspective of a "cut-throat competition" among federal states in the U.S. led to the suggestion of a federal intervention to save states from themselves.⁷⁶ Under this perspective, it is assumed that, given the specific nature of public goods, competition among States would lead to a "race to the bottom," of an eminently destructive character, which would subject States to a situation where they would not cooperate, even knowing that cooperation would be more beneficial than competition. In the case of tax competition, even if it would be better for States to maintain taxation levels, they would choose not to do so, fearing that other States would adopt tax incentives to attract investments. Those who share this perspective

---

68. R. S. Avi-Yonah. "All of a Piece of Throughout: the four ages of U.S. international taxation," 25 *Virginia Tax Review* 313 (2005), p. 334.
69. *See* C. Tiebout, "A pure theory of local expenditures," *The Journal of Political Economy*, 64, no. 5, (1956), pp. 416–424.
70. *See* G. Brennan and J. Buchanan *The Power to Tax: analytical foundations of a fiscal constitution*, (Indianapolis, Liberty Fund, 2000), p. 46.
71. *See* G. Brennan and J. Buchanan *The Power to Tax: analytical foundations of a fiscal constitution*, (Indianapolis, Liberty Fund, 2000), p. 200.
72. *See* W. Oates and R. Schwab. "Economic Competition Among Jurisdictions: efficiency enhancing or distortion inducing?," 35 *Journal of Public Economics* (1988), p. 334.
73. *See* C. Tiebout, "A pure theory of local expenditures," *The Journal of Political Economy*, 64, no. 5 (1956), pp. 416–424.
74. *See* G. Brennan and J. Buchanan *The Power to Tax: analytical foundations of a fiscal constitution*, (Indianapolis, Liberty Fund, 2000), p. 200 and ss. Compare with: W. Oates and R. Schwab. "Economic Competition Among Jurisdictions: efficiency enhancing or distortion inducing?," 35 *Journal of Public Economics* (1988), p. 342.
75. *See* W. Oates and R. Schwab. "Economic Competition Among Jurisdictions: efficiency enhancing or distortion inducing?," 35 *Journal of Public Economics* (1988), p. 335.
76. *See* ACIR (Advisory Commission on Intergovernmental Relations), *Regional Growth: interstate tax competition*, (Washington: Comission Report, 1981), p. 10.

argue that States should sign agreements granting minimal standards of State action, which, if signed between private companies would certainly be subject to antitrust sanctions.[77]

Even if prevailing, the argument that competition among States would necessarily imply distortions is not convincing. If residents of a State are actually concerned with the effect of tax competition over public services, then tax competition entails real burdens over citizens. It is not clear the extent to which citizens would tolerate and endorse a competitive behavior of the State, in the detriment of efficient public services provision. Tax competition promotes the diversity of Governments and tax systems, increasing local efficiencies.[78] In summary, the opposition to tax competition relies on two main economic arguments: (i) allowing tax competition would generate few efficiency gains; and (ii) such efficiency gains would not overcome the social loss arising from the decreasing of tax collection.[79]

As from the Harmful Tax Competition report,[80] tax competition between States has been put into perspective. The scope of this report is the behavior of jurisdictions which, by means of low taxation of mobile activities, distort the "actual" flow of investments, reduces the integrity of tax structures and transfer the tax burden to less mobile elements, such as labor.[81] This report was the first step towards more comprehensive harmonization measures such as those brought by the BEPS Project.

The Action Plan argues that "taxation is at the core of countries' sovereignty, but the interaction of domestic tax rules in some cases leads to gaps and frictions."[82] Such gaps would consist on the non-taxation of profits where "value is created." The BEPS Project, then, through coordinated measures, is intended to "realign" taxation with value creation.[83] The expression "realigning" is very interesting, because it implies that taxation has once been "aligned" with value creation.

Thus, the BEPS rhetoric is often structured as follows: (i) international taxation used to be aligned with value creation; (ii) subsequent events, mostly attributable to globalization, have distorted international taxation; (iii) in order to "realign" taxation with value creation, States must cooperate, and apply the measures suggested by the BEPS Project. For instance, as argued in the Final Report on Action 6, if the measures

---

77. See J. Roin. "Competition and Evasion: Another Perspective on International Tax Competition," 89 *The Georgetown Law Journal* (2000), p. 546.
78. See J. Roin. "Competition and Evasion: Another Perspective on International Tax Competition," 89 *The Georgetown Law Journal* (2000), p. 553.
79. See R. S. Avi-Yonah. "Globalization, Tax Competition, and the Fiscal Crisis of the Welfare State," 113 *Harvard Law Review* 7 (2000), pp. 1644–1647. This position is also held by the International Monetary Fund ("IMF"), which deems tax incentives as largely inefficient (*See* J. Stotsky, "Summary of IMF Tax Policy Advice," in *Tax Policy Handbook* (Washington: FMI, 1995), pp. 279–283). For a similar position, *see* Y. Brauner, "The Future of Tax Incentives for Developing Countries," *in* Y. Brauner, M. Stewart. *Tax, Law and Development* (Edward Elgar Publishing, Massachusetts, 2013) pp. 25–56.
80. *See* OECD. *Harmful tax competition*, Paris: OECD, 1998.
81. *See* OECD, *Harmful tax competition*, supra., p. 16.
82. OCDE (2013), Action Plan on Base Erosion and Profit Shifting, OECD Publishing, available at http://dx.doi.org/10.1787/9789264202719-en, access on July 22, 2016.
83. "Realigning taxation with economic activities and value creation" is a recurrent expression in many of the BEPS documents.

regarding the prevention of granting of treaty benefits in inappropriate circumstances are applied, "it is expected that profits will be reported where the economic activities that generate them are carried out and where value is created."[84] This reasoning grants that further discussion on inter-nations equity is avoided.

Curiously enough, the measures suggested are mostly intended to amplify taxing rights in the State of residence. Despite the consolidated interpretation of the arm's length standard set forth in Article 9 of the OECD-MC, by means of an aggressive interpretation, the BEPS Project intends to shift the provision to a "value creation" paradigm, which is not necessarily compatible with the arm's length as agreed by the Contracting States in several tax treaties[85] or with the jurisprudence of the European Court of Justice.[86] The outcome of this new interpretation is shifting taxation to capital exporting countries, which are, as per the BEPS Project reasoning, often the countries where value is created.[87]

Value creation, as per the BEPS Project, is attributed to "assets used, risks assumed and functions performed." This mantra is far from being able to determine in any and every case where value is created and works rather as a formula to deny the importance of demand (market) for value creation even though, as mentioned above, taxation where consumption occurs was the very reason for the whole BEPS movement. As a consequence, as "economic allegiance" and "neutrality," "value creation" is nothing more than a narrow view of the justifications for allocating tax jurisdiction, intended to amplify the taxing rights of the State of residence.

Some scholars intend to take one step further. In another text, Professor Avi-Yonah points out there would be a natural convergence of income tax rates among States, mostly due to tax competition. In his understanding, the BEPS Project would present "a chance to go further."[88] After considering that the European Union (EU) has never succeeded in coordinating tax rates, due to the diversity among its members (a factor which would also be present among the OECD and UN members), he poses that the G20 would present a different opportunity.[89] Unlike the other organizations, the G20 is composed of great capital exporters, which are residence to 90% of world's multinational enterprises. Hence, G20 members could commit to taxing their multinationals in a worldwide basis at a rate between 20% and 30%. In this case, no member

---

84. OECD (2015), Preventing the Granting of Treaty Benefits in Inappropriate Circumstances, Action 6 – 2015 Final Report, OECD/G20 Base Erosion and Profit Shifting Project, OECD Publishing, Paris, p. 3, available at http://dx.doi.org/10.1787/9789264241695-en, access on July 22, 2016.
85. See L.E. Schoueri, "Arm's Length: Beyond the Guidelines of the OECD," 69 *Bulletin for International Taxation* 12 (2015), pp. 690–716.
86. See W. Schön, "Transfer Pricing Issues of BEPS in the Light of EU Law," 3 *British Tax Review* (2015).
87. For examples on these outcomes, see L.E. Schoueri, "Arm's Length: Beyond the Guidelines of the OECD," 69 *Bulletin for International Taxation* 12 (2015), pp. 690–716.
88. See R. S. Avi-Yonah. "Is it Time to Coordinate Corporate Tax Rates? A Note on Horst," *Public Law and Legal Theory Research Paper* Series, Paper No. 382 (2014), p. 2. The author argues that "*multinationals compete with each other across national borders, and no country wishes to put its multinationals at a competitive disadvantage. Because of this, corporate tax rates tend to move in unison.*"
89. A primitive version of these ideas where already present in his seminal article AVI-YONAH, "Globalization, tax competition...," *supra.*, p. 1610.

of the G20 would have to raise their rates, and only Argentina, Brazil, France, Italy, India, and the USA would have to reduce them. He concludes that Horst's utopia, consisting on simultaneously obtaining CIN and CEN, could be "closer to reality than many economists and policy makers believe."[90] This is a simplistic approach, which does not consider peculiarities of tax systems. For instance, although Brazil taxes its companies on a (relatively) high rate (34%), dividends paid by such companies are exempt from further taxation. Therefore, if Brazil would reduce its corporate tax rate to the suggested 30% limit, companies would have an effective advantage, since their overall burden (including taxation of dividends) would be lower than those located in countries which opt for taxing dividends.

Harmful tax competition is present where the taxation in a given State may be considered too low.[91] Even though one may question the parameters under which a "too low" taxation may be characterized, such identification certainly present some limits.[92] Policies that are merely different cannot always be considered harmful. The abovementioned Brazilian policy not to tax dividends can be a good example thereof. In other words, there is a long path to conclude that harmful tax competition issues should be solved by means of harmonization.

Those who contend the need for harmonization seem to believe that economic globalization should not affect the social consensus reached with respect to the financing of public services, apparently not taking into account that many States have not taken part in such consensus, and are still not prepared to do so. They seem to believe that cooperation between States could bring benefits, such as the efficiency arising from neutrality, the possibility of taxing capital instead of labor and the equity which is allegedly present in a scenario without tax competition.[93]

Even in the context of a federation, harmonization is questioned: in the U.S., the difference in tax burdens was considered fundamental for the characterization of the federation.[94] When one refers to a sovereign State, the importance of taxation is even greater. Avi-Yonah, who sustains increasing harmonization measures, stresses the importance of preserving the capacity of each democratic State to determine the size of its public sector.[95] It is not clear, however, how a State could be subject to

---

90. *See* R.S. Avi-Yonah. "Is it Time to Coordinate Corporate Tax Rates? A Note on Horst," *Public Law and Legal Theory Research Paper* Series, Paper No. 382 (2014), pp. 2–3.
91. J. Roin. "Competition and Evasion: Another Perspective on International Tax Competition," 89 *The Georgetown Law Journal* (2000), p. 553.
92. *See* J. Roin. "Competition and Evasion: Another Perspective on International Tax Competition," 89 *The Georgetown Law Journal* (2000), p. 553.
93. *See* T. Dagan. "The Costs of International Tax Cooperation," *Bar-Ilan University Faculty of Law*, Working Paper No. 1-03 (2013), p. 23.
94. In ACIR's Report it is argued that *"Differences in state and local tax rates and tax burdens are fundamental to the American federal system. Geography, the pattern of settlement, tradition, and politics dictate place-to-place differences in tax and spending activities. A federal effort to intervene in the hope of muting these differences and their effects on industrial location is not likely to succeed." See* ACIR (Advisory Commission on Intergovernmental Relations), *Regional Growth: interstate tax competition*, (Washington: Comission Report, 1981), p. 23.
95. *See* R.S. Avi-Yonah. "Globalization, Tax Competition, and the Fiscal Crisis of the Welfare State," 113 *Harvard Law Review* 7 (2000), pp. 1573–1676 (1576).

harmonization measures and, at the same time, preserve its capacity of determining the size of its public sector.

It is also important to highlight the existence of hidden costs in adopting such "consensual" harmonization measures. If, on the one hand, harmonization allows some states to keep the structure of their welfare State, on the other hand, it also prevents other States, namely the developing countries, from establishing levels of taxation which are compatible with the level of development of their public sector. The transition from tax competition to multilaterally agreed harmonization does nothing more than transferring power to States with a privileged position in such negotiations.[96]

The only alternative that would completely eliminate tax competition is harmonization, which can only be consensually achieved, since regulatory competition is inescapable.[97] The focus on harmonization, however, brings more harm than good. Even though such proposal would allow States to collect more taxes, such increasing of tax revenues would not be necessarily desirable. Some authors consider that harmonization would produce the same effects as a cartel, reducing the efficiency due to the lack of competition: rent-seeking behavior would give rise to government waste.[98] Daniel Shaviro contends that, as companies do not need to please their consumers if they are able to create cartels, also governments will resort to tax harmonization in order to reduce competitive pressures.[99]

§3.03 SOVEREIGNTY AND INTER-NATIONS EQUITY

Recent OECD moves are seen as "implicitly proposing a theory of sovereignty that does not support absolute autonomy in taxation."[100] Under OECD's view, cooperation would be a form of supporting "the effective fiscal sovereignty of countries over the design of their tax systems."[101]

Sovereignty can be generally defined as the competence and power of the State to make autonomous choices[102] free from outside interference.[103] Its core meaning is the

---

96. See T. Dagan. "The Costs of International Tax Cooperation," *Bar-Ilan University Faculty of Law*, Working Paper No. 1-03 (2013), p. 23.
97. See J. Roin. "Competition and Evasion: Another Perspective on International Tax Competition," 89 *The Georgetown Law Journal* (2000), p. 603.
98. See T. Dagan. "The Costs of International Tax Cooperation," *Bar-Ilan University Faculty of Law*, Working Paper No. 1-03 (2013), p. 25.
99. D. Shaviro. "Some Observations Concerning Multi-Jurisdictional Tax Competition," *New York University Law School*, Public Law and Legal Theory Working Paper No. 13, 2000, pp. 19-20.
100. A. Christians. "Sovereignty, Taxation and Social Contract," 18 *Minnesota Journal of International Law* 99 (2009), p. 148.
101. OECD, *Towards Global tax co-operation: Report to the 2000 Ministerial Council Meeting and Recommendations by the Committee on Fiscal Affairs* (2000), p. 5.
102. See S. Besson, "The authority of International Law – Lifting the State Veil" 31 *Sidney Law Review* 343 (2009), p. 372.
103. See M. J. Kelly, "Pulling at the threads of Westphalia: 'Involuntary Sovereignty Waiver' – revolutionary international legal theory or return to rule by the great powers?" 10 *UCLA Journal of International Law and Foreign Affairs* 361 (2005), p. 363.

exercise of supreme authority within a territory.[104] Sovereignty implies independence: every Nation is free to manage its domestic and external affairs solely guided by its will, to enact the legislation it wishes and to choose its own system of administration,[105] as well the size of its public sector and the benefits it grants to its citizens.

Mostly due to its historical relation with national sovereignty, law has been "among the least global of social phenomena."[106] International lawyers have not responded uniformly to the consequences of globalization and cannot be expected to do so.[107] Likewise, political theorists diverge with respect to the nature and consequences of anarchy, the possibility and effects of international cooperation, the priority of State goals and the whole of institutions and regimes in international relations.[108] Such divergences certainly engender different conclusions with respect to the content of sovereignty.

Despite the lack of consensus with regard to the precise contours of sovereignty, it is certainly not the same as equality of rights and duties before international law.[109] There are several examples of unbalanced treaties which do not represent any violation to international law, such as peace treaties signed by defeated Nations after a war. As a consequence, it has already been regarded as a "purely legal construct, not something which value is to be assumed as a first principle of normative analysis."[110]

A realistic approach implies the recognition of sovereignty as a merely formal concept. Sovereignty should not be confused with actual independence in political, military, economic, or technological matters. In these areas, it may be possible that a given State is not able to approve and enforce certain norms, which more powerful States are able to accomplish. The actual inequality among Nations is irrelevant for the purpose the legal concept of sovereignty.[111] In other words, sovereignty does not imply fairness. In fact, this is one explanation for the little relevance of inter-nations equity in actual legislative measures on international taxation.

Indeed, inter-nations equity has never played a significant role in the international allocation of taxing rights, despite the significant contributions of scholars in this field.[112] As a consequence of the democratic principle, States are incentivized to

---

104. See. D. Philpott, *Sovereignty*, in Stanford Encyclopedia of Philosophy (Edward N. Zalta ed., 2003), available in http://plato.stanford.edu/entries/sovereignty/, accesses on July 8, 2016.
105. See H. Morgenthau, A política entre as nações (trad. O. Biato, São Paulo, ed. UNB, 2003), p. 572.
106. F. Schauer, *The Politics and Incentives of Legal Transplantation*, in J.S. Nye Jr. & J.D. Donahue (Eds), Governance in a Globalizing World 253 (2000).
107. P. Alston, "The Myopia of the Handmaidens: International Lawyers and Globalization," 3 *European Journal of International Law* (1997), pp. 435–448.
108. See D.A. Baldwin, "Neoliberalism, Neorealism, and World Politics," *in* D.A. Baldwin (ed.), *Neorealism and Neoliberalism: The Contemporary Debate* (New York: Columbia University Press, 1993), pp. 3–8.
109. See H. Morgenthau, A política entre as nações (trad. O. Biato, São Paulo, ed. UNB, 2003), 576.
110. See S. Besson, "The authority of International Law – Lifting the State Veil" 31 *Sidney Law Review* 343 (2009), p. 373.
111. H. Morgenthau, A política entre as nações (trad. O. Biato, São Paulo, ed. UNB, 2003), 576.
112. See K. Vogel, "World-wide vs. Source Taxation of Income – A Review and Reevaluation of Arguments," *in* S; Mclure; Musgrave et al, *Influence of Tax Differentials on International Competitiveness* (Amsterdam Kluwer, 1989), pp. 117–166 (119).

prioritize the interests of their citizens, instead of seeking global justice,[113] and there are generally no deviations from this expected behavior.[114] The centrality of the Nation State is still an undeniable fact and has led to rather skeptic statements on the impossibility of determining what would be a fair outcome under the perspective of inter-nations equity.[115] After all, "we regard our obligation for the well-being of our fellow citizens as more pressing than for people in need elsewhere in the world."[116]

The assumption that States behave like egoistic value maximizers is common to most theories on international relations.[117] Value maximization is inherent to States' negotiations and the current international tax scenario has already been described as "polluted by power play and deception," which are the "two striking elements that can be detected in the actual struggle for international tax justice."[118] In this context, it is difficult to believe in any other positive duty arising from sovereignty than of non-interference in the execution of the external policies of other Nations.[119] Absent a treaty provision, no State has the right to tell another one which legislation it should approve and follow.

The redistribution of tax revenues from "poorer to the richer signatory countries" is the main effect of signing Double Tax Conventions (DTCs) modeled after the OECD-MC.[120] The only exception to this shifting of income would be the adoption of exemptions as a method of preventing double taxation or of tax sparing clauses: absent such provisions, tax treaties would be unable to significantly encourage Foreign Direct Investment (FDI) in developing countries.[121] Tax sparing, however, has been expressly discouraged by the OECD.[122]

Keohane defines multilateralism as "a practice of coordinating national policies in groups of three or more states, through ad hoc arrangements or by means of institutions."[123] Building consensus around coordination in international tax issues is a difficult task. States still present fundamental economic and political differences, which decisively affect the way they perceive taxation. There are still huge gaps

---

113. *See* M. J. Graetz, "Taxing International Income: inadequate principles, outdated concepts, and unsatisfactory policies," 54 *Tax Law Review* 261 (2001), pp. 280–281.
114. *See* J. Roin, "Taxation without Coordination," 31 *The Journal of Legal Studies* 61 (2002).
115. *See* W. Schön. "International Tax Coordination for a Second-Best World (Part I)," 1 *World Tax Journal* 67 (2009), p. 93.
116. *See* M. J. Graetz, "Taxing International Income: inadequate principles, outdated concepts, and unsatisfactory policies," 54 *Tax Law Review* 261 (2001), pp. 277–278.
117. *See* D. A. Baldwin, "Neoliberalism, Neorealism, and World Politics," *in* D.A. Baldwin (ed.), *Neorealism and Neoliberalism: The Contemporary Debate* (New York: Columbia University Press, 1993), p. 9.
118. P. Essers, "International Tax Justice between Machiavelli and Habermas," *Bulletin for International Taxation* (2014), p. 54.
119. H. Morgenthau, A política entre as nações (trad. O. Biato, São Paulo, ed. UNB, 2003), 573.
120. *See* T. Dagan, "The Tax Treaties Myth," 32 *NYU Journal of International Law and Politics* 939 (2000).
121. The author also acknowledges other incentives arising from tax treaties other than the reduction of the tax burden, such as investor certainty and reduction of bureaucratic barriers. *See* T. Dagan, "The Tax Treaties Myth," 32 *NYU Journal of International Law and Politics* 939 (2000), p. 52.
122. OECD, Tax Sparing: A Reconsideration (OECD Publishing, 1998).
123. R. Keohane, "Multilateralism: an Agenda for Research," 45 *International Journal* 4 (1990), p. 731.

regarding the level of development and capital flows between developed and non-developed States. Hence, the perceptions of the Four Economists remain true: "the proportion presenting a true compromise for country A and the rest of the world may be adopted which is inappropriate for the relations of country B to the rest of the world."[124]

Unfortunately, their conveniently optimistic prediction that the industrialization of developing countries would make the distinction between debtor and creditor countries more tenuous – thus bringing consensus around the principle of residence[125] – was nothing more than an illusory prophecy.

The same disillusion in also present in current debates. The problem is well summarized by Ricardo García, who questions whether the current multilateral efforts carried out by the OECD are not actually consecrating "the traditional 'status quo' anchored in the division between developed and non-developed countries."[126] The stability of the allocation of taxing rights along the years evidences that the theoretical approaches have operated "more as convenient support for pre-existing policy preferences than the real reason for policy changes."[127] There is no reason to conclude that this is different in the context of the cooperative approach of the OECD, which, after all, "always has been and has viewed itself as the representative of the interests of its members – the club of the rich countries."

As economic allegiance and neutrality, the rhetoric in favor of tax cooperation and against tax avoidance as justification towards the elimination of tax competition operates in a rather clear sense: increasing of tax collection in capital exporting countries. In the BEPS Project, States are called to cooperate in favor of the traditional allocation of taxing rights. As evidenced by the negotiations on exchange of information and by the (lack of) measures regarding the digital economy, all efforts are being made to keep the allocation of taxing rights as it has been since the 1920s.

[A] Information Exchange in the Brazilian Context

The current response to the fiscal crisis of the welfare State is mostly a response to the revenue crisis in developed countries. In relative terms, developed countries have been hit much harder by the financial crisis.[128] Therefore, answers as exchange of information, country-by-country reporting, concerns with sophisticated financial instruments, intangibles and so on are mostly the kind of answers that developed countries want: those are the most pressing issues for them.

The rest of the world still has much more to explore. Of course developing countries will benefit from exchange of information, but relatively much less than

---

124. The Four Economists Report, p. 4050.
125. *Id., ibid.*
126. R. Garcia Antón. "The 21st Century Multilateralism in International Taxation: the emperor's new clothes?" 2 *World Tax Journal* (2016), p. 148.
127. R. S. Avi-Yonah. "All of a Piece of Throughout: the four ages of U.S. international taxation," 25 *Virginia Tax Review* 313 (2005), p. 317.
128. Y. Brauner. "What the BEPS," 16 *Florida Tax Review* 2 (2014), p. 64.

developed countries. Developing countries still have potential to benefit from measures which do not demand cooperation.[129] Left aside issues of corruption and rent-seeking behavior (which are surely the most pressing issues), investing in the capacity of tax agents, for instance, would allow States to collect more from complicated transfer pricing transactions, and to pursue more objective and effective outcomes in terms of GAAR application. Developing rules for the allocation of profits to permanent establishments is yet a measure to be explored in many countries and this could also be a source of tax revenues. On the contrary, it is doubtful whether country-by-country reporting will be of any use in some jurisdictions.

Hence it may seem that, while negotiating bank information from their citizens, developing countries have bargained very poorly, perhaps taken by the anti-avoidance speech. After all, they had something that developed States really wanted and the reciprocity was not an equivalent exchange: exchange of information benefits developed countries much more than developing countries in terms of revenue collection.

Another possible (and more probable) conclusion for the lack of resistance in developing countries for adhering to information exchange is that, due to pressures from the OECD and the much more straight-forward message of FATCA, these countries did not have any bargaining position at all: not adhering to the developed countries proposal was not a serious option.

Sovereignty does not grant any State enforceable measures against economic and political pressure. In some cases, even if it could be inferred from the policy (or from Constitutional norms) of a given country that it would not adhere to a given proposal, it may be led to accept all sorts of measures fearing sanctions and retaliation from stronger economies or a negative response from market agents.

In Brazil, bank secrecy is protected by Article 5, items X and XII, of the Federal Constitution. If one reads the seventy-seven items of the list of fundamental rights in Article 5 of the Federal Constitution, one can reasonably conclude that in no case shall the right to bank secrecy be restricted. There is not a single sentence therein authorizing the violation of bank secrecy for the purpose of collection of taxes. The only exception would be for the purpose of criminal investigation. Article 5, item XII, authorizes the violation of communication and data secrecy, upon the authorization of a Judge, for the purposes of a criminal investigation. In this reasoning, it would be concluded that the right of the taxpayer to bank secrecy cannot be restricted, unless for the purpose of a criminal investigation.

However, a more restrictive interpretation to taxpayers' rights is also possible. Article 145, § 1, of the Constitution, sets forth that, for the purpose of implementing the principle of the ability-to-pay, the tax administration has the authority to "identify, provided that the individual rights are respected and in the terms of legislation, the assets, income and economic activity of the taxpayer."

Under this reasoning, one may find grounds for the tax administration to try and disclose the bank data of the taxpayer, for the purposes of the collection of taxes. This

---

129. L. E. Schoueri and R. A. Galendi Jr., "Transparência Fiscal e Reciprocidade nas Perspectivas Interna e Internacional", in: V. O. Rocha, *Grandes Questões Atuais do Direito Tributário*, vol. 19 (São Paulo, Dialética, 2015), pp. 248–287.

interpretation demands, however, further attention. The expression "provided that the individual rights are respected," certainly recalls Article 5 and the fundamental rights included therein. In this sense, the proportionality test should be applied in this interpretation, as means of weighing bank secrecy granted by Article 5, XII, and the ability-to-pay, set forth in Article 145, § 1.

Despite these provisions, Article 6, of Complementary Law No. 105/01 granted the authorities of Municipalities, States, and the Union the power to exam bank information of the taxpayer during a tax assessment. There is no further requirement for such violation to bank secrecy. The mere event of a tax investigation is enough for the tax authority to restrict the taxpayers' right to bank secrecy, upon its own discretion.

The constitutionality of this provision could be challenged. When applying the proportionality test, one may conclude that, despite being "adequate," the measure provided by the legislation is not "necessary." Necessity implies concluding that there are no other possible measures to achieve the intent pursued ("collection of taxes") without applying a less severe restriction to the fundamental right ("bank secrecy"). The possibility of a tax officer having access to bank information upon her/his own discretion is tremendously restrictive and there are certainly other less aggressive measures to provide means for the collection of taxes.

One of them is submitting the disclosure of bank information to a previous judicial authorization. This was essentially the applicable regime prior to the enactment of Complementary Law No. 105/01. According to a previous case judged by the Supreme Court, tax authorities would not have the power to violate a taxpayer's bank secrecy within the purposes of a tax assessment, without previous authorization of a Judicial Court.[130] In this decision, the Court considered that the Judiciary is the only legitimate power to authorize the disclosure of information protected by bank secrecy. Justice Ricardo Lewandowski had considered that "the Judiciary is the superior guardian of the fundamental rights." This understanding was endorsed by Justice Marco Aurelio, according to whom the attributions of the Judiciary cannot be transferred to the agencies of the Executive Branch. However, this decision of the Supreme Court was not applicable *erga omnes* and therefore other taxpayers were not granted the right of having their bank secrecy protected.

Additionally, the preparedness of the tax administrations of developing countries to comply with an automatic exchange of information system is an issue of serious concern.[131] First, because there is no guarantee that such countries will be able to efficiently use the information. Second, technological barriers may be detrimental to efficient revenue collection. Also, one may include the independence of tax authorities in relation to delinquent taxpayers as a point of concern, given that the corruption of

---

130. Supreme Court, Extraordinary Appeal No. 389.808/PR, Reporting Justice Marco Aurélio, decided on December 15, 2010.
131. K. Baisalbayeva, *Counteracting Tax Evasion and Avoidance (Focus on Non-compliance by High-Net-Worth Individuals)*, in R. Petruzzi K. Spies (Eds), Tax Policy Challenges in the 21st Century, Series on International Tax Law (M. Lang (Ed)), vol. 86, pp. 365–389 (385).

public and private agents may be challenging to the effective combating of tax evasion.[132]

Despite this background, in June 2015, the Brazilian Congress approved the Intergovernmental Agreement (IGA) for the implementation of the FATCA. The IGA approved is based on Model 1A, whereby the financial institutions exchange information with their own Governments, which further carry out the exchange of information with the other contracting State. Brazil has also signed and approved the Multilateral Convention on Mutual Administrative Assistance in Tax Matters.

In 2016, the Supreme Court rushed to settle the issue of the constitutionality of the Brazilian legislation in an Extraordinary Appeal, with an *erga omnes* effect. Against expectations based on the Courts previous decision, the relevant provisions were deemed to be compatible with the Federal Constitution.[133] Thus, one may conclude that tax authorities do not need a judicial authorization to access bank accounts in Brazil.

Regardless of the reasoning expected, considering the relevant constitutional provisions, the Court held that, due to an unwritten "fundamental duty to pay taxes," the tax administration should be granted the effective means to tax the individuals, which would include the power granted by Complementary Law No. 105/01. After long references to international trends and quotations of the work of international organizations on the issue, the proportionality test of the provisions was not carried out, being the access to bank data considered essential for the effectiveness of the tax administration.

The Supreme Court decision may well be attributed to a judicial activist trend that has taken the Court in the last decade.[134] In any case, one may not say that the decision to adhere to exchange of information was not a sovereign choice, with which not only the Executive, but also the Legislative and the Judiciary have agreed. Questioning its legitimacy would be a matter of questioning the legitimacy of an activist interpretation of the Constitution, not compliant with its text and spirit. However, even considering the important role of economic and political pressure for this outcome, no breach to sovereignty can be argued in such cases.

[B] The Challenges of the Digital Economy

One of the events that neither the Four Economists nor Mitchell Carroll could be expected to foresee was the extent to which technology would change economic relations. As a consequence, it is obvious that problems arising from the digital economy cannot (and should not) be solved by means of hermeneutics, as the OECD

---

132. K. Baisalbayeva, *Counteracting Tax Evasion and Avoidance (Focus on Non-compliance by High-Net-Worth Individuals)*, in R. Petruzzi K. Spies (Eds), Tax Policy Challenges in the 21st Century, Series on International Tax Law (M. Lang (Ed)), vol. 86, pp. 365–389 (386).
133. Supreme Court, Extraordinary Appeal No. 601.314/SP, Reporting Justice Edson Fachin.
134. *See*, on judicial activism in Brazil, C. A. Azevedo Campos, *Dimensões do Ativismo Judicial do STF*, (Rio de Janeiro, Forense, 2014).

has for long tried to do, but require a new form of allocation of taxing rights.[135] The need for physical presence to attract jurisdiction is a tremendous anachronism on which developed countries conveniently rely. Therefore, scholars have recently provided relevant contributions to "justify the exercise of the taxing jurisdiction by the market country" in respect of income arising from the digital economy.[136]

The Final Report of Action 1 is the clearest signal that the BEPS Project is not even slightly committed with inter-nations equity. OECD's trend towards understating the relevance of the digital economy is repeated in Action 1, which considers that "broader direct tax challenges currently raised by the digital economy are expected to be mitigated once the BEPS measures are implemented." Again, the BEPS reasoning is repeated: make taxpayers comply with the current tax regime and wherever arises from this compliance will be fair.

Action 1 considered some responses to the challenges of the digital economy: (i) the creation of a new nexus to cover situations in which there is significant digital presence in the source State; (ii) the enactment of withholding taxes in digital economy transactions; (iii) the charging of an equalization levy, which would be levied in cases of significant digital presence. Such proposals would surely affect the allocation of taxing rights. However, even though they were examined in the context of Action 1, the Final Report has not recommended any of them, because "measures developed in the BEPS Project will have a substantial impact on BEPS issues previously identified in the digital economy." As concluded by the Final Report, "certain BEPS measures will mitigate some aspects of the broader tax challenges," and "consumption taxes will be levied effectively in the market country."[137]

Essentially, while concrete proposals on direct taxation in the digital economy were expected, the Report changed the subject, recommending countries "to apply the principles of the International VAT/GST Guidelines for the collection of VAT on cross-border B2C supplies of services and intangibles and consider the introduction of the collection mechanisms included therein." In summary, the only proposal actually recommended by the BEPS Project is not a measure on direct taxation. With respect to the other three proposals, which would in fact influence the allocation of jurisdiction, the Final Report considers that countries could "introduce any of the options in their domestic laws as additional safeguards against BEPS, provided they respect existing treaty obligations, or in their bilateral tax treaties."[138]

---

135. See R. A. Galendi Jr. and G. S. Galdino, Desafios da Economia Digital: do problema hermenêutico ao desequilíbrio na alocação de jurisdição, In: M. L. Gomes and L. E. Schoueri (coord.), A tributação internacional na Era Pós-BEPS: soluções globais e peculiaridades de países em desenvolvimento, vol. 3 (Lumen Juris, Rio de Janeiro, 2016).
136. P. Hongler; P. Pistone. "Blueprints for a New PE Nexus to Tax Business Income in the Era of the Digital Economy," IBFD White Papers, Amsterdam, IBFD, 2015, p. 18.
137. OECD (2015), Addressing the Tax Challenges of the Digital Economy, Action 1 – 2015 Final Report, OECD/G20 Base Erosion and Profit Shifting Project, OECD Publishing, Paris, p. 148, available at http://dx.doi.org/10.1787/9789264241046-en, access on July 22, 2016.
138. OECD (2015), Addressing the Tax Challenges of the Digital Economy, Action 1 – 2015 Final Report, OECD/G20 Base Erosion and Profit Shifting Project, OECD Publishing, Paris, p. 148, available at http://dx.doi.org/10.1787/9789264241046-en, access on July 22, 2016.

The BEPS Project could have been an opportunity to acknowledge the importance of the demand for the creation of value. However, the Project has chosen to consider only the supply side, and refused measures aimed at implementing a more comprehensive notion of creation of value. Such justification then imitates the role formerly played by economic allegiance and CEN, as means to justify residence taxation.

The Project has also shown that the anti-avoidance rhetoric was developed as an effective means to avoid relevant debates on allocation of jurisdiction. The most extreme example is that one of the most relevant actions of a Project dealing with "profit shifting" ended up presenting a solution based on indirect taxation.

Scholars have shown that there are feasible alternatives to substantially change the allocation of taxing rights as a response to fundamental changes brought by the digital economy.[139] These changes encompass recognizing factors that "arise in the market country and that can influence the performance of business and value creation arising in such context."[140] In fact, as argued by Brauner, "source has never been about moral or economic correctness, but rather about legitimacy and practicality."[141]

§3.04 CONCLUSION

Mostly in the context in which companies are not accused of being illegal, but of being immoral, combating abusive behavior is essentially confronting conducts that deviate from a given understanding of what the ideal system should be. The absence of a democratically approved international tax code implies that such claims of immorality are grounded on an unwritten conception of allocation of taxing rights, as constructed almost a century ago, in a context of dominance of the main economies.

Globalization has brought us to a scenario where making taxpayers pay their fair share is not sufficient: it is central to rethink or perhaps reinvent the system to which taxpayers shall comply. This reform requires a straightforward debate on what international taxation is primarily about: allocation of taxing rights. Such debate must be freed from the blurred rhetoric on tax avoidance, in order to bring inter-nations equity back to the scope of international debates.

Sovereign countries are contributing to enforce the tax regime envisaged in the BEPS Project: administrative cooperation is the first step towards the crystallization of the regime. Nevertheless, the regime which is being crystallized is grounded on a narrow view of the justifications for the allocation of taxing rights and once all the tools to implement it are available, the space for debating it will be even tighter.

Where sovereignty does not imply fairness, by cooperating, States that deem the current regime unfair are progressively losing leverage in future negotiations. Once administrative cooperation is consolidated, without actual changes in inter-nations equity, it is doubtful whether building further consensus will be possible. As a

---

139. *See* Y. Brauner and A. Baez, "Withholding Taxes in the Service of BEPS Action 1: Address the Tax Challenges of the Digital Economy," *IBFD White Papers,* Amsterdam, IBFD, 2015.
140. P. Hongler; P. Pistone. "Blueprints for a New PE Nexus to Tax Business Income in the Era of the Digital Economy," *IBFD White Papers,* Amsterdam, IBFD, 2015, p. 19.
141. Y. Brauner. "What the BEPS," 16 *Florida Tax Review* 2 (2014), p. 68.

consequence, just as it is impossible to segregate the preoccupations with abusive behavior from the debate on the allocation of tax revenues, it is impossible to segregate the discussions on administrative cooperation from the broader concerns with the justification of the tax regime.

CHAPTER 4
An Essay on BEPS, Sovereignty, and Taxation

Yariv Brauner

§4.01 INTRODUCTION

Sovereignty is often used in international tax discourse as a hand grenade to shut down difficult discussion. It is very common to hear arguments about the "tax sovereignty" of countries when they do not wish to adhere to international norms or obligations that they deem disadvantageous.[1] Yet the same tax sovereignty is relied upon when powerful states use their weight, either independently or corroboratively, to gain advantages in the global competition over scarce tax revenues, even to the detriment of other states.[2]

A good example for this can be found in the rhetoric surrounding the recent Base Erosion and Profit Shifting ("BEPS") project orchestrated by the G-20 and led by the Organisation for Economic Co-operation and Development (OECD).[3] The project was a political response to the public (and media) demand that corporations pay their fair share of taxes; the public pressure being instigated by the recent exposé regarding the aggressive tax schemes which have become commonplace in big corporations. Being a rushed political project, BEPS did not have clear goals or a defined scope; it generally targeted corporate transactions deemed abusive by many countries, and specific rules

---

1. *See*, e.g., Papali'i T. Scanlan, Globalization and Tax-Related Issues: What are the Concerns? In Commonwealth Secretariat, Rajiv Biswas, Ed., *International Tax Competition: Globalisation and Fiscal Sovereignty*, Commonwealth Secretariat, London (2002), 43.
2. *See* OECD, Addressing Base Erosion and Profit Shifting (2013), http://www.oecd.org/tax/addressing-base-erosion-and-profit-shifting-9789264192744-en.htm.
3. *See Id.*, and OECD, Action Plan on Base Erosion and Profit Shifting (2013), http://www.oecd.org/ctp/BEPSActionPlan.pdf. The Final reports are available electronically; *BEPS 2015 Final Reports*, OECD.org, http://www.oecd.org/tax/beps-2015-final-reports.htm.

that were considered either inadequate or ineffective in a mini-reform of the international tax regime.[4]

A key insight of BEPS has been that more cross-state coordination of tax policies is required due to the interdependency of nations operating on the global market. The OECD promoted therefore more coordination in the name of tax sovereignty preservation, arguing that dispersive, unilateral action would leave all nations in vulnerable positions vis-à-vis the all-powerful corporations; this would in turn lead to diminished capabilities with respect to raising legitimate revenues.[5]

In response, some countries and various commentators argue that BEPS impinges on the tax sovereignty of nations when it centralizes the functions and harmonizes the norms of the international tax regime.[6] This critique was directed at the fact that the OECD, which was very much under attack prior to BEPS, has used the project to strengthen its institutional power with the stakeholders (most countries, including non-OECD members).[7] Post BEPS implementation efforts by the EU received a similar response.[8]

Yet, this protean use of the term sovereignty is problematic. The notion of 'sovereignty' has evolved over the years and now has a range of context specific meanings. The term seems to metamorphose with contextual changes, from the domestic setting to the cross-border context; in political science and in law (for somewhat different purposes); and, of course, in politics and diplomacy with little boundaries or organizing principles.[9] The addition of the prefix 'tax' forming the term 'tax sovereignty' seems to have had the effect of causing governments to believe they have carte blanche to implement tax policies without external constraints. This is not the case.

Sovereignty in its modern form is used often, yet is not often used carefully in debates concerning policy and international relations. The modern use of sovereignty is rooted in an aversion to anarchy, which Jean Bodin, the intellectual father of the notion argued could only be avoided if the ultimate power would lie with a single,

---

4. For a discussion of the incoherent, dual purpose of BEPS, see, e.g., Yariv Brauner, What the BEPS?, 16 Fla. Tax Rev. 55 (2014).
5. See OECD, Addressing BEPS, *supra* note 1.
6. See, e.g., http://www.freedomandprosperity.org/files/OECD/ctc-OECDFundingBEPS-2016-05-1 2.pdf (May 12, 2016); Jason J. Fichtner and Adam N. Michel, The OECD's Conquest of the United States: Understanding the Costs and Consequences of the BEPS Project and Tax Harmonization, Mercatus Center (George Mason University, March, 2016); Laurens van Apeldoorn, BEPS, Tax Sovereignty and Global Justice, Critical Review of International Social and Political Philosophy (Online, Aug. 19, 2016).
7. See, e.g., Philip Baker, Is There a Cure for BEPS?, 5 British Tax Rev. (2013) at 605; Most notably, China and India have challenged the OECD primarily through vocal participation as observers in OECD proceedings, and Brazil through an adoption of norms decidedly different and often explicitly rejected by the OECD. See, e.g., Yariv Brauner & Pasquale Pistone, Ed., BRICS and the International Tax Regime (IBFD, 2015).
8. Malta's finance minister, Edward Scicluna, in opposition to the EU Transparency package said that Malta will not cede sovereignty to the EC, and pledged that Malta will resist any attempt by the EC to reduce sovereignty over its own fiscal affairs. See Mossak Fonseca website (Feb. 3, 2016), at: http://www.mossfon.com/news/malta-refuses-to-cede-tax-sovereignty/.
9. See, e.g., Stephen D. Krasner, Problematic Sovereignty: Contested Rules and Political Possibilities (Columbia University Press, 2012), 1–12.

clearly defined entity.[10] It is easy to observe that even in our complex, globalizing world, five centuries later, Bodin's idea remains useful and states are still the key components of our political systems. Yet, the core of sovereignty is in the context of fundamental questions such as war and peace, basic human ethics, etc. Simply put, in this context a country is sovereign or is not sovereign; there is no middle ground if one wishes to maintain the stability of the political system.[11] This does not mean that a sovereign is not limited at all in its actions; it is clearly limited by general ethics and by fundamental international law norms. Nevertheless, a sovereign cannot be limited by the law or action of another sovereign, unless it chooses to accept such limitations.

Given the scope of the sovereignty doctrine, appears the argument that sovereignty does not give countries *carte blanche* to tax as they wish, without international intervention (even if we assume that such taxation is domestically legitimate – let us say democratically decided – and appropriate in terms of basic human rights) seems, on the face of it, to contradict the very heart of the sovereignty notion. However, if there truly was a dichotomy, we would probably be living in a world that most of us would not like. The majority of us would be poor or oppressed (or, more likely both).

More nuanced articulations of sovereignty soften the impact of the notion, including a component of responsibility of the sovereign to the welfare of its subjects or a responsibility to a more general body, perhaps even all living creatures based on various structures, such as a social contract, legitimacy, etc.[12] These constructs are all useful in policy discourse yet it is not clear what sovereignty really adds here: perhaps a welfare discussion should focus on welfare, a global efficiency discussion on maximization, a moral discussion on ethics, and so on.

This chapter consequently argues that international tax discourse would benefit greatly if participants simply refrained from making sovereignty-based assertions. A precise use of the notion of sovereignty is unlikely to advance the discourse, yet an imprecise, protean use of the term is sure to impede it.

This chapter does not conceptually reject a more nuanced view of the rights of nations to justifiably resist compliance with standards or act to amend the operation of the regime. It uses the BEPS project to demonstrate its claim, not as a critique of the project, but rather with the view of informing its potentially successful outcomes. It therefore points to the benefit of, for instance, thinking about sovereignty in its original, rather minimal form – the prevention of political chaos – to support a gradual and balanced process of enhancing the coordination of tax policies among countries. This process is essential required for the survival of the international tax regime as has been observed by the BEPS project, yet it seems almost impossible to jumpstart. Despite the theoretical contribution made by such thinking,[13] the chapter still argues

---

10. *See*, e.g., Jean Bodin, On Sovereignty (Julian H. Franklin, Ed.), Cambridge Univ. Press, 1992. *See also* Francis H. Hinsley, Sovereignty, 2nd. Ed., Cambridge Univ. Press, 1986.
11. *See also* Robert Jackson, Sovereignty in World Politics: A Glance at the Conceptual and Historical Landscape, 47 Pol. Stud. 431 (1999),449.
12. *See*, Allison Christians, Sovereignty, Taxation, and Social Contract, 18 Minn. J. Int'l L. 99 (2009).
13. The article acknowledges and even agrees with a few very thoughtful works of this kind, such as *Id.*, Diane M. Ring, What's at Stake in the Sovereignty Debate?: International Tax and the Nation State, 49 Va. J. Int'l L. 155 (2008), and Diane M. Ring, Democracy, Sovereignty and Tax

that a less protean, less colloquial use of sovereignty is more likely to continue to dominate the international tax policy discourse, and therefore it would be more desirable to refrain from accepting sovereignty as a safe-word in international tax policy discourse.

Following this introduction, the chapter concisely tracks the roots of the modern notion of sovereignty, followed by an examination of its place in the contemporary international tax regime. The fourth section demonstrates the issues raised by this chapter through examples from the BEPS project finally concluding with a modest proposal to reformulate the discourse without resorting to sovereignty-based arguments.

§4.02 SOVEREIGNTY

The notion of sovereignty dates back a very long time. One could identify a clear use of the notion in an articulation of the rule of law principle already in Roman law, yet until modern times the notion has gone through various transformations, eventually leading to the modern understanding of the sovereignty of the people reflected through the leadership, typically, yet not necessarily, the democratic government.

Sovereignty indicates supreme power over a political entity ("polity"), such as the nation state, on which this chapter focuses. In its most simple form sovereignty means that the sovereign has full power to govern the relevant state (territory) without interference; most importantly, without interference from other countries or governments. This principle is the foundation on which the idea that all nations are equal is built. The monopoly that the sovereign has over power is absolute, yet this does not mean that the sovereign can simply do whatever she wants. Early in the modern era the conflicts between the state and the church clouded the notion of sovereignty, yet modern articulations of sovereignty accept that the sovereign is the ultimate power within the confines of an accepted, legitimate ethical system.[14] In addition, the power of the sovereign is protected in the appropriate context it was granted to her; in a democracy it would clearly be the good of the nation and civil order. It would be useful to note the historic point that first and foremost sovereignty was deemed to be necessary, and eventually became a fundamental part of international law, in order to ensure public order and safety. Civil chaos was also the primary concern of Bodin who first articulated the modern concept of sovereignty.[15] It is natural therefore to trigger sovereign power and concerns in the contexts of territorial disputes, the use of force,

---

Competition: The Role of Tax Sovereignty in Shaping Tax Cooperation, 9 Fla. Tax Rev. 555 (2009). Yet, again, country actions, especially in the context of the BEPS project demonstrate that a serious, substantive discourse on the future of coordination of tax policies that is based on a responsible, focused use of the term is probably unlikely, as this essay demonstrates.

14. This modern understanding stems from the original conflict between divine and civil law that eventually was settled in sovereignty being part of the law, civil law, while religion, morality and similar aspects became a matter of ethics, the bases of the system within which a sovereign may apply her power. See, e.g., Hinsley, Id., 69–71.

15. See, e.g., Hinsley, Id., 119–125, referring to Jean Bodin, De la république (1576).

and similar issues. Resorting to sovereignty claims in economic issues is less obvious despite the very ubiquitous colloquial use of the term in public discourse.

The confinement of the sovereign power may be viewed as conflicted with the very definition of sovereignty as the sole, superior power or law within a nation. Yet, again, the purpose of sovereignty, this grant of such superior powers, was to prevent chaos and permit the populous, the true sovereign, to live life as expected. Note, the idea behind sovereignty is not to maximize the welfare of a society, but to maintain order in society that is a precondition to any set of policies taken for the maximization of welfare or any other goal of a society.[16]

The same Bodin was also the first to make sense of modern sovereignty in the relations between nations, when he rejected the dominant view of international law as subject to divine or natural law, shifting the focus on what we would now call treaty law, i.e., the mutual acts of various sovereigns.[17] In this sense natural law, to the extent applicable (and the debate over that is beyond the scope of this chapter), is also part of the surrounding (ethical) system within which and subject to which the sovereign operates. Note that Bodin has not endorsed the international law he envisioned, but merely noted its necessity. Subsequently, Bodin's concepts were developed, most notably by Grotius and his followers in the founding scholarship of public international law that focused on issues of war, peace and the use of force.[18]

One may perceive such categories as limiting the scope of sovereignty in contradiction of total power however this is not the case. Bodin's categorization is very important for the purposes of this chapter since, somewhat ironically the international tax regime is rarely about ethical claims or any related natural law issues but rather about the division of tax bases among nations. This division is based merely on negotiation and in this sense it is arbitrary and based very much on powers that states can lord over one another. Below, the chapter discusses how and why nations camouflage this truth and the implications of this camouflage for our discussion, yet the main point stands: the very ubiquitous claim that a fiscal action of one or several states infringes upon the sovereignty of others is nonsensical when sovereignty is understood following Bodin's insights and formulations. This issue is related to a common critique of sovereignty in our globalized world: that sovereignty does not fit the complex reality within which we now operate, a world in which the description of a single, ultimate authority is both unrealistic and undesirable, and that the new, open global economy creates a reality where nations are increasingly dependent on each other (a very relevant challenge to international taxation as is further elaborated on below) and therefore cannot be viewed as sovereign since no-authority truly has omnipotence within its territory; power is dispersed, hence modern states cannot be viewed as sovereign powers in the "old" sense. This critique, again, mixes the traditional view of sovereignty with its confused, colloquial use or interpretation of the notion.[19] The basic response to these claims is that the state remains the fundamental

---

16. *See*, e.g., Hinsley, *Id.*, 121–122.
17. *See*, e.g., Hinsley, *Id.*, 180–183.
18. *See*, e.g., Hinsley, *Id.*, 189–191.
19. *See*, e.g., Hinsley, *Id.*, 217–220.

unit in international affairs and increasingly so, making the necessity of a single decision and law maker essential for each territory. The rest of this chapter further establishes this claim.

In conclusion, the core of the sovereignty idea is in the necessity of having an entity with superior power in a state, and setting the law there with no interference from outside the state. This necessity is based on the need for order in society, ensuring the society has a chance to prosper which must be its aim, regardless of the political system. Most importantly, sovereignty does not mean that the sovereign can do whatever she pleases, as the notion of sovereignty is not relevant for the content or manner of the use of the power.[20] Finally, the sovereign operates within the confines of a system, with ethics and perhaps other fundamental bases, which one may view as potentially constraining its absolute powers.

§4.03 THE INTERNATIONAL TAX REGIME

The current international tax regime is constructed of over 3,000 bilateral tax treaties that apply and hence regulate the taxation of the large majority of cross-border business and investment.[21] These treaties are meaningfully standard. Scholars estimate that around 70% of the language of all tax treaties is taken from a single source: the OECD model tax convention (as amended from time to time).[22] The OECD Model dominates current tax treaty law and hence the normative baseline of the international tax regime.

The standardization of international tax law is not confined, however, to tax treaty law. In the last century, the international tax laws of essentially all of the world's countries have significantly converged.[23] Such convergence occurred not only in income taxes, on which this chapter focuses, but also more generally in fiscal devices and polices.[24] Much of this convergence can be attributed to tax treaties and their standardization,[25] yet some of it relates to norms that are merely tangential, or not at all related to treaty norms.[26]

Such standardization has not amounted to much harmonization, however. An international tax regime has emerged but has remained a primarily soft-law based

---

20. *See*, e.g., Hinsley, *Id.*, 217–218.
21. *See*, e.g., Reuven S. Avi-Yonah, Commentary, 53 Tax L. Rev. 167, 169 (1999) (explaining that the regime is constructed around the network of bilateral tax treaties, essentially all of which are modeled after the OECD Model Tax Convention). The original acknowledgment of the existence of such a regime was in Reuven S. Avi-Yonah, The Structure of International Taxation: A Proposal for Simplification, 74 Tex. L. Rev. 1301 (1996).
22. *See*, e.g., Michael Lang, Pasquale Pistone, & Josef Schuch, The Impact of the OECD and Un Model Conventions on Bilateral Tax Treaties (Cambridge University Press, 2012).
23. *See* Yariv Brauner, An International Tax Regime in Crystallization, 56 Tax L. Rev. 259 (2003).
24. A more general review of this convergence is, however, beyond the scope of this article and will have to wait for another occasion.
25. The most salient example for this phenomenon is perhaps the almost universal use of the permanent establishment ("PE") concept for the taxation of business income of foreigners.
26. The almost universal convergence of source rules is one example of this phenomenon. *See*, e.g., *supra* note 18.

regime.[27] The convergence has attracted some scholars to examine whether this regime had reached a customary international law status,[28] yet such a conclusion is yet to be reached and remains primarily a desirable goal (for some). Numerous differences among tax laws still exist, many of which are difficult to rationalize. Some of such differences have facilitated aggressive corporate tax planning of the kind that triggered the launch of the BEPS project. A fundamental insight of this project was that countries cannot proceed to make completely independent tax policies due to the interdependence of their economies.[29] It is difficult for countries to quickly act on this insight and enhance coordination of their tax policies since, despite the convergence of norms, at its core the international tax regime is based on competition, not cooperation. The international tax regime is not institutionalized; it includes no strong supranational norms (if any); it does not have a mandatory dispute resolution device; and, by design, legal action taken pursuant to the regime is decisively unilateral and not cooperative. This should not be surprising since it was primarily constructed by the world's strongest economic powers and enthusiasts of market theory, following the so-called Washington consensus.[30] The international tax regime evolved with the apparent aim of perfecting such competition rather than curbing it. Unsurprisingly, it remained a soft legal regime with no established international forum or supranational, evolving body of law. Some scholars disputed the mere existence of the regime, or the utility of referring to it as such, based on its lack of coherence and structure.[31]

International tax scholarship has also been dominated, by the perceived binary choice between competition and harmonization. Since no one seriously wished for a global tax government, and surely no one believed that countries would agree to it, harmonization was generally rejected outright.[32] The sovereignty harm rhetoric was often used to support this rejection. Consequently, the regime stuck to reliance on

---

27. See, e.g., Allison Christians, Hard Law & Soft Law in International Taxation, 25 Wisc. Int'l L. J. (2007); Diane Ring, Who is Making International Tax Policy? International Organizations as Power Players in a High Stakes World, 33 Fordham Int'l L. J. 649; Hugh J. Ault, Reflections on the Role of the OECD in Developing International Tax Norms, 34 Brook. J. Int'l L. 757 (2009); Jose M. Calderón, The OECD Transfer Pricing Guidelines as a Source of Tax Law: Is Globalization Reaching the Tax Law?, 35 Intertax 4 (2007); Alberto Vega, International Governance Through Soft Law: The Case of the OECD Transfer Pricing Guidelines, TransState Working Paper, No. 163. (2012), available at http://hdl.handle.net/11858/00-001M-0000-000E-78E6-3.
28. See, e.g., Reuven S. Avi-Yonah, International Tax As International Law: An Analysis of the International Tax Regime (2007).
29. See Yariv Brauner, What the BEPS...? 16 Fla. Tax Rev. 55 (2014).
30. See John Williamson, "What Washington Means by Policy Reform" in John Williamson, ed., Latin American Readjustment: How Much Has Happened (Washington: Institute for International Economics, 1989). For reflection on the evolution of the term and its symbolism see Pedro-Pablo Kuczynski & John Williamson, eds., After the Washington Consensus (Washington: Institute for International Economics, 2003).
31. See, e.g., H. David Rosenbloom, International Tax Arbitrage and the "International Tax System," The David R. Tillinghast Lecture, NYU School of Law (Oct. 1, 1998), in 53 Tax L. Rev. 137 (1999).
32. See, e.g., Dagan, Tsilly, The Tax Treaties Myth, 32 New York University J. Int'l Law & Pol. 939 (2000); Tsilly Dagan, The Costs of International Tax Cooperation, In E. Benvenisti, G. Nolte and D. Barak-Erez (eds.), Globalization and the Welfare State (Springer, 2002), 49; Julie Roin, Taxation Without Coordination, 31 J. Legal Stud. 61 (2002); Julie Roin, Competition and Evasion: Another Perspective on International Tax Competition, 89 Geo. L.J. 543 (2001).

competition, primarily based on the unquestioned belief in the invisible forces behind markets and their vague pie (welfare) maximization properties. A more sophisticated support of competition as a basis for the international tax regime developed due to political distrust of cooperation at the international level.[33] Such approaches view even the current, soft regime as a powerful cartel in the service of the more powerful at the expense of the less powerful countries. The core of this critique is its distrust of the OECD, the rich countries club that has been the caretaker of the international tax regime. The OECD dominates the regime through its exclusive powers over the OECD Model that permits it to set the agenda for all developments of the regime. Yet, more fundamentally, the norms contained in the OECD Model are biased in favor of residence taxation that benefits countries that are better-off, such as the OECD Member States.[34] Any further harmonization, goes the claim, would have to be based on this bias, further fixating the dominance of the rich countries over all others.

Critics of the competition framework respond to these arguments by noting that it is the current regime and framework that had assured the dominance of the rich countries and their control over the international tax regime. Further competition would not give voice to the less powerful economies that do not compete on a level playing field with the rich countries or even amongst themselves. The competition framework limits policy choices that may assist developing countries to grow and develop, and even collect sufficient revenue to sustain their policies. Only cooperation at some level would allow these countries to make free and rational policy choices. This approach may be based on general notions of fairness or equity, yet it may also be based on interests that may be mutual to both developed and developing productive countries, all of which suffer from poor revenue collection. Such lost revenue may be found in inappropriate tax planning that uses non-productive, sometimes called "tax haven," jurisdictions for the benefit of a few flesh-and-bloods at the eventual expense of many others. The BEPS project reflects a realization that more coordination and even some harmonization may be beneficial to both developed and developing (productive) countries.

Recent developments have posed challenges to the international tax regime, adding to the above-mentioned difficulties it faces. Well-known recent geopolitical changes have been particularly important in this regard. The general criticism of the OECD and its dominance over the international tax regime became much more focused as some of the developing countries who are not members of the OECD begun emerging and acquiring both economic and political powers. Most notably, the BRICS countries, led by India and China gained strong positions in the global market and began demanding a corresponding voice in the policymaking process. The OECD had anticipated the importance of communicating with non-Member States long before these developments and had launched an observation program for such countries. Yet, the power to observe proceedings was not sufficient for countries that started viewing

---

33. *See* Tsilly Dagan, BRICS: Theoretical Framework and the Potential of Cooperation, in Brauner & Pistone, BRICS, *supra* note 4, 15.
34. But, *see*, e.g., Ekkehart Reimer, 5 + 7 = odd, Fla. Tax Rev. (forthcoming) (arguing for excessive concessions by the OECD in favor of so-called source countries).

themselves as world leaders, especially when for most purposes their participation has not resulted in significant enough (for them) changes in the division of tax bases and other norms. The demand for more taxation at source, conflicted with the opposite trend to eliminate taxation at source in favor of residence taxation that had always been the hallmark of OECD tax policy and a consequence of the competition framework of the international tax regime. Some countries have unilaterally departed from some of the prior universal norms of the international tax regime to assert their tax jurisdiction and views of appropriate division of tax bases.[35]

At the same time, past economic powers have lost some or, in some cases, most of their power, or, at least in the case of the United States, their superpower. Today even the United States cannot dominate any international tax policy discussion. Globalization and the recent Global Financial Crisis resulted in the starvation of revenue even among the most developed countries and a lack of power to independently regenerate their collection powers. The first response to this crisis focused on collection and the most traditional, conservative tax treaty law measure of information exchange. The theory was that an enhanced and cheap exchange of information, coupled with the destruction of bank secrecy would eliminate most abusive tax planning regimes and restore the power of the old international tax regime. Yet, the nature of the global market, of information and contemporary tax planning was that the rich economies could not implement this solution alone. The power effectively shifted, at least in part, to the G-20 organization where some OECD members are not members and some emerging economies who are not OECD members have an equal voice to that of the traditional powers. The outcome was the "Global Forum."[36] The BEPS project, reviewed in the next section, was the next step. The G-20 took the initiative, although in doing so, it required the cooperation of the OECD who in turn would be charged with following the pattern set by the Global Forum.

The same phenomena resulted not only in political challenges to the international tax regime but also in direct challenges to the efficacy of the norms. New trends, such as: electronic commerce, the ascent of intangibles, the increased use of sophisticated financial instruments, including derivatives, in the increasingly mobile global capital markets, and the rise of MNEs facilitated by globalization, have all dumbfounded the prevailing norms that had been established in a simpler, "smaller," brick-and-mortar world. For much of these transactions not only the norms but also the structural foundations of the international tax regimes, such as the *Source v. Residence* dichotomy became apparently inadequate.

These challenges to the norms of the regime tested its efficacy, especially when they coincided with a global economic downturn that created serious revenue

---

35. For example, China lost the battle over locational savings, yet continued to pursue it under domestic laws despite its rejection by the BEPS project. *See*, e.g., Ryan Finley, Panel Expects Rising Transfer Pricing Compliance Burdens in China 2015 WTD 211-6. *See also* the renewed collection demand by India of Vodafone following the litigation regarding India's exceptional (from OECD norms) taxation of indirect share transfers. *See*, e.g., Stephanie Soong Johnson, India Renews $2.1 Billion Vodafone Tax Demand, 2016 WTD 31-5.
36. The Global Forum on Transparency and Exchange of Information for Tax Purposes. *See* website at http://www.oecd.org/tax/transparency/.

pressures in most countries. These pressures culminated with the BEPS project and the apparent mixed actions by many nations that on the one hand seem to agree that enhanced coordination of tax policies is desirable for them, and spend time and energy participating in fora promoting these ideas, yet on the other hand engage in new unilateral actions that appear to be diametrically opposite to coordination efforts. Next, the chapter demonstrates this conflict through a few examples taken from BEPS.

§4.04 BEPS AND THE SOVEREIGNTY CLAIM

The chapter now turns to examining the perceived conflicts between tax sovereignty and efforts to enhance coordination in the international tax regime, using examples from the BEPS project and its aftermath.

[A] BEPS Action 2 (Neutralize the Effects of Hybrid Mismatch Arrangements)

Action item 2 addresses the very essence of BEPS, the tax planning schemes exploiting differences between the laws of the jurisdictions involved to minimize taxation in an inappropriate manner. Here is the core base erosion issue. Another articulation of it is the complaint about so-called stateless income, or income not fully taxed in any jurisdiction. Yet, it is not clear what is inappropriate in this context? Taxpayers cannot be blamed for organizing their affairs in manners that take advantage of mere differences in tax laws, as this is the essence of all tax planning, and some differences are clearly intentional; part of the tax competition that is at the core of the international tax regime. One could try to distinguish between general taxation at low rates and preferential no taxation or low taxation, yet this distinction often becomes merely semantic. It is very difficult to justify this complaint in a regime that is based on competition, in which tax competition is the core value rather than the pathology. In this regime it would be very difficult to distinguish between acceptable and "harmful" tax competition, and indeed prior attempts to do that failed. Even "easy" cases that some may argue that they fail an obvious smell test do not suffer universal condemnation. Perhaps the closest to this is the "cash box" example in the BEPS transfer pricing reports, yet even on this case there is no clear consensus. The simple reason for this is that consensus requires coordination (as acknowledged by BEPS), yet meaningful coordination is antithetical to the international tax regime and its competition ethos. The deeper issue is that there is no agreement on common principles regarding tax jurisdiction. The OECD residence/source dichotomy is quite dominant but it is not based on a substantive rationale; it is not natural law, and it is definitely not based on any robust economic principles despite its presentation as economically meaningful. Here, again, BEPS promised to improve the regime and base it on "value creation;" vague as it may be at least it could have served as a good starting point for a substantive discourse, yet the OECD stirred the project away from it, and kept course based on administrative ease that eventually resolved none of the core issues.

Chapter 4: An Essay on BEPS, Sovereignty, and Taxation   §4.04[A]

Note that even the little coordination provided by tax treaties is manifestly incomplete. There are many instances of double taxation not resolved by tax treaty norms since the competing jurisdictions could not agree to resolve them. Certain conflicts of qualifications and conflicts regarding corporate residence are examples.[37] This chapter argues that BEPS has not substantively changed this picture, and its addition of minimum standards cannot be viewed as improving coordination in the regime.

Hybrid mismatches are perhaps the most obvious example for BEPS issues. It is difficult to stomach such mismatches in an international tax regime since they present income that one feels obvious that it should be taxed and is not. It is not taxed either because it is "stateless," it is generated by a hybrid entity or it is characterized differently in different jurisdictions. Only a double non-taxation perspective could provide a workable framework for identifying what is inappropriate in tax planning that relies on mismatches.

The final action 2 report clearly identifies the problem created by hybrid mismatches as one of double non-taxation, yet it chooses to recommend a two pronged solution that does not include a clear articulation of double non-taxation as a fundamental principle of the international tax regime or tax treaties; a principle that regardless of its desirability could at least guide future development of standards of application and operative rules to combat the undesirable consequences of hybrid mismatch arrangement.

Instead, the report recommends domestic and model treaty law amendments.[38] This approach demonstrates a clear preference towards a minimal scope for the BEPS project and a rejection of the opportunity it presents for a comprehensive international tax reform. One may argue that the OECD has taken a "pragmatic" approach, yet this would merely be camouflaging the clear policy choice taken by the OECD on this matter in favor of maintaining a competition based regime. It would also be a clear retreat from the general obligation of the OECD to the fundamental insights of BEPS: the emphasis on domestic anti-abuse rules all but eliminates the commitment to a collaborative approach, relying primarily on ad-hoc, unilateral measures with no innovation, as the recommendations replicate work already launched by the OECD in the pre-BEPS era.[39]

Part I of the report includes a set of specific recommendations based on domestic law changes to combat payments made under hybrid financial instruments, or by a hybrid entity or hybrid mismatches imported into a third jurisdiction. The idea here is to establish a set of best practices, based on the theory that if all countries follow such practices hybrid mismatches would not result in undesirable outcomes. Yet, even the report itself seems not to be convinced that that would happen and hence it proposes alternative, "defensive" domestic anti-abuse rules that would be effective in cases

---

37. *See*, e.g., OECD Model Commentary on conflict of qualifications, Art. 23A and 23B, para. 32.
38. OECD, Neutralising the Effects of Hybrid Mismatch Arrangements, Action 2 – 2015 Final Report (Oct. 5, 2015), available at http://www.oecd.org/tax/neutralising-the-effects-of-hybrid-mismatch-arrangements-action-2-2015-final-report-9789264241138-en.htm.
39. OECD, Hybrid Mismatch Arrangements: Tax Policy and Compliance Issues, (May 3, 2012), available at http://www.oecd.org/ctp/aggressive/HYBRIDS_ENG_Final_October2012.pdf.

where relevant countries do not follow the first-order recommendations. The OECD does not explain why it expects that countries would follow its best practices, ignoring self-interest, best self-assessment of the desirable rules and the possibility of defection by other countries. The provision of the defensive rules is proof that the OECD does not believe that progress towards resolution of the lack of coordination leading to BEPS and hybrid tax planning can truly be made. One is left puzzling how that is different from the current state of affairs.

Yet, the content of these proposed best practices lacks any logic or reason, and would not even rely on a double non-taxation framework. The OECD simply chose one set of countries (generally the residences of the payors) to make concessions over others (generally the residences of the payees) without any explanation or analysis of the consequences of these choices. It is all neatly set in elaborate tables, but nothing is provided in terms of the rationale, or even an assessment of the winners or losers from the recommendations. The solutions provided by the OECD are merely instrumental and propose to demonstrate that something is being done, but not more than that. Why would then countries follow these recommendations unless they expect to accidentally "win," and even then their winning is conditional upon the "loser" country decision to follow the rules as well for reasons unfathomable. Of course, even arbitrary arrangements could work in a well-coordinated regime when participants believe that overall they would benefit from such a regime, yet this is not the case here. The action 2 recommendations are not part of a future multilateral treaty, but rather to be implemented unilaterally by countries, so they could easily defect with essentially no consequences, and one should expect many of them to do exactly that.

It is the stubborn reluctance to deal with principles that haunts this action item that may eventually be the focus of attention being the most direct articulation of BEPS style planning. The OECD is attracted to the appeal of the so-called single tax principle, and more specifically the view of double taxation and double non-taxation as parallel problems. Yet, as already mentioned, the implementation of this view in practice is problematic, and the OECD approach to action 2 is pragmatic, since requiring a jurisdiction to concede taxation is very different from requiring it to tax when it does not wish to. In the latter case revenue may be lost, yet a promise of more investment and a better competitive position ensues, while in the latter it gets some revenue, if any, in exchange for a worse competitive position (we know that it is worse since the country had already made that decision when it chose not to tax). The actual recommendation is to primarily deny the deduction, not to tax the not-included income, yet the impact is similar. Domestically, this choice could be worse than reluctant inclusions, since identical transactions would get a deduction in the purely domestic setting but not across-borders, distorting domestic tax policies.

A tax sovereignty claim may be used in this context to support whatever position taken by a country. Of course, a country may do nothing, taking the simple position that action 2 does not obligate it to do anything, or just keep silent about it. This seems at this point to be the most popular approach. Tax sovereignty may be used to support such inaction simply due to lack of interest or benefit to a country. Other countries may comply with the action 2 recommendation and deny deductions for hybrid mismatches. Such a rule may be adjusted to be narrower or wider depending on the country. Tax sovereignty may support this action and fend arguments of discrimination, using anti-abuse reasoning and tax sovereignty to protect one's base. A country may similarly use the action 2 defensive mechanism as the primary rule or indeed as a defensive mechanism to justify discriminatory taxation in hybrid mismatches circumstances, again, based on anti-BEPS rationale. It is not difficult to observe that tax sovereignty may be used to support whatever action is desired. The lack of strong consensus relieves countries from being subject to a meaningful international law and no one thinks that all countries will simply comply with BEPS in a single, universal manner. It is easy to observe that the tax sovereignty argument is useless in this context. This is not surprising since action 2 asks a country to take a leap of faith and act against its interests (not to tax) and tax, with potentially detrimental consequences to inbound investment with no clear payoff.

The second part of the action 2 report complements the first part by addressing the difficulty of establishing corporate residence, an unresolved issue to date.[40] Its solution is to drop the current proposed general and tie-breaking rule of place of effective management and replace it by a case-by-case analysis. This is not unreasonable since the current rule had no chance of implementation in the first place, yet, to replace it with a no-test (case-by-case analysis) cannot project progress. This no-solution signals a weakness of the BEPS project. It is obvious to all that corporate residence, like corporations, is a legal metaphor, perhaps necessary for the proper application of a corporate tax system. Therefore, it is also obvious that an objective, or meaningful rule simply cannot be established for corporate residence. Countries use different rules for a variety of operative, instrumental purposes, but not based on any "truths."[41] Therefore, there is no substantive basis for countries to convince each other to standardize these rules and fight BEPS.[42] Any standard rule will do if fighting BEPS is the goal so long as all agree to use the same rule and in a consistent manner. Since different rules have different winners and losers it would be difficult to choose among them – indeed, the BEPS project failed to do exactly that. But, one thing is clear: progress can be made only by consensus. In that BEPS had failed. A somewhat similar difficulty concerns the taxation of partnerships. The old debate between the entity and aggregate approaches to partnerships is similarly fruitless, as there is obviously no right and wrong. The action 2 report recommends to implement the 1999 OECD partnership report[43] in the form of a model convention provision and commentary. The problem here is that the OECD's partnership report has made little progress in the fifteen years since it was published, with much criticism and now the OECD promises that it will really work once all of the countries adopted it. Again, no progress was made on this

---

40. See, e.g., Omri Y. Marian, Jurisdiction to Tax Corporations, 54 Boston College L. Rev. 1613 (2013).
41. Id.
42. Therefore, a case-by-case analysis is meaningless here if countries disagree about the parameters of the analysis.
43. See OECD, The Application of the OECD Model Tax Convention to Partnerships (OECD, Issues in International Taxation, No. 6, 1999); and Michael Lang, The Application of the OECD Model Tax Convention to Partnerships: A Critical Analysis of the Report Prepared by the OECD Committee on Fiscal Affairs (Linde Verlag Wien, 2000).

matter. The corporate residence and partnership taxation issues demonstrate the futility of the tax sovereignty debate even better than the core hybrid mismatches issue. On the one hand, tax sovereignty rhetoric supports acting in the narrow interest of a country, yet, on the other hand, this may eventually hurt the country, especially when compared with a potentially beneficial consensus arrangement. The core decision in this context must be whether a country predicts that an international effort to standardize a norm is feasible or not. The sovereignty arguments adds nothing to this core question and may only obscure it.

[B] Action 13 (Guidance on Transfer Pricing Documentation and Country-by-Country Reporting)

The most tangible achievement of BEPS, and perhaps its only real contribution to the evolution of the international tax regime is the introduction of standard transfer pricing documentation. Transfer pricing regulation intends to keep MNE in check, requiring them to establish transfer prices based on arm's length (i.e., market) analysis and document their position contemporaneously. The documentation requirement fixes the taxpayers' positions and limits their options. Despite the inherent bilateral (or more) nature of transfer prices, the rules and reporting apply on unilateral bases with no coordination or a strong requirement of consistency. This is strange in a regime that applies an essentially universal standard and applies in multiple countries in parallel to the same transactions. Despite its inherent bilateral nature, the transfer-pricing regime is applied unilaterally, consistent with the competition-based international tax regime. This may be viewed as a manifestation of tax sovereignty, but also as a concession to an international standard set and forcefully protected by the dominant OECD. One must acknowledge that from the perspective of a country that wishes to apply rules that deviate from the universal standard, its enforcement by the OECD is clearly a worse violation of its sovereignty.

In any event, action 13 seeks to fix some of this anomaly by standardizing the documentation requirements. The final report establishes a three-tier reporting regime.[44] A master file includes information that would be necessary for the implementation of the rules in every relevant country. A standard form would avoid duplication, and hence reduce the costs of compliance and prevent inconsistent reporting. A country file would complement the master file with more particular information that may be relevant to specific countries only or that is uniquely required by one involved country but not by another for legitimate reasons. Finally, a standard CbC report would provide an overview of the entire business of the taxpayer in the different relevant countries in order to give individual countries a better perspective on the specific country reporting relevant to them and how it fits the general structure and strategy of the taxpayer. Such reporting would also encourage consistency in compliance and filing.

---

44. OECD, Transfer Pricing Documentation and Country-by-Country Reporting, Action 13 – 2015 Final Report, available at http://www.oecd.org/tax/transfer-pricing-documentation-and-country-by-country-reporting-action-13-2015-final-report-9789264241480-en.htm.

Chapter 4: An Essay on BEPS, Sovereignty, and Taxation   §4.04[B]

This standard three tier reporting should improve the consistency of transfer pricing compliance, which one would expect to be inherent to this norm yet has been neglected in the current competition-based international tax regime. It would obviously be consistent with the single tax principle, or, more pointedly, would assist in avoiding untaxed "gaps" in income reporting as a result of inconsistent transfer pricing positions. It would reduce the costs of compliance and enforcement, especially for countries with insufficient budgets for sophisticated enforcement of transfer pricing. It would prevent biased reporting, either due to taxpayers' interests or power positions of certain countries. Finally, it would centralize the control over the transfer-pricing regime, and therefore set the stage to opportunities for coordination of policies and enforcement.

The CbC report is the single true innovation of BEPS today. Yet, the conservative forces within the project had fought to decimate its scope, supposedly in the name of protecting taxpayers' data.[45] Whether corporate tax data should be confidential at all is beyond the scope of this chapter,[46] yet it is clear that the conservative forces have succeeded in significantly limiting the scope of the CbC report to information that is generally already available or could be available to most sophisticated, well-funded tax authorities. Moreover, the same forces dictated that the report shall be available only to the tax authorities, keeping the information confidential. Finally, the same forces succeeded in adding a clarification that the CbC report would not directly be used for tax assessment but only for risk assessment purposes, i.e., to identify problems. Such clarification aims primarily at the prevention of deviation from arm's length and resort to formulary apportionment.

The sovereignty perspective on action 13 and especially on the CbC reporting is particularly interesting. This is a real achievement of BEPS: a truly standard reporting regime. On its face, it violates simple tax sovereignty since the reporting regime is dictated by an external polity, not the state, yet action 13 leaves space for domestic law to make idiosyncratic reporting requirements that will find a place in a local file that is part of the scheme. The question is therefore whether the requirements beyond the domestic requirements should be viewed as a violation of tax sovereignty, as action 13 does not limit the powers of a country to make its own requirements. Nominally, external requirements may be viewed as acceptable due to the sovereignty rights of other countries within which jurisdiction an MNE operates. A corporation will not be subject to effective extraterritorial burden unless it operates extraterritorially. But, one may argue that CbC reporting goes beyond what a country would demand of "its" MNE, perhaps base on an articulation of (exclusive) sovereignty based on residence. Yet, even this would be a very weak argument, since when a country decides not to cooperate, perhaps by simply not requiring CbC reporting from its MNE, there is no

---

45. For arguments in favor of confidentiality, *see* the Final Action 13 Report, *Id.*; and David Ernick, Will Public Disclosure of Country-by-Country Reporting Data Become Mandatory? BNA News (Jun. 8, 2015).
46. But, it would be naïve to assume that it can be kept secret. *See*, e.g., Brauner, What the BEPS? *supra* note 4; Andrew Goodall, U.K Paves the Way for Public CbC Reporting but Stresses Multilateral Approach, 2016 WTD 173-5 (Sept. 7, 2016); Tax Notes, European Legislators Call for Public CbC Reporting 2016 WTD 125-19 (Jun. 29, 2016).

sanction. But, other countries may, and are likely to demand such reports from "foreign" MNE operating within their jurisdiction, making non-cooperation a rather futile move. The United States is trying to maintain the bilateral nature of CbC reporting exchange, yet the self-policing nature of the reporting scheme should not be defeated even by the United States, and it seems that the government has essentially acknowledged that.

CbC reporting is an example for a true standard with meaningful purpose and content that once accepted by enough countries mandate coordination and does not raise meaningful sovereignty issues, unless one uses an extreme articulation of the notion of sovereignty.

[C] Action 14 (Making Dispute Resolution Mechanisms More Effective)

An international legal regime is often measured by the efficacy of its dispute resolution regime. The current, soft, non-legalistic MAP regime has undoubtedly been proven successful for the forming years of the regime. Its non-mandatory nature reduced the perceived threat posed by the international tax regime to the tax sovereignty of the participating nations.[47] It also has not prevented the convergence of the international tax rules, even if it had not contributed much to their development. Many fundamental disputes have actually been resolved without resort to tax wars, a non-trivial achievement. Yet, in recent years it became increasingly apparent that progress is required. A quicker, cheaper and more decisive regime is needed. Scarcity of revenue, increased competition for investment, globalization and decentralization of power, and the increasing complexity and sophistication of global business require a more resolute regime that would contribute rather than just adhere to the universal norms.

Pre-BEPS OECD project has resulted in a recommendation for mandatory "baseball" arbitration to be added to the MAP in cases that the latter fails to resolve in an acceptable timeframe.[48] Some countries have adopted this recommendation, yet despite the relative success that the solution apparently enjoy, only few treaties had been concluded based on this recommendation.[49] This failure exacerbated BEPS on the one hand and unjust treatments of some taxpayers who could not get relief on the other hand. The BEPS project chose to take another go at it and employed its first insight to organize a relatively large,[50] yet not complete group of countries that now commit to adoption of mandatory arbitration in all of their treaties. Success in adopting a

---

47. *See*, e.g., Robert A. Green, Antilegalistic Approaches to Resolving Disputes Between Governments: A Comparison of the International Tax and Trade Regimes, 23 Yale J. Int'l L. 79 (1998).
48. *See*, e.g., OECD, Improving the Resolution of Tax Treaty Disputes (Report adopted by the Committee on Fiscal Affairs on Jan. 30, 2007), available at http://www.oecd.org/ctp/dispute/38055311.pdf.
49. *See* OECD, Making Dispute Resolution Mechanisms More Effective, Action 14 – 2015 Final Report, available at http://www.oecd.org/tax/making-dispute-resolution-mechanisms-more-effective-action-14-2015-final-report-9789264241633-en.htm.
50. Encouragingly, the OECD notes that these countries were involved in 90% of outstanding MAP cases at the end of 2013. *See* final report, *Id.*, page 10.

multilateral instrument of the kind described next may prove to be important for a chance of success in realizing such commitment.

Hand in hand with action 15 that is discussed next, action 14 is viewed as the biggest threat to tax sovereignty in BEPS. Interestingly, one may argue that it is viewed as a bigger threat than action 15 even though action 15 visions multilateral action that inherently leaves less power to individual jurisdictions in comparison to bilateral arbitration. Nonetheless, many fewer countries have subscribed to the idea of mandatory arbitration to date compared to the multilateral instrument. The arguments made in this context are that MAP leaves wide discretion in the hands of sovereign states, while arbitration is likely to be dominated by the richest, most powerful nations. With MAP, the weaker nations may simply say no, with perhaps some negative consequences, yet with no harm to their sovereignty. The domination of the richest nations may be manifested in the baseline legal norms used in arbitration (these are, however, already the current rules of the international tax regime), in the resources, monetary and others, available to them in the process, and, perhaps most conspicuously, in the dominance of the richest countries over the pool of "experts" that may serve as arbitrators. The latter complaint is perhaps the most commonly heard against mandatory arbitration. Yet, note that the same countries have agreed to similar arrangements in other economic circumstances, such as trade and investment, and there it has not been difficult to find arbitrators representing the relevant regions. Some may articulate the refusal to support mandatory tax arbitration in sovereignty protection terms that many believe apply more forcefully in the tax area in comparison to trade and investment. Yet, in terms of self-interest and even in terms of control over the outcomes, it is very unclear that weaker countries fare better under MAP, especially when large MNE taxpayers are concerned. This chapter argues that sovereignty has very little to do with this opposition to mandatory arbitration. It is really the lack of trust that drives the refusal of developing countries to support the developed countries' promotion of mandatory arbitration. The current impasse on mandatory arbitration proves again that when framed in sovereignty terms the international tax discourse cannot progress, especially when sovereignty has little to do with the real issues. The chapter argues that if framed as a trust issue it would be much easier to make progress on dispute resolution in general and mandatory arbitration in particular. The international trade and investment regimes have gone through similar phases and lessons may be learned from the progress they made and obstacles they had (and to some extent still have) to overcome.

[D] Action 15 (Developing a Multilateral Instrument to Modify Bilateral Tax Treaties)

Enhanced coordination of tax laws and policies is the key insight of the BEPS project: countries are now unable to unilaterally apply their tax system, independent of all other countries. The so intuitive notion of national sovereignty at its most fundamental level – tax policymaking, collection and enforcement – has brutally crashed. Even the strongest countries in the world found themselves vulnerable. Resort to a multilateral solution was almost inevitable against this background. Action item 15 was charged therefore in assessing the feasibility of adopting such an instrument. Despite the longstanding opposition of many countries and experts to the notion, the action item 15 report clarifies that such an instrument is both legally and practically feasible.[51] This is dramatic enough, yet the report has exceeded its mandate to merely issue a report, and proceeded to work on the implementation of the instrument.

The final action 15 report uses language consistent with the minimal view of BEPS to promote the adoption of the multilateral instrument. It explains that to be effective the BEPS recommendations must be implemented quickly, cheaply, in a synchronized manner and coherently. This is impossible in the current paradigm of pure bilateral negotiation and conclusion of tax treaties. The BEPS project took advantage of its political support to conclude that its charge could only be met if such an instrument is adopted. The perceived instrument does change the bilateral nature of tax treaties; it only streamlines standard amendments to tax treaties such as those required by BEPS, and prevents the elaborate give and take nature of bilateral treaty negotiations and negotiations' budget constraints from standing in the way of success in realizing these goals. The report realizes the possibility of partial or gradual adoption of the multilateral instrument.[52] Such flexibility makes the instrument more appealing (or less intimidating) and most importantly sidesteps the all-or-nothing approach that so typified the debate over multilateralism in taxation. Naturally, the success of the instrument would depend on the size of its early adopters. One does not need to be an expert game theorist to conclude that a multilateral instrument is inevitable if any progress is to be made in the regime that is based on bilateral tax treaties. The alternative, of course is a multilateral regime (or chaos...) that, again, requires wide multilateral cooperation. Again, sovereignty has little to contribute to this issue, as the question is solely whether countries will be willing to engage in this multilateral experiment to avoid chaos. One is reminded of Bodin and the origins of the modern concept of sovereignty – the prevention of political chaos. One could not therefore honestly resist the multilateral instrument based on sovereignty alone.

[E] Post BEPS EU Action

The EU has provided the boldest BEPS (project) supporting move with its Anti-Tax Avoidance package adopted by the European Commission on January 28, 2016. This is the single implementation measure, beyond individual items adopted sporadically in some countries, that takes a BEPS-plus approach with multiple measures. It included four documents: a proposal for an Anti-Tax-Avoidance Directive,[53] a Communication

---

51. OECD, Developing a Multilateral Instrument to Modify Bilateral Tax Treaties, Action 15 – 2015 Final Report, available at http://www.oecd.org/tax/developing-a-multilateral-instrument-to-modify-bilateral-tax-treaties-action-15-2015-final-report-9789264241688-en.htm.
52. *See also* Yariv Brauner, An International Tax Regime in Crystallization, 56 Tax L. Rev. 259 (2003).
53. COM (2016) 23 final. Proposal for a Council Directive laying down rules against tax avoidance practices that directly affect the functioning of the internal market.

on an external strategy for effective taxation,[54] an amendment to the Directive on mutual assistance to apply automatic exchange of information to country-by-country reporting,[55] and a recommendation to add to tax treaties the "genuine economic activity" caveat to the Principal Purpose Test ("PPT").[56] The package is an interpretation of some of the BEPS final reports and their implementation in European law. It is a rather bold or aggressive interpretation of the anti-avoidance elements of the BEPS reports, and it is attempting standardization of this interpretation throughout the EU at the same time that some EU countries have been the prime violators of the BEPS promise of standardization. These countries famously "jumped the gun" on various matters, such as the U.K. diverted profits tax, the various new patent box regimes, and similar actions, making this countering action by the commission very interesting and internally controversial.

The directive proposal included six measures: an interest limitation rule, an exit taxation provision, a switch-over clause, a general anti-abuse rule, Controlled Foreign Companies ("CFC") legislation, and a hybrid mismatches rule. One can immediately observe that only some of these measures are following BEPS recommendations (the hybrid mismatches rule), some promote ideas on which BEPS had not reached consensus (the CFC rules) and some may be in the spirit of BEPS as interpreted by the commission yet not part of the BEPS action plan (switch-over clause). These measures may be viewed as allocation rules and as such may be legitimate under EU law, yet when viewed from the more relevant prism of anti-avoidance rules the picture is different. The proposals faced challenges with EU law, including the fundamental freedoms. Moreover, the directive indirectly shifts competence on anti-avoidance matters from the Member States to the EU, yet the range of possibilities permitted by the directive would make harmonization here very difficult. Moreover, some of the measures go beyond BEPS, adopting norms that even within BEPS countries could not agree to, such as making CbC reports publicly available. It is very questionable whether it is possible to view this package as a step toward more coordination or as a first shot in a battle to push the comprehensive reform elements in BEPS forward in the implementation stage overcoming some of the shortcomings during the design period of the Project.

Naturally, the United States would view this push as just another European aggression in addition to the state aid investigations that generated suspicion of a looming tax war between the EU and the United States. But, the internal EU problems may be more threatening for the European commission. For example, Malta's finance minister, Edward Scicluna, said in opposition to the package that Malta will not cede sovereignty to the EC, and pledged that Malta will resist any attempt by the EC to

---

54. COM (2016) 24 final, Communication from the Commission to the European Parliament and the Council.
55. COM (2016) 25 final. Proposal for a Council Directive amending Directive 2011/16/EU as regards mandatory automatic exchange of information in the field of taxation.
56. COM (2016) 271 final, Commission Recommendation of 28.1.2016 on the implementation of measures against tax treaty abuse.

reduce sovereignty over its own fiscal affairs.[57] This is quite interesting since the whole European project is about ceding sovereignty (in its simplest form) to the Union in exchange for stability, growth, and peace. Yet, one should note that in the direct (income) tax area the European Member States simply refused to cede sovereignty to the Union. Some of this had been proven moot since the so-called fundamental freedoms required some harmonization of tax norms anyway, but no direct, positive agreement was reached among the Member States on most matters (putting aside the directives focusing on withholding taxes and mergers for a moment). Against this background the new package is a very bold movement by the European commission in a direction that the Member States have not authorized. Moreover, the reliance on BEPS make the source of the changes proposed external to the Union which further puts into question the authority for such a bold harmonization proposal.

Yet, the core of this debate is political, not legal. One can make good legal argument for both sides, even if some are more convincing than others, but that may not be relevant. Again, a simplistic use of sovereignty will probably lead nowhere. As mentioned, single Member States may oppose the package based on their sovereign rights not conceded, while the commission will point to the constitutional arrangement of the Union and its own obligation to ensure the effective function of the single market, which, it will undoubtedly argue necessitates taking bold measures against MNE that engage in BEPS. Interestingly, though, reminding us of the origins of the modern articulation of sovereignty may be useful in this context. Bodin's concern about political chaos may be relevant in this context, so, although simplistic use of competing sovereignty claims may not be helpful, one could ask whether the EU anti-avoidance package is justified based on a concern that otherwise political chaos would ensue. To the extent it is, and tests such as proportionality, supported by economic and empirical studies, may come into mind as productive in this context. This chapter does not pretend to engage in an analysis of European law or policy, yet it wishes to point to the meaning of the use of sovereignty claims in the context of BEPS, the mistake in casual use of the term and possible benefits of a more meaningful understanding of the notion. Next, the chapter concludes, further emphasizing these points.

§4.05 CONCLUSION

This chapter demonstrated that the casual use of the notion of sovereignty in the international tax discourse in general and the BEPS context in particular is useless.[58] Competing ideas and policy paths can equally draft sovereignty to support their cause, and they often do. Most importantly, the competition framework that defines the current international tax regime cannot accommodate serious sovereignty claims, since

---

57. *See* Mossak Fonseca website (Feb. 3, 2016), at: http://www.mossfon.com/news/malta-refuses-to-cede-tax-sovereignty/.
58. The words of Zbigniew Brzezinski come into mind: "Sovereignty is a word that is used often but it has really no specific meaning. Sovereignty today is nominal. Any number of countries that are sovereign are sovereign only nominally and relatively."

at its core competition results in winners and losers and simple losing cannot justify claims about sovereignty infringement. A state may argue that anti-competitive measures, such as cartelistic behavior of strong countries (OECD) or simple violations of the rules of the game via bullying or blunt violations of international obligations infringe upon its sovereignty, yet there really is no remedy for such state beyond retaliation, if possible, in collusion with other countries. Conversely, countries may coordinate action with the intent of perfecting competition (BEPS). They may argue that not cooperating with them infringes upon their sovereignty, etc. Again, their success eventually depends on their power to coerce cooperation, and the notion of sovereignty adds nothing to that beyond obscuring what really goes on.

In a competing, coordination-based regime, of the kind perhaps imagined by the original BEPS documents, should again have no use for sovereignty. Even if all countries agreed that more coordination is required there will be temptation to defect, especially when the current (former) regime was competition based. Enforcement of an agreement to cooperate will certainly be countered by sovereignty claims, and a debate over which is superior – this latter claim or the international agreement establishing a common baseline that acceptably put boundaries to sovereignty claims – is clearly going to be fruitless, and, again, will depend on the relative political and economic powers and interests involved.

One may however try a different approach that corresponds, as already mentioned, with the origins of the modern notion of sovereignty. Following Bodin, one could establish an instrumental role for sovereignty in the process of improving cooperation and coordination of tax policies among productive (non-tax haven) countries. This role would be to balance claims and serve as a safeguard against political (in this case international) chaos. This approach may be helpful to secure more cooperation of hesitant parties and a balanced solution that provides enough space for competition and growth, yet within acceptable boundaries that would ensure at least an opportunity for all participants to succeed; an opportunity that is evidently not available at the present, hence the vast participation in the BEPS project.

Part II Challenge to the Foundational Principles of Source and Residence

CHAPTER 5
Evaluating BEPS

Reuven S. Avi-Yonah & Haiyan Xu

§5.01 INTRODUCTION: THE FINANCIAL CRISIS AND INEQUALITY

The financial crisis of 2008 and the Great Recession that followed have raised anew the problem of how to address a growing inequality both between the rich and everybody else within countries, and between developed and developing countries. Both dimensions of inequality, the intra- and inter-country ones, have risen in this century, and the Great Recession has made both problems worse. The current rise of populism in both the United States (U.S.) and in Europe and the vehement reactions to a tide of migrants from poorer to richer countries show how these two problems are intertwined.

Sixteen years ago, the first author wrote about the challenge that globalization and tax competition pose to the fiscal viability of the post-World War II welfare state.[1] He pointed out that if tax avoidance by multinational corporations is allowed to undermine the ability of both developed and developing countries to provide adequate social insurance for their citizens, a violent reaction against globalization may ensue that risks ending this era of opening borders, just like World War I ended the previous era of globalization a century ago. In 2016, we worry that the lack of adequate response to the Great Recession is leading to the rise of violent anti-globalization sentiments on both the right and the left, embodied in the U.S. by the success of Bernie Sanders and Donald Trump and in Europe by an even more virulent rejection of the open border policies the EU has stood for.

It is imperative for the West to find ways to strengthen the ability of the state to provide adequate social insurance and to reduce inequality before these forces lead to the closing of the borders and to pressures that could result in World War III. But the response so far has unfortunately not been adequate.

---

1. Reuven S. Avi-Yonah, Globalization, Tax Competition, and the Fiscal Crisis of the Welfare State, Harvard Law Review, Vol. 113, 2000, p. 1573.

Following the financial crisis and ensuing austerity, politicians discovered the problem of tax avoidance. In response, the Organisation for Economic Co-operation and Development (OECD) and G20 launched the Base Erosion and Profit Shifting (BEPS) project in 2013, and this has in October, 2015 culminated with the release of a series of action steps that the OECD and G20 countries have undertaken to adopt.[2] OECD Secretary-General Angel Gurria has stated that "Base erosion and profit shifting affects all countries, not only economically, but also as a matter of trust. BEPS is depriving countries of precious resources to jump-start growth, tackle the effects of the global economic crisis, and create more and better opportunities for all. But beyond this, BEPS has been also eroding the trust of citizens in the fairness of tax systems worldwide. *The measures we are presenting today represent the most fundamental changes to international tax rules in almost a century: they will put an end to double non-taxation, facilitate a better alignment of taxation with economic activity and value creation, and when fully implemented, these measures will render BEPS-inspired tax planning structures ineffective.*"[3]

Is Mr. Gurria justified in his optimism? We do not think so. These efforts are commendable and to some extent have an impact. But in our opinion, they are inadequate. The basic problem is that they take as a given the fundamental consensus underlying the international tax regime, also known as the "benefits principle." Under the benefits principle, active (business) income should be taxed primarily at source while passive (investment) income should be taxed primarily at residence. This

---

2. On BEPS *see*, e.g., Ault, Hugh J., Some Reflections on the OECD and the Sources of International Tax Principles (July 1, 2013). Reprinted from Tax Notes International, Vol. 70, No. 12, June 17, 2013, p. 1195; Working Paper of the Max Planck Institute for Tax Law and Public Finance No. 2013-03. Available at SSRN: http://ssrn.com/abstract=2287834 or http://dx.doi.org/10.2139/ssrn.2287834; Dharmapala, Dhammika, What Do We Know About Base Erosion and Profit Shifting? A Review of the Empirical Literature (September 3, 2014). Illinois Public Law Research Paper No. 14-23; University of Chicago Coase-Sandor Institute for Law & Economics Research Paper No. 702. Available at SSRN: http://ssrn.com/abstract=2373549 or http://dx.doi.org/10.2139/ssrn.2373549; Brauner, Yariv, What the BEPS? (March 12, 2014). Available at SSRN: http://ssrn.com/abstract=2408034 or http://dx.doi.org/10.2139/ssrn.2408034; Ault, Hugh J. and Schoen, Wolfgang and Shay, Stephen E., Base Erosion and Profit Shifting: A Roadmap for Reform (June 1, 2014). Bulletin for International Taxation, Vol. 68, 2014, p. 275; Boston College Law School Legal Studies Research Paper No. 324. Available at SSRN: http://ssrn.com/abstract=2459646; Dharmapala, Dhammika, Base Erosion and Profit Shifting: A Simple Conceptual Framework (September 25, 2014). University of Chicago Coase-Sandor Institute for Law & Economics Research Paper No. 703. Available at SSRN: http://ssrn.com/abstract=2497770; Vann, Richard J., Policy Forum: The Policy Underpinnings of the BEPS Project-Preserving the International Corporate Income Tax? (August 20, 2014). Canadian Tax Journal, Vol. 62, No. 2, 2014, pp. 433–441; Sydney Law School Research Paper No. 14/77. Available at SSRN: http://ssrn.com/abstract=2483619; Shaviro, Daniel, The Crossroads versus the Seesaw: Getting a "Fix" on Recent International Tax Policy Developments (July 1, 2015). NYU School of Law, Public Law Research Paper No. 15-20; NYU Law and Economics Research Paper No. 15-11. Available at SSRN: http://ssrn.com/abstract=2605144 or http://dx.doi.org/10.2139/ssrn.2605144; Rosenzweig, Adam H., Building a Framework for a Post-BEPS World (June 24, 2014). Tax Notes International, Vol. 74, No. 12, 2014. Available at SSRN: http://ssrn.com/abstract=2463259; Grinberg, Itai, Breaking BEPS: The New International Tax Diplomacy (September 1, 2015). Available at SSRN: http://ssrn.com/abstract=2652894 or http://dx.doi.org/10.2139/ssrn.2652894.
3. OECD, Centre for Tax Policy and Administration, OECD presents outputs of OECD.G20 BEPS Project for discussion at G20 Finance Ministers meeting, October 5, 2015.

Chapter 5: Evaluating BEPS §5.01

compromise between the claims of residence and source countries was reached by the four economists in 1923 and still serves as the foundation of the international tax regime. It is embedded in over 3,000 bilateral tax treaties and in the domestic laws of the U.S. and most other countries. Not surprisingly, it is also reflected in BEPS, which is an attempt to improve source-based taxation of active income.

In our opinion, this consensus should be reconsidered in light of current realities. The shortcomings of BEPS are directly related to its reliance on the benefits principle, because upholding it requires cooperation by too many jurisdictions.

The original rationale for the benefits principle was that economists in the 1920s believed that active (business) income was earned primarily in the country of source, because that is where business activity took place, while passive (investment) income was earned primarily in the country of residence, because that is where the capital invested was accumulated. Economists no longer believe in the validity of this analysis, because most types of income have more than one source.

Nevertheless, the common view (including, until recently, our own) is that the benefits principle still makes sense, because most active income is earned by corporations and most passive income is earned by individuals. Since individual residence is meaningful in a way that corporate residence is not, it makes sense to tax individuals on a residence basis and corporations on a source basis.

This system functioned reasonable well until the 1980s. For active income, it could generally not be earned without taxation by source countries, because corporate investments by multinationals were generally immobile and tax competition was limited in scope. The *Dupont* case (1979) is a good illustration of the limits of tax planning in the pre-globalization era: It involved a multinational manufacturing goods in the U.S. and selling them in Europe, and both activities were subject to high levels of taxation. Dupont tried to avoid this result by routing the sales through a Swiss subsidiary, but the U.S. court rejected this attempt, and Subpart F was enacted in part to prevent it from happening again. The underlying assumption behind the Subpart F compromise (1962) was that active income would be taxed at source, and therefore it was not problematic to permit deferral of active income while taxing passive income and base company income currently.

But these constraints started to erode in the 1980s. Multinationals became much more mobile as the focus shifted from heavy manufacturing to services and intangibles. The result was tax competition as multinationals became able to pit one country against another. By 1995 Intel, which builds a new chip factory every other year, was able to boast that tax competition enabled it not to pay any foreign tax as it pitted Israel against Ireland and Mexico against Costa Rica as new plant locations, earning tax holidays in all of them.

The result has been that by the early twenty-first century most cross-border income is untaxed. In the case of multinationals, this is because the source jurisdiction either lacks the authority to tax because in the age of electronic commerce it is easy to avoid the required physical presence in the source country; or because source jurisdictions grant tax holidays to multinationals. Residence jurisdictions do not tax active income currently for fear that multinationals will establish their headquarters elsewhere, as the current U.S. inversion saga confirms.

While the BEPS project is helpful, it is unlikely to solve the underlying issues described above. The project only addresses artificial profit shifting, not tax competition, and it only applies to the OECD and G20, not to the many source countries outside these two organizations. Thus, it is likely that multinationals can avoid BEPS by sourcing income in countries that are not subject to it.

Fundamentally, if the income tax is to be preserved in the twenty-first century, multilateral solutions are needed. BEPS represents an attempt at such a solution, but it is hampered by the focus on source jurisdictions for active income. There are too many source jurisdictions, since multinationals operate globally.

Thus, in our opinion it is time to re-evaluate the benefits principle. Most of the current issues can be solved if we taxed active income primarily at residence. About 90% of large multinationals are headquartered in the G20, and none of those countries have a tax rate below 20%, so if they taxed their multinationals currently on a coordinated basis and restricted the ability to move out most of the problem would be resolved.

We would therefore suggest that we reconsider the benefits principle in light of the reality of globalization. We should tax active income primarily at residence.[4]

Importantly, like under current rules, this does not preclude the alternative. Once active income is taxed at residence, a credit can be given to source country taxes if the source country responds to the limitation of tax competition by re-imposing its tax. But the key is that the income has already been taxed, so that no double non-taxation ensues even if source countries choose not to tax in the case of active income.

The following unpacks this analysis in more detail. Section §5.02 analyzes the BEPS response to corporate tax avoidance and its limitations. Section §5.03 develops the alternative of taxing active income primarily at residence. Section §5.04 concludes.

§5.02 THE LIMITS OF THE BEPS PROJECT

On October 5, 2015, the OECD and G20 released the final BEPS package of thirteen reports, which cover fifteen actions. It was only two years since the G20 leaders endorsed the ambitious and comprehensive Action Plan to address BEPS at the meeting in St. Petersburg on September 5-6, 2013.

The BEPS package represents the first substantial – and overdue – renovation of the international tax standards in almost a century.[5] The BEPS package is an unprecedented turning point in the history of international tax law. The mission of the BEPS package is to align the location of taxable profits with the location of economic activities and value creation. Some generally accepted principles of international tax

---

4. We also believe that passive income should be taxed primarily at source, because there are far fewer source jurisdictions for portfolio investment than residence jurisdictions, and cooperation of tax havens is not required. *See* Reuven Avi-Yonah and Haiyan Xu, Taxation after the Crisis: Why BEPS and MAATM are Inadequate Responses, and What Should be Done about it (2016), available on SSRN.
5. OECD (2015), Explanatory Statement, OECD/G20 Base Erosion and Profit Shifting Project, OECD, p. 5.

Chapter 5: Evaluating BEPS §5.02[A]

law, including the single tax principle, the benefit principle, the anti-discrimination principle and the transparency principle have been reflected in many respects.

Despite considerable progress, there are many shortcomings with the BEPS project due to the short two-year framework. Hence, the BEPS project is not the final destination of international tax law reform. In fact, it is the first step toward the modernization of global tax governance in the long run.

[A] New Shoes on the Old Road: An Old Approach for the New Destination

The primary problem with the BEPS project is that although the new destination has been redefined, new principles and new rules have not been truly established for the new direction, and the old principles have been strengthened by a patch up of current rules.

The core principle of international tax law is the single tax principle, which requires eradication of both double taxation and double non-taxation. Unfortunately, both the governments and the MNEshave been active in fighting against the double taxation, and have ignored another danger of double non-taxation. Therefore, the main theme of traditional international tax law has been eradication of double taxation, instead of double non-taxation.

Based on the single tax principle, the mission of the BEPS project is to prevent and eliminate the double non-taxation. As the G20 leaders pointed out the new principle, "profits should be taxed where economic activities deriving the profits are performed and where value is created."[6] Therefore, the new direction of international tax law reform in the context of BEPS project is to safeguard the single tax principle by fighting against the BEPS.

It is well known that the rickety international tax regime, including rules and underlying principles, is one of the primary root causes of BEPS opportunities. Therefore, the new direction demands revolutionary changes to current approaches. The ideal roadmap for the BEPS project is supposed to replace the old principles with a new principle, and to redesign the rules based on the requirement of the new principle.

Unfortunately, many old principles of international tax law have been preserved and continued in the final BEPS package. The mixture of new principle and old principles has substantially compromised the value of the new principle, and made the legal reform of international tax look more like the patch-up of existing rules and principles. The reason is pretty obvious. On the one hand, it is impossible to abolish or even reconsider the dysfunctional current rules, which have been favored by some large countries and MNEs. On the other hand, it is mandatory to change the current rules to some extent, because of the emerging political pressure against BEPS schemes.

Given the fact that two years are very short for serious in-depth research, debate and negotiation, given the strong tradition and interest groups desire to keep the

---

6. Tax Annex to the St Petersburg Declaration, September 2013.

continuity of old principles, given the global voice for closing up the BEPS opportunities, the architect of the BEPS project has no choice but to patch up some loopholes of current rules, instead of fundamental restructuring of current regime.

As a result, complete renovation of current international tax law did not happen, and genuine new rules guided by the new principle have not been formulated. Moreover, the patch-up work has produced many more complex, discretionary, uncertain, costly and in many cases contradictory rules. There are two possible negative consequences. First, it is difficult to translate all the new rules into the reality. Second, even if the BEPS project is implemented as outlined and promised in the book, it is still possible for the creation of either new BEPS opportunities on the part of MNEs, or arbitrariness on the part of tax authorities.

In addition to adhering to the independent entity principle and rejection of the new principle of single unitary entity, the BEPS project is also silent on the basic concepts of residence and source, and where profit should be considered to be earned. As the existing rules based on the old principles have been strengthened, and new rules based on the new principle have not been established, the BEPS project is not so revolutionary and fundamental as it appears at the first sight.

The ironic fact is that the patch up of current rules in the BEPS project was made in the name of new mission and new principle. However, because of the inconsistencies and conflicts between the new principle and old principles, the new principle of international tax law has been compromised or undermined by the strengthened current rules based on old principles. Without the support of new principle and new rules, it is very challenging to achieve the new destination of aligning the taxation of MNE profits with economic activity.

[B] The Survival and Continuity of Notional and Illusionary Independent Entity Principle and Arm's Length Principle

The traditional international tax law is designed and interpreted based on the assumption that the various constituent entities or members of MNE group are independent of each other and conduct transactions with each other at arm's length.

While criticizing the independent entity theory as fundamental flaw of the existing rules, the BEPS Monitoring Group identified a new but implied approach in the G20 mandate to treat the corporate group of a MNE as a single firm, and ensure that its tax base is attributed according to its real activities in each country.[7] This means that the new destination of taxing MNEs "where economic activities take place and value is created" is unlikely to be achieved, without treating the MNE group as a single firm.

In principle, the optimal long-term solution is the single unitary entity principle. In our view, the G20 mandate could be interpreted as both a new direction and a new guiding philosophy, which requires all the BEPS actions should serve the purpose of taxing MNEs where economic activities take place and value is created in the most

---

7. The BEPS Monitoring Group (BMG), "Overall Evaluation of the G20/OECD Base Erosion and Profit Shifting (BEPS) Project." Available at: https://bepsmonitoringgroup.wordpress.com.

Chapter 5: Evaluating BEPS §5.02[B]

efficient manner. Guided by the brand new philosophy, the principle of single unitary entity, and the basic concepts of residence and source need to be established as the cornerstones to support the design, interpretation, and implementation of new measures in the BEPS package.

Unfortunately, the BEPS project refused to make the implied principle explicit, but has continued to emphasize the independent entity principle, while attempting to counteract its harmful consequences. Consequently, the BEPS outputs fail to provide a coherent and comprehensive approach, and offer instead proposals for a patch-up of existing rules, making them even more contradictory and complex.[8]

According to our observation, virtually all the new rules of the BEPS package are still built on the notional principle of independent entity. By its very nature, the untouchable principle of arm's length ultimately derives from the root of independent entity theory. Additionally, many other flawed rules including weak controlled foreign corporations (CFC) rule; territorial and deferral systems are also indirectly but closely connected with the independent entity principle.

The orthodoxy of independent entity taxation has two basic assumptions. First, the members of the MNE group are regarded as equal, separate, and independent legal persons. Namely, the members of MNE group are reasonable legal entities. From the perspective of corporate law, the fiction of independent entity in the context of corporate group derives from the orthodoxy of shareholder's limited liability and the corporate independent status as legal persons in the traditional corporate law. Second, the contracts between the related parties in the corporate group are freely negotiated at arm's length, and the terms of the contract are fair and reasonable dealings. In short, both the entities and the transactions in the corporate group are reasonable, therefore legal, and moral.

However, the two beautiful and attractive assumptions do not make sense, and they do not really exist in the commercial reality. The primary commercial reality is that multinational corporate group operates more like a single, unitary entity or enterprise rather than separate independent entities or enterprises. This is made possible by the controlling power of the parent corporation. As traditional international tax law stubbornly insists on the old concept of independent entity, the MNEs have been encouraged to incorporate dozens and even hundreds of affiliates all over the world to undertake aggressive BEPS schemes. The more subsidiaries or members in the MNE family, the stronger the parent corporation in reducing the overall transaction cost, and advance the profitability of the group as a whole. Why?

The answer is very simple. All the commercial activities of the subsidiaries and affiliates are under the effectively direct or indirect control from the parent corporation. Therefore, the profits or benefits could be unlimited by separate but coordinated operations of business under the uniform controlling power. On the other hand, the principle of independent entity could better protect the MNEs from unlimited risks and liabilities of group members towards bona fide third parties including the tax authorities. Therefore, the legal risks and liabilities of corporate group are limited by law,

---

8. The BEPS Monitoring Group (BMG), "Overall Evaluation of the G20/OECD Base Erosion and Profit Shifting (BEPS) Project." Available at: https://bepsmonitoringgroup.wordpress.com.

because there is no joint and several liability between and among the group members unless otherwise agreed by the corporate group members.

Because of the controlling power of the parent corporation on the top of the pyramid of the complicated corporate structure, like a smart spider on the center of grand network of corporate groups, it is unlikely to find real arm's length transaction in the reality. In fact, the related party contracts within the corporate group are always concluded without seriously free, competitive, and transparent bargainings and negotiations.

If the BEPS project is designed on the principle of single unitary entity, the BEPS counter-measure will be much more simple and effective, as inter-group transactions will be disregarded, and the profit or tax base will be attributed to its real activities which generate the profit and create the value in the jurisdictions.

Unfortunately, many actions of the BEPS project, including but not confined to Action 2 on hybrid mismatches, Action 7 on PE, and Actions 8–10 on transfer pricing, heavily rely on the legal fictions of independent entity and arm's length transactions. This is understandable given the difficulty of implementing a coherent unitary tax system in a short time frame, but it means that the goals of BEPS are unlikely to be achieved.

[C] The Survival and Continuity of the Problematic Benefit Principle

The OECD declared that, the goal of BEPS package is "to tackle BEPS structures by comprehensively addressing their root causes rather than merely the symptoms. Once the measures are implemented, many schemes facilitating double non-taxation will be curtailed."[9] Therefore, a key question is whether all root causes, instead of symptoms, have been addressed?

In our opinion, one of the root causes is traditional benefit principle, which has guided the allocation of global profits in the past decades, and has created many BEPS opportunities. Unfortunately, the BEPS project failed in replacing the benefit principle. Instead, the BEPS package was still designed based on residence jurisdictions for passive income and source jurisdictions for active income.

As articulated in this chapter, our argument is that BEPS concerns will be more effectively tacked if active income is primarily taxed at residence. This new philosophy will help to build a new international tax governance framework of win-win, which will benefit both developed countries and developing countries. Moreover, the conflicts between the domestic demand for tax revenue and domestic policy to attract foreign direct investment will be better balanced, and the MNEs and domestic firms will be offered a level playing field.

Many scholars have realized the significance of the renovation of basic principles of current international tax law. As Mindy Herzfeld argued observed, "attempts at coordination cannot be successful unless there is agreement on an underlying set of

---

9. OECD (2015), *Explanatory Statement*, OECD/G20 Base Erosion and Profit Shifting Project, OECD, p. 5.

principles for allocating the revenue of global citizens (including natural persons and legal entities). A more rigorous effort to develop such a clear and agreed upon set of principles which rests on economic, philosophic and fairness grounds is needed."[10]

[D] Limited Inclusiveness and Multilateralism

Global challenges need global solution. BEPS, as a global concern, is made possible by uncoordinated tax rules at domestic and international levels. Therefore, the global solutions need to be based on inclusive and multilateral global governance. This means each and every country should be offered equal opportunity and equal weight to shape the outcome of the global solutions.

Although OECD/G20 have made great efforts in organizing many non-member countries and Non-governmental Organization (NGOs) to participate in the development of the BEPS package, the inclusiveness and multilateralism of the BEPS project is limited for a number of reasons.

First, the undisputed fact is that major OECD countries dominated the formulation of the BEPS package in the process of discussions and negotiations. As OECD countries are all developed countries, it is inevitable that the BEPS project is mainly a result of compromise between the rich countries. For instance, weak measures on CFCs, interest deductibility and innovation box schemes are favored particularly by the United Kingdom (U.K.).[11]

Second, although over sixty countries were directly involved in the process of the BEPS project, they only account for less than one-third of 193 UN members.[12] As MNEs have their taxable presence around the globe, including the non-participating countries, the effectiveness of the BEPS project is very limited. The tax competitions between participating countries and non-participating countries will continue. The race to the bottom and the unilateral actions taken by any jurisdiction could hurt all the countries in the world.

Third, although some developing countries were consulted for the BEPS project, it does not necessarily mean that their core proposals were finally accepted by the BEPS package. As observed by independent commentators, some key OECD countries opposed and succeeded in blocking the institutional reform proposal from developing countries at the Third International Conference on "Financing for Development."[13]

Fourth, less influential participating countries and more than 120 non-participating counties might be hurt due to the effect of negative spill-over arising from the implementation of the BEPS project in the future. They are weak not only because of their limited influence in the renovation of the current rules, but also because of their limited experience and resources to enforce the BEPS actions.

---

10. Mindy Herzfeld, "The Limits of Tax Coordination," working draft, October 11, 2015.
11. The BEPS Monitoring Group (BMG), "Overall Evaluation of the G20/OECD Base Erosion and Profit Shifting (BEPS) Project," p. 3. Available at: https://bepsmonitoringgroup.wordpress.com.
12. http://www.un.org/depts/dhl/unms/whatisms.shtml#states.
13. The BEPS Monitoring Group (BMG), "Overall Evaluation of the G20/OECD Base Erosion and Profit Shifting (BEPS) Project." Available at: https://bepsmonitoringgroup.wordpress.com.

Fifth, the process of public debate and consulting was relatively insufficient. BEPS Monitoring Group, an active tax justice advocate, complains that they have been vastly outnumbered by the army of paid tax advisers and representatives of multinational enterprises.[14] Although stakeholder interest, including invaluable interactions with business and civil society, saw more than 12,000 pages of comments received on the twenty-three discussion drafts published and discussed at eleven public consultations,[15] it is unknown to what extent these valuable proposals have been adopted by the BEPS package. More importantly, detailed reasons for rejecting different proposals have not been published.

Given the fact that it is impossible to guarantee that countries and stakeholders really had the equal opportunity to influence and shape the outcome of the BEPS package on really equal footing, OECD and/or G20 is not the truly global platform for comprehensive reform of international tax law. To transform the current BEPS project into truly global, coherent, coordinated and inclusive actions, the UN should undertake the leadership in the next stage of international tax law reform.

The third paragraph of Article 1 of the Charter of the UN recognizes that the third purpose of the UN is to achieve international cooperation in solving international problems of an economic, social, cultural, or humanitarian character. The fourth paragraph of Article 1 of the Charter of the UN recognizes its fourth purposes is to be a center for harmonizing the actions of nations in the attainment of these common ends.

We believe that the UN will be more qualified, impartial, transparent, credible and influential than the OECD/G20 in rewriting and renovating the international tax rules including the BEPS counter-measures. All UN members have the right to be heard and represented in the process of international tax law reform. As the working group of the UN, the UN Tax committee is expected to make great difference in this regard.

We urge that the UN Convention of Anti-BEPS should be made as the cornerstone of the global response to BEPS in a more coherent, inclusive and multilateral manner. Compared with the partial multilateral approach of OEC/G20, the global BEPS actions launched by the UN will better address the BEPS concerns and restore the integrity of international tax principles of single tax, neutrality, transparency, fairness.

[E] The limits of Action 1

Action 1 was unable to propose all the solutions to the BEPS concerns in the digital economy for the following two reasons.

The first reason is that although the digital economy has exacerbated BEPS risks, it has not generated genuinely unique BEPS issues. Almost every BEPS issue is directly or indirectly relevant to digital economy. Additionally, all the BEPS actions interconnect and interact with each other in the digital economy. Therefore, the ideal Action 1 report is supposed to focus on universal philosophy and methodology of the BEPS

---

14. *Ibid.*
15. OECD (2015), Explanatory Statement, OECD/G20 Base Erosion and Profit Shifting Project, OECD., p. 5.

project from the perspective of digital economy. It is challenging and unwise for the TFDE to produce some unique measures in parallel with other measures of the BEPS project.

The second reason is that the staggered time frame of the BEPS Project makes it impossible for TFDE to foresee and analyze the effectiveness of the future BEPS package in addressing BEPS concerns in the digital economy in advance. For the same reason, it is difficult for TFDE to evaluate the ultimate scope of the more systemic tax challenges in the area of nexus, data, and characterization, and potential options to address them.

However, the limit of Action 1 report could be overcome by continuing research on the broader tax challenges of the digital economy, and by proposing detailed and viable options to address those challenges, with appropriate focus on multi-sided business models and the participation of users and consumers in value creation. On the one hand, TFDE need to assist the implementation of other BEPS actions, such as Action 3 on CFC rules, Action 7 on artificial avoidance of PE, Actions 8-10 on transfer pricing. On the other hand, TFDE should update the Action 1 report based on the experience, performance and outcomes of the BEPS Project.

As planned by TFDE, a supplementary report reflecting the outcomes of the continuing work will be finalized by December 2015.[16] We doubt whether the intended outcomes of the BEPS project would be available for assessment, given the fact that the implementation of the fifteen actions is a lengthy process domestically and internationally. In our opinion, the Action 1 report should be updated regularly based on the changing business models of digital economy.

[F] The limits of Action 2

The solutions of Action 2 are soft recommendations, instead of minimum standards. Although countries have agreed to a general tax policy direction in neutralizing the effects of hybrid mismatch arrangements, it is difficult to achieve the agreements on minimum standards at this stage. As a result, the Action 2 has to choose a common approach to encourage the countries to converge over time through the implementation of the recommendation at the levels of internal law and bilateral treaties.

However, it is not clear how long it will take the countries to converge in a harmonized way, because changes of domestic law are up to the free choice of sovereign states, based on the consideration of complex factors including different legal traditions. Some jurisdictions might wish to continue to treat certain instrument as indebtedness, while some jurisdiction might continue to treat it as equity. For similar reasons, some jurisdictions will continue to treat certain hybrid entities and reverse hybrid entities as fiscally transparent conduits, while some jurisdictions will continue to treat them as separately taxable entities.

---

16. OECD (2014), *Addressing the Tax Challenges of the Digital Economy*, OECD/G20 Base Erosion and Profit Shifting Project, OECD Publishing, p. 21. http://dx.doi.org/10.1787/9789264218789-en.

Therefore, if a few countries are very slow in the convergence process, the whole process of convergence will be delayed. Although all countries may argue that their own measures or paths are consistent with the right direction of the BEPS project, the real consequences might depart from the direction originally decided by the BEPS project. Even worse, it is possible that a few jurisdictions will return to the race to the bottom. In this event, the original direction of neutralizing the effects of hybrid mismatch arrangements might be compromised in some jurisdictions.

Our proposal is that the international community needs to replace the common approach by global minimum standards in the near future. To better coordinate the Action 2 with other relevant Actions, in particular on interest expense deduction limitations, CFC rules and treaty shopping, the latter Actions should be also upgraded.

[G] The limits of Action 3

Strong CFC rules are supposed to play an important role in tackling BEPS schemes. The Action 3 should serve as a backstop to transfer pricing and other rules. Unfortunately, the CFC rules in the Action 3 are very weak. The building blocks in this Action are very soft, weak recommendations based on best practices, instead of hard minimum standards. In particular, the threshold for defining CFC income is very low.

The reason for the weak CFC rules could be explained by the stubborn insistence on the tax incentives by some OECD countries in particular the U.K. According to BEPS Monitoring Group, the U.K. and other countries "belie their assertions that they wish to see effective solutions to the problem of taxation of MNEs."[17]

Therefore, it is very difficult to expect that the Action 3 will effectively reduce and deter the motivation of MNEs to abuse the system of exemption or deferral of tax on foreign income, and to shift income from operating affiliates in source jurisdictions to the tax havens. Moreover, it is also likely for the race to the bottom to continue to attract the headquarters of MNEs, and hurt all the countries in the end. On the one hand, traditional tax havens will feel free to continue their behaviors. On the other hand, other countries will be motivated to adopt low effective tax rates on foreign income or exempting such income altogether to attract foreign direct capital.

Although the compromise is inevitable in the process of developing Action 3, the OECD/G20 should seek the win-win solution by maximizing the common denominator of international tax. We urge the international community to strength the weak CFC rules of Action 3, and to adopt full-inclusion CFC rules in the future. Of course, the recommendations should be replaced by minimum standards.

[H] The Limits of Action 4

As lower transaction cost and more business opportunities are the core features and advantages of the corporate group, it is extremely abnormal and even ridiculous for the

---

17. The BEPS Monitoring Group (BMG), "Overall Evaluation of the G20/OECD Base Erosion and Profit Shifting (BEPS) Project." Available at: https://bepsmonitoringgroup.wordpress.com.

interest deductions to be greater in aggregate than each corporate group's consolidated interest costs to third parties. Theoretically speaking, if the interest cost of intra-group loans is unreasonably higher than the loans from third parties, the group and its members would reduce the interest loans.

But the reality does not support this logic. One of the pressure areas for the BEPS concerns is that intra-group debt usually exceeds the firm's overall borrowing from third parties, and the interest deductibility is almost out of control. Therefore, the limitation of deductions of interest should be strong enough to root out the BEPS opportunities.

Unfortunately, the Action 4 Report is not minimum standard. Its philosophy is to facilitate the convergence of national rules in the area of interest deductibility. Therefore, its success is entirely dependent upon voluntary coordination between and among countries in enacting new domestic rules. If the progress of implementation and operation of the recommendations is not satisfactory as anticipated, the effectiveness of this Action will be compromised. It is very challenging for the jurisdictions to address excessive deductible payments and address competitiveness considerations at the same time, and to ensure that appropriate interest expense limitations do not themselves lead to double taxation.

More problematic is the substance of Action 4, which prioritized an interest deduction cap within a suggested band of 10%–30%, with the option of using apportioned consolidated interest costs if they are higher. Such a recommendation is not as powerful and strong as the audience anticipated. Moreover, the formula of fixed cap does not match best with every sector and firm. That is why the Action 4 report recognizes the need to develop suitable and specific rules that address BEPS risks in banking and insurance industries. Although it does make sense to respect the specific features of banking and insurance industries, other industries might also claim the special treatments from the BEPS project. It is not realistic to design the specific rules for every firm, industry or sector.

Before the proposal of a fixed cap was adopted, there were also other better proposals. For instance, based on the doctrine of unitary entity, a proposal suggested apportionment of the MNE group's consolidated interest expenses based on EBITDA (earnings before interest, deductions and amortization), figures for which are readily available. However, the initial proposals have been watered down to recommendations prioritizing a fixed cap.[18]

We strongly urge that the bottom line of international tax law reform is that interest deductions may not be greater in aggregate than each corporate group's consolidated interest costs to third parties.

Anyway, the recommendations in Action 4 do not prohibit the countries from seeking better alternative solutions for effective control of interest deductibility. If the countries really have no other choice but to follow the default recommendation of fixed cap on deductions, they should use the lowest limit to deter aggressive interest deductions by MNEs. In fact, even the lowest limit still falls in the range of unrelated

---

18. The BEPS Monitoring Group (BMG), "Overall Evaluation of the G20/OECD Base Erosion and Profit Shifting (BEPS) Project." Available at: https://bepsmonitoringgroup.wordpress.com.

loans. Of course, coordination is always important to prevent the MNEs from defeating all the countries by abusing the different rules around the world.

[I] The Limits of Action 5

The harmful tax practices proliferating in many countries represent the major form of race to the bottom. Such practices have triggered and increased numerous BEPS opportunities. Hence, Action 5 is designed to effectively reverse the history of beggar-thy-neighbor, which damage all countries, including the jurisdiction having harmful tax practices.

Different from the Actions 2-4, the Action 5 sets out a minimum standard in terms of substance and transparency, and includes the results of the application of the elaborated substantial activity and transparency factors to a number of preferential regimes. Unfortunately, Action 5 is still very weak and even disappointing, as it continued the traditional but unsuccessful approach.

First, the effectiveness of implementation of Action 5 is still up to voluntary self-regulation and self-monitoring by individual countries. No one is able to bite her own nose. Irrational developed and developing countries could be addicted to harmful practices, in the name of national competitiveness or attracting international capital.

Second, although the work of the Forum on Harmful Tax Practices (FHTP) will be refocused to develop more effective solutions, no penalty could be imposed by FHTP. In fact, all forty-three preferential regimes reviewed by the FHTP were inconsistent with the nexus approach.[19] However, there is no effective penalty against the violators. It is very challenging for all countries to voluntarily bring their IP regimes into compliance with the nexus approach.

Third, the application of the broad and general principles of "nexus" and "substance" to innovation boxes might create different and divergent standards and interpretations in different countries. The consideration of national competitiveness or specific domestic circumstances might lead to new forms of harmful preference regimes.

Fourth, some developed countries have set bad examples for the developing countries in fighting against the harmful practices. As observed by BEPS Monitoring Group, the U.K.'s strong defense of its patent box introduced in 2012 resulted in a compromise agreed with Germany, based on a "modified nexus approach," and a transition to the new standard by 2021; other countries quickly announced that they would introduce their own schemes (Ireland, Italy, Switzerland), and business pressures have led to proposals elsewhere also (Germany, U.S.).[20]

As the harmful tax practices always end up hurting every country, we urge the international community to abandon the voluntary self-policing model, and to

---

19. Joint Committee on Taxation, *Background, Summary, and Implications of the OECD/G20 Base Erosion and Profit Shifting Project* (JCX-139-15), November 30, 2015, p. 21. This document can also be found on the Joint Committee on Taxation website at www.jct.gov.
20. The BEPS Monitoring Group (BMG), "Overall Evaluation of the G20/OECD Base Erosion and Profit Shifting (BEPS) Project." Available at: https://bepsmonitoringgroup.wordpress.com.

establish mandatory monitoring model based on transparency, accountability, condemnation and even economic sanctions depending on the seriousness of the harmful schemes. Harmful tax practices are unjustified and immoral. They are against the core value of international tax law. Therefore, it is inadequate, and even inappropriate to require countries to conduct cost-benefit analyses of the harmful incentives. In fact, many addicted countries still attempt to acquire the limited selfish benefit at the price of negative spillovers on the other countries. The harmful tax practices themselves have demonstrated the failure of voluntary self-policing approach.

Of course, all countries should be encouraged to behave themselves in terms of higher standard of transparency, monitoring, review and accountability of tax incentives. If a country really wants to win the trust from the global community, it must take the firm initiative in this regards. To activate the monitoring function of FHTP, the mechanism of transparent investigation, impartial peer review, reasonable reward and adequate sanction will be indispensable.

[J] The Limits of Action 6

Although the three-part approach adopted by the Action 6 will help to counter treaty abuse, either LoB article or PPT provision has its own pros and cons. Although the LoB article is easily understood and applied, a proliferation of treaty-specific varieties of LoB articles would lead to over complexity in the treaties or domestic legislation.

Although the PPT provision is general enough to cover all the treaty shopping schemes, its interpretation and application heavily depend on discretionary decisions of the tax authorities or the courts. Therefore, the success of PPT article relies on the individual country's competence, expertise and resources, especially the useful information relevant to the treaty shopping behaviors. Unfortunately, many developing countries do not have the necessary capacity and information resources to make the best use of the PPT provision. To offer useful guidance and reference to the developing countries, we urge the OECD/G20 to publish all the latest decided cases or rulings on the PPT article on a regular basis.

To sharpen the competence of developing countries in applying the anti-abuse clauses, spontaneous, systematic exchange of information between treaty partners should be established to ascertain the pre-requisites for the taxpayer to enjoy treaty benefits. Of course, a more ambitious, global, spontaneous, comprehensive and systematic platform for exchange of BEPS data between and among all jurisdictions should be created in the future. CbCR is one of the important parts of this data bank.

Although the countries may vary substantially from each other in terms of the legislation framework, judicial interpretation tools and administrative ability, all countries involved should do their best in endorsing the minimum standard of protection against treaty shopping. In this way, the model treaty provisions included in the Action 6 report will be better adapted to the specificities of individual states and the circumstances of the negotiation of bilateral conventions.

To reduce the treaty renegotiation cost and prevent the emergence of new treaty shopping platforms, a clear and effective anti-abuse provision should be incorporated as the core article of the proposed multilateral convention.

Finally, another important issue is the policy considerations relevant to treaty entitlement of collective investment vehicles (CIVs) and non-CIV funds.[21] The OECD will continue to evaluate issues related to entitlement to treaty benefits by certain types of investment funds by early 2016.[22] But it is challenging to achieve a satisfied consensus on some key issues, as there are different definitions of CIV in different jurisdictions. Furthermore, CIV may be organized in different forms, including partnerships, agreements, trusts, or incorporated entities.

[K] The Limits of Action 7

Although Action 7 developed changes to the definition of PE in Article 5 of the OECD Model Tax Convention, the changes are not substantially innovative. This is because the definition of taxable presence still rests on the obsolete PE concept, which requires physical presence for a period of six or twelve months in relation to the particular activity generating the profit attributable to it.

Both the traditional PE definition and the proposed changes in Action 7 are based on the independent entity principle. Without disconnection between the taxable presence and the independent entity principle, it is unlikely to make groundbreaking progress in changing the definition of PE.

Action 7 only targets abuse of the PE definition, instead of rewriting the definition of PE itself. However, not all forms of abuse are covered in this Action. The anti-fragmentation rule in Action 7 is only applicable to artificial fragmentation of sales functions, but not to the artificial fragmentation of non-sales-related functions. This means that MNEs will be free to continue fragmentations of non-sales-related functions, and attribute higher profits to tax havens.

According to the findings of the BEPS Monitoring Group, the proposals of Action 7 could only affect some MNEs such as those engaged in internet-based selling and which own warehouses in the country of sales. However, the proposals would not deal with sales of immaterial products, or services, so they would affect physical but not electronic books, and DVDs but not streaming services. In fact, the MNEs have already restructured their production chains to separate basic manufacturing, which can be allocated a "routine" profit, from functions such as R&D or design, which may be considered high-value-adding, and can be located where they will be lightly taxed.[23]

---

21. OECD (2014), Preventing the Granting of Treaty Benefits in Inappropriate Circumstances, OECD/G20 Base Erosion and Profit Shifting Project, OECD Publishing, p. 20. http://dx.doi.org/10.1787/9789264219120-en.
22. Joint Committee on Taxation, *Background, Summary, and Implications of the OECD/G20 Base Erosion and Profit Shifting Project* (JCX-139-15), November 30, 2015, p. 22.
23. The BEPS Monitoring Group (BMG), "Overall Evaluation of the G20/OECD Base Erosion and Profit Shifting (BEPS) Project." Available at: https://bepsmonitoringgroup.files.wordpress.com/2015/10/general-evaluation.pdf.

Even the rules against artificial fragmentation of sales functions have some loopholes. For instance, although an entity will be deemed to have a PE, if activities can be said to be "preparatory or auxiliary" to sales, the terms "preparatory or auxiliary" are not clearly defined. Therefore, uncertainties and disputes are likely to arise in the future.

It should be noted that there are different legal rules in the agency, especially the indirect agency in the civil law families and the common law families. Different jurisdictions may have different definitions of the agent. In European civil law jurisdictions, a commissionaire acts in their own name for the account of a principal, but no relationship is created between the customer and the principal. As a commissionaire is not generally viewed as a dependent agent by virtue of the commissionaire status, the activities and place of business of a commissionaire are not attributed to the principal in civil law jurisdictions. However, such arrangement could create agency in common law countries.[24] Therefore, the anti-fragmentation rule should adopt a functional approach, which should be compatible with the different legal traditions of agency law in different countries.

According to the Action 7 report, follow-up works will be undertaken to provide additional guidance on profit attribution to the PEs resulting from the proposed changes, and to incorporate the proposed changes into the Model Tax Convention.[25] For the latter work, additional clarification on the new treaty wording should be provided, any unintended consequences of the changes should be addressed, and the BEPS issue related to the global trading of financial products should be considered.

We urge that the limited scope of the anti-fragmentation rule will be expanded to cover all the schemes of abuse of the PE definition. If possible, the continuing work should also reconsider the fundamental weakness of the "functionally separate entity" approach and reorient the future reform of anti-fragmentation based on the single and unitary entity principle.

[L] The Limits of Actions 8–10

Actions 8–10 are the most important part of the BEPS project in addressing related party transactions of MNEs. Of course, the transferring pricing documentation requirements in Action 13 are also closely relevant to these three actions. The purpose of Actions 8–10 is to assure that transfer-pricing outcomes are in line with value creation. The proposals on transfer pricing have made extensive revisions to the OECD Transfer Pricing Guidelines, which in fact will further strengthen the discretionary power for tax authorities to adjust them. Many proposals take the form of international standards, which could have some direct effects as international "soft law."

---

24. https://en.wikipedia.org/wiki/Commissionaire. For more details of the differences of agency law between the civil law jurisdiction and the common law jurisdiction, *see also*, The Research on the Agency Law in the Common Law Jurisdiction (YING MEI DAI LI FA YAN JIU), by Haiyan Xu, Press of Law, Beijing, 2000.
25. OECD (2015), Explanatory Statement, OECD/G20 Base Erosion and Profit Shifting Project, OECD., p. 8.

Although the goal is totally correct, the approach of Actions 8–10 is very problematic. The solutions still focus on patch up of the dysfunctional rules built on the arm's length principle, which again is rooted in the principle of separate independent entity. According to the arm's length principle, all intra-group transactions are supposed to be rational and reasonable as commercial transactions between unrelated parties in comparable economic circumstances.

To implement the arm's length principle, Actions 8–10 made transfer-pricing rules more sophisticated and complex, so as to authorize tax authorities to re-characterize the related party transactions within the MNE group. To find the available comparables, the tax authorities are required to make careful, informed judgment in good faith based on subjective analysis of detailed facts and circumstances relevant to the functions, assets and risks actually undertaken by different group members located in different jurisdictions.

As the approach of Actions 8–10 is inevitably subjective and discretionary, the real effect of attribution of the tax base of MNEs will rely on the interactive bargaining and negotiation between MNEs and tax authorities. If the game is not fair enough, either under-taxation or over-taxation will arise. To avoid under-taxation, tax authorities will tend to maximize their discretionary power of re-characterizing, which might lead to the strong opposition from the MNE taxpayers. For the similar reasoning, to avoid over-taxation, MNEs might upgrade their aggressive BEPS schemes. As a result, both enforcement and compliance costs will be increased, and more disputes will be created. Moreover, as the subjective judgment will be made independently and separately by different national authorities, different jurisdictions might make conflicting re-characterization conclusions on the same intra-group transaction.

The complicated and uncertain approach of re-characterizing intra-group transactions is most challenging for the developing countries, as they do not have the necessary resources and expertise to administer the revised version of Transfer Pricing Guidelines. Of course, it is also very costly or even impossible for the developed countries to search for really precise and genuine comparables. Although the G20 Development Working Group promised to help the developing countries to deal with the problem of lack of comparables, it is not clear whether a simple, effective win-win solution on pricing method will be made available in the near future. We do not wish to see any form of one-sided solutions, including purely subjective discretion favored by tax authorities, and purely notational transfer pricing method favored by MNEs.

As indicated earlier, the principle of the separate independent entity and the principle of arm's length are at most beautiful legal fictions, which do not actually exist in the commercial reality. In fact, even the terms of transactions between independent and unrelated parties are not necessarily fair and reasonable, if the two parties do not have equivalent negotiation powers on a level playing field. As the comparability analysis is not practical and feasible as anticipated, we propose the formulary apportionment system based on the single unitary entity principle. In other words, MNE group will be treated as single and unitary entity, and all intra-group transactions will be disregarded. Compared with the approach of separate entity, this route will be more simple, direct and effective in addressing the BEPS concerns arising from intra-group related party transactions.

In fact, the OECD has already noticed the proposed alternative income allocation systems, including formula based systems. Unfortunately, the OECD finally refused to replace the current transfer pricing system. The reason is not the flaw of the proposed alternatives, but the familiarity with the current approach and the reluctance to switch to new approach by launching ambitious reform. In the words of the OECD, "the importance of concerted action and the practical difficulties associated with agreeing to and implementing the details of a new system consistently across all countries mean that, rather than seeking to the best course is to directly address the flaws in the current system, in particular with respect to returns related to intangible assets, risk and over-capitalization."[26]

As early as 2013, the OECD claimed that "there is consensus among governments that moving to a system of formulary apportionment of profits is not a viable way forward; it is also unclear that the behavioral changes companies might adopt in response to the use of a formula would lead to investment decisions that are more efficient and tax-neutral than under a separate entity approach."[27]

Although the U.S. and some other states stubbornly defended and insisted on the dysfunctional arm's length principle for transfer pricing adjustments and resisted alternatives,[28] there is no credible evidence to indicate that thirty-four OECD members have reached clear and concrete agreement on unanimously opposing the system of formulary apportionment of profits based on the single entity principle. Moreover, there are no scientific research findings to indicate that the single entity approach has more weakness and less strength than separate entity approach.

To offer easy, certain, clear and predictable solutions to the BEPS concerns arising from transfer pricing, over the longer term formulary apportionment methodology should be adopted, and the allocation of assets, payroll, sales and other factors need to be restructured and weighted. This will better allocate the tax base of MNE according to the location where economic activities and value creation take place. To make the formulary apportionment approach successful and sustainable, the principle of separate independent entity needs to be replaced by the principle of single unitary entity.

[M] The Limits of Action 11

Although the final report of Action 11 conducted in-depth research on measuring and monitoring BEPS and offered recommendations on collecting and disseminating data to facilitate analysis of BEPS, there are some weakness which need to be improved.

For instance, this report emphasizes that analysis of BEPS should not rely on any one indicator, and requires that the indicators should be viewed collectively to determine the scale and scope of BEPS. It is impossible for each of the six indicators to have equal weight in each and every jurisdiction. Unfortunately, this report has not

---

26. Action Plan on Base Erosion and Profit Shifting – © OECD 2013, p. 20.
27. Action Plan on Base Erosion and Profit Shifting – © OECD 2013, p. 14.
28. The BEPS Monitoring Group (BMG), "Overall Evaluation of the G20/OECD Base Erosion and Profit Shifting (BEPS) Project." Available at: https://bepsmonitoringgroup.wordpress.com.

offered a scientific and reliable formula of differentiating the separate weights of the six indicators suitable for the jurisdictions.

This Report offers recommendations concerning data collection and dissemination to facilitate the analysis of BEPS for participating countries, and proposes to collect new data under Actions 5, 12, and 13. However, this report has not proposed to publish the CbCRs worldwide, so as to make the transfer pricing information available to all the countries and the public.

We are living in a society of big data. Unfortunately, this report has not offered satisfactory big data solution for the countries to use in a digital society. We believe that it is necessary to develop the big data deployment strategy, and set up a global BEPS data bank as the basic platform for collecting, exchanging, disseminating and analyzing of BEPS information all over the world.

[N] The Limits of Action 12

The purpose of Action 12 report is to enable the governments to have early access to information, and to quickly respond to systemic tax risks through informed risk assessment, audits or changes to legislation or tax policies.

However, the recommendations on requirements for taxpayers to disclose their aggressive tax planning arrangements are not minimum standards. Countries are free to decide whether or not to introduce mandatory disclosure regimes. Currently, only seven countries[29] have mandatory disclosure regime in their domestic legislation.

As the recommendations are not universally mandatory, it is easy for the MNEs to avoid the mandatory requirements in certain jurisdictions by incorporation in another jurisdiction without such requirements. It is also possible for the jurisdictions to join the race to the bottom by refusing to adopt mandatory disclosure regime.

In our opinion, mandatory disclosure rules should be introduced to each and every jurisdiction, and the liabilities for violation of the mandatory disclosure rules should be designed and enforced in fair and transparent manner.

[O] The Limits of Action 13

The annual CbCR is the most important measure in Action 13 to ensure the minimum transparency of transfer pricing. However, there are some limits with it.

First, the threshold of EUR 750 million of annual consolidated group revenue is unreasonably high for the major MNEs in developing countries, although this threshold is tailor made for the need of developed countries. Such threshold will exclude many large MNEs from the CbCR requirement, and deprive developing countries of the access to the information of MNEs below the threshold. In fact, many large MNES have annual consolidated group revenue less than EUR 750 million. Needless to say, some large MNEs will be motivated enough to manipulate their group revenue to a level of

---

29. Ireland, Israel, Korea, Portugal, South Africa, U.K., and U.S.

less than EUR 750 million. In our opinion, all MNEs should be subject to CbCR requirement.

Second, all the transfer pricing documents are only required to be submitted to the tax authorities, but not to the public and civil society organizations. It seems that the philosophy of this institutional arrangement is to preserve the confidentiality of the information and to ensure the appropriate use by the government. However, the commercial confidentiality is not strong enough to defeat the right of the public to information of BEPS. The relevant stakeholders and the public need to have access to the MNEs' transfer pricing documentation. The reason is very simple, BEPS could hurt other taxpayers and stakeholders in relevant jurisdictions. We believe that the BEPS concerns will be more effectively addressed with the active and informed participation of the stakeholders and the public based on disclosed transfer pricing. Under the public pressure and support, the domestic legislatures and tax authorities will be more diligent and competent in tackling the BEPS issues. Of course, a high level of transparency will also benefit the MNEs, as it will significantly reduce compliance burden, and will improve their public image of credibility in terms of BEPS concerns.

Third, the CbCRs are only required to file with the tax authority of the MNE's ultimate parent entity's jurisdiction, instead of all the tax authorities of the jurisdictions where the MNEs have taxable business presences. To ensure rapid availability of CbCRs, we urge the CbCRs to be shared automatically and simultaneously between and among all the interested jurisdictions which have good reason to believe the existence of taxable presences by MNEs. Of course, if the MNEs' transfer pricing documentation is made available to the public, the double standards will be totally rooted out.

Fourth, although the content of the CbCRs covers the major issues of transfer pricing, it is difficult to exhaust all the data needed by tax authorities to assess the BEPS concerns arising from transfer pricing. Therefore, necessary data should be added into the CbCRs on a regular basis.

[P]   The Limits of Action 14

The mutual agreement procedure (MAP) is the ideal win-win platform to effectively resolve treaty-related disputes between two countries. However, the MAP does not always work effectively, because any party in the dispute could block the MAP unilaterally. Unfortunately, the Action 14 has not offered remedies for the deadlock of MAP.

In fact, mandatory arbitration is the suitable remedy for the MAP deadlock. However, the Action 14 has not proposed the minimum standard of mandatory arbitration. At most, this Action encourages the inclusion of arbitration as an optional provision in the multilateral instruments. As some jurisdictions might exclude the arbitration clause in their bilateral and multilateral tax treaties, mandatory binding arbitration should be included in all bilateral and multilateral tax treaties.

It is important to note that mandatory binding arbitration should be supported by clear and predictable substantive rules, due process of law, and impartial and competent arbitrators. In our opinion, each party may freely appoint one arbitrator. If the two parties are unable to collaborate in choosing the chief arbitrator, the arbitration body may appoint the chief arbitrator.

[Q] The Limits of Action 15

The goal of Action 15 is to streamline the implementation of the tax treaty-related BEPS measures by drafting a multilateral instrument.[30] Although this Action represents a significant step towards multilateralism, the proposed multilateral instrument has not been provided for debate. To make the multilateral instrument coherent, inclusive and feasible, the developing process should be open and transparent. Namely, the negotiations should be really on equal footing, the proposals should be published, all relevant stakeholders should be heard, and public debate should be meaningful.

However, participation in developing the multilateral instrument is voluntary, and participating country are not obligated to sign it.[31] This liberal approach intends to encourage more countries to participate in the development process. However, it is uncertain how many countries will sign it in the end. If the participating countries are obligated to sign the multilateral instrument, many countries will be not interested in participation. This dilemma reflects inadequate multilateralism represented by the OECD. Therefore, we believe that UN is the most qualified multilateralism platform to develop a universally binding multilateral instrument to address BEPS.

§5.03 RECONSIDERING THE INTERNATIONAL TAX REGIME: A MULTILATERAL SOLUTION

As stated above, in our opinion it is time to re-evaluate the benefits principle. Most of the current issues can be solved if we taxed active income primarily at residence. About 90% of large multinationals are headquartered in the G20, and none of those countries have a tax rate below 20%, so if they taxed their multinationals currently on a coordinated basis and restricted the ability to move out most of the problem would be resolved.

There are three common critiques of the above approach. First, it is said that it violates certain economic neutrality norms and is therefore less efficient that territoriality (i.e., each country only taxing the income of the multinational earned within it). Second, adopting the proposed global approach is said to harm the competitive position of any given country's multinationals. Third, adopting the proposed approach will, it is said, provide an incentive for multinationals to shift their residence to tax havens.

---

30. OECD (2014), Developing a Multilateral Instrument to Modify Bilateral Tax Treaties, OECD/G20 Base Erosion and Profit Shifting Project, OECD Publishing, p. 10. http://dx.doi.org/10.1787/9789264219250-en.
31. Joint Committee on Taxation, *Background, Summary, and Implications of the OECD/G20 Base Erosion and Profit Shifting Project* (JCX-139-15), November 30, 2015, p. 32.

[A] Neutrality

There are three types of neutrality arguments that apply to cross-border investment. The two traditional ones are capital export neutrality (CEN) and capital import neutrality (CIN). CEN requires neutrality in the location of investment between the residence and source jurisdictions, and therefore supports taxing multinationals on a global basis as envisaged above. CIN requires neutrality between two different investors in a third jurisdiction (which is assumed to impose no tax) and therefore requires territoriality if the other jurisdiction taxes on a territorial basis.

It is often said that CEN and CIN are mutually incompatible in a world with different tax rates, and therefore a choice must be made. Traditionally, CEN was regarded as more important than CIN because investment locations were shown to be more sensitive to tax rates than the rate of savings, and CIN was considered to affect the rate of savings in each resident jurisdiction. But in the current environment where the tax rates of most OECD countries have converged, if the above multilateral proposal is adopted it is possible to achieve both CEN and CIN simultaneously.

A new variant of the neutrality argument is capital ownership neutrality (CON), which focuses on the multinational itself and not on its investors. It is said that multinationals exist because of ownership advantages that render them more efficient than their competitors. If one multinational is subject to a higher effective tax rate than a competitor because of global taxation, then it may be forced to forego an investment in a third country even if it is the more efficient one. But if the proposed solution is adopted on a multilateral basis, then all likely competitors will be taxed in the same way and CON can be preserved as well.

[B] Competitiveness

Historically, the main argument against adopting the Kennedy proposal and similar unilateral proposals is that they would put U.S.-based multinationals at a competitive disadvantage because multinationals from other countries are not subject to the same type of rule. The first author has always found this argument less than persuasive for several reasons: (a) it is not clear that competitiveness is a meaningful economic concept, or that the U.S. as a country should care particularly about the competitiveness of multinationals resident in it (as opposed to the competitiveness of the U.S. economy as a whole or of its population); (b) the same argument was made in 1961, where U.S.-based multinationals clearly dominated the globe, as in more recent years when their position was less dominant; (c) there is no evidence that current U.S. rules, which deviate from the global norm of territoriality and impose tax on some foreign source income of U.S.-based multinationals, have injured those multinationals in any significant way. In fact, empirical studies suggest that EU-based multinationals and U.S.-based multinationals pay similar effective tax rates even though the former benefit from territoriality and the latter do not (Avi-Yonah and Lahav, 2012).

But even if competitiveness is a valid argument (and it clearly carries weight among politicians), if a multilateral approach is adopted it loses its force. As stated above, about 90% of large multinationals are resident in OECD countries, and the others are mostly resident in large developing countries that may also be willing to join a multilateral approach. Under these circumstances, there will be no competitive disadvantage to any residence country that adopts the global approach unless it stems from its domestic corporate tax rate. As suggested above, the U.S. is an outlier in this regard because its corporate tax rate of 35% is significantly above the OECD average. In the context of adopting such a reform the U.S. can and should reduce its rate on a revenue neutral basis.

[C]   Corporate Expatriations

The last argument against taxing multinationals on a global basis is that the tax can be avoided by shifting the residence of the multinational to a jurisdiction that does not impose such a tax. In fact, we are currently in the midst of another wave of "inversions," or corporate expatriations, out of the U.S. because of the high U.S. corporate tax rate.

But this argument assumes that there are other jurisdictions that the multinational can move to. If all OECD countries adopt the proposal, most of the likely destinations disappear (again, assuming this is coupled with a reduction in the U.S. corporate tax rate). There are good business reasons why the headquarters of almost all multinationals are in OECD countries, and those reasons will militate against a move outside the OECD.

A move to a tax haven may be possible if residence is defined as place of incorporation. But as suggested above corporate residence should be defined as location of the corporate headquarters, and those are much less likely to be moveable to tax havens because corporate management are not likely to want to relocate there and other facilities that usually follow the headquarters location, such as research and development, cannot easily be moved there. For the same reasons, it is unlikely that new multinationals can be founded in tax havens outside the OECD and G20 countries.

Thus, it seems that none of the common arguments against taxing multinationals on a current basis is valid if one assumes that this approach can be adopted on a multilateral basis. The key question is therefore whether a multilateral approach is realistic, which is discussed below.

[D]   Can the Proposal Be Adopted?

By this point, we hope the reader will be convinced that: (a) current taxation of all multinationals on a global basis is the preferred approach, (b) *if* such taxation can be adopted on a multilateral basis, then all the usual arguments against its unilateral adoption by any country disappear. This is an unusual situation because in most tax policy debates there are good arguments on either side. In this case, however, the case in favor of multilateral current taxation would seem to be quite convincing, with no significant drawbacks if it can be achieved.

But, the reader is likely to object, this assumes that a multilateral approach is possible on such a sensitive issue as taxation. What is the evidence that this is in fact the case?

In order to assess whether multilateral action is possible, it is first necessary to establish the interests of the parties involved. Tax competition for Foreign Direct Investment (FDI) typically involves a MNE deciding which countries are possible investment locations from a non-tax point of view, that is, taking into account location, infrastructure, education, political stability, and other factors. Once the MNE has established a list of plausible countries, it then approaches these countries and asks what they would be willing to offer it in return for the investment. The countries then engage in a bidding war to grant tax reductions, culminating in the winner receiving the investment. Frequently, more than one country is able to get the investment.

Under these circumstances it is clear that the investment would be made in any case, whether or not the tax incentive is granted. The tax incentives are therefore a pure windfall for the MNE. If the countries could find a way to coordinate their approaches, they would still get the investment but without the tax cost.

Thus, it is in the interest of most countries to coordinate their approaches to prevent this type of tax competition. The same rationale obtains for capital exporting jurisdictions like the large countries in OECD. They would prefer to tax their MNEs on a current basis, but are constrained from doing so because of the competitiveness and expatriation concerns outlined above.

Thus, in our opinion all OECD member countries would benefit from a multilateral approach. Capital exporting countries could obtain revenues from their MNEs without concerns about harming their competitiveness or MNEs migrating to other OECD countries. Capital importing countries could obtain FDI without concern that if they do not grant tax holidays the investment would end up in other countries. In the latter case, if all OECD and G20 countries were on board, the limits on tax competition would apply outside the OECD as well since almost all MNEs are based in these countries. Countries outside the OECD/G20 would have no incentive to grant tax holidays against their own interest if the income were taxed in the residence country of the MNE, since in that case there would be no benefit to the MNE from the tax holiday.

In addition, if the proposal above were adopted, this would also help alleviate the current opposition by MNEs and some countries to country-by-country reporting, which is being considered by OECD as part of the BEPS project. Since MNEs would obtain credit for taxes levied by source countries under the proposal, they should be less hostile to country-by-country reporting, which is designed to aid source countries collect their fair share of taxes.

If the interests of the countries are aligned, what has prevented multilateral action so far? In our opinion, it is primarily because of lobbying by the MNEs themselves. They are the primary beneficiaries from the status quo and they have successfully lobbied both countries and the OECD against meaningful reform.

A useful contrast is to examine a case in which the countries and MNEs were aligned. Prior to 1977, there were no domestic limits on MNEs paying bribes overseas to obtain contracts from corrupt government officials. In 1977, following several scandals, the U.S. enacted the Foreign Corrupt Practices Act, which imposed criminal sanctions on such bribes by U.S.-based MNEs and their executives. Predictably, U.S. MNEs complained that this ban put them at a competitive disadvantage, especially when other countries like Germany permitted foreign bribes to be deducted for domestic tax purposes.

Somewhat surprisingly, the outcome was not relaxation of the U.S. law. Instead, the Clinton administration successfully pushed the OECD to adopt the same provisions as part of a binding, multilateral treaty, which eliminated the competitive disadvantage issue.

The key reason for this success is that not only were the interests of the countries aligned; the MNEs did not like paying bribes either and therefore lobbied in favor of the provision. This will not be the case for tax, where the MNEs are already pushing back against the OECD BEPS project. However, there have been instances in the past where resistance by MNEs has been overcome.

In the case of corporate tax avoidance, we think the best way forward is unilateral U.S. action. The precedent is the adoption of the CFC rules, which proves (among other examples) that such action can be both possible and effective in pushing other countries to adopt similar rules.

Before 1961, no country taxed the foreign source income of subsidiaries of its multinationals, because residence countries believed they lacked both source and residence jurisdiction over foreign source income of foreign corporations. However, in 1961 the Kennedy Administration proposed taxing all income of CFCs by using a deemed dividend mechanism that was copied from the Foreign Personal Holding Company (FPHC) rules.

While this proposal was rejected, the resulting compromise (Subpart F, 1962) aimed at taxing income of CFCs that was unlikely to be taxed by source countries either because it was mobile and could be earned anywhere (passive income) or because it was structured to be earned in low-tax jurisdictions (base company income).

Initially, the adoption of Subpart F seemed to have put U.S.-based multinationals at a competitive disadvantage, because no other country had such rules. But gradually this picture changed. The U.S. was followed by Germany (1972), Canada (1975), Japan (1978), France (1980), U.K. (1984), New Zealand (1988), Australia (1990), Sweden (1990), Norway (1992), Denmark (1995), Finland (1995), Indonesia (1995), Portugal (1995), Spain (1995), Hungary (1997), Mexico (1997), South Africa (1997), South Korea (1997), Argentina (1999), Brazil (2000), Italy (2000), Estonia (2000), Israel (2003), Turkey (2006), and China (2008). Many other countries, such as India, are considering adopting such rules. As a result, most of our trading partners now have CFC rules.

Moreover, the later adopters improved on the U.S. in two principal ways. First, they rejected the deemed dividend mechanism, which can lead to many unforeseen complications, in favor of taxing the shareholders on a pass-through basis. Second, they generally explicitly incorporate the effective foreign tax rate into the determination whether a CFC will be subject to current tax. This is better than the U.S. rule that is based solely on the type of income, because after 1980 it became quite easy to earn active income that is not subject to tax.

The result is that the CFCs of EU-based multinationals are currently generally subject to tax at similar or higher rates than U.S.-based ones, despite the non-taxation of dividends from active income under territoriality. This is therefore a classic example of constructive unilateralism. The U.S. led and others followed, and the end result is that most multinationals are subject to similar effective tax rates, with no competitive disadvantage or advantage. The result is a world in which there is much less double non-taxation than in the absence of CFC rules.

Unfortunately, in the U.S. Subpart F has been critically undermined by the adoption of check the box and the CFC to CFC exception, resulting in USD 2 trillion of low-taxed accumulated earnings offshore by U.S. multinationals. This cannot happen in other countries with tougher CFC rules, and is a major part of the explanation why despite rampant tax competition most OECD members did not see the sharp drops in overall corporate tax revenues that are seen in developing countries.

The main argument in favor of territoriality (i.e., exempting dividends paid by U.S. CFCs from tax upon receipt by their parents) is the lock-out problem. About USD 2 trillion in low-taxed foreign source income are in CFCs that cannot repatriate them because of the 35% tax on repatriations and the absence of foreign tax credits. We know this is a real problem because of the effectiveness of the 2004–2005 amnesty and because of various attempts by multinationals to avoid the rule (e.g., via inversions, "killer Bs," short-term loans, etc.).

But it is less clear that the solution is a participation exemption. Why not abolish deferral and let the dividends flow back tax-free?

We would argue that this is a good opportunity for "constructive unilateralism." No G20 country has a corporate tax rate below 20%. If we reduced the corporate tax to, say, 28%, and at the same time abolished deferral, the likely response by other G20 members like Germany or France would be to follow suit. They need the extra revenue more than we do, and concerns about competitiveness would be alleviated by the U.S. move, like they were in the original CFC context.

It should be remembered that the other G20 have more effective CFC rules than we do, and those CFC rules already act as a de fact worldwide system with a minimum tax: If the foreign tax is below a set level (e.g., 25% in Germany or 20% in Japan), the CFC rules kick in to tax the income. The result is that there is much less lock out because most low-taxed foreign income is taxed by the CFC rules. The change to a worldwide system would be much less radical than usually envisaged. This is why for both the U.K. and Japan there was no significant increase in repatriations after they adopted territoriality in 2009.

But should the U.S. not adopt a minimum but lower tax on foreign source income for competitiveness reasons? This is what both the Obama and Camp proposals envisage. Obama suggests a 28% corporate tax on domestic profits and a 19% tax on foreign income, while Camp proposed a 25% tax on domestic profits and a 12.5%–15% tax on foreign income.

The problem, of course, is that such a gap would still encourage U.S.-based MNEs to shift profits overseas, with no repatriation tax to deter them. We can always fall back to such a system if needed. But for now we would suggest taxing all income at the same rate, and if that rate has to be lower, so be it. As long as it is above 20% we do not think we will be outside G20 norms, and a rate in the 20%–25% range will not put our MNEs at a significant competitive disadvantage given the effective minimum tax imposed by the CFC rules of our trading partners.

It is impossible to predict what will happen, but the history described above suggests that there is a good chance that other G20 countries will follow us if we abolish deferral at a lower rate.[32] And if that happens, all the usual objections to worldwide taxation (competitiveness, inversions, and the various neutralities) lose their force. We do not think there is a significant risk involved in this move, and the potential upside is quite large.

§5.04 CONCLUSION

The benefits principle should be reconsidered in light of the reality of globalization. We should tax active income primarily at residence. This will enable the large economies to address corporate tax avoidance.

If nothing is done, multinationals will avoid the corporate tax. If that happens, ordinary middle class Americans will be reluctant to pay their taxes. Our tax system is built around voluntary cooperation; if most Americans refused to cooperate, the IRS could not force them to do so. As the Greek experience has recently demonstrated, once a tax culture of non-payment is established, it is very hard to change. We need to do something about avoidance before it is too late.

---

32. *See* the most recent proposal of the EU Commission to tax currently CFC profits that are subject to an effective tax rate below 40% of the residence country rate if over 50% of the CFC's income is either passive or derived from sales to related parties. Council of the European Union Doc. 14544/15 (December 2, 2015) and Dec 14544/15 Add 1 (December 2, 2015), Art. 9.

CHAPTER 6
Jurisdictional Excesses in BEPS' Times: National Appropriation of an Enhanced Global Tax Basis

Guillermo O. Teijeiro

Nowadays there is an increasingly perceived desire of governments to stretch international law principles on personal or economic nexus, as well as on the reachable tax basis either to enhance their share in income from traditional across-the-border businesses, or to grasp income coming from stateless business manifestations, such as the digital economy or private commercial use of satellites in outer space. These trends will probably deepen in coming years as a result of the states' competition on the increased global tax basis arising from BEPS efforts.

The purpose of this work is to analyze and evaluate certain current realities which apparently contravene international legal principles concerning the states' scope of tax jurisdiction in the international context, as an alert against other potential excesses that might arise in the post-BEPS era. With that aim, the analysis will be focused on: (i) full inclusion CFC rules under Brazilian tax law, (ii) indirect Vodafone-type taxation of capital gains, (iii) attribution of notional income to commodity exporters, under aggressive versions of the so-called Sixth (transfer pricing) Method, and (iv) withholding taxes or alternative schemes aimed at reaching digital economy income.

§6.01 FULL INCLUSION CFC RULES UNDER BRAZILIAN TAX LAW: ABSENCE OF MINIMAL PERSONAL CONNECTION

The Report of the Experts to the League of Nations (1923) provided that taxation of business income should stay with the state of residence of the entity, except when the latter carries out activities in another state through a permanent establishment ("PE").

This basic principle together with the separate legal personality of foreign companies are two essential elements of International General and treaty Law.

Controlled foreign corporation ("CFC") or foreign investment fund ("FIF") regimes developed over the last fifty years complement those principles; they have been designed to avoid perceived abuses of tax deferral which erode the national tax basis, through foreign entities organized in haven or preferred jurisdictions without a worthy purpose, and where accumulated profits are maintained almost indefinitely. CFC/FIF regimes have been admitted by the custom (*opinio iuris*) of the international community as long as certain commonly shared extremes are met. The common extremes to which these regimes are conditioned upon to be deemed compatible with the separate legal personality of foreign entities are: (i) the shift of easily re-allocable (*tainted*) income, including passive (interest, dividends, royalties, rents, and capital gains) or trading income; and (ii) the shift of tainted income to a foreign entity that is subject to a privileged tax regime (of a general or specific nature), whether defined objectively or by comparison to the level of taxation at the shareholders' home country. Control and minimal individual equity participation are conditions under CFC regimes, but may not be so under FIF-type rules.

CFC/FIF regimes of widespread acceptance do not allow to attribute to the shareholders business income obtained by a controlled or related entity in a non-privileged foreign jurisdiction.

Article 74 of Medida Provisoria ("MP") 2158-34-01 (re-edited on August 24, 2001 as 2158-35/01), complementing Article 43 of the Código Tributário Nacional (CTN) established that in relation to corporate income tax and social contribution on income (Contribuição Social sobre o Lucro Líquido ("CSLL")), the income obtained by foreign-controlled or related companies is deemed available, and hence is attributed to the Brazilian parent or participating entity on a current basis, as of the date of closing of the year in which the income accrued to the foreign entity.[1]

The rule applied to all kinds of income regardless of its nature, e.g., including business income, and regardless of the level of taxation at which the income is subject at source; therefore, the Brazilian rules do not consist of a typical CFC regime consented by international custom and the commentaries to the OECD Model Convention ("OECD MC"). Moreover, Brazilian CFC rules contradict the Commentary to Article 1, paragraph 26 of the OECD MC and concurrent principles embodied therein, as the rule does not solely apply to certain tainted income, (e.g., passive, base company income and/or income subject to a preferential regime) but to all income of a foreign related or controlled entity. Besides, the Brazilian rules may not be deemed a special

---

1. On these rules *see, inter alia*, Xavier A., Direito Tributario Internacional do Brasil, 7th edition, Editora Forense, Sao Paulo, 2010, p. 374 ss; Xavier A., Permicao Fiscal as Empresas Brasileiras, Valor Económico, February 15, 2012; Duque Estrada R., E Improvisora Revisao da en de Tributacao Internacional, Consultor Tributario, January 12, 2012; Teijeiro G. & Catao M., Ficcoes jurídicas e tributacao, Estadao, April 2, 2012; Freitas de Moraes E. Castro, Brazilian CFC Rules: Background and Status after Eagle II Case, Latin America Law & Business Report, vol. 18, # 3, March 2010, p. 12 ss.

Chapter 6: Jurisdictional Excesses in BEPS' Times §6.01

anti-abuse rule ("SAAR") of general application in the international community, and, therefore, are not legitimized by the *opinio iuris* under this perspective either.

The Brazilian CFC regime is a highly peculiar and exceptional set of the rules that removes the legal dividing line between legal entities – i.e., the foreign subsidiary and its Brazilian parent company – which is beyond the aim of protecting the Brazilian tax basis. The purpose of that regime is to tax business income of a foreign entity currently in the hand of the Brazilian shareholders – business income that is otherwise not taxable under generally accepted principles of International General and treaty Law.

As it can be seen below, after a Copernican twist from older precedents, more recent judicial decisions have recognized the incompatibility of the Brazilian CFC rules and double taxation treaties ("DTTs"), giving prevalence to the DTTs over domestic CFC rules; but no similar decision with *erga homes* effects outside the umbrella of DTTs has been issued, therefore the issue of taxing currently business income of a foreign subsidiary in a non-privileged jurisdiction under MP 2158-35/01 remained open.

In January 2012, the Economic Administrative Court of the Nation ("CARF") issued a procedural decision rejecting (in second instance) a claim from Vale do Rio Doce (the largest Brazilian mining company), in a tax litigation of enormous economic significance. In essence, the case focused on the interpretation and application of Article 74 of MP 2158-35/0 in the context of the treaties then in force with Belgium, Denmark and Luxembourg.

In its 2012 decision CARF followed, as a *dictum*, the judicial doctrine previously established *in re Banco Itaú S.A.* (September 19, 2009), and confirmed the earlier decision issued in *Vale* by the Federal Court in Rio de Janeiro, sustaining that MP 2158-35/01 did not contradict DTTs executed by Brazil, since Article 7 of the DTTs refers to business income of controlled or related entities residing in treaty-partner countries, and not to the income added to the tax accrued in Brazil by the parent or related company by application of the equity accounting method *(método de equivalência patrimonial)*.

The argument is, in fact, a game of words that attempt to hide the use of a legal fiction to attribute to the Brazilian parent business income accrued to a foreign related entity (its actual beneficiary), with the purpose of taxing – in hands of the parent – current income of a foreign legal person on which Brazil lacks jurisdiction to tax.

In other words, holding that there is no conflict between Brazilian DTTs and Article 74 of the MP 2158-35/01 – since, in the absence of an effective distribution, the MP leads to tax not business but income of other nature in the hands of the parent company – is an euphemism that may not hide the facts nor allow to circumvent the application of the relevant rules of International general and treaty Law. When business income derived by a subsidiary is currently taxed at the level of the Brazilian parent company in the absence of a profit distribution, the separate legal identity of the entities is unlawfully ignored; in other words, the corporate veil is disregarded without a justifying reason (as it would be the case of protecting the domestic basis in the presence of tainted income); and this is extraterritorial (ultra vires) taxation not only incompatible with Article 7 of DTTs, but with the basic division of jurisdiction among states under international Law.[2]

The position embodied in Article 74 of MP 2158-35/01: (i) contradicts the intention shared by the DTT's Contracting States of avoiding double taxation, even beyond the strict framework of juridical double taxation; and (ii) by resorting to a legal fiction, it ends up creating a new taxpayer or economic unit (parent/subsidiary unit), partially beyond the reach of the Brazilian tax jurisdiction, since it implies encompassing in the parent's taxable basis business income undoubtedly derived by a separate corporate entity residing in the other Contracting State. This fictional taxpayer (economic unit) and the attribution to it of income generated by a separate foreign legal entity contradicts basic and undisputed principles of treaty law regarding covered persons and allocation of profits (arm's length principle) in a setting that – to the extent applicable to business income not subject to preferential treatment – clearly goes beyond the aim of protecting the erosion of the domestic taxable basis.

On April 10, 2013, *in re Confederación Nacional de Industrias, ADI 2558*, The Brazilian CFC Regime was at stake before the *Supremo Tribunal Federal ("STF")*.

In ADI 2558, the Supremo decided with *erga omnes* effect, that: (i) CFC rules are unconstitutional as applied to foreign related companies (participated in less than 50% of their capital) residing in non-privileged jurisdictions; (ii) CFC rules are constitutional as applied to foreign-controlled entities residing in tax-haven jurisdictions; and (iii) the retrospective application of CFC rules to profits obtained before 2001, as provided for in MP 2158-35/01, was also unconstitutional. The issue of the nature of the deemed distributed income (e.g., business income) was not expressly discussed.

The constitutionality of the CFC system as applied to foreign-controlled entities in non-privileged jurisdictions, as well as to related entities domiciled in tax haven jurisdictions was not decided and, hence, remained an open issue. The issue of whether the Brazilian CFC system was compatible with Article 7 and other related clauses and principles of DTTs in force (e.g., the discussion in the Vale case) also remained open after ADI 2558.

In the case involving *Embraco*, also decided in ADI 2558, the constitutionality of the CFC regime as applied to foreign-controlled entities domiciled in non-privileged jurisdictions was upheld; again, without addressing the issue of the nature of the income concerned (whether business or passive income). This decision, however, did not have the effect of a precedent (*stare decisis*) as it was taken by simple majority (two judges were absent: Judge Fux, and the yet to be appointed new judge in substitution of retired judge Ayres Britto).

As of the date of ADI 2558, there was no final decision in the case of most Brazilian MNEs, either because *Embraco* was not definitive (nor had the value of a precedent), or because the issue of the compatibility of the CFC system with DTT provisions was not even addressed. These two types of cases were, by far, the richest from an international taxation viewpoint, since as anticipated current taxation of

---

2. *See* Teijeiro G.O., *Ficciones Jurídicas y Jurisdicción Tributaria Internacional*, Revista de Tributación AAEF, N° 25, 2012, p. 45 ss; Teijeiro G.O. and Vinhas Catao M., *Ficcoes Juridicas e Tributacao*, O Estado de S. Paulo, April 2, 2012.

Chapter 6: Jurisdictional Excesses in BEPS' Times §6.01

business income obtained by foreign-controlled legal entities is arguably an extraterritorial (ultra vires) application of Brazilian taxation.

Pending a judicial decision of said matter, the Brazilian Executive Branch issued MP 627/13, dated November 11, 2013, altering the design of the CFC regime as previously contemplated in MP 2158-35/01 but not its essentials. In accordance to MP 627/13: (i) income (including business income obtained in a non-preferential tax jurisdiction) is kept as deemed realized income currently in the hands of the Brazilian parent (at the time it accrued to the foreign entity) regardless of whether distributed as a dividend; (ii) payment of the tax can be deferred up to the time of actual distribution or eight years, whichever occurs first, with interest thereon (at LIBOR rates) so that, at the end of the relevant period, interest must be added up to the amount of income tax to be paid over to the government (as if it were being paid in arrears).

In other words the extraterritorial effect of the Brazilian CFC rules remained unchanged (although disguised) in MP 627; and the system became even more aggressive since current taxation also applied to income of indirect foreign-controlled entities. Charging interest thereon as from the accrual period implies that, in economic terms, the separate legal personality of the entity residing in a treaty-partner country is not respected but merely tolerated, in order to allow postponement of a tax which remained due on a yearly basis regardless of a distribution.

After a quite prolonged Congressional discussion, MP 627/13 was passed as Law 12,973, published in the Official Gazette on May 14, 2014. As far as the CFC regime is concerned, the new design outlined in the preceding paragraph was retained (with some minor changes) in Articles 77–92 of said Law.

Meanwhile, the *Vale* case progressed as follows: on February 14, 2014, the *Superior Tribunal de Justiça* ("STJ") approved a partial procedural surrender and waiver of rights submitted by Vale, for years 2003 to 2012, aimed at benefitting from the payment program provided for in the *Programa nacional de recuperacao fiscal* enacted by law 12,865/13. This procedural surrender did not include the on-going discussion on the conflicting nature of the CFC regime with Brazilian DTTs. Finally, on April 24, 2014, the STJ decided that the CFC regime (as contemplated in MP 2158-35/01) was not applicable to Vale's subsidiaries organized in Brazil treaty-partner countries (Belgium, Denmark, and Luxembourg).[3]

In addressing CFC regimes, BEPS Draft Report on Action 3 (*Designing Effective Controlled Foreign Company Rules*) recognized (Chapter 5) the existence of two approaches concerning the definition of CFC income: a full inclusion system which treats all income earned by a CFC as CFC attributable income regardless of its character (i.e., passive or business income), and the widespread partial inclusion system which only attributes certain types of income earned by a CFC. As the Draft Report also

---

3. STJ Recurso especial 1.925.709 RJ (2012/01-10520-7), *Companhia Vale do Rio Doce*, April 24, 2014. In the same sense, in *Petrobras*, decided in October 2014, CARF upheld a *Recurso Voluntário*, and sustained that business profits obtained by a controlled foreign corporation in The Netherlands were not subject to taxation on an accrual basis in the hands of the Brazilian parent company in accordance to Art. 74, MP 2.158-35/01, because of Dutch exclusive tax jurisdiction on said income obtained by an entity with separate legal personality domiciled in The Netherlands.

recognized, under full inclusion systems there is no need to separately define CFC income, but such an approach catches categories of income that do not raise specific profit shifting concerns (i.e., operational or business income). Thus, such approach is meaningless from a BEPS policy point of view.

Notwithstanding the foregoing, the Final Report (Executive Summary and Chapter 4) contemplated full inclusion systems as an option, and though recommended that CFC rules include a definition of CFC income (setting out a non-exhaustive list of approaches or combination of approaches that could be used), did not expressly banned full inclusion approaches from the available alternatives, thus leaving open the chance that domestic rules implement a Brazilian-type extraterritorial approach.[4]

§6.02 INDIRECT TAXATION OF CAPITAL GAINS: ABSENCE OF A MINIMAL ECONOMIC CONNECTION: *VODAFONE* AND *SANOFI PASTEUR* CASES

Vodafone is a well-known Indian tax case which maintained the attention of the international business community in recent years, not only because of the intrinsic significance of the discussion, but also for the immediate contagious effect that the Indian Tax authorities' position spread to legislation of a number of other jurisdiction such as Chile, China, Israel, and Peru.

The case concerned the acquisition by Vodafone, a Dutch company, from Hutchinson (HTIL, a Cayman Islands company), of the shares in CGP, another company in the Cayman Islands. The acquired company (CGP) indirectly owned a controlling stake in Hutchinson Essar, an Indian operator of telephone services in India.

Based on a possible interpretation of Indian income tax rules, the tax authorities argued that the transfer of the shares in the foreign company acquired (CGP) was equivalent to the transfer of assets in India belonging to Hutchinson Essar, and, therefore, in the role of acquirer, Vodafone should have withheld applicable Indian income tax on the capital gain obtained by the transferor (HTIL). In other words, it was discussed if India had sufficient nexus, and, hence, jurisdiction to tax gains from the sale of shares in a foreign company (CGP) obtained by another foreign company (HTIL), by the mere fact that the target (CGP) possessed indirectly, through a chain of holdings, shares in an Indian operating company with assets located in India.

In a significant judgment dated January 20, 2012, the Supreme Court of India reversed an earlier ruling from the Supreme Court of Bombay and decided the dispute in favor of Vodafone. Along the process, Vodafone had sustained the lack of jurisdiction of the Indian Treasury to tax income from the transfer of shares in a foreign company, executed by and between a nonresident seller and a nonresident buyer, due to the lack of sufficient territorial nexus with India. In upholding Vodafone's position, the Supreme Court of India applied undisputable principles of International Law

---

4. OECD Final Report on Action 3, *Designing Effective Controlled Foreign Company Rules*, 2015 http://www.keepeek.com/Digital-Asset-Management/oecd/taxation/designing-effective-contro lled-foreign-company-rules-action-3-2015-final-report.

requiring a minimal connection between the nonresident alien taxpayer and the taxing jurisdiction to legitimize the latter's exercise of tax jurisdiction.

From the Vodafone case, it follows that the connection with the taxing state should be actual and cannot be built or construed on the basis of a legal fiction utilized to expand the state's tax jurisdiction beyond acceptable limits under international law. In other words, in defining the territorial reach of a tax, income that is not actually sourced in the territory may not be deemed to have originated within the taxing jurisdiction. The judgment also provides that deeming the income to have originated in the taxing jurisdiction would imply extraterritorial or *ultra vires* taxation, conflict with the proper legal balance among states, and originate a potential double or multiple taxation that cannot be remedied in accordance with the rules of existing DTTs.[5]

A similar reasoning was applied by the Andhra High Court in *Sanofi Pasteur Holding* ("Sanofi"), although under the umbrella of the DTT between France and India. In this case, which was decided on February 15, 2013, it was held that retrospective amendments to the Indian Income Tax Act had no impact on a genuine transaction covered by an existing DTT.[6]

The facts of the case involved a share acquisition between a French company, as purchaser, two French companies as sellers, and a French target (holding) having a participation in an Indian operating company. Sanofi purchased an 80.37% participation and a 19.63% participation in ShanH, from sellers, Merieux Alliance (MA) and Groupe Industrial Marcel Dassault (GMID), respectively. ShanH, in turn, held an 82.5% participation in Shantha Biotechnics Limited (SBL), an Indian company. The court decision rejected the Indian Treasury's claim because of the lack of nexus of the transaction with India, and the conflict of the domestic rules with DTT rules.

Among its considerations, the Court observed that ShanH, as holding, had a business purpose in itself – its main object was to serve as a an investment vehicle for foreign direct investment in India – and this had been done by participating in SBL. It was additionally argued that the receipt of dividends by ShanH as shareholder in SBL, during the holding period, reaffirmed that ShanH was a separate entity subject to Indian withholding on said dividends. The court also indicated that ShanH was not established for the purpose of avoiding capital gain liability in India, and that the Indian tax authorities had not been able to evidence otherwise, so that piercing the corporate veil was not justified in the case. It was further sustained that under de DTT, ShanH's controlling participation in SBL could not be distinguished from its shareholding, and hence, could not be taxed as a separate asset in India. Finally, the Court understood that the amended provisions of the Indian Income Tax Act of 1961 were intended to prevent tax avoidance and, in the case, they conflicted with the applicable DTT so that could not be applied to Sanofi.

---

5. *See* Teijeiro G.O., *Ficciones Jurídicas y Jurisdicción Tributaria Internacional*, Revista de Tributación AAEF, N° 25, 2012, p. 45 ss. Please note that the Indian rule at stake applies objectively; i.e., regardless of whether a tax avoidance objective was sought by the taxpayer. The appreciation might have been different if by application of GAARs or SAARs and in the presence of a sham, gains were attributed to a taxpayer having an economic attachment with the taxing State.
6. *See* Saran S., *Sanofi Pasteur Case: A Comprehensive Analysis*, Tax India, May 29, 2014.

The decision in this case was perceived as an harmonious interpretation of the post-Vodafone amendments to the Income Tax Act of 1961, and the provisions of the DTT between India and France.

As regards the Vodafone decision, the Indian Government first intended to apply the amendment introduced to the Income Tax Act retrospectively (to the periods covered by the 2012 Supreme Court decision), and after a recommendation from the government-appointed Shone Commission suggesting otherwise, started non-binding negotiations to settle the case which, at the end, reached no conclusion. As a result, on April 13, 2014, Vodafone sought arbitration remedy under the Bilateral Investment Promotion and Protection Agreement between India and the Netherlands.[7]

Indirect capital gain taxation in Latin American countries (Perú, Chile) was discussed at length in the IFA Regional Congress which took place in Santa Cruz de la Sierra, Bolivia, in early May 2014. Both the Peruvian and Chilean legislation applies regardless of evidence on the existence of a tax avoidance purpose (the legislation does not work as a special anti-avoidance rule), so that the *ultra vires* taint of this type of regime, first introduced in other latitudes, is replicated in these Latin American attempts.[8]

§6.03 THE SIXTH METHOD OF TRANSFER PRICING: A LATIN AMERICAN EXPERIMENT ATTRIBUTING ADDITIONAL NOTIONAL INCOME TO COMMODITY EXPORTERS

Chapter II of the OECD Transfer Pricing Guidelines for Multinational Enterprises and Tax Administrations (pre-BEPS version) contained a discussion of five transfer pricing ("TP") methods that could be applied to establish whether the conditions of related-party transactions were consistent with the arm's length principle. These five methods consist of three traditional transaction methods: the comparable uncontrolled price method ("CUP"), the resale price method, and the cost plus method; and two transactional profit methods: the transactional net margin method and the transactional profit split method. These TP methods represented the then existing international consensus on the manner of applying the arm's length principle, so that, as expressed in the Guidelines, states were encouraged to make the methods available in their domestic rules and to apply them in accordance with the Guidelines, to minimize the risk of double taxation.[9]

---

7. *See* Wagh S., *Vodafone Tax Saga, Episode II: India Strikes Back*, New Europe, September 29–October 5, 2013; and Fronda A., International Tax Review, ITR Premium, *Vodafone and Nokia Switch Tactics in Attempt to Resolve Indian Tax Disputes*, May 22, 2014.
8. To *see* power point presentations, go to Seminar C *Transferencia indirecta de activos y planificación fiscal* in www.ifabolivia2014.com/pages/general/program.aspx [and click *descargar* (download)]. As regards indirect taxation of capital gains in the context of BEPS and low-income countries, particularly in extractive industries (citing the cases of Mauritania and Mozambique), *see Part 2 of a Report to G20 Development working Group on the Impact of BEPS in low income countries*, August 13, 2014, section 4, a), where it is called for further work, in consultation with the IMF, to identify policy options to tackle abusive cases.
9. OECD Transfer pricing Guidelines for Multinational Enterprises and Tax Administrations, July, 2010.

Reference to a Sixth Method in OECD BEPS documents is first found in the OECD Report on the impact of BEPS on low-income countries,[10] where it was mentioned that in connection with the issue of lack of data for TP comparability analysis, some developing countries have shown an interest in approaches that operate in a way similar to the Sixth Method referred to in section 3(a) of the same Report, i.e., use of quoted prices in the relevant transparent markets.[11] Associated recommendations call for BEPS Actions 4 and 10 to take into account developing countries' issues.

On December 16, 2014, OECD released a discussion draft under BEPS Action 10, discussing the transfer pricing aspects of cross border commodity transactions. This document also made express reference to the Sixth Method and proposed a working framework with a twofold objective: (i) to clarify that CUP can be an appropriate TP method for commodity transactions between associated enterprises, and that quoted or publicly available prices can be used under CUP as a reference to determine the arm's length price for the controlled commodity transaction; and (ii) provide additional guidance on the adoption of a deemed pricing date for commodity transactions between associated enterprises in the absence of evidence of the actual pricing date agreed by the parties to the transactions.

The Sixth Method had spread over Latin America since its inclusion in the Argentine Income Tax Law in 2003.[12] Under Argentine law, the Sixth Method applied and still applies to the export of commodities (i.e., cereals, oilseeds, hydrocarbons and their derivatives, and, in general, all goods quoted in a transparent market).

Whenever commodities are exported to related final purchasers, through a foreign trading entity that is not the final purchaser of the goods, the transactions are not deemed made at arm's length conditions and, hence, are to be adjusted by applying the quoted price of the goods in the transparent relevant market as of the date of loading, regardless of the price agreed upon between the exporter and the foreign trader, unless the latter is higher.[13]

The Sixth Method consists of imputing to the exporter a notional gross income equivalent to the market price difference occurring between the date on which the transaction takes place and the date of loading. Therefore, the Sixth Method is not a typical TP adjustment which, based on pre-BEPS Guidelines' basic principles, would have led to compare the agreed upon price with the quoted price as of the date of the export contract.

The attribution of such notional income to the exporter under the Sixth Method is an attempt to enlarge the domestic tax basis extraterritorially by ignoring the design of the transaction as a two-segment deal, and in a way that is incompatible with the

---

10. *See* note 83, section 4, b).
11. The Sixth Method is described in this section by reference to the Zambian legislation to assess the value of commodities (sale of metals or precious metals) between related parties, according to which the price is the monthly average quoted price on metal exchange markets.
12. Article 15, ITL, as amended by Law 25,784. Other countries using some form of the Sixth Method in the region are: Uruguay, Peru, Bolivia, Dominican Republic, Ecuador, Paraguay, and Brazil.
13. In a bull market, the adjustment might be illustrated as follows: (i) agreed upon price (USD/ton) 99; (ii) quoted price at loading (USD/ton) 108; (iii) difference per ton. 9; (iv) quantity 100; (v) export price adjustment (USD) 900.

existence of the foreign trader's assessment of its income by computing a purchase price as of the date of execution of the contract. Moreover, under DTTs, the adding of such notional income contravenes Article 9 (associated enterprises), creating potential economic double taxation which might not be remedied by correlative adjustments provided for in that article. In this sense, it is worth noting that the Sixth Method applied whenever export transactions are made using a triangular structure and regardless of whether the intermediary trading is organized in a foreign preferred-tax jurisdiction or haven. Thus, it allows the state of the exporter to soak up taxable basis otherwise belonging to a foreign jurisdiction under the excuse of a TP adjustment, which it is not such since it consists of adding notional income deemed realized by the mere passing of time after the date of the contract, and by a reference (market price at loading) that is absolutely disassociated with the foreign counterpart's cost of acquisition.[14] Moreover, in a down market the lowering of the price between the execution date and the loading date is not considered.

The Uruguayan Sixth Method follows the Argentine rules almost verbatim. The Peruvian regulations are more flexible since they allow taking the market price at loading as one among other alternatives, including: (i) the average market price within the four previous and the four subsequent months from loading; (ii) the market price at the date of execution of the agreement; or (iii) the average market price within the thirty-day period after execution. Moreover, the method does not apply with regard to hedged transactions, or transactions entered into with international traders meeting conditions similar to those contemplated under Argentine tax law for the same purpose. The Sixth Method as applied in the Dominican Republic, Ecuador, and Paraguay mandates using the market price at loading, unless the foreign trader meets certain specified conditions for exclusion of the application of the method.

The Brazilian's TP system of adjustments on the export of commodities,[15] instead, mandates to apply the quoted price in the relevant transparent market as of the date of the transaction, whenever exports are made to foreign related counterparties or purchasers subject to a preferential tax regime. This is much more in line with traditional OECD TP Guidelines since the adjustment is made on the basis of the market price as of the date of the transaction (which functions as a CUP), and regardless of whether the transactions are made straight to the final purchaser or through a foreign intermediary trader.

The OECD Discussion Draft followed, in substance, the line of the Brazilian system (the Sixth Method as a variation of CUP). The discussion draft made clear that its principal purpose was to allow the use of the quoted or publicly available price at execution date as reference to assess the market price for the export of commodities to

---

14. The Sixth Method under the Argentine ITL does not apply as long as certain statutory parameters are complied with simultaneously [Articles 15, 8 a), b) and c)]. These relate to evidence of the trading's substance (risk, assets and functions commensurate to the volumes transacted), and meeting of the following ratios: (i) passive income may not be higher than 50% of total income; (ii) purchases and sales of goods from and to Argentina may not be higher than 50% of all purchases and sales, (iii) purchases and sales to the group related entities (less purchases and sales with the Argentine counterpart) may not be higher than 30% of total purchases and sales.
15. Article 34, *Instrução Normativa* RFB 1312 as amended by RFB 1395/13.

a foreign related party. Moreover, in accordance with the discussion draft, the adoption of a different date (deemed pricing date) would be allowed only in two exceptional cases: (i) when pricing at execution date is inconsistent with the facts and circumstances of the case; or (ii) in the absence of evidence on the execution date by the parties to the transaction. Comments received on the discussion draft and the public discussion that took place March 19-20, 2015, endorsed this approach, and the final Report receipted it, thus couching the issue within traditional TP principles.[16] As a result, in the coming years, it could be expected a progressive adaptation of Latin American legislation on the Sixth Method to the TP post-BEPS directives.

§6.04 THE CASE OF THE DIGITAL ECONOMY UNDER BEPS ACTION 1: EXTRATERRITORIALITY OF SPECIAL WITHHOLDING OR EQUALIZATION LEVIES

The post-BEPS international tax scenario is in transition to a stage where the domestic tax base will be much better protected against erosion and profit-shifting than it was in pre-BEPS times. The international tax system, however, is not yet stable,[17] and despite OECD's efforts to uniform national responses within BEPS's implementation stage, it is a fact that simultaneous OECD-G20, EU, and unilateral state's efforts under the BEPS label, frequently collide among them and/or with more fundamental international tax principles. For a variety of reason, this is quite apparent concerning domestic experiments on the digital economy.

Only seventeen years ago, at the Munich IFA Congress, discussions centered on whether a server – as automated equipment without personnel – might constitute a PE under the OECD MC. Three years later, the 2003 version of the OECD MC included in the Commentaries to Article 5, paragraph 7, subparagraphs 42.1-42.10, the first and unique comments thus far on e-commerce, making the location of the server the pivotal concept meeting the physical (objective) presence test of the PE concept. The experience soon revealed that the location of the server meant nothing as regards activity in a given market, as that location might be and usually is absolutely dissociated with the market location and, hence, the new comments soon became outdated and useless.

Borderless digital economy's business models are nowadays much more rich, complex, and sophisticated than e-commerce state-of-the-art manifestations in 2003; and still the digital economy is a moving target hardly graspable by traditional residence and source concepts, at home and market jurisdictions.

---

16. BEPS Final Report, Actions 8 to 10, *Aligning Transfer Pricing Outcomes with Value Creation* (commodities).
17. In an article published last year, I alerted on the instability of the current world tax scenario, based on a number of different but confluent circumstances including, *inter alia*, potential inter-country tax imbalances coming from the perceived intention of governments to grasp income from borderless activities – such as the various manifestations on the digital economy – whether at residence or at the customers' jurisdictions (accord., Teijeiro, *Opening the Pandora's Box in the International Tax Field* (First Part), Tax Planning International Review, volume 42, #4, April 2015, p. 4 ss.).

The Final Report on BEPS Action 1 (*Addressing the Tax Challenges of the digital Economy*) and corresponding final reports, illustrate the direct tax challenges posed by the digital economy to market jurisdictions as well as the limited scope of the traditional PE concept as a tool to allocate income obtained therefrom to destination countries. The BEPS Report's response to the issues fell short to be a comprehensive approach and lacked a uniform recommendation to be implemented, somehow allowing inter-nation imbalances to rise. This is of course a significant issue in industrial and emerging countries as well.[18]

Approaches for a comprehensive response are indeed highlighted in Chapter 7 of the Final Report on Action 1 (i.e., the significant economic presence test, a withholding tax on digital transactions, and an equalization levy) but none was adopted nor uniformly recommended. Moreover, the main features of the three options were foremost meagerly described, so the application at the national level might show great variances, as the already started domestication process in selected jurisdictions shows.[19]

The significant economic presence test would create a taxable presence at the market jurisdiction on the basis of factors that evidence a purposeful and sustained interaction with the economy of that country via technology and other automated tools, such as a local domain name and a local website or digital platform, availability of a local payment option; or even user-based factors, including monthly active users (MAU) in the country, the regular conclusion of online contracts with resident users, and the volume of digital content collected from resident users and customers.[20]

As anticipated, an option contemplated in the final report is a standalone gross-basis final withholding tax on digital transactions, i.e., payments to nonresident providers of goods and services ordered online (digital sales transactions), under certain specific conditions.[21] This alternative raises a number of questions, including

---

18. Back in 2015, and pending the appearance of the final Reports, I had also observed that should the BEPS Project failed at the end to impose uniform principles on the taxation of the digital economy, chances were certain that countries would attempt to stretch source rules and business presence tests beyond the application of the traditional PE concept, or even depart completely from it to try alternative paths for taxation such as formulary apportionment or destination-based corporate tax, just to mention a couple of them. (Accord. Teijeiro, *id.* note 1, (Third Part), Tax Planning International Review, volume 42, #6, June 2015, at pp. 9–10). Following the release of the Final Report on Action 1, fears concerning future unilateral and uncoordinated country responses that might lead to jurisdictional overlaps and cascade taxation in the digital economy area deepened.
19. Although the work on the digital economy taxation will continue, meaningful revisions of the alternative options should not be expected before 2020; this is a period long enough to observe the appearance of diverging and even contradicting experiments at the national level.
20. absent the physical presence requirement, proper of the *brick and mortar* traditional businesses, the test is more close to Anglo-Saxon concepts such as *trade or business* or *doing business in* (as opposed to doing business with) of the U.S. and U.K. domestic tax systems, respectively. The report also recommended that the digital and user-based factors (to be chosen in accordance with the features and characteristics of the particular market) be also combined with a revenue factor, i.e., revenues obtained from remote transactions into the country in excess of a revenue threshold, in order to ensure that only cases of significant economic presence are covered.
21. In this case the definition of the transaction covered, as well as of the definition of the local collecting agent [e.g., the customer (for B2B or B2G transactions) or a third-party payment processing intermediary (for B2C transactions)] are crucial design element to be considered.

that: (i) direct taxation of foreign automated internet sales and services might be deemed to lack sufficient nexus with the taxing jurisdiction, unless a significant economic presence is detected, (ii) the market jurisdiction may consider income from foreign sales of tangible goods and/or foreign services into the country to be foreign source income, in which case taxation of remote online similar sales and services would be incoherent with the treatment afforded to traditional inbound sale and service income; and (iii) a withholding tax on digital transactions from abroad might conflict with treaty law commitments (particularly the treatment of business income).

Based on the foregoing, The U.K. Diverged Profit Tax (DPT) was designed as a levy which is applied separately from the income tax, and, hence, aimed at bypassing challenges coming from the fact that income tax treaty rules would still treat income from inbound sales and services as foreign source (as well as EU law – applicable at the time – and trade obligations).[22]

The U.K. DPT standalone gross-basis final withholding tax on digital transactions still raises serious doubts on its international legitimacy: Is it enough to change the *nomen iuris* of a tax and resort to a fictional source rule (a SAAR or deemed PE) to go beyond business income jurisdictional principles under international treaty law? Is it international tax jurisdiction on business income a concept extendable beyond the traditional carved-in-stone PE paradigm, which has remained untouched even under the OECD-G20 BEPS Project? Is the U.K. DPT a manifest evidence that the BEPS' outcome on the taxation of the digital economy fell short to address the inherent international tax issues?

The third and final alternative presented by the Final Report on BEPS Action 1 was the creation of an equalization levy, e.g., under the form of an excise tax applied if and when it is determined the existence of a significant economic presence, or on all remote sales transactions entered into with customers in a market jurisdiction.

An example of this tool is the Indian 6% equalization tax that came into effect on June 1, 2016; the tax was conceived as a levy separate from the income tax applicable on every consideration received by nonresidents from Indian tax residents for the provision of online advertisement, digital advertising space, or other similar online advertisement services. The levy is to be withheld by Indian residents from the consideration paid to nonresident service providers.[23]

Aside from the fact that the equalization levy, by its own nature, does not allow the crediting against income tax at the nonresident's home country (an issue shared with withholding taxes designed as separate levies such as the U.K. DPT), a much more

---

22. On DPT *see, inter alia*, Baker, *Diverted Profits Tax: A Partial Response*, British Tax Review, volume 2, 2015, pp. 167–171; Neidle, *The Diverted Profits Tax: Flawed by Design*, British Tax Review, volume 2, 2015, pp. 147–166; Self, *The UK's New Diverted Profits Tax: Compliance with EU Law*, Intertax, volume 43, no, 4, 2015, pp. 333–336.
23. Parekh and Wagh, International tax proposals in Budget 2016 – India's "Digital Tax" googly!, The Tax Booster; Teijeiro, *Detecting clouds before the Post-BEPS storm becomes uncontrolled*, and *Once more on a short-of-expectation BEPS outcome and the erratic domestication of a weak guidance: The case of the digital economy*, Kluwer International Tax Blog, March 30, and August 29, 2016, respectively; Gupta, *Equalisation Levy is not so equal*, August 13, 2016 Https://www.linkedIn.com/pulse/equalisation-levy-so-equal-ca-rohit-gupta-. Wagh, The Taxation of Digital Transactions in India: The New Equalization Levy, Bulletin IBFD, September 2016, p. 538 ss.

fundamental jurisdictional issue taints this levy and makes it highly controversial: It is a well-settled principle that international income tax jurisdiction may not be asserted on a legal fiction; and that is precisely how the levy functions when advertising expenses incurred by Indian residents are deemed a succedaneums of actual activity in India by the nonresident recipient of the payments.[24] In this context, the query is, again, whether just by changing the *nomen iuris* of the tax the levy is able to overcome an *ultra vires* taint under international general and treaty tax law.[25] As in the case of the U.K. DPT, profound doubts persist on whether these levies are easily legitimated under international jurisdictional principles.

Even assuming that, hypothetically, the equalization levy passes an income-type jurisdictional scrutiny, it is not hard to imagine the aggregate over-taxation that would result from the simultaneous application of similar levies by market jurisdictions, not to mention the potential overlap with VAT on the importation of services.

At this point, looking at all the difficulties inherent to the application of traditional jurisdictional principles to the taxation of income from the digital economy, one may well wonder whether it would not be better to start considering a migration to a destination-based corporate tax model, a still untested but highly attractive alternative to tax income from the digital economy.[26]

Meanwhile, unless until the taxation of the digital economy is reassessed, something that apparently will not happen until 2020, national conflicting experiments will be repeated without a meaningful, solid, and uniform conceptual basis, and, consequently, with grave consequences to the industry in terms of multiple, cascade taxation. Moreover, with the present lack of definitions, the expected rapid irruption of the emerging economies trying to grasp a wider basis from borderless digital economy income may end up in a worldwide tax chaos, with serious damages to the tax administrations in terms of harmful tax competition, and the business sector as well.

§6.05 FINAL COMMENTS

The adoption of full inclusion Brazilian-type CFC regimes encompassing foreign business income derived by controlled or affiliated entities in non-privileged jurisdictions (including treaty-partner jurisdictions); the indirect taxation of capital gains under Vodafone-like statutes and precedents; peculiar TP methods, such as the Sixth Method under its more aggressive variances, and digital economy national experiments based on BEPS's outcomes, are just a few relevant examples of how, by resorting to legal fictions, states try to enlarge the scope of their personal or economic nexus, or to

---

24. This principle was clearly stated by the Indian Supreme Court *in re Vodafone*, January 20, 2012.
25. The Report of the Committee on Taxation of E-Commerce (dated on February 2016, and prepared by the Committee on Taxation of E-Commerce formed by the Central Board of Direct Taxes, Department of Revenue, Ministry of Finance, Government of India), found no possible challenges on this basis.
26. *See* on point, Devereaux and de la Feria, *Designing and Implementing a Destination-Based Corporate Tax*, Oxford University Centre for business Taxation, WP 14/07, May, 2014; reproduced in Tax Notes International, May, 2015.

grasp taxable events and bases beyond their proper reach under well-settled international law rules and principles.

It is quite clear that Brazilian CFC rules have a scope of application that goes far beyond that of similar regimes around the world, and, most significantly, are ill-conceived since they apply regardless of the nature of the income obtained (not merely tainted income as commonly understood), or the level of taxation borne in the residence country of the foreign affiliate. In other words, the CFC rules are denaturalized as a legitimate mechanism to fight the use of foreign base companies, and as such, unlawfully disregard the separate legal and tax existence of corporate entities organized in accordance with the laws of the incorporation country. They are simply revenue-geared provisions aimed at taxing currently in the home country of the parent company, business income of foreign direct or indirect subsidiaries or related entities taxed abroad at comparable corporate income tax rates. Aside from the issue of whether these rules originate juridical or economic double taxation (OECD MC Commentaries' approach), it is undeniable that they imply extraterritorial taxation that confronts one of the basic paradigms of contemporaneous international treaty taxation (i.e., the recognition of the separate personality of legal entities, and the exclusive allocation of business income to the residence state, in the absence of a PE situated in the source state). Moreover, by disregarding the foreign legal entity's separate existence without a fundamental reason, CFC rules in Brazil conspire against the exercise of fiscal sovereignty by third states under international law. The proliferation of these regimes by unilateral initiatives, if it ever occurs, might alter significantly the global jurisdictional balance and inter-nation equity among states.

Vodafone-type indirect taxation of capital gains is an *ultra vires* exercise of tax jurisdiction based on a legal fiction that does not warrant the minimum link or nexus required by international law to tax nonresident aliens. Unfortunately, and despite Vodafone and subsequent judicial developments in India curtailing this trend, indirect taxation has been highly contagious and has spread fast as demonstrated by the incorporation of similar rules in China, Israel, as well as in Chile and Peru in the Latin American region. Further proliferation is still to be expected since the use of techniques to avoid the payment of taxes when assets situated in emerging economies are sold is a common concern, as evidenced in the report on the impact of BEPS in low-income countries. However, it would be highly advisable that source countries resort to sham doctrines, domestic GAARs, or even SAARs, to combat the excesses, setting aside initiatives which, as conceived (i.e., applied regardless of the evidence of a tax avoidance purposes), contravene longstanding undisputable jurisdictional principles, with foreseeable detrimental global economic effects (double taxation).[27]

The TP Sixth Method on commodities exports, which under certain conditions allow the state of the exporter to tax notional income (on account of or substitute for income presumably derived by foreign trading entities in a commercialization chain), create potential economic double taxation beyond the reach of correlative adjustments allowed under Article 9 of DTTs. If, with the purpose of overcoming the lack of

---

27. Fortunately, the recent tax reform passed in Colombia (Law 1819, dated December 29, 2016) did not follow the trend initiated in Latin America by Peru and Chile.

comparables in low-income countries, some form of the Sixth Method is finally adopted under BEPS for low-income countries, it would be most desirable that the form to be adopted be in line with Actions 8–10 final recommendations which set aside the unwarranted (more aggressive) existing national versions of the method, and, as a general rule, simply endorsed to use transparent market prices as of the date of execution of the transactions.

Unless until the taxation of the digital economy is reassessed, something that apparently will not happen until 2020, national conflicting experiments will be repeated without a meaningful, solid, and uniform conceptual and legal basis, and, consequently, with grave consequences to the economic sector in terms of multiple, cascade taxation. Moreover, the forthcoming irruption in the field of emerging economies may end up in a worldwide tax chaos of unilateral diverging measures and countermeasures.

This is an area of taxation where there is still time to react and reconsider a more precise and uniform response aligned with longstanding international law jurisdictional principles which, at the same time, preserves the industry from the risks of multiple layers of taxation (the otherwise undesired result under the current post-BEPS status). The proposed 2020 revision should be speed up as much as possible and meanwhile it would be highly desirable to reach a commitment under the umbrella of G20/OECD inclusive framework not to advance with digital economy domestic taxation until the proposed revision process is terminated and a new, superseding outcome is released.

Examples of jurisdictional excesses may be replicated in a number of areas and by the use of different techniques in developing economies, which are notably and justifiably concerned by practices that might erode the income tax basis at source. These include creative interpretations of ambiguous texts of DTTs to calculate foreign technical services otherwise ruled by Article 7, or the royalty clause (Article 12), as it is the case in Brazil and Colombia; defensive domestic source rules on technical services broadly construed by the courts to tax services rendered from abroad in the place of destination or utilization (source state), relegating the application of a competing rule taxing services income generally in the place of performance;[28] and aggressive GAARs and SAARs on cross-the-border transactions, as well as increased source-source conflicts because of the choosing of the financial or economic source criteria solely based on revenue-collection interest without a reasonably concerted basis.

In a highly unstable tax world, the G20/OECD BEPS initiative in its current implementation stage acquire a huge dimension and a decisive aligning influence not only to domesticate BEPS new paradigms but to preserve basic international jurisdictional paradigms, including: (i) minimum (actual) connection requirement to assert jurisdiction over nonresidents; (ii) attribution of the income basis on the grounds of

---

28. This is the case in Argentina where a special rule taxing technical services at destination (Art. 12, ITL), is construed by the courts to embrace all type of services; see Supreme Court of justice, in *Hidroeléctrica El Chocón S.A. c/ DGI*, dated September 9, 2013 (http://sjconsulta.csjn.gov.ar/sjconsulta/documentos/verUnicoDocumentoLink.html?idAnalisis=704276).

residence and source; (ii) recognition of the juridical separate personality of legal entities, and the exclusive allocation of business income to the residence state absent a PE in the source state; and (iii) the arm's length principle and the application of correcting transfer pricing adjustments, if and when required. In the field of international tax jurisdiction, breaking apart from longstanding, universally shared principles might lead to cascading taxation with catastrophic effects on trade and investments.

CHAPTER 7
Taxing the Consumption of Digital Goods

Aleksandra Bal

§7.01 INTRODUCTION

A major characteristic of the modern economy is its shift to the intangible. Dematerialized content has become a major source of economic value, transforming the way companies are organized and transactions carried out. Last century witnessed the emergence of new business models and markets centred around the concept of digital goods.

In simple terms, digital goods are goods that can be fully expressed in electronic format so that their creation, transfer and consumption can be executed based on an electronic infrastructure such as the Internet.[1] They possess some characteristics that distinguish them from traditional physical goods. They are indestructible, easily transmutable and cheaply reproducible. The majority of them are experience goods, meaning that their quality can be evaluated only after usage.

Digital goods have placed strains on consumption taxes throughout the world. The evolution of technology has dramatically increased the ability of private consumers to shop online and the ability of businesses to sell to consumers around the world without the need to be present physically in the consumer's country. As consumption taxes were conceived at the time when commerce meant local traders selling products to consumers in their brick-and-mortar shops, technological advances and the proliferation of digital goods have made it necessary to revisit the existing rules.

---

1. C. Loebbecke, *Digital Goods: An Economic Perspecitve*, available at: http://www.mtm.uni-koeln. de/team-loebbecke-publications-book-chapters/Chapt-024-2002-%20Digital%20Goods%20An%2 0Economic%20Perspective-scan.pdf; S. Choi, D. Stahl & A. Whinston, *The Economics of Electronic Commerce*, ch. 2 (Macmillan Technical Publishing 1997); T. Rayna, *Understanding the Challenges of the Digital Economy: The Nature of Digital Goods*, available at: http://comstrat.org/fic/revue _telech/816/CS71_RAYNA.pdf.

Digital goods were the subject of many initiatives undertaken at both international and national levels in the last few years. The international debate in respect of taxation issues arising from electronic commerce was largely driven by the Organisation for Economic Co-operation and Development (OECD's) Committee on Fiscal Affairs (CFA). OECD's first major policy document was the framework for the taxation of electronic commerce, which was presented at the Ottawa conference in October 1998.[2] The framework was followed by several implementing guidelines.[3] More recently, OECD recognized jurisdictional challenges of the digital economy in its Base Erosion and Profit Shifting (BEPS) initiative.[4] BEPS Action 1 called upon the examination of 'the application of source rules, and how to ensure the effective collection of VAT/GST with respect to the cross-border supply of digital goods and services'.[5] The Consolidated Value Added Tax / Goods and Services Tax (VAT/GST) Guidelines, adopted by the OECD member countries in November 2015, set the international standard for the VAT treatment of cross-border transactions in intangibles by making recommendations regarding their place of supply[6] and collection mechanisms.[7] OECD recommended that where it is not necessary for the supplier and customer to be in the

---

2. OECD, *A Borderless World: Realizing the Potential of Global Electronic Commerce* (OECD 1998). The Ottawa Report (1998) concluded that the same principles that governments apply to the taxation of conventional commerce should apply to electronic commerce. These principles included the well-known tax policy concepts of neutrality, efficiency, certainty, simplicity, effectiveness, fairness and flexibility. New legislative measures were not precluded, provided that they were intended to assist in the application of the existing taxation principles and not to impose a discriminatory tax treatment of electronic commerce transactions. The Ottawa Report (1998) recommended treating the supply of digitized products as a supply of services and to tax it in the country of consumption. International consensus had to be sought on the circumstances under which supplies were held to be consumed in a jurisdiction. Countries were advised to examine the use of reverse charge mechanism, self-assessment or other equivalent mechanisms for digital supplies acquired from suppliers outside the country.
3. OECD, *Report by the Consumption Tax Technical Advisory Group* (OECD 2000); OECD, *Report by the Technology Technical Advisory Group* (OECD 2000); OECD, *Taxation and Electronic Commerce: Implementation the Ottawa Taxation Framework Conditions* (OECD 2001); OECD, *Consumption Tax Aspects of Electronic Commerce* (OECD 2001).
4. OECD, *Action Plan on Base Erosion and Profit Shifting* (OECD 2013). The fundamental idea behind the BEPS project was concerns about multinational enterprises (MNEs) being able to avoid tax by artificially separating income from activities that generate it. The BEPS Action Plan set out 15 Actions to counteract commonly employed BEPS strategies and designated tax challenges of the digital economy as Action 1. On 24 March 2014, the OECD published a discussion draft on Action 1 and on 16 September 2014 the final report was released.
5. OECD, *Addressing the Tax Challenges of the Digital Economy. Action 1: 2014 Deliverable* (2014), available at: www.oecd.org/tax/addressing-the-tax-challenges-of-the-digital-economy-97892642 18789-en.htm.
6. The terms 'place of supply' and 'place of taxation' are often used interchangeably. However, in some tax systems (e.g., in New Zealand), determining the place of supply is the first step in determining the place of taxation. The place of supply determines which jurisdiction has the right to tax, whereas the place of taxation is the country where the tax is levied. In the European Union, a two-step approach is applied to the supply of goods: in the case of exports, the exporting country is the place of supply but the place of taxation is somewhere else since in the exporting country the supply is zero rated. For services, a one-step approach applies, i.e., the place of supply is equivalent to the place of taxation. *See* A. Cockfield et al., *Taxing Global Digital Commerce* p. 244 (Kluwer 2013).
7. OECD, *International VAT/GST Guidelines* (OECD 2015).

Chapter 7: Taxing the Consumption of Digital Goods §7.02[A]

same location when the services are supplied, the jurisdiction in which the customer has his usual residence should have taxing rights. In order to collect GST on these supplies, non-resident suppliers should be required to register and file GST returns in the jurisdiction of the consumer's usual residence. The OECD's approach has been followed by many jurisdictions, such as Member States of the European Union (EU),[8] Norway, South Korea, Japan, Switzerland, South Africa and New Zealand. Australia is currently in the process of introducing similar rules.

The aim of this chapter is to investigate the concept of digital goods and to examine what can be interfered about the taxation of digital goods from the concept of sovereignty.[9] Section §7.02 provides the necessary context and briefly discusses the rules applicable to the taxation of digital goods in the EU, Australia and New Zealand. Section §7.03 proceeds with a more detailed examination of the concept of digital goods. Section §7.04 defines the concept of sovereignty and examines how it is affected by supplies of digital goods. The final section concludes.

§7.02 LEGAL FRAMEWORK

[A] European Union

EU VAT is levied on supplies of goods and services by a taxable person acting as such. A supply of goods is defined as the transfer of the right to dispose of tangible property as owner.[10] A supply of services is defined residually as any transaction which is not a supply of goods.[11] An important category of services are electronically supplied services (commonly referred to as 'digital supplies' or 'online services'). They are defined as services delivered over the Internet or an electronic network, the nature of which renders their supply essentially automated, involving minimum human intervention and impossible in the absence of information technology.[12]

---

8. The European Union was the pioneer of adopting the destination-based taxation of business-to-consumer supplies of services and introducing simplified registration mechanisms. Originally, many supplies of services were subject to VAT at origin, i.e., in the Member State where the service provider was established. This was a logical solution at the time when most services were provided domestically. Due to the rapid increase in the volume of cross-border services, it was recognized that the origin-based approach distorted competition in favour of business activity in low-tax countries. To increase the application of the destination principle, the European Union introduced a major amendment to the place-of-supply rules in 2008 (Council Directive 2008/8/EC of 12 February 2008 amending Directive 2006/112/EC as regards the place of supply of services, OJ L 44 (2008)). This reform, commonly referred to as the 'VAT Package', implemented changes to the rules on the place of taxation of services over the period 2010–2015.
9. This chapter focuses on the taxation of business-to-consumer (B2C) supplies as business-to-business (B2B) supplies do not involve final consumption. Since only private individuals are capable of having a personal sphere, only they can be engaged in consumption. Businesses do not have personal needs; they purchase and use goods but do not consume them.
10. Article 14(1) Council Directive 2006/112/EC of 28 November 2006 on the common system of value added tax, OJ L347/1 (2006) (hereinafter referred to as the VAT Directive (2006/112).
11. Article 24 VAT Directive (2006/112).
12. Article 7(1) VAT Implementing Regulation (282/2011).

Under the place-of-supply rules applicable as from 1 January 2015, all supplies of electronic services are subject to the VAT rules of the country of the customer.[13] In order to establish who has to account for the VAT due, in EU scenarios, it is necessary to distinguish between business-to-business (B2B) and business-to-consumer (B2C) transactions. In the EU, the supplier may regard his customer as a business (taxable person) if the customer has communicated his VAT identification number to him and the supplier has verified its validity or if the customer has demonstrated that he is in the process of registering for VAT.[14] If the customer is located outside the EU, his status is not relevant since the supply is outside the scope of EU VAT.

The reverse charge mechanism[15] applies to cross-border supplies to businesses (i.e., the VAT liability is shifted to the customer who accounts for VAT on the supply in his VAT return), whereas a simplified registration mechanism (One Stop Shop (OSS)/Mini One Stop Shop (MOSS) scheme) may be used in respect of cross-border supplies of electronic services to EU final consumers. In the latter case, since the reverse charge cannot be applied, the supplier must determine where his customers are established, have a permanent address or usually reside in order to apply the correct VAT rate.[16] To assist suppliers with the identification of the location of their non-taxable customer, the Commission has issued a detailed regulatory framework consisting of the VAT Implementing Regulation (282/2011), which establishes a number of

---

13. Article 44 VAT Directive (2006/112) (the default place-of-supply rule for B2B services), Arts 58 and 59 VAT Directive (2006/112) (for supplies to non-taxable persons). However, under Art. 59a of the VAT Directive (2006/112), Member States may exercise the option of levying VAT where consumption actually occurs. A 'use and enjoyment' clause may be applied by Member States to electronic services supplied by EU suppliers to both private and business customers. It allows Member States to consider that services supplied within their territory or in third countries are supplied, respectively, outside the European Union or within their territory if this is where those services are effectively used and enjoyed.
14. Article 18(1) Council Implementing Regulation 282/2011 of 15 March 2011 laying down implementing measures for Directive 2006/112/EC on the common system of value added tax, OJ L77/1 (2011), as amended by Council Implementing Regulation (EU) 1042/2013 of 7 October 2013 amending Implementing Regulation (EU) 282/2011 as regards the place of supply of services, OJ L284 (2013). The amended version of the Council Implementing Regulation 282/2011 is hereinafter referred to as the VAT Implementing Regulation (282/2011).

    According to Art. 18(2) of the VAT Implementing Regulation (282/2011), if no VAT identification number has been communicated, the supplier *may* regard his customer as a non-taxable person, irrespective of any information to the contrary. The purpose of this provision is to provide certainty for the supplier as to the status of the customer by disregarding information other than the VAT identification number. The use of 'may' makes it optional for the supplier to use this provision. If the supplier does not know the VAT identification number of the customer but has other evidence to substantiate his status as a taxable person, the supplier may issue an invoice without VAT and apply the reverse charge mechanism. In such a scenario, he assumes the risk for the incorrect status determination and will be held liable for VAT payment if his determination turns out to be wrong.
15. Article 196 VAT Directive (2006/112).
16. The term 'established' refers to non-registered legal persons and the terms 'permanent address' and 'usual residence' refer to non-taxable natural persons. A permanent address of a natural person is the address entered in the population or similar register, or the address indicated by that person to the relevant tax authorities, unless there is evidence that this address does not reflect reality. The place where a natural person usually resides is the place where that natural person usually lives as a result of personal and occupational ties. Where the occupational ties are in a country different from that of the personal ties, or where no occupational ties exist, the place

rebuttable presumptions and an evidence rule, supplemented by more detailed explanations in the non-binding Explanatory Notes.[17] Under the presumptions laid down in the VAT Implementing Regulation (282/2011), electronic services that are provided at, for example, a Wi-Fi hot spot, an Internet café, a restaurant or a hotel lobby, are presumed to be supplied at those places.[18] Also, non-taxable persons are presumed to be established or resident at the place of installation of the fixed landline through which they receive the services or in the country whose code is mentioned on the SIM card when they receive the services through a mobile network.[19] According to the evidence rule, it is assumed that the customer is established at the place identified on the basis of two items of non-contradictory evidence (e.g., billing address, bank details, IP address or other commercially relevant information).[20]

The OSS scheme was introduced on 1 July 2003 to avoid a situation in which, for the purpose of having to account for VAT on B2C electronic services in a maximum of twenty-eight Member States, non-EU suppliers must be registered in all of those Member States. Under this scheme, the non-EU supplier can register and account for VAT in a single Member State, but applies the VAT rate of the customer's Member State.[21] EU suppliers of electronic services to EU final consumers have the option to use a similar arrangement (the MOSS), i.e., to register and remit VAT only in the Member State of their establishment. The MOSS regime is optional; however, a taxable person that chooses to use the scheme must apply it in all relevant Member States. The scheme cannot be applied to supplies of electronic services in the Member State where the taxable person is established; such supplies must be declared in the domestic VAT return.

In certain circumstances, responsibility for the collection and remittance of VAT on supplies of electronic services may be shifted from the supplier to the operator. Article 9a(1) of the VAT Implementing Regulation (282/2011) introduces a rebuttable presumption that a taxable person who takes part in the supply of electronic services is acting in his own name but on behalf of the provider of those services. This means that the intermediary party is deemed to act as a 'commissionaire', i.e., to have received and supplied the services itself.[22] The presumption does not apply to taxable persons who solely provide payment-processing services (e.g., credit card companies).[23] Shifting the responsibility for VAT liability to platform operators and

---

of usual residence shall be determined by personal ties that show close links between the natural person and a place where he is living (Arts 12 and 13 VAT Implementing Regulation (282/2011)).

17. See European Commission, *Explanatory Notes on the EU VAT Changes to the Place of Supply of Telecommunications, Broadcasting and Electronic Services That Enter into Force in 2015* (3 April 2014).
18. Article 24a VAT Implementing Regulation (282/2011).
19. Article 24b VAT Implementing Regulation (282/2011).
20. Article 24d and 24f VAT Implementing Regulation (282/2011).
21. The One Stop Shop Scheme cannot be used by non-EU suppliers that are already registered in the European Union (e.g., because they receive services that are effectively used and enjoyed in a Member State or perform intra-Community supplies of goods). See Art. 358a VAT Directive (2006/112).
22. For commissionaire arrangements, see Art. 28 VAT Directive (2006/112).
23. Article 9a(3) VAT Implementing Regulation (282/2011).

distributors is aimed at minimizing compliance costs. Platform operators typically have greater knowledge about their customer base, are larger in scale and generally are better able to comply with regulatory requirements in the countries in which their distribution services are available than providers of electronic content that is distributed via online platforms.

[B] Australia

Australian GST law does not adopt the usual practice of dividing taxable supplies into supplies of goods and services. A supply is defined to mean 'any form of supply whatsoever'.[24] The objects of supplies are referred to as things.[25] For cross-border purposes, things are divided into 'goods', 'real property' and everything else. To determine the place of taxation, it first needs to be considered whether a supply is 'connected with Australia'.[26] If a supply is connected with Australia, the place of taxation can still be abroad due to the application of the rules on GST-free exports and consumption outside Australia. For supplies not connected with Australia, the supply will still be taxed in Australia if it is considered an inbound service or importation of goods.

Under current Australian law, things (which are not goods or real property) imported by Australian consumers are not subject to Australian GST. Thus, the consumption of digital products provided by non-resident suppliers is not currently caught by the GST rules. This results in forgone GST revenue and places domestic businesses, which generally have to charge and remit GST on digital products and services they provide to Australian consumers, at a tax disadvantage compared to overseas businesses.

In the 2015–2016 Budget, the Government announced that it would extend GST to cross-border supplies of digital products and other services imported by consumers with effect from 1 July 2017 (the proposal was frequently referred to as a 'Netflix tax' as it was made after Netflix started providing services to Australian consumers without charging GST).[27] Legislation giving effect to this measure (Tax and Superannuation Laws Amendment (2016 Measures No. 1) Act 2016) received Royal Assent on 5 May 2016. The amendments to the Australian law are broadly modelled on similar rules currently in operation in the EU.

Under the new law, overseas companies selling digital products and other services will be required to register, collect and remit GST on their sales to Australian

---

24. Section 9-10(1) GST Act 1999.
25. A 'thing' is defined as 'anything that can be supplies or imported'. Section 195-1 GST Act 1999.
26. Where the term 'Australia' is used, it refers to the 'indirect tax zone' as defined in section 195-1 of the GST Act 1999. With effect from 1 July 2015, the term 'Australia' has been replaced in nearly all instances within the GST legislation with the term 'indirect tax zone'. The change has been made by the Treasury Legislation Amendment (Repeal Day) Act 2015. 'Indirect tax zone' means Australia, but does not include external territories and certain offshore areas.
27. http://www.budget.gov.au/2015-16/content/bp2/download/BP2_consolidated.pdf.

consumers. GST will not only be imposed on inbound intangible consumer supplies,[28] such as digital content, games and software, but will also extend to consultancy and professional services performed offshore for customers in Australia. Overseas entities will be able to elect to have limited registration for GST purposes without being able to access input tax credits. Only supplies made to consumers will be caught: B2B transactions will not be affected by the new rules. The new law requires suppliers to take reasonable steps to ascertain whether the recipients of their supplies are Australian consumers. After taking those steps, the suppliers must reasonably believe that their customers are Australian customers. The new law recognizes that a supplier should be able to rely on its existing business systems and processes for forming this conclusion.

In some circumstances, responsibility for GST liability that arises under the new law may be shifted from the supplier to the operator of an electronic distribution service for services provided through the electronic distribution service he operates. This may happen if the operator controls any of the key elements of the supply, such as delivery, charging or terms and conditions. As a result of being treated as making the supply, the operator will be liable for the GST on the supply and the supply will be included in his GST turnover for all purposes, including whether they are required to be registered for GST.

[C] New Zealand

In New Zealand, supplies of goods and services as well as importation are subject to GST.[29] The concept of goods includes both tangible and intangible property as it is defined to mean 'all kinds of personal and real property' except money and choses in action. Services are defined by reference to what is not goods.[30] To determine the place of taxation, New Zealand applies different rules for resident and non-resident suppliers. All supplies by residents are considered to take place in New Zealand but the zero-rating rules are used to remove outbound and foreign supplies from the tax net. In contrast, supplies by non-residents are considered to take place outside New Zealand and the reverse charge mechanism for imported services is used to ensure that services consumed within New Zealand are subject to tax there. Until 1 October 2016, digital services provided by non-residents to New Zealand consumers were not subject to tax in New Zealand.

As from 1 October 2016, offshore suppliers providing cross-border remote services to New Zealand resident consumers are required to register and charge GST on those supplies.[31] The non-resident supplier must treat a customer as a New Zealand resident on the basis of two non-conflicting pieces of evidence that support the

---

28. A supply is an inbound intangible consumer supply if it is a supply of anything other than goods or real property that is not done wholly in the indirect tax zone or made through an enterprise the supplier carries on in the indirect tax zone.
29. Section 8(1) and 12(1) GST Act 1985.
30. Section 2(1) GST Act 1985.
31. Taxation (Residential Land Withholding Tax, GST on Online Services, and Student Loans) Act 2016.

conclusion the person is resident in New Zealand.[32] Non-resident suppliers are required to register and file GST returns when their supplies of remote services to New Zealand consumers exceed NZD 60,000 in a twelve-month period. Supplies to New Zealand GST-registered businesses only count towards this threshold if the parties agree that the supply is zero-rated. A simplified 'pay-only' registration system has been made available to offshore suppliers who are only required to return GST and who do not have any New Zealand GST costs to claim back. When certain conditions are satisfied, operators of electronic marketplaces (such as an app store) are required to register and return GST on supplies made through the marketplace instead of the underlying supplier.

§7.03 THE CONCEPT OF DIGITAL GOODS

[A] Introductory Remarks

The key feature of the digital economy is the digitalization of previously existing goods and the development of new purely digital goods. Digital goods are intangible goods that are stored, delivered and used in electronic format. They are delivered to customers through e-mail or downloaded from the Internet.

There is a large body of literature on the taxation of the digital economy and electronic commerce, evaluating different national and international approaches and searching for best practices.[33] However, hardly any publication provides a detailed examination of the characteristics of digital goods. Since sound policy rules can be developed once the underlying phenomenon is properly understood, this section discusses the concept of digital goods and its use for consumption tax purposes in the EU, Australia and New Zealand.

[B] General Definition

The main characteristics of digital goods are indestructibility, easy reproducibility and transmutability.[34] Digital goods are indestructible, i.e., they are not subject to wearing

---

32. The items of evidence include: the person's billing address; the internet protocol (IP) address of the device used by the person or another geo-location method; the person's bank details, including the account the person uses for payment or the billing address held by the bank; the mobile country code (MCC) of the international mobile subscriber identity (IMSI) stored on the subscriber identity module (SIM) card used by the person; the location of the person's fixed landline through which the service is supplied to them; and other commercially relevant information.
33. For example, R.L. Doernberg et al., *Electronic Commerce and Multijurisdictional Taxation* (Kluwer Law International 2001); B. Westberg, *Cross-border Taxation of E-commerce* (IBFD 2002); R.L. Doernberg & L. Hinnekens, *Electronic Commerce and International Taxation* (Kluwer Law International 1999); S. Basu, *Global Perspectives on E-commerce Taxation Law* (Aldershot Ashgate 2007); R.A. Westin, *International Taxation of Electronic Commerce* (Kluwer Law International 2007); A. Cockfield et al., *Taxing Global Digital Commerce* (Kluwer 2013).
34. This section is based on Loebbecke, *supra* n. 1; Choi, *supra* n. 1 and Rayna, *supra* n. 1.

out from usage. The quality of a digital product does not degrade no matter how long or how often it is used. Although the media used to store and distribute digital goods are prone to failure and have a finite life expectancy, digital goods can last forever. Although the creation of digital goods may require high fixed costs, they can be subsequently replicated at no cost and transferred without delay to almost everywhere. Transmutability means that the content of digital products can be changed instantly. Such goods can be customized and manipulated more easily than physical goods. Given the high degree of customizability, consumers are frequently involved in the production of digital goods, for example, by making decisions about the content, mode of display or transformation.

Digital goods are frequently classified as public goods. Public goods share two important properties: they are both non-rival in consumption and non-excludable in usage. A good is non-rival in consumption if the consumption activity of each person does not decrease the quantity of good available in the economy. As digital goods can be copied without any loss of quality at very low costs, the consumption activity of one consumer does not decrease the potential consumption of other consumers. A good is non-excludable if no one can be prevented from consuming it. Although producers of digital goods initially have the ability to directly exclude certain consumers (e.g. by preventing downloads if people do not pay) and enforce copyright by legal means, it proves to be more and more difficult to prevent unauthorized persons from using digital products. Anybody owning a digital good becomes a potential supplier of this good. As the number of people owning the good grows, the number of consumers able to obtain the good from other consumers rather than from the producer rises.

Based on the customer's ability to judge the value of a product, goods are divided into search and experience goods. The quality of search goods can be determined without actually using them. In contrast, the value of experience goods cannot be determined prior to purchase. The fact that digital goods are experience goods is related to their content. Although consumers can acquire sufficient information on the technical characteristics of digital goods without experiencing them, the value obtained from these attributes remains unknown or uncertain. Moreover, the value of the content of some digital goods is so subjective that it is impossible for consumers to obtain full information on the goods without experiencing them.

Based on the characteristics, the following conclusions can be drawn:

- since digital goods are indestructible, they can be consumed multiple times ('unlimited consumption');
- since digital goods are easily transferable and movable, consumption follows the consumer who can use them anywhere ('multiple destination');
- digital goods can be re-produced and sold by consumers whose activity of reproducing and distributing digital goods may easily qualify as an entrepreneurial one.

[C] Definition for Indirect Tax Purposes

The OECD VAT/GST Guidelines do not explicitly mention digital goods but apply a broad definition of internationally traded services and intangibles. They define a supply of services or intangibles as a supply where one party does something for, or gives something (other than something tangible) to, another party or refrains from doing something for another party, for consideration.[35] The previous OECD reports also focused on a broad category of cross-border supplies of services and intangible property capable of delivery from a remote location.[36]

Some countries follow the OECD approach and do not provide for detailed definitions of digital goods. In New Zealand, a broad definition of remote services is used for the purposes of taxing supplies made by overseas businesses to New Zealand consumers. A remote service is defined as a 'service where, at the time of the performance of the service, there is no necessary connection between the physical location of the recipient and the place of physical performance.' Non-digital services, such as consulting, accounting and legal services, can also be supplied as remote services. Australia does not distinguish a separate category of digital goods (or electronic services) either but applies uniform rules to all inbound intangible consumer supplies, which are defined as supplies of anything other than goods or real property that are not done wholly in the indirect tax zone or made through an enterprise the supplier carries on in the indirect tax zone.

The EU took a different approach. Under EU VAT legislation, digital goods (called 'electronically supplied services' for VAT purposes) are a separate category of services. They are defined as services delivered over the Internet or an electronic network, the nature of which renders their supply essentially automated, involving minimum human intervention and impossible in the absence of information technology.[37] A non-exhaustive list of those services provided in the VAT Implementing Regulation (282/2011) includes, *inter alia*, the supply of digitized products (movies, music, games), services automatically generated from a computer via the Internet or an electronic network, in response to specific data input by the recipient, Internet Service Packages (ISP) of information in which the telecommunications component forms an ancillary and subordinate part, website hosting, remote systems administration, online data warehousing, accessing the digitized content of books and other electronic publications, the provision of advertising space, use of search engines and Internet directories and automated distance teaching (except where the Internet or similar electronic network is used as a tool simply for communication between the teacher and student).[38]

The correct classification of goods or services for EU VAT purposes is extremely important as it determines the applicable place-of-supply rules, VAT rates and exemptions. For example, the VAT Directive (2006/112) allows for the application of reduced

---

35. VAT/GST Guidelines, *supra* n. 7, at p. 27.
36. For example, OECD, *Consumption Tax Aspects of Electronic Commerce* p. 10 (OECD 2001).
37. Article 7(1) VAT Implementing Regulation (282/2011).
38. Article 7(2) and Annex 1 VAT Implementing Regulation (282/2011).

Chapter 7: Taxing the Consumption of Digital Goods §7.03[C]

rates to 'books on all physical means of support'. However, books in a digitalized format cannot benefit from a reduced VAT rate as 'the reduced rates shall not apply to electronically supplied services'.[39]

The VAT treatment of books and e-books has been the subject of a lively debate in the EU. Despite the clear wording of the VAT Directive (2006/112), France and Luxembourg started applying the reduced rate to electronic books, giving publishers established in those countries an enormous commercial advantage over their competitors. This was so because, until 31 December 2014, supplies of electronic services to final consumers were governed by the VAT law of the country of the supplier. Both countries claimed that the electronic format was an alternative physical means of support and that a different treatment of books and e-books violated the principle of neutrality. The European Commission started an infringement procedure against both countries and the Court of Justice of the European Union (CJEU) ruled in favour of the Commission, stating that the supply of electronic books cannot be subject to the reduced rate.[40]

On 11 September 2014, the CJEU gave its decision in *K Oy* (Case C-219/13) regarding the question of whether or not reduced rates for printed books should also be applied to books published on another physical medium (i.e., books sold on CD-ROM or USB sticks).[41] The case was referred to the CJEU by the Finnish Supreme Administrative Court and the issue raised was whether this apparently different treatment of similar products complied with the principle of fiscal neutrality. The CJEU ruled that it is up to national courts to decide whether printed books and books on other physical mediums are sufficiently different from each other to justify the application of a reduced rate of VAT to one but not the other. National courts have to assess the issue from the point of view of an 'average consumer'. Thus, if a national court concludes that printed books and books on other means of support achieve substantially the same purpose from the perspective of an average consumer in that Member State, then the court will have no choice but to rule that the same VAT treatment must be applied to both.

In her decision of 8 September 2016,[42] in the *RPO* case (C-390/15), Advocate General Juliane Kokott concluded that the different treatment of digital publications and those supplied on physical means of support does not amount to an infringement of the principle of equal treatment. It is up to the EU legislature, not the Court of Justice, to assess whether these publications are in competition with each other.

Between July and September 2016, the European Commission held an open public consultation on the application of reduced VAT rates to electronically supplied

---

39. Article 98(2) VAT Directive (2006/112). It is interesting to observe that the European Union applies higher tax rates to digital goods than to their equivalent in printed form, whereas digital goods are treated more favourably than their printed counterparts in the United States (i.e., they are not subject to tax in many states and their inter-state supply escapes taxation if the seller lacks nexus in the state of the recipient).
40. CJEU, 5 March 2015, Case C-479/13, *European Commission v. French Republic* and CJEU, 5 March 2015, Case C-502/13, *European Commission v. Grand Duchy of Luxemburg*.
41. CJEU, 11 September 2014, Case C-219/13, *K Oy v. Veronsaajien oikeudenvalvontayksikkö, Valtiovarainministeriö*.
42. AG Opinion, 8 September 2016, Case C-390/15, *Rzecznik Praw Obywatelskich (RPO)*.

publications. Some 858 stakeholders responded to the consultation, whereby 94% of the respondents agreed that Member States should be allowed to apply a reduced VAT rate to e-books and 88% of the respondents agreed that Member States should be allowed to apply a reduced VAT rate to e-newspapers and e-periodicals.[43] Following the view of the majority of the respondents, on 1 December 2016, the European Commission announced its intention to enable Member States to apply the same VAT rate to e-publications as that applicable for their printed equivalents, removing provisions that excluded e-publications from the favourable tax treatment allowed for traditional printed publications.

In this context, a question arises whether the application of a different rate to books and electronic books is in breach of the principle of VAT neutrality. Base on the CJEU case law, the principle of VAT neutrality prevents the application of a different VAT treatment to similar supplies or to non-similar supplies that are in competition with one another so that a different tax treatment would be likely to affect consumers' decisions.[44] As both print and e-books provide identical content, it would seem logical to allow both of them to benefit from the reduced rate. However, their functionalities may render them not similar products. E-books require a reader or a different electronic devise to access their content, they offer additional functionalities (search options, hyperlinks) and do not take any physical space. If based on their accessibility, storability and functionality, it is concluded that e-books are different from print books, it must be determined whether both types are offered in competition with one another. This must be assessed against the consumer's experience[45] and economic reality.[46] A survey conducted by PwC indicated that the driver for purchases of a book is its content and it is irrelevant whether the book is in a print or digital format.[47] It remains to be seen whether other research will confirm this conclusion.

---

43. European Commission, *Summary Report Responses received on The Commission's consultation on reduced VAT rates for electronically supplied publications* (October 2016), https://circabc.europa.eu/sd/a/64320cf4-021f-48e3-941b-b34224ec2290/Summary%20Report.pdf.
44. CJEU, 10 November 2011, Case C-259/10, *Commissioners for Her Majesty's Revenue and Customs v. The Rank Group PLC*); CJEU, 19 July 2012, Case C-33/11, *A Oy*.
45. CJEU, 11 September 2014, Case C-219/13, *K Oy v. Veronsaajien oikeudenvalvontayksikkö, Valtiovarainministeriö*: 'To determine whether goods or services are similar, account must be taken primarily of the point of view of a typical consumer. Goods or services are similar where they have similar characteristics and meet the same needs from the point of view of consumers, the test being whether their use is comparable, and where the differences between them do not have a significant influence on the decision of the average consumer to use one or the other of those goods or services' and 'as the average consumer's assessment is liable to vary according to the different degree of penetration of new technologies in each national market and the degree of access to the technical equipment enabling the consumer to make use of books published on physical supports other than paper, it is the average consumer in each Member State who must be taken as a reference'.
46. CJEU, 23 April 2009, Case C-357/07, *The Queen on the application of TNT Post UK Ltd v. The Commissioners of Her Majesty's Revenue & Customs and Royal Mail Group Ltd*: 'the assessment of the comparability of the services supplied hinges not only on the comparison of individual services, but on the context in which those services are supplied'.
47. PwC, *Media Trend Outlook: E-books on the Rise* (May 2014).

Chapter 7: Taxing the Consumption of Digital Goods §7.04[A]

The EU definition is narrower than the OECD recommendations and does not cover several types of services that are capable of delivery from a remote location. Several components of the EU definition ('essentially automated' or 'minimum human intervention') are vague and may give rise to classification problems. By including the requirement of 'minimum human intervention', the provision of distance teaching (i.e., remote participation in live online classes) and computer repair services, both of which are made entirely via the Internet, do not qualify as electronically supplied services. This may create artificial and unnecessary distinctions among similar intangible products. Since the definition of digital goods is used in a cross-border context, it should not be difficult to interpret by non-resident suppliers who are not familiar with EU VAT legislation. Therefore, this chapter advocates the adoption of a broad and simple definition to capture all supplies of digital goods by non-residents. The OECD provided a good example of such as definition when it referred to 'services and intangible property capable of delivery from a remote location'.

§7.04 DESIGN ISSUES AND SOVEREIGNTY

[A] Concept of Sovereignty

Under the traditional view, states are entitled to self-determination in most regulatory matters. They are said to have supreme and exclusive rule over their own people within their territorial borders. With regard to taxation, this traditional view means that states have the right to decide through political means and democratic processes whether and how to tax an activity that occurs within their territories and people who are deemed to be their residents or citizens. Decisions about the tax system should be made by national governments independent of outside interference.[48]

However, in the twentieth century, sovereignty ceased to be equated with complete state autonomy in tax matters.[49] Sovereignty includes a responsibility to the international community and a duty to respect the sovereign right of other states. This shift in meaning occurred due to the work of the OECD to curb harmful tax competition. OECD believed that countries have a duty to comply with certain standards of transparency and information exchange and to abstain from providing facilities that permit tax evasion and encourage non-compliance with the tax laws of other countries. States cannot design their tax system as they please. The concept of sovereignty includes respect for sovereignty of other countries.

---

48. For the concept of sovereignty, *see* A. Christians, *Sovereignty, Taxation and Social Contract*, 18 Minn. J. Int'l L. 99 (2009); M. Graetz, *Taxing International Income: Inadequate Principles, Outdated Concepts, and Unsatisfactory Policies*, 54 Tax L. Rev. 261 (2001); P.B. Musgrave, *Sovereignty, Entitlement, and Cooperation in International Taxation*, 26 Brook. J. Int'l L. 1335 (2001); P. Genschel, *Globalization and the Transformation of the Tax State*, 13 Eur. Rev. 53 (2005).
49. Christians, *supra* n. 48, at p. 101.

[B] Intra-jurisdictional Reach

Sovereignty implies that states must make decisions about their jurisdictional reach. Since people's activities overlap territorial boundaries, more than one state may have a legitimate claim to tax certain activities. For income tax purposes, the source of the income and the residence of the taxpayer are generally recognized as legitimate grounds for an assertion of jurisdiction to levy tax. In the context of consumption tax, the choice of jurisdiction to tax is governed by two principles: the principle of origin and the principle of destination.[50]

Under the origin principle, countries levy VAT on the value created within their own borders (i.e., exports are taxed on the same basis and at the same rate as local supplies and imports are exempt with the right to deduct input VAT). Where the value chain crosses several jurisdictions, the total amount of tax reflects the various rates applicable in countries where a value is added, clearly favouring production in low-tax jurisdictions.[51] A commonly made mistake is to confuse the origin principle with the supplier's location. Equating the origin of a supply with the place where the supplier is established would disregard the fact that certain supplies bear no relationship with the place where the supplier is established (e.g., supplies related to immovable property or supplies of transport services). Thus, the origin principle should be properly understood as ensuring that the country from which the supply is made has the right to assert jurisdiction to tax the supply.

Under the destination principle, the total tax paid in relation to a supply is determined by the rules applicable in the jurisdiction to which a supply is made and all revenue accrues to that country (i.e., exports are exempt with refund of input taxes, and imports are taxed on the same basis and with the same rates as local production). The key difference between both principles is that the destination principle ensures that all consumption within a particular jurisdiction is treated in the same way, whereas the origin principle makes sure that consumers from different jurisdictions are on an even footing.

From the point of view of formal sovereignty, there are no restrictions on the type of tax rules that states adopt. What is deemed appropriate changes over time through the acceptance of practices by some states. Currently, there is a widespread consensus that the destination principle is the proper way to tax international trade.[52] Since the object of VAT/GST is to tax consumption, the country where consumption takes place should have the right to assert jurisdiction to tax.

In theory, in a destination-based VAT system, the place-of-supply rules should identify the place of actual consumption. However, in most cases, the supplier is not able to identify such a place at the time of the supply since the person who will 'consume' the goods or services may not necessarily be the purchaser or at the time of

---

50. VAT/GST Guidelines, *supra* n. 7.
51. If all countries had identical VAT systems, the origin and destination principles would become equivalent.
52. VAT/GST Guidelines, *supra* n. 7, at p. 27; A. Schenk & O. Oldman, *Value Added Tax: A Comparative Approach* p. 35 (Cambridge University Press 2007).

Chapter 7: Taxing the Consumption of Digital Goods §7.04[B]

the supply it may not be sure where the goods will actually be consumed. Consumption taxes are imposed as transaction taxes, meaning that the amount of tax must be determined as soon as the consumer makes the expenditure, irrespective of when and how the goods will be used later on. The term 'consumption' merely indicates who bears the tax burden. As the decision about the place of taxation must be made at the time of the transaction, all destination-based VAT systems use various proxies (e.g., the place where services are used and enjoyed, the permanent address or the usual residence of the customer) to predict with reasonable accuracy the place where goods and services are likely to be consumed.

In the context of digital goods, the application of the destination principle triggers two important questions: first, whether it is possible (at least in theory) to determine the destination of digital goods (i.e., the place where the consumption of digital goods occurs); and, second, what proxies can be used to identify that place.

Identifying the place where digital goods are actually consumed is not an easy task. Digital goods bear no relationship with a particular geographical location. They can be moved and consumed many times without delay or transport costs. The consumer can access them everywhere (although sometimes access to the Internet is necessary). Digital goods follow the consumer: he can use them both at the place of his usual residence and during his trips abroad. Since one single place of consumption of digital goods cannot be determined, the use of the traditional concepts of origin and destination seems to be questionable in the context of digital goods. If something can be consumed everywhere, it makes little sense to designate one of these multiple locations as destination of the supply.

Even though digital goods can be consumed multiple times and at multiple locations and thus do not have a single destination, for the correct application of tax, a place of taxation needs to be determined. There must be mechanisms in place to identify where a transaction takes place and those mechanisms should aim to identify a location where a digital good is most often likely to be consumed. In this context, a question arises whether the use of multiple proxies and presumptions to establish the place of taxation (e.g., place of performance, place of use of enjoyment, customer's residence) is preferable or one simple rule would be sufficient.

In the EU, the place of taxation of electronic services supplied to a non-taxable person should be the place where the customer is established, has his permanent address or usually resides.[53] In order to determine that place, the VAT Implementing Regulation (282/2011) has introduced a number of presumptions, which unfortunately often contradict the main rule rather than clarify its application.[54] For example, for electronic services supplied at a location, such as a Wi-Fi hot spot, an internet café, a restaurant or a hotel lobby, it shall be presumed that the customer is established, has his permanent address or usually resides at the place of that location and that the service is effectively used and enjoyed there.[55] Similarly, for services provided through

---

53. Article 58 VAT Directive (2006/112).
54. For a critical evaluation of the presumptions, see A.M. Bal, *The Myth of Taxing Cloud Computing under EU VAT*, 25 Intl. VAT Monitor 6 (2014), Journals IBFD.
55. Article 24a VAT Implementing Regulation (282/2011).

mobile networks, it shall be presumed that the place where the customer is located is the country identified by the mobile country code of the SIM card used when receiving those services.[56] Both presumptions (which can be rebutted on the basis of three non-contradictory evidence items)[57] aim at identifying a location that does not seem to bear any relationship to the main rule mentioned in the VAT Directive (2006/112). For services not covered by a specific presumption, the customer will be presumed to belong at the place identified by the supplier on the basis of two items of non-contradictory evidence (such as the customer's billing address, he Internet Protocol (IP) address of the device used by the customer or any method of geo-location, bank details or other commercially relevant information). The application of some of the evidence items may also lead to a different result than the main legislative rule. For example, the IP address indicates the place where the customer is located at the time of the transaction and which may be different from the customer's usual residence. Despite this inconsistency, the VAT Explanatory Notes state that all presumptions should be interpreted consistently with the rules set by the VAT Directive.[58] It remains unclear how to achieve that.

The VAT Explanatory Notes admit the possibility of a clash between presumptions and provide that in order to determine which one should prevail, a factual assessment of the supply should be made and the supplier should collect all available information.[59] If there is a conflict among the items of evidence collected, priority is to be given to the place that best ensures taxation at the place of actual consumption of the services. In cases where items of evidence are contradictory, verification by the supplier on a regular basis is more needed.[60]

The EU have constructed an impressive regulatory framework that seeks to tax electronic services at the place of their actual consumption although as shown earlier in this section there is hardly ever a single place where a digital good is consumed. By introducing a number of presumptions whose application may lead to different results that that of the main legislative rule, the VAT system for taxing electronic services became more complex and less transparent. The rules for identifying the place of supply are difficult to comply with and their application cannot be effectively checked by the tax authorities. Thus, the complex regulatory framework fails to meet the objectives of efficiency, simplicity and certainty, which the rules on the taxation of electronic commerce should follow.[61]

Since there is rarely a single place of consumption of digital goods, it makes little sense to use a wide variety of proxies and presumptions to seek to determine one. The example of the EU shows that the application of multiple presumptions does not guarantee correct results and adds to the complexity of the regulatory framework. The

---

56. Article 24b VAT Implementing Regulation (282/2011).
57. A supplier is not obliged to rebut a presumption. Even though there can be evidence to the contrary, the supplier may, for determining the place where the customer belongs, decide to rely on the presumption and disregard evidence to the contrary.
58. Explanatory Notes, *supra* n. 17, at p. 54.
59. Explanatory Notes, *supra* n. 17, at p. 62.
60. Explanatory Notes, *supra* n. 17, at p. 72.
61. OECD, *supra* n. 2.

requirement to use a large number of proxies is based on the assumption that suppliers can verify information provided by their customers on a transaction-by-transaction basis. Whereas this may work well for conventional supplies, this assumption does not hold true in a digital context where suppliers cannot obtain all relevant information in a timely fashion to carry out transaction-based assessments. Depending on the factual circumstances surrounding each supply of digital goods is unrealistic. For this reason, the use of a single rule could be considered a viable alternative. As consumers most often consume digital goods in their country of residence, the consumer residence should be used to determine the place of taxation of digital goods. For suppliers, it will be easier to comply with one rule than a multitude of presumptions that may give rise to conflicting results. Such a rule may not identify correctly the place of actual consumption in all cases, but provides a good approximation. As suppliers use different business models, they should be allowed to identify the place of residence based on the information they usually collect or that which is available in their commercial records. In Australia, the new GST law recognizes that a supplier should be able to rely on its existing business systems and processes for determining the place where his consumers are resident.

[C] Tax Collection

The ability to collect the tax due is part of a country's sovereignty. The question 'how to collect the tax due?' is as important as 'which country has the right to levy tax?' Enacting legislation that will subject supplies of digital goods to resident consumers to VAT/GST seems to be a relatively easy task compared to the challenge of how to collect the tax due.

There is a widespread consensus that the most effective approach to ensure collection of VAT/GST on supplies of digital goods by non-residents is to require the non-resident supplier to register and account for VAT in the jurisdiction of taxation.[62] A number of such systems are already in operation around the world.[63] Other mechanisms for tax collection on cross-border supplies, such as VAT self-assessment by final consumers have proven ineffective. In the absence of effective enforcement mechanisms, consumers are unlikely to comply.

The biggest disadvantage of simplified registration systems is that they rely on the voluntary compliance of the supplier. If the supplier does not register and remit VAT/GST, the tax administration will hardly ever know that a taxable supply took place. Detailed information on such cross-border supplies (which is necessary to determine the tax liability) can only be obtained after audits in the country of the supplier have been carried out and the tax authorities of the supplier's country have communicated their findings.

To encourage voluntary compliance by non-residents, the simplified registration systems should be as user-friendly and easy to apply as possible. They should rely on

---

62. VAT/GST Guidelines, *supra* n. 7, at. p. 50.
63. For example, in the European Union, Norway, South Africa, Korea (Rep.).

electronic communication and electronic payment facilities. The information requested from foreign suppliers (for both registration and submitting returns) should be limited to the absolutely necessary details. The design of the national tax systems is an important aspect in fostering compliance. A complicated tax system might turn into a market access barrier or an incentive for non-compliance. To facilitate compliance, countries should make available online all information necessary to register, calculate tax liability and submit tax returns, preferably in the language of their major trading partners.[64]

An important design question is whether a registration threshold should be introduced for non-resident suppliers using the simplified registration mechanism. The OECD VAT/GST Guidelines do not contain a clear recommendation on that matter but recommend striking a balance between the compliance costs for non-residents and the need to level the playing field between resident and non-resident businesses. Relieving suppliers from the obligation to register in countries where their sales are of negligible value is not likely to cause net losses of revenue in light of the offsetting expenses. Currently, there is no 'small seller exemption' for supplies of cross-border electronic services in the EU. This means that foreign suppliers must be aware of the local VAT rules even if they perform a single transaction in one Member State. In New Zealand, a threshold of NZD 60,000 will be introduced.

It is questionable whether the fact that tax collection in cross-border scenarios is reliant on voluntary compliance by non-resident suppliers is acceptable from a neutrality and competition perspective in the long term. Without effective supervision and enforcement, there is a risk of non-taxation that threatens to distort competition. If tax rules are not linked to a real possibility of enforcement, taxpayers are unlikely to comply. To ensure tax collection in the country of destination, the enforcement capacity of tax authorities needs to be reinforced through enhanced international cooperation. In the EU, a supranational legal framework for exchange of VAT information is already in place.[65] Data on cross-border B2B supplies of services is stored and made available through the electronic VAT Information Exchange System (VIES): the supplier has to submit, to the tax authorities of his country of establishment, a recapitulative statement containing information on his intra-EU supplies and their recipients and this information becomes automatically available to the tax authorities of the country of his recipients. However, no similar system is in place in relation to B2C supplies, which rely on voluntary compliance by non-resident suppliers. Both EU and non-EU countries can make use of the existing instruments on exchange of information and assistance in tax collection, such as the Convention on Mutual Administrative Assistance in Tax Matters, tax information exchange agreements, and tax treaties based on the OECD or UN Model Convention (Articles 26 and 27 apply to

---

64. VAT/GST Guidelines, *supra* n. 7, at p. 53.
65. Council Regulation (EU) No 904/2010 of 7 October 2010 on administrative cooperation and combating fraud in the field of value added tax and Council Directive 2010/24/EU of 16 March 2010 concerning mutual assistance for the recovery of claims relating to taxes, duties and other measures.

all taxes, including VAT/GST). Countries would be more willing to exchange information and answer requests of other jurisdictions if a revenue sharing was introduced. This would mean that the tax of the country of supplier is entitled to retain a proportion of the VAT revenues due to the country where the final consumer is resident. Revenue sharing is well established in the EU in respect of customs duties, and is already provided for in the initial period of the MOSS (30% in 2015 and 2016, and 15% in 2017 and 2018).

Digital goods are traded on the global marketplace. Such a market can never be subject to full control by the tax authorities. If the collection of tax on the supplies of digital goods is to be reliant on voluntary compliance by non-resident suppliers without the presence of effective domestic enforcement mechanisms, suppliers must be provided with incentives to comply and countries must be encouraged to cooperate. The former could be achieved by simple registration and reporting mechanisms, whereas the latter by revenue sharing system.

§7.05 SUMMARY

Consumption taxation of cross-border supplies of digital goods is a major issue faced by all countries that operate a VAT/GST system. Many countries have already enacted special rules for digital goods supplied by non-resident businesses to local customers and others are in the process of implementing them. OECD recognized the challenges of tax collection on cross-border digital supplies in its BEPS Action 1 and issued comprehensive VAT/GST Guidelines to assist countries in the implementation of rules to ensure effective tax collection.

Regardless of their content, digital goods have three fundamental economic characteristics: they are indestructible (durable), easily reproducible and easily transmutable. Due to those features, they can be consumed multiple times by multiple locations. Some countries (Australia and New Zealand) have followed the OECD VAT/GST Guidelines and implemented a broad definition of digital goods for the purposes of taxing intangible supplies by foreign businesses to local consumers, whereas others (the EU) apply additional criteria that may give rise to artificial and unnecessary distinctions among similar intangible products.

Form a sovereignty point of view, it is of crucial importance to determine which country has the right to levy tax and how to ensure effective tax collection. Regarding the entitlement to levy tax, there is a widespread consensus that the destination principle is the correct way to tax consumption. However, the place-of-taxation rules should take into account that there is rarely a single place of consumption of digital goods that can be used by consumers multiple times and at multiple locations. Even the application of multiple proxies and presumptions will not guarantee the correct determination of the place of taxation. Therefore, this chapter advocates the use of a simple rule that provides a good approximation of the place of actual consumption and is relatively easy to apply by non-resident suppliers: the place of taxation should be determined on the basis of the consumer's usual residence.

The most effective approach to collect VAT/GST on supplies of digital goods by non-residents is to require the non-resident supplier to register and account for VAT in the jurisdiction of taxation. To ensure that the tax due is actually collected, suppliers must be provided with incentives to comply (such as simple registration systems and availability of information to determine the tax liability) and countries must be encouraged to cooperate (e.g., by a system of revenue sharing).

PART III   Acceptance and Implementation of Consensus by Differently-Situated States

CHAPTER 8

The Birth of a New International Tax Framework and the Role of Developing Countries

Natalia Quiñones

Many of the traditional paradigms of international taxation have changed radically in a relatively short timeframe. Starting from the automatic exchange of information and the peer-review system, down to multilateralism in the setting of international tax standards, we are now witnessing the birth of a new international tax framework. Although the final shape of the framework is still uncertain, we must acknowledge at this point that it is having a very significant influence in the way countries are reforming their domestic and treaty rules regarding the tax treatment of cross-border situations.

The new international tax framework may be described as a new set of common principles, standards, and regulating bodies, all codified in different sources of international tax law. The birth of this new framework is marked by the base erosion and profit shifting (BEPS) project, endorsed by G-20 countries and administered by the Organisation for Economic Co-operation and Development (OECD). Underlying the BEPS project is the political desire to revamp the international tax system, perceived as outdated and inefficient in dealing with the global economic forces of the twenty-first century (OECD, 2013a). According to the OECD (OECD, 2013b), the project and framework are also designed to guarantee that income earned by multinational enterprises (MNEs) does not remain untaxed because of legal structures that take advantages of mismatches in treaties and the domestic legislation of different countries, and that taxes are generally 'aligned with value creation'.

At the centre of this framework are the OECD and G-20 countries, but the role of the developing world is still unclear. Most statements by the OECD and G-20 claim that the new international tax standards and governing bodies will be drawn within an 'inclusive framework' (IMF, OECD, WB, & UN, 2016; G-20 Finance Ministers, 2015; OECD, 2015b) that has taken and will take into account the interests and realities of developing countries (OECD, 2016). However, recent literature has suggested that this framework may not reflect in practice the realities and needs of most low- and middle-income countries (Brauner, 2014; García, 2016; Mehta, 2014; Mosquera, 2015). If what these authors claim is true, and even if the inclusive framework has done a good job in serving the interests of developing countries, it is now crucial to understand how developing countries may take advantage of the new international tax architecture to ensure that their voices are truly shaping the standards, and that the knowledge gap between developing and developed is getting narrower instead of wider.

Because of the BEPS project, the OECD has emerged as the leading institution, charged with the tasks of diagnosing the shortcomings of the current system (OECD, 2013a), of formulating an action plan to address these shortcomings (OECD, 2013b) and of proposing a new set of rules and standards to implement the Action Plan (OECD, 2015b). The Action Plan recognized the need to establish a global framework in which developed, emerging, and developing countries had to cooperate in order to guarantee a successful outcome in addressing existing challenges related to BEPS (OECD, 2013b). Representatives of a few developing countries were thus invited to the BEPS process in an attempt to ensure that the results of the action plan would be perceived as legitimate in a global context, especially when Action 15 of the Action Plan calls for a multilateral treaty (OECD, 2013b; OECD, 2015a) that can only be successful if a significant number of countries across the different regions agree to sign and ratify the instrument, as we will discuss below (G-20 Finance Ministers, 2015). Some authors have questioned that this inclusion of non-OECD developing countries in the negotiation of BEPS outcomes provides legitimacy to the project (García, 2016; Mosquera, 2016), and many insist on the need for a change of the administering body for the UN (Avi-Yonah & Xu, 2016; García, 2016; Mosquera, 2015; Ocampo, 2015; Picciotto, 2013) precisely because of this lack of legitimacy.

The fact that the OECD is leading the structuring of the new international tax architecture has created a tension in the developing world that has been clearly recognized and voiced by a part of the literature. A 2014 report by Tax Justice Network mentioned that:

> 'This will create tensions with developing countries, which participate in the BEPS process and its promise of producing remedies for the shortcomings in the international tax system, and on the other hand feel the pressure to assert their own fiscal sovereignty, conscious that a club of rich countries may be seeking to protect primarily its own membership first.' (Mehta, 2014)

The exclusion of most countries from the decision-making process is largely voiced as an additional element of tension (Brauner, 2014; Ocampo, 2015; Pistone, 2013), even when the implementation phase is promised to include all desiring countries on equal footing (OECD, 2016c).

In view of the tensions mentioned in recent literature, and in view of the statements of the OECD regarding the importance of a 'global' implementation of BEPS, it is necessary to examine how developing countries are integrating into the new international tax framework, and whether the current form of inclusion is sustainable in the long run. This chapter will discuss the importance of developing countries in the new international framework, and it will examine the way in which they have been involved in the building of the new international tax architecture until now. Finally, it will propose that actively participating in a multilateral dispute resolution framework will in fact enhance the protection of the sovereign interests of developing countries and will achieve the desirable function of rapidly narrowing the knowledge gap between both worlds.

§8.01 WHY DEVELOPING COUNTRIES ARE FUNDAMENTAL TO THE FUNCTIONING OF THE NEW FRAMEWORK

Developing and emerging countries, understood for purposes of this chapter as low- and middle-income countries as defined by the World Bank, represent a large portion of the world in terms of population, resources, and of course, potential sovereign legislators that could jeopardize the G-20/OECD bets of global cooperation and transparency to prevent the erosion of national revenue by MNE's (Ocampo, 2015; Sadiq, 2013). The 2013 BEPS report systematically showed that asymmetries between domestic tax legislation are the main source of BEPS by MNEs (OECD, 2013a), and thus the Action Plan called for enhanced cooperation and coordination between countries to ensure a consistent approach to key items that were creating opportunities for reducing taxes due on a multinational economic operation (OECD, 2013b).

The OECD (2015; 2016) and the G-20 Ministers of Finance (G-20 Finance Ministers, 2015) recognized that the need for a consistent application of rules and standards cannot refer only to the implementation of BEPS in the developed world. In fact, MNEs currently operate in a world where significant consumer markets are located in emerging and developing countries, and the globalized economy has provided easy access to legal and tax regimes in small countries where there are virtually no business reasons to even consider as places of incorporation in the strategy of a MNE. It is precisely in these jurisdictions where the incentives for tax competition in the form of a race to the bottom are the highest (Dagan, 2015). Evidently, it is exactly this competition which creates the opportunities for BEPS, and which has prevented the implementation of true multilateralism in the area of tax.

Thus, the overarching aim of tax coordination and transparency as set forth in the BEPS project requires the millimetric cooperation of all actors involved in global trade in order to prevent a massive increase in international tax disputes. As this absolute uniformity in the adoption and interpretation of the soft-law recommendations developed by the OECD seems unattainable in the present state of things (De Pietro, 2015), developing countries are being 'encouraged' to sign the multilateral instrument proposed in action 15 (OECD, 2015a), along with joining the 'inclusive framework' for the consistent implementation of BEPS minimum standards and best practices (OECD, 2016a; OECD, 2016b).

The inclusive framework requires, firstly, that countries 'commit to the comprehensive BEPS Package and its consistent implementation' (OECD, 2016b), so that they can enjoy the benefits of having a voice in the monitoring process and, if new standards were to be developed, in the setting of such standards. After the first meeting of the inclusive framework, the OECD had recruited more than eighty countries that were willing to commit (OECD, 2016c). This, of course, serves as an additional argument for pressing developing countries into joining, as the dynamic mainly replicates the pressure exerted by the Global Forum on Tax Transparency and the Exchange of Information (the Global Forum) for the adoption of the exchange of information standards (Pistone, 2014).

During 2016, we have seen the OECD release flyers inviting countries to participate and 'protect your [their] tax rate' and the taskforce on tax and development travelling to all meetings of regional tax administration associations (ATAF, CIAT, etc.) to promote the inclusive framework; even multilateral organizations like the IMF and the World Bank are travelling around the globe promoting their tool-kits for the consistent implementation of BEPS in low and middle-income countries. All these efforts are built on the clear assumption that achieving tax transparency and coordination in a way that leaves no room for MNEs to rely on different treatments for a single transaction or situation, definitely requires the full engagement of developing countries.

Now that the BEPS project has called for a new multilateralism (OECD, 2015a), developing countries face the decision of cooperating in the framework of the BEPS project as designed by the OECD or, as Dagan has suggested, refraining from 'cartel cooperation' (Dagan, 2015). Although the OECD insists on the fact the inclusive framework and multilateral instrument will cause the voices of developing countries to be heard at last (OECD, 2016b), it is clear that the standards to be implemented have already been set, and developing countries did not have much of a say (Brauner, 2014), as they were either minorities or had other political interests at hand that prevented them from opposing the majority opinions in the standard-setting process (Mosquera, 2015). This is the case of, for example, Colombia, which participated in the BEPS project from the start, but had a priority interest of joining the OECD rather than defending the interests of the emerging and developing world.

The fact that their voices were not relevant enough can also be verified in the substance of the outcomes reached in BEPS. The alignment of taxation with value creation, set up as an objective in the Action Plan (OECD, 2013b), was never truly reviewed, as the entire analysis was performed on the assumption of the source-residence dichotomy, which has created the imbalance in the distribution of international taxes in the first place. Moreover, keeping the Authorized OECD Approach (AOA) in the attribution of profits to a PE has even resulted in frustrating the purpose of the outcomes presented in Action 7, which extended the scope of agency PE to benefit source states. Furthermore, the fact that the consumer market was ignored as a value driver in actions 8-10 also shows that the position of developing countries was not welcome within the OECD BEPS analysis. This, of course, has resulted in disparities

Chapter 8: The Birth of a New International Tax Framework §8.01

in the adoption of BEPS, as is the case of the Indian equalization levy, which they claim is aligned with BEPS recommendations for action 1, while also giving India the opportunity to protect its tax base understood as the profits associated with Indian consumers (Sengupta, 2016).

As to the concern for eliminating opportunities for 'double non taxation', many of the solutions proposed in the outcomes of the BEPS action plan create a residual right to tax in the residence (often developed) state in order to compensate for the absence of taxation in the source (often emerging or developing) state; this is the empirical outcome of the recommendations for actions 2, 3, and 4, among others (OECD, 2015c). In the absence of coordination with the developing world, these new residual rights to tax created by the BEPS recommendations and their adoption by G-20 and OECD countries would amount to multiple taxation on the same income, or in some cases, to null taxation due to the lack of information on the activities and tax regime of the MNE in the source state. The same is true for Action 5, which now requires peer-review approval of preferential regimes, in spite of the fact that developing countries will most often face severe difficulties in dismantling tax benefits granted to attract investment (this is especially true amongst countries with a legal stability regime).

This lack of input legitimacy (Mosquera, 2015) is not necessarily recognized by all. On the contrary, the OECD has claimed that the presence of emerging countries like Colombia should be enough to legitimize the standard-setting process (OECD, 2016b). Furthermore, the inclusive framework documents seem to adhere to the view that output legitimacy consisting on the common desire of developed and developing countries of protecting their tax base is reason enough for developing countries to choose cooperation in the form of adhesion to the inclusive framework (OECD, 2016a; OECD, 2016b).

In the context of BEPS, this rhetoric of cooperation that Dagan heavily criticizes is of course born of two main concerns: on the one hand, the concern for an eventual migration of investment towards countries that do not implement measures to counteract BEPS; and on the other hand, the concern for closing every loop-hole that will allow for 'double non-taxation'. The first concern is not a small concern, and it particularly affects developing countries, where investment is more sensitive to changes in policy. As some authors have pointed out, the developing countries that choose to implement harsh measures to counter BEPS, may loose investment to neighbouring countries that choose not to cooperate or that delay the adoption of BEPS recommendations (Quinones, Prologo, 2016).

As per the above, we can conclude that developing and emerging countries are crucial to the success of the BEPS project, which is why the OECD is investing so much in convincing countries to join the inclusive framework. But convincing countries to join the inclusive framework is by no means the end of the road to ensuring a successful BEPS implementation. Indeed, in a more ironic scenario, formal cooperation by developing countries could still lead to an undesirable increase in international tax disputes, as even when countries accept the standards, domestic implementation always brings the possibility of different interpretations by tax administration officials and domestic courts.

§8.02 CURRENT INVOLVEMENT IN THE INTERNATIONAL TAX ARCHITECTURE: SUBSTANTIVE OR FORMAL MULTILATERALISM

Although the OECD has insisted on the substantiality of the BEPS inclusive framework with terms such as 'equal footing' and 'level playing field' for developing countries, several voices have claimed that the new framework is only inclusive on a superficial level, while unilateral or bilateral behaviour persists in shaping the standards promoted by the BEPS project (Brauner, 2014; García, 2016; Mosquera, 2015).The purpose of this section is to analyse whether the inclusion of a large number of developing countries and jurisdictions in the inclusive framework is enough to transcend formal multilateralism, or if the BEPS multilateralism must be recognized, as an author cleverly stated, as the emperor's new clothes. If this were the case, developing countries would have to develop a different strategy to ensure that their participation in the new international tax framework is substantive and that their perspective may effectively be reflected in the shaping of the newly created standards.

Now that the standards have been set, developing countries have the possibility of joining the inclusive framework mentioned above, and of negotiating the language of the multilateral instrument proposed in Action 15 of the BEPS Action Plan. As mentioned before, this possibility has already been embraced by a number of developing countries, adding up to a total of eighty-two jurisdictions as of July, 2016 (OECD, 2016c). Many of these countries are developing or emerging countries, and their hope is that by implementing the agreements reached by the OECD in the outcomes of the BEPS Action Plan will increase their revenues and their capacity. However, the first promise is not necessarily true, as Dagan recently argued (2015). Besides, it will be difficult to assess an objective increase in revenue, as it would have to be measured against a scenario where the state had not agreed to cooperate in the multilateralism proposed by the OECD.

It could in fact be argued that developing countries cannot be better off with the current concept of source-residence taxation, but rather with some form of unitary taxation (Avi-Yonah & Xu, 2016; Picciotto, 2013) that could privilege immovable factors such as the place where consumers are located (billing address for purposes of the digital economy) and the place where natural resources are being extracted. This approach, of course, has not been discussed even remotely in the inclusive framework, given that it would entail a structural revamp of the traditional pillars of international taxation. This form of profit allocation, which deserves a separate study that is beyond the scope of this work, would be very likely to raise more revenue for developing countries and truly realign profits with value creation, as the OECD purports to intend.

The second promise, on the other hand, is not an innocent promise. Furthering training and capacity for developing countries has been the focus of multilateral organizations (IMF, OECD, WB, & UN, 2016) and of the OECD taskforce for Tax and Development (OECD, 2016a). Training programmes and developing country tool kits, however, are mainly focused on guaranteeing that developing countries will implement BEPS recommendations in a consistent fashion, rather than in transferring knowledge in a way that will allow tax administrations and developing country leaders to form their own opinions and autonomously determine what is most convenient for their country or region at a given time. This training, in fact, may rather be viewed as a form of fiscal colonialism (Sanders, 2002), where developed countries impose their views on developing countries through *teaching* them how to analyse different issues on international taxation (Picciotto, 2013).

This biased inclusion of developing countries in the agenda can be paralleled with the lukewarm actions taken to strengthen the UN. Ocampo harshly criticized these actions, because the Addis Ababa Conference on Financing for Development had a proposal to establish an intergovernmental tax body within the United Nations (UN) to replace the current UN Committee of Experts. The proposed body would be charged with the task of coordinating tax cooperation between countries, given the limited possibilities of an effective democratic decision-making process in the OECD, an organization run by the elite of the most powerful nations. However, developed countries blocked the proposal, mainly because 'These countries insist that tax cooperation should take place exclusively under the leadership of the OECD, a body that they control'. (Ocampo, 2015). Again, behind the formal support consisting in the decision to enhance the financing of the UN Committee of experts and to increase meetings there is a masked will to continue to dominate the international tax decision-making inside the OECD (Picciotto, 2013).

This 'club diplomacy' (García, 2016) is thus certainly far from achieving the results of a substantive multilateralism, where a truly democratic decision-making process would be the basis for resolving the challenges of international taxation today. The merely formal inclusion of developing countries in the inclusive framework and the blocking of efforts to turn the UN Committee into a truly equipped and inclusive administering body are proof of the lack of a substantial influence of developing countries in the shaping of the international tax architecture as of now. It is for this reason that we may conclude that the current involvement of developing countries in the international tax architecture responds to a formal multilateralism where the OECD countries are running the show (García, 2016; Picciotto, 2013).

What is most serious about this landscape is that the OECD continues to assert that they are an inclusive platform that is effectively taking into account the view and challenges of developing countries. The fact that they have taken care of showing the world that developing countries are sitting at the table definitely makes it harder to question the legitimacy of the current form of multilateralism established by the developed world, as most organizations exercising political pressure will take these efforts as a sufficient inclusion of the world's poorest and emerging economies, without looking deeper into the actual power that they can exert as formal members of an inclusive framework where everything has already been decided.

Furthermore, although the OECD and the G-20 insist on the output legitimacy of the inclusive framework in the sense of developing countries as sharing an objective of preventing base erosion (OECD, 2016a; OECD, 2016b), the fact that the standards and the system as a whole are mainly based on bilateral tax treaties −in turn based on the residence-source dichotomy- also poses a question of whether countries may effectively expect to make more money from cooperation within the BEPS inclusive framework (Dagan, 2000; Brauner, 2014). In face of this uncertainty, it would seem wise to look for additional benefits that developing countries could derive from cooperation, as we will discuss in the following section.

As the inclusive framework is insufficient in terms of an effective influence over the international tax framework, it is suggested that developing countries should indeed try harder to give their voice effective power in the post-standard-setting phase, as it is there that the true shaping of international tax will take place. In fact, it is our contention that the application and interpretation of the standards is what will ultimately shape international tax law, which is precisely why the OECD is still investing profuse resources in ensuring a consistent adoption of the standards and best practices by all jurisdictions participating in the inclusive framework. But in order for BEPS to achieve the consistency desired in their documents (OECD, 2016b) and to prevent the chaos of unilateral arbitrary positions taken by judges and tax administrations in different countries, it is clear that a global dispute resolution body must be set up, as we will discuss in the following section.

§8.03 DISPUTE RESOLUTION AND SOVEREIGNTY IN A POST-BEPS WORLD

The paradigm shift that the OECD is proposing in the BEPS project involves a fundamental change in the way that tax sovereignty is perceived and defined. Indeed, domestic tax rules and international tax policy were traditionally perceived as the core of sovereignty in the Westphalian conception (Dietsch, 2015), so that countries only limited their domestic taxing powers in the context of a bilateral negotiation. Before the crusade for tax transparency gained momentum, the only known international tax standard was the alleviation of double juridical taxation. The soft-law paradigms to achieve this – the OECD Model Convention and the less popular UN Model – were based on majority consensus that took several years to be modified in any sense. Besides, most countries in fact deviated from the models in their own individual negotiations (Lang, Pistone, Schuch & Staringer, 2012).

The solutions proposed in the BEPS outcome reports now call for a new level of coordination, one that unmistakably requires a greater cession of sovereignty by all nations, in favour of peer-review bodies and, hopefully, an international dispute resolution body. Some authors claim that this new coordination may not favour developing countries (Dagan, 2015; García Antón, 2016), and the previous section showed that the current involvement in the inclusive framework cannot guarantee a substantive influence (or even substantial benefits) for developing countries. Nonetheless, it would seem at this point that clinging to sovereignty in the traditional Westphalian sense of the word will probably result in strong peer pressure that will eventually lead to forced compliance, as was the case with the exchange of information and the peer-review system developed by the Global Forum. This shall not mean, however, that developing countries have no option other than complying with the standards set by the OECD. Rather, the proposal is to shift the claim of sovereignty towards a new dispute resolution body, where developing country representatives will be able to exert a truly substantive influence through the decisions issued in this body.

In BEPS times, Westphalian national tax sovereignty is being challenged in different fronts, including limitations to what has been called 'preferential tax regimes' (OECD, 2015b), which could involve the very popular tax holidays approved by congressmen in exchange for votes or campaign financing. These challenges have even been extended to action 14 on dispute resolution, especially in the context of developing countries (Lennard, 2014). We submit that, quite to the contrary, participation of developing countries in international tax-dispute resolution may enhance their sovereignty understood as the ability to exert an autonomous influence on the shaping of international tax rules and standards.

Some authors have expressed their fear of the chaotic scenario that might result from disparity in the interpretation and application of the standards (Brauner, 2014; García, 2016). This fear is certainly not unfounded, as we are seeing diversity in the implementation of BEPS even in Europe, where many of the core OECD countries are located. One example of this is the UK diverted profits tax (DPT), or even at the community level with the ATAD directive, which was precisely intended to provide a uniform application of BEPS within the twenty-eight European Union members. If the disparity in the application of BEPS is having such scope within Europe, it is to be expected that developing countries may create further disparities that will naturally result in an increase of international tax disputes.

As mentioned before, the overarching aim of consistency in BEPS requires a coherent implementation and interpretation of all recommendations issued, whether as minimum standards or as best practices. This coherency can only be reached if taxpayers and tax administrations have access to an organ or institution where they can complain of inconsistent applications of a standard by another country, with the purpose of obtaining a public ruling/opinion that may clarify how the standard is to be applied in a specific situation. And the peer-review group hosted by the OECD seems like an inadequate platform given the analysis performed in the above section, where developing countries only enjoy a formal inclusion and where developed countries have an almost exclusive initiative to set or change a standard.

An independent or UN-sponsored dispute resolution body would then seem ideal in this context, especially when it can guarantee that developing countries will have a substantial representation amongst the justices/arbitrators/mediators or, in general, in the set of persons that issue the opinions. Precisely, opening the possibility for the presence of technical experts in a truly international body may also ensure that developing country interests will be protected from biased interpretations of existing standards. The proposal for an international organization has already been sketched by different authors in legal and political research in the past century and in more recent years (Picciotto, 2013; Rixen, 2016; Sawyer, 2009), but again none of them have truly taken into account the realities of developing countries. This may be due, at least in part, to the fact that there is no data available to describe those realities in the post-BEPS era.

The full participation of developing countries in a body like this one may in fact enhance the current form of multilateralism, as dispute resolution has often been the key to the successful application of multilateral instruments even when countries as powerful as the US have abstained from ratification (García, 2016). These examples include the UN Convention on the Law of the Sea and the Nordic Treaty, among others. Besides, this is a change that is still possible in the current framework, where many developing countries have already decided to participate and can join together to promote this initiative as a logical extension of the peer-review group once the multilateral treaty has been finalized.

Some authors have argued that developing countries face several difficulties in joining international disputes resolution bodies (Lennard, 2014). However, this contention still lacks supporting data from actual developing countries, which is why we suggest the procurement of baseline data on these perceived difficulties in order to make more accurate representations on the situation of developing countries, and how the international dispute resolution body may be shaped in order to overcome real existing difficulties in the developing world. Based on this data, the international dispute resolution body may be delineated with decisions regarding availability of ADR solutions (binding and non-binding), the rules for the application of each of these solutions (baseball arbitration, technical requirements to be eligible as arbitrator/mediator, cost schemes, publicity, value of precedent, etc.). If this body is indeed successful in representing developing country interests, we may finally arrive at a stable framework where the desired consistency in the application of international tax standards may be achieved (Quinones, 2014).

Finally, taking into account that the offering of training within the inclusive framework (IMF, OECD, WB, & UN, 2016; OECD, 2016b) will not provide developing countries with the necessary elements to make autonomous decisions on what is convenient for them, joining a truly multilateral dispute resolution body may actually provide a desirable surplus for developing countries. The need to obtain training and the general perception on the lack of capacity in developing countries (which is yet to be evaluated with field data), are rooted on the large knowledge gap between developed and developing countries in matters of international taxation. This gap has in turn resulted from the lack of publicity in international tax decisions (Christians, 2012; Picciotto, 2013) –arbitration where available, MAPs, APAs, etc.-, and from the lack of translations of soft-law instruments into Spanish and other developing country languages. This is especially true in the international tax context, where soft-law has traditionally played a fundamental role in the international tax practice, and where it remains a key to a coordinated application of the standards (Pichhadze, 2015).

If the international tax-dispute resolution body that we hereby propose engages in public decision-making, the probability is that not only developing countries but also taxpayers and advisors world-wide will have the opportunity to build knowledge in a way that allows for independent determination of how to face the challenges of international taxation, without having to blindly accept what the OECD throws their way.

§8.04 CONCLUSIONS

This chapter set out to analyse the role of developing countries in the new international tax framework. In this context, we have seen that developing countries are indeed fundamental for the success of BEPS, inasmuch as international tax coordination and transparency requires their commitment to a consistent application of the standards. As fundamental players in the international tax framework, developing countries have been invited to join an inclusive framework led by the OECD.

In the second section of the chapter we showed that this form of multilateralism is not substantive, as developing countries do not have an effective power to influence the shaping of international tax rules and standards, nor to take the initiative in proposing changes in current standards and effectively taking the decision to change. We also may conclude that the promises offered to developing countries of increasing revenue and obtaining training must be looked at with some degree of suspicion as to the real benefits that developing countries may derive from cooperation within the inclusive framework.

Finally, given that the current form of inclusion within the international tax framework is insufficient to outweigh the burden of ceding more sovereignty, we propose that developing countries should focus their efforts in obtaining a substantive participation in a global dispute resolution body that will ultimately shape international tax law through its opinions. This will not only ensure that the cession of sovereignty is worthwhile for all developing countries, but also that the multilateral network as a whole will have a higher chance of success because of the possibility of reaching consistency and coherence in the application and interpretation of the international tax standards and best practices.

References

Avi-Yonah, R., & Xu, H. (2016). Global Taxation after the Crisis: Why BEPS and MAATM are Inadequate Responses, and What Can Be Done About It. *U of Michigan Public Law Research Paper* (494), 1–51.

Brauner, Y. (2014). What the BEPS? *Florida Tax Review, 16* (2), 55–115.

Christians, A. (2012). How Nations Share. *Indiana Law Journal, 87*, 1407–1453.

Dagan, T. (2015). BRICS- The Potential of Cooperation. In Y. Brauner, & P. Pistone, *BRICs and the Emergence of International Tax Coordination*. Amsterdam: IBFD.

Dagan, T. (2000). The Tax Treaties Myth. *NYU Journal of International Law and Politics, 32* (939), 2–53.

De Pietro, C. (2015). Tax Treaty Override and the Need for Coordination between Legal Systems: Safeguarding the Effectiveness of International Law. *World Tax Journal, 7* (1), 73–97.

Dietsch, P. (2015). *Catching Capital: The Ethics of Tax Competition*. Oxford: Oxford University Press.

G-20 Finance Ministers. (2015). Communiqué G20 Finance Ministers and Central Bank Governors Meeting 4–5 September 2015, Ankara, Turkey. *Bankarstvo, 44* (4), 144–155.

García, R. (2016). The 21st Century Multilateralism in International Taxation: The Emperor's New Clothes? *World Tax Journal, 8* (2).

IMF, OECD, WB, & UN. (2016). *The Platform for Collaboration on Tax: Concept Note.* Washington DC: Wrold Bank Group.
Lang, M., Pistone, P., Schuch, J., & Staringer, C. (2012). *The Impact of the UN and OECD Model Tax Conventions on Bilateral Tax Treaties.* Cambridge: Cambridge University Press.
Lennard, M. (2014). International Tax Arbitration and Developing Countries. In A. Rovine, *Contemporary Issues in International Arbitration and Mediation:* (pp. 437-459). New York: Fordham University Press.
Mehta, K. (2014). *The OECD's BEPS Process and Developing Countries – a Way Forward.* Chesham Bucks: Tax Justice Network.
Mosquera, I.J. (2015). Legitimacy and the Making of International Tax Law: The Challenges of Multilateralism. *World Tax Journal, 7* (3), 343-382.
Ocampo, J. A. (2015). *Evaluation of the Independent Commission for the Reform of International Corporate Taxation for the Base Erosion and Profit-Shifting Project of the G20 and OECD.* New York: ICRICT.
OECD. (2013b). *Action Plan on Base Erosion and Profit Shifting.* Paris: OECD Publishing.
OECD. (2013a). *Addressing Base Erosion and Profit Shifting.* Paris: OECD Publishing.
OECD. (2016b). *Background Brief Inclusive Framework for BEPS Implementation.* Paris: OECD Publishing.
OECD. (2016a). *Co-Chair Statement on the Meeting of the OECD Task Force on Tax and Development on Base Erosion and Profit Shifting (BEPS).* Paris: OECD Publishing.
OECD. (2015a). *Developing a Multilateral Instrument to Modify Bilateral Tax Treaties.* Paris: OECD Publishing.
OECD. (2015c). *Executive Summaries 2015 Final Reports.* Paris: OECD Publishing.
OECD. (2015b). *Explanatory Statement OECD/G20 Base Erosion and Profit Shifting Project.* Paris: OECD Publishing.
OECD. (2016c). *Inclusive Framework Composition- July 15, 2016.* Paris: OECD Publishing.
Picciotto, S. (2013). *Is the International TAx System Fit for Purpose, Especially for Developing Countries?* International Centre for Tax and Development. Brighton: Institute of Development Studies.
Pichhadze, A. (2015). Exposing Unaddressed Issues in the OECD's BEPS Project: What About the Roles and Implications of Contract Interpretation Law and Private International Law in the Transfer Pricing Arm's Length Comparability Analysis? *World Tax Journal, 7,* 383-416.
Pistone, P. (2014). Coordinating the Action of Regional and Global Players during the Shift from Bilateralism to Multilateralism in International Tax Law. *World Tax Journal,* 3-9.
Quinones, N. (2014). International Tax Arbitration as an ADR Solution in a Time of Global Demands. In A. Rovine, *Contemprorary Issues in International Taxation and Mediation* (pp. 459-471). New York: Fordham University Press.
Quinones, N. (2016). Prologo. In M.E. Gutierrez, & N. Quinones, *Resulados del Plan de Acción BEPS y su aplicación en Colombia* (pp. 7-11). Bogota: ICDT.

Rixen, T. (2016). Institutional Reform of Global Tax Governance: A Proposal. In P. D. (Eds), *Global Tax Governance What Is Wrong with it and How to Fix It* (pp. 325–351). Colchester, UK: ECPR Press.

Sadiq, K. (2013). A Nation's Role in Addressing Base Erosion and Profit Shifting: Sovereignty in Relation to Transfer Pricing. *New Zealand Journal of Taxation Law and Policy, 19* (4), 343–363.

Sanders, R. (2002). The Fight Against Fiscal Colonialism the OECD and Small Jurisdictions. *The Roundtable* (365), 325–248.

Sawyer, A. (2009). *Developing a World Tax Organization: The Way Forward.* Birmingham: Fiscal Publications Press.

Sengupta, D. (23 March 2016). The Indian Equalization Levy. *Tax India International,* pp. 1–5.

CHAPTER 9
The Other Side of BEPS: "Imperial Taxation" and "International Tax Imperialism"

Sergio André Rocha

§9.01 INTRODUCTION

After almost a century orbiting around the basic principles laid down by the 1928 League of Nations draft convention on double taxation, the international taxation field has been shaken by an unexpected and unstoppable force called base erosion and profit shifting (BEPS).

Looking back in history, one will notice that the birth and development of international taxation is intrinsically connected with the creation of Income Tax and with the economic crises that have challenged mankind over the years.

Even though some rudimentary forms of income taxation can be traced far back in time, modern income taxation is actually a creation dating from the 1800s and early 1900s.

In England, Income Tax was first established in 1799 to support the war against Napoleon.[1] However, after more than a century during which the tax was in and out of validity, it was finally and firmly enacted in 1907. According to Charles Adams, "By 1910, British income taxes evolved to where they are today."[2]

The United States of America enacted its first Income Tax in 1862. In 1895, the Supreme Court decided that the tax was unconstitutional because tax revenues had to be shared among the states. In 1909, a new tax was created, which was considered to

---

1. James Coffield, A *Popular History of Taxation: From Ancient to Modern Times* (Longman, 1970) p. 90.
2. Charles Adams, *For Good and Evil: The Impact of Taxes in the Course of Civilization* (Madison Books, 2001) p. 364.

be an "excise tax" and upheld by the Supreme Court.³ Only after the 16th Amendment to the Constitution,⁴ was the Income Tax definitely established in the United States in 1913.⁵

French Income Tax was created a little later – 1914.⁶ According to Professor Guy Gest, "The first French income tax system was instituted by three statutes in 1914 and 1917. It was a mixture of the then English and Prussian systems in that it was characterized by the imposition of seven flat rates on seven different scheduler categories of income (almost the same as today) at the first level and progressive tax on the total of incomes from all scheduler categories accrued to or received by the taxpayer at the second level."⁷

In the German states, Income Tax was created in the nineteenth century. In Prussia, for instance, the tax was first enacted in 1851. Income Tax was later reformed in 1891.⁸ In Professor Wolfgang Schön's words, "The history of modern income taxation in Germany starts with the Prussian Income Tax Act of 1891, which introduced a systematic 'source-based' approach to income taxation. Due to the heavy financial burden of the World War I, the legislative power was shifted to the German Reich by the Weimar Constitution of 1919."⁹

Income Taxation arrived a little later in Latin America. The tax was created in 1922 in Brazil¹⁰ and only by 1932 in Argentina.¹¹

These brief comments about the birth of income taxation obviously do not touch on the controversies surrounding its appearance. It is known that the creation of the Income Tax has incurred strong opposition in all jurisdictions where it was implemented for the first time. Instead, these initial remarks are intended to place the consolidation of the Income Tax historically at the beginning of the twentieth century.

This chronology is important in making the connection between the initial impetus for the development of income taxation and the first steps of international taxation. The tax cooperation treaty signed between France and Belgium in 1843 is singled out by some authors as one of the first tax treaties ever signed.¹² Later, in 1899,

---

3. Richard L. Doernberg, Howard E. Abrams, and Don A. Leatherman, *Federal Income Taxation of Corporations and Partnerships* (Wolters Kluwer, 2009) p. 3.
4. Seligman commented on the proposition of the 16th Amendment to the U.S. Constitution. See Edwin R.A. Seligman, *The Income Tax: A Study of the History, Theory, and Practice of the Income Taxation at Home and Abroad* (The Lawbook Exchange, 1914) pp. 590–627.
5. See James Coffield, *A Popular History of Taxation: From Ancient to Modern Times* (Longman, 1970) pp. 230–232; Carlos Araújo Leonetti, "Breve Histórico da Tributação da Renda," Ubaldo Cesar Balthazar (ed.), *O Tributo na História: Da Antiguidade à Globalização* (Fundação Boiteux, 2006) pp. 273–274.
6. See Louis Trotabas and Jean-Marie Cotteret, *Droit Fiscal* (Dalloz, 1997) p. 145; Jacques Grosclaude and Philippe Marchessou, *Droit Fiscal Général* (Dalloz, 2003) p. 47.
7. Guy Gest, "France," Hugh J. Ault and Brian J. Arnold (eds.), *Comparative Income Taxation: A Structural Analysis*, 2nd Ed. (Kluwer Law International, 2004) p. 37.
8. Ferdinand H. M. Grapperhaus, *Tax Tales From the Second Millennium* (IBFD, 2009) p. 66.
9. Wolfgang Schön, "Germany," Hugh J. Ault and Brian J. Arnold (eds.), *Comparative Income Taxation: A Structural Analysis*, 2nd Ed. (Kluwer Law International, 2004) p. 53.
10. See Benedito Ferreira, *A História da Tributação no Brasil: Causas e Efeitos* (Brasília, 1986) p. 75.
11. See Dino Jarach, *Finanzas Públicas y Derecho Tributario* (Abeledo-Perrot, 1996) p. 529.
12. See Sunita Jogarajan, *Prelude to the International Tax Treaty Network: 1815–1914 Early Tax Treaties and the Conditions for Action* (Oxford Journal of Legal Studies, 2011) p. 9.

Chapter 9: The Other Side of BEPS §9.01

the first double tax convention was signed between Prussia and the Austro-Hungarian Empire. The treaty became necessary after the Austro-Hungarian Empire created its income tax in 1896.[13]

Accordingly, international taxation as it is known today evolved only after the introduction of income taxation as one of the most relevant sources of state revenue. Starting in the twentieth century, western states have organized themselves in such a way that most public revenues are derived from the collection of taxes and not from the exploitation of government property.[14] The importance of income taxation as a source of revenue for modern states – and its weight as a burden on taxpayers – rendered inevitable the development of an instrument to allow countries to share tax revenues and to protect taxpayers against double taxation.

Therefore, the stimulus for the first double tax conventions, which occurred before World War I, was the birth of income taxation. This fact alone shows that – even though modern tax conventions have purposes other than simply avoiding double taxation[15] – there is an unbreakable bond between international taxation and the Income Tax.[16]

Although income taxation is at the core of International Tax Law, the creation of Income Tax alone did not provide sufficient momentum for the development of this field. Indeed, the development of the so-called International Tax Regime[17] is even more consequence of economic chaos and crisis.

If we single out the most important moments for the growth and development of international taxation standards, we will certainly recall the role that the two world wars had in this process.[18]

Indeed, the first great initiative for the development of international taxation followed the end of World War I and the devastation that it provoked throughout Europe. Therefore, one can make a connection between the work of the League of Nations and the economic challenges posed by the end of the conflict.

World War II had a similar impact. It triggered the creation of the Organisation for European Economic Co-operation (OEEC), which was later transformed into the Organisation for Economic Co-operation and Development (OECD). Given that it was up to the OECD to pick-up the work regarding international taxation from where the League of Nations left it, this points once again to the close connection between the end of the war and the focus on the development of international taxation standards.

---

13. See Sunita Jogarajan, Prelude to the International Tax Treaty Network: 1815–1914 Early Tax Treaties and the Conditions for Action (Oxford Journal of Legal Studies, 2011) p. 12; Christian Freiherr von Roenne, "The Very Beginning – The First Tax Treaties," Thomas Ecker and Gernot Ressler (eds.), History of Tax Treaties: The Relevance of the OECD Documents for the Interpretation of Tax Treaties (Linde, 2011) pp. 24–26.
14. See José Casalta Nabais, O Dever Fundamental de Pagar Impostos (Almedina, 1998) pp. 199–204.
15. See Sergio André Rocha, Interpretation of Double Taxation Conventions: General Theory and Brazilian Perspective (Kluwer, 2009) pp. 6–17.
16. See Adolfo Atchabahian, Derecho Tributario Internacional (Horacio García Belsunce, Tratado de Tributación, Astrea, 2003) p. 529.
17. On the "International Tax Regime," see: Reuven S. Avi-Yohah, International Tax as International Law: An Analysis of the International Tax Regime (Cambridge University Press, 2007).
18. See Alberto Xavier, Direito Tributário Internacional do Brasil, 8th Ed. (Forense, 2015) p. 75.

History has recently repeated itself. The latest proposed changes in international taxation – which are putting in check long-standing paradigms of this area – are a direct consequence of the global economic crisis that has shaken the world since 2008, and which has impacts still being felt around the globe.

The global economic crisis has forced countries to review their positions on the taxation of cross-border transactions. And it has fostered the largest global reaction against so-called aggressive tax planning in history. At the core of this global reaction is the OECD/G-20 BEPS Project.

Public attention has been focused on large multinationals as culprits, which have been tried and found guilty in the court of public opinion. Moreover, this strong view that large multinationals – and possibly even companies in general – are engaged in "aggressive tax planning" has triggered a reaction from countries that in some cases might be as aggressive as the problem that it intended to counteract.

This development leads us to what we call "Imperial Taxation." This is a view of basic taxation principles such that they can become more protective of the states themselves and less protective of taxpayers.

On the other hand, even though reference is made to the OECD/G-20 BEPS Project, perhaps it would be more accurate to refer to it as the OECD BEPS Project. Even though the G-20 economies have politically backed the Project, it was indeed developed inside the OECD. Yariv Brauner's words seem completely accurate, when he states that, "The OECD was not only charged by the G20 to lead the BEPS project with no supervision beyond the highest political levels but also succeeded in positioning itself as an independent partner to the G20, taking ownership of the project rather than acting in a subordinate role."[19] And Allison Christians perfectly depicts the current international tax political context:

> "Yet despite the specter of the G20 as a 'new model of multilateral engagement', the United States and Europe continue to dominate a virtually impervious institutional architecture of tax policymaking in the form of the Organisation for Economic Cooperation and Development (OECD), an international network of thirty of the world's wealthiest countries. The OECD has long enjoyed a position of central importance in formulating and disseminating tax policy norms, labeling itself the 'market leader in developing [tax] standards and guidelines.' This characterization is widely recognized as accurate and probably impervious to change. The emergence of the G20 as an economic policy leader does not alter this architecture, but provides an opportunity to syndicate OECD policy positions under the new, more inclusive and representative label of G20-endorsed 'internationally agreed tax standards.' To date, the financial crisis and G20 diplomatic leadership have helped the United States and Europe achieve existing tax policy aims by enlisting new support for an existing process of OECD-led tax policy development."
>
> "As a result, the financial crisis may have elevated developing countries to a more prominent policy leadership position in the G20, but G20 leadership may not

---

19. Yariv Brauner, "Transfer Pricing Aspects of Intangibles: The Cost Contribution Arrangement Model," Michael Lang, Alfred Storck, and Raffaele Petruzzi (eds.), *Transfer Pricing in a Post-BEPS World* (Kluwer, 2016) p. 100.

provide developing countries with a meaningful voice in global tax policy dialogue. Even so, the rising prominence of the G20 signals that creating opportunities for developing countries to have such a voice is a priority, whether during a time of crisis or beyond. The institutional shift to the G20 thus may have little impact on the current distribution of tax policymaking power, but it may create an institutional infrastructure from which developing countries may exert more influence in the OECD and other institutions where tax policy norms emerge. Understanding the dynamics of leadership in global tax policy therefore requires an examination of the relative capacities of leadership from the G20 and the OECD, as well as other institutions that play a role in influencing the direction of tax reform efforts. That is the aim of this Article. Part I explores the pressure on tax policy that arose from the financial crisis and examines the respective roles played by the G20 and the OECD in tax policymaking during the crisis. Part II compares the institutional capacities of the G20 and the OECD in developing and disseminating tax policy norms, and analyzes the interplay of leadership between these institutions. Part III asks whether and how developing countries can influence tax policy more effectively through the G20."[20]

It is well known that in October 2015, the OECD released the final reports on the fifteen BEPS Actions, which provide several recommendations on how countries should deal with BEPS issues.

Reviewing the BEPS Action Plan, and the OECD's recommendations regarding its Actions, is not the focus of this chapter. What is relevant is that the OECD's BEPS Project recommendations seem to be more and more connected with discussions regarding "harmonization" and "coordination," which is only natural considering its global reach.

This raises the question as to who should perform the coordination role.

It is well known that the OECD is not an internationally independent organ, but rather an association of a certain group of countries. This puts in question whether the OECD's leadership in this matter can be considered independent from the special interests of its member countries.

It is true that the OECD has been trying to attract more and more countries into the debates connected to the BEPS Project – especially after the introduction of its "inclusive framework." Notwithstanding, it is unclear whether such countries – which are not OECD or even G-20 members – will actually have a strong voice in shaping the final outcomes of the Project, or will have the liberty to decide whether or not to implement the OECD's recommendations.

In this context, there is another aspect of BEPS that should be carefully considered – especially by developing countries – which this author will refer to as "International Tax Imperialism."

Beginning with the dawn of international taxation, passing through the League of Nations' meetings in Mexico (1943) and London (1946), and continuing until current times, there has been a long-standing conflict between developing countries and

---

20. Allison Christians, "Taxation in a Time of Crisis: Policy Leadership from the OECD to the G20" (2010) 5 (1) *Northwestern Journal of Law & Social Policy*, pp. 19-20.

developed countries regarding the sharing of tax revenues that derive from cross-border transactions.[21]

Therefore, if developing and developed countries have different views regarding the criteria for assigning taxing rights globally – and if the reshaping of the "International Tax Regime" is being chaired by the OECD and developed economies – there is justifiable concern that changes to the "International Tax Regime" might be implemented in a way that further benefits developed countries to the detriment of developing nations.

This chapter focuses on commenting on these two aspects: (i) the current environment that is leading us to some sort of "Imperial Taxation"; and (ii) whether the BEPS Project might actually foster some sort of "International Tax Imperialism." This term being understood to mean the exportation of developed countries tax patterns to developing economies in way that favor the former.

One formal note: in this chapter, all direct quotations of texts not originally written in English have been freely translated into English by this author.

§9.02 DEVELOPMENT OF "IMPERIAL TAXATION" IN THE POST-BEPS WORLD

In 2015, people around the globe celebrated the 800th anniversary of the *Magna Carta Libertatum*. This is considered to be the first constitutional-like document that established restrictions on a sovereign's basically unlimited power.

The symbolic relevance of the *Magna Carta* has survived the test of time throughout the centuries because it challenged dogmas (such as "the king can do no wrong") that marked absolutism. As pointed out by Thomas Cooley:

> For several hundred years, however, changes had from time to time been made in the common-law principles by means of statutes. Originally the purpose of general statutes was mainly to declare and reaffirm such common-law principles as, by reason of usurpations and abuses, had come to be of doubtful force, and which, therefore, needed to be authoritatively announced, that king and subject alike might understand and observe them. Such as the purpose of the first great statute, promulgated at a time when the legislative power was exercised by the king alone, and which is still known as the Magna Carta of King John.[22]

In the *Magna Carta*, one can find the earliest origins of the protection of citizens' rights against state power – which is at the base of the bills of rights found in modern

---

21. There are authors such as João Francisco Bianco and Ramon Tomazela Santos who argue that the source/residence conflict has been overcome (*see* João Francisco Bianco and Ramon Tomazela Santos, "A Change of Paradigm in International Tax Law: Article 7 of Tax Treaties and the Need to Resolve the Source versus Residence Dichotomy," (2016) 70 (3) *Bulletin for International Taxation*. This chapter does not subscribe to such views. The author's position is that current international taxation is still marked by the conflict between source and residence. *See* Veronika Daurer. *Tax Treaties and Developing Countries* (Kluwer, 2014) pp. 22–28.
22. Thomas M. Cooley, *A Treatise on the Constitutional Limitations Which Rest Upon the Legislative Power of the United States of the American Union* (Little, Brown, and Company, 1883) p. 31.

constitutions and human rights treaties. It is also the *Magna Carta* that marks the development of the principle of no taxation without representation.[23]

No doubt, taxation is one of the areas where the balance between the legitimate exercise of government power and the illegitimate violation of citizens' rights is most challenging.

In current times, the use of the word "citizen" is significant since the term "taxpayer" (as a legal category) has been demonized by some sectors of the media, local governments, and international organizations.

Yes. Before being taxpayers we are all citizens. Even legal entities are ultimately comprised of people.

The transformation of most modern states into fiscal states[24] – i.e., states that depend on tax collection to obtain the resources to fund all their activities – has changed the nature of the obligation to pay taxes. Some authors have begun to argue that there is a fundamental or constitutional obligation to pay taxes.[25] Important works from authors such as Liam Murphy and Thomas Nagel[26] and Stephen Holmes and Cass Sunstein[27] highlight that there is no "pre-tax" income because one's capacity to generate income is dependent on a state's infrastructure paid for by taxes.

However, this line of thought, to which this author subscribes, has been used to support an inversion of the whole structure of tax systems. Legal principles that are, at their core, protections of taxpayers against the state have been transformed into protections for the state against taxpayers.

Consider, for instance, the principle of transparency, which is at the center of modern constitutional, administrative, financial, and tax law.[28] It is, first and foremost, a protection for the citizens against the state. It establishes as a goal a state of affairs that guarantees full disclosure of a government's actions to its citizens.

The principle of transparency is not a one-way street. It also applies to citizens and requires disclosure and combating opaque situations that prevent the due application of laws in general. Nevertheless, one should not forget: State and government transparency come first. Ricardo Lobo Torres has analyzed the principle of transparency from a Brazilian perspective. However, his lesson can also be applied in the realm of international taxation:

> Tax transparency is an implicit constitutional principle. It establishes that financial activity needs to evolve in accordance with standards such as clarity, openness, and simplicity. Therefore, it is directed to the state and to society, to international

---

23. Thomas M. Cooley, *The General Principles of Constitutional Law in the United States of America* (Little, Brown, and Company, 1883) pp. 6–7.
24. *See* José Casalta Nabais, *O Dever Fundamental de Pagar Impostos* (Almedina, 1998) pp. 191–221; Sergio André Rocha, *Processo Administrativo Fiscal: Controle Administrativo do Lançamento Tributário*, 4th Ed. (Lumen Juris, 2010) pp. 6–9.
25. *See* José Casalta Nabais, *O Dever Fundamental de Pagar Impostos* (Almedina, 1998) p. 185.
26. Liam Murphy and Thomas Nagel, *The Myth of Ownership* (Oxford University Press, 2002) pp. 31–37.
27. Stephen Holmes and Cass R. Sunstein, *The Cost of Rights: Why Liberty Depends on Taxes* (W. W. Norton & Company, 1999) pp. 35–76.
28. *See* Sergio André Rocha, *Troca Internacional de Informações para Fins Fiscais* (QuartierLatin, 2015) pp. 58–62.

financial organs and to non-governmental entities. It orients and contains problems regarding the preparation of public budgets and their responsible management, the creation of rules against abusive tax planning, the end of bank secrecy, and the fight against corruption.[29]

This maxim seems to have been forgotten by those entities now in charge of reshaping the "International Tax Regime."

Some of the most relevant criticism directed towards the work on transparency and exchange of information that is coordinated by the Global Forum on Transparency and Exchange of Information (hereinafter "Global Forum") is that it has ascribed very little importance to the protection of taxpayer's rights in its crusade to ensure transparency.[30] Regarding transparency, the BEPS Project approach is also not exempt from such criticism.

In October 2015, the New York University School of Law hosted the annual David R. Tillinghast Lecture on International Taxation. The speaker was Pascal Saint-Amans, the well-known Director of the OECD's Centre for Tax Policy and Administration as well as the ultimate coordinator of the BEPS Project.

At the end of the 43rd minute of the speech (which is available on YouTube), Saint-Amans stated that, "Transparency, from my perspective, is transparency from the taxpayer to the Tax Administration, and maybe the other way around as well. You know that there is an Action related to more transparency from the Tax Administrations to the taxpayer and that is the Action 14 on Mutual Agreement Procedures."[31]

With all due respect to Saint-Amans' position, he could not be more wrong.

As previously mentioned, it is impossible to think about the principle of transparency as a legal standard directed first to citizens and only secondarily – if at all – to state and government officials.

We must be very careful with discourses that justify the eclipse of taxpayers' rights that have been gained after centuries of struggle in the war against an archenemy, whether such an archenemy is terrorism, weapons and drugs trafficking, or the surprisingly deemed public enemy no. 1 of countries: multinational enterprises.

In current times, which have been marked by financial crises and the fall of the welfare state (in those countries that have had one), multinationals have been tried and found guilty in the court of public opinion for struggles that common people are facing in their day-to-day lives. Not poor management by state administrations. Not government corruption scandals. But multinationals?

States diminish themselves in face of the all-mighty multinationals. It is claimed that the fight against such powerful enemies requires a new approach to international taxation that puts the protection of taxpayers' rights in second place. The stage is set.

---

29. Ricardo Lobo Torres, *Tratado de Direito Constitucional, Financeiro e Tributário: Valores e Princípios Constitucionais Tributários* (Renovar, 2005) v. II, pp. 243–244.
30. *See* Sergio André Rocha, "Exchange of Tax-Related Information and the Protection of Taxpayer Rights: General Comments and the Brazilian Perspective" (2016) 70 (9) *Bulletin for International Taxation*, pp. 502–503.
31. Available at https://www.youtube.com/watch?v = K8V_6j1gx-k.

Chapter 9: The Other Side of BEPS §9.02

This viewpoint clearly underlies the current approaches to transparency and exchange of information. Taxpayers' notification rights are seen as potential obstacles to effectiveness in the exchange of information and therefore should be ignored.

The first problem with this line of thought is that states are not the weak link compared to multinationals – especially those states that are OECD member countries. The problem is that they operate under the maxim "each man – in this case, each country – for itself."

To some extent, the BEPS Project is an attempt by states to show that they can put aside domestic interests and work together in a coordinated fashion. Whether this will prevail remains to be seen.

However, states should have started by pointing their fingers at themselves. If there is "aggressive tax planning," they are as much to blame for it as large multinationals. As noted by Hugh J. Ault, Wolfgang Schön, and Stephen E. Shay, "MNE behavior is only one side of the coin. International profit shifting and base erosion envisaged by large business enterprises would be ineffective without countries offering preferential tax rules, including low/no tax regimes for particular taxpayers or income categories and benign provisions on profit measurement. To put it differently: MNE tax avoidance is just the flipside of harmful tax competition."[32] This is also the position of authors such as Gema Patón Garcia,[33] Luís Eduardo Schoueri,[34] and Heleno Taveira Tôrres.[35]

The reshaping of fundamental tax principles and the limiting of taxpayers' rights can lead to what this author terms "Imperial Taxation." This produces our greatest concern: how the "regular Joes" – small, mid-size, and even large domestic companies and small multinational corporations – will be affected. We should make no mistake: once legal principles have been mutilated and taxpayers' rights overturned, effects will be felt by all taxpayers of all sizes – humans and legal entities alike.

The public discourse that states are "in dire need of tax revenues" should not be directed only to multinationals. For instance, the notion that transparency is more an *obligation* of taxpayers than their *right* has profound domestic tax implications.

The financial crises and their impacts on countries' budgets have triggered a significant change in the relationship between states and taxpayers. For instance, in Portugal the crisis was used to justify an attempt to overcome basic taxpayers' rights, such as the right not to be charged new or increased taxes in the same fiscal year these

---

32. Hugh J. Ault, Wolfgang Schön, and Stephen E. Shay, "Base Erosion and Profit Shifting: A Roadmap for Reform," (2014) 68 (8) *Bulletin for International Taxation*, p. 276.
33. Gema Patón Garcia, "Análisis de las Medidas Españolas Alineadas con el Plan de Acción BEPS: Desafíos en la Implementación e Incidencia en Latinoamérica," ILADT, *Memorias de las XXVII Jornadas Latinoamericanas de Derecho Tributario* (ILADT, 2015) p. 186.
34. Luís Eduardo Schoueri, "O Projeto BEPS: Ainda uma Estratégia Militar," Marcus Livio Gomes and Luís Eduardo Schoueri (eds.), *A Tributação Internacional na Era Pós-BEPS* (Lumen Juris, 2016) v. I, p. 30.
35. Heleno Taveira Tôrres, *Direito Tributário Internacional: Planejamento Tributário e Operações Transnacionais* (Revista dos Tribunais, 2001) p. 68.

taxes were created or increased. Naturally, this move was argued based on the country's state of financial emergency.[36]

The role played by the public opinion is also very dangerous. The "Scarlet Letter" that was initially hung on multinationals is easily passed along to other taxpayers, damning the entrepreneurial class as a whole.

Financial need and people on the streets is a dangerous combination in the hands of populist governments and can pose a threat to taxpayers' rights. Brazil's current situation is a perfect example. Under huge budgetary pressure, taxes are being created or increased – not always in accordance with constitutional provisions – thereby putting taxpayers' ability to pay at risk.

Both the Global Forum's and BEPS' work share a common feature: they are aimed at optimizing states' tax collection. The taxpayer – the citizen – is not in their focus. This is unacceptable. There is nothing more urgent than recovering the taxpayers' protagonist role in taxation, where they rightfully belong. This does not mean that tax authorities' focus is completely misguided. It only means that they need to find a way to achieve their rightful objectives without leaving taxpayers' rights behind.

§9.03 "INTERNATIONAL TAX REGIME" AND "INTERNATIONAL TAX IMPERIALISM"

From a historical perspective, "imperialism" refers to the control by more economically and militarily developed nations over less developed countries. The word "imperialism" is often used to refer to the "colonization" of African, Asian, and Latin American countries by European countries.

The attempt to export an "International Tax Regime" to developing countries can be considered a form of "International Tax Imperialism." Even the concept of "developing countries" is arbitrary, since it encompasses countries with significantly different economic and political features.

As used in this chapter, "International Tax Imperialism" means the transformation of certain tax criteria that favor the interests of developed economies into international tax standards that become considered as basic principles of international taxation.

In a previous article, the author used as an example of "International Tax Imperialism" the defense of the so-called principle of the permanent establishment[37] to assign taxing rights to source countries.[38] As stated in that article:

---

36. *See* Suzana Tavares da Silva, Sustentabilidade e solidariedade em tempos de crise, José Casalta Nabais and Suzana Tavares da Silva (eds.), *Sustentabilidade Fiscal em Tempos de Crise* (Almedina, 2011) pp. 61–91.
37. *See* Alexander Hemmelrath, "Article 7. Business Profits," Klaus Vogel (ed.), *On Double Taxation Conventions*, 3rd Ed. (Kluwer Law International, 1998) pp. 399–400; Carlo Garbarino, *Manuale di Tassazione Internazionale* (IPSOA, 2005) p. 163; Alberto Xavier, *Direito Tributário Internacional do Brasil*, 7th Ed. (Forense, 2010) pp. 551–552; Ekkehart Reimer, "Article 7. Business Profits," Ekkehart Reimer and Alexander Rust (eds.), *Klaus Vogel on Double Taxation Conventions*, 4th Ed. (Kluwer, 2015) v. I, p. 501.
38. Sergio André Rocha, "International Fiscal Imperialism and the 'Principle' of the Permanent Establishion," (2014) 68 (2) *Bulletin for International Taxation*, pp. 83–87.

"Calderón Carrero (2004) also describes the rule under article 7(1) of the OECD Model as 'one of the great principles of international taxation in relation to the taxation of business income', adding that justification may be found in the fact that 'an enterprise of one contracting state that carries on business in another state does not participate to a significant extent in the 'economic life' of the other state, unless it operates in its territory through a permanent establishment'. The same justification appears in the Commentary on Article 7 of the OECD Model (2010)."

"There are no grounds for contesting, and this is certainly not our intention in this article, the fact that the 'principle of the permanent establishment' is a valid and coherent criterion for the distribution of taxing rights between countries that sign a tax treaty. However, it seems that it is nothing more than a reasonable criterion; certainly not a fundamental principle of international tax law."

"It is evident that by stating that this 'principle' is a fundamental rule of international taxation, the intention is to eliminate the possible consideration of other criteria that are also legally valid and coherent for the taxation of business profits – such as taxation, whether exclusive or concurrent, of such earnings by the source country – an argument that has constantly been raised by developing countries, especially Latin American ones."[39]

The notion that passive income should only – or mostly – be taxed at the state of residence is another example of the transformation of one possible taxing standard into "the standard" for assigning the "fair share of tax" among countries.

It is fairly clear that the OECD has usually been the number one "spokesperson" for the developed countries' interests, and its Model Tax Convention is the formalization of the standards that favor such countries.

This situation led to the development of the UN Model Convention. However, this Model fell short in protecting developing countries rights. As well noted by Francisco Dornelles (who served as Brazil's representative in the committee that drafted the UN Model), the decision to use the OECD Model as a basis and to maintain the requirement of a permanent establishment to allow taxation at source in the case of business profits significantly reduced the capacity of the UN Model to protect the interests of developing countries.[40]

The attempt by countries to seek to impose their fiscal policies through the monopolization of international organizations is not surprising. It is a common feature in the history of mankind. Another feature that can be observed is what we call "theoretical tax imperialism."

With the considerable growth of International Tax Law in recent years, researchers from developing countries have been devoting more and more time to works prepared abroad. Students and researchers have been taking courses abroad and bringing back to their home countries the results of their international experience. LLM

---

39. Sergio André Rocha, "International Fiscal Imperialism and the 'Principle' of the Permanent Establishment," (2014) 68 (2) *Bulletin for International Taxation*, pp. 84–85.
40. *See* Francisco Dornelles, "O Modelo da ONU para Eliminar a Dupla Tributação da Renda e os Países em Desenvolvimento," Agostinho Toffoli Tavolaro et. al. (eds.), *Princípios Tributários no Direito Brasileiro: Estudos em Homenagem a Gilberto de Ulhôa Canto* (Forense, 1988) pp. 195–232.

programs on international taxation in the United States and throughout Europe are packed with students from Latin America, Africa, and other developing regions.

This interchange is extremely positive for the development of a body of national legal principles. However, for this purpose, it is important that this "importation" of foreign research and ideas be carried out in a critical manner – without the wholesale substitution of national doctrine for international doctrine and allowing room for the former to incorporate the phenomenon of international taxation in light of its own context.

In part, "tax colonization" is also a consequence of the incestuous relation between academic research and legal tax practice in developing countries.

Unlike developed countries, it is extremely rare in developing ones to find academics that are devoted full-time to academic activities. More often than not, academics are also lawyers, who are heavily engaged in defending clients against charges from local tax authorities. Therefore, there is little concern with whether the country should be allowed to levy taxes or not. The focus, instead, is to eliminate source taxation.

Besides this fact, which compromises academic independence, there is another one that is even more grave. In some countries – and this is the case with Brazil – international tax literature is not even mostly produced by academics, but by practitioners. These experts are usually not concerned with international tax policy issues or with whether their countries should be entitled to more taxing rights in the international taxation scheme. Nearly universally, practitioners tend to be more concerned with their client's interests than with national tax policy.

The consequence of this state of affairs is "colonized" tax literature, that sometimes (uncritically) reproduces foreign opinions and standards without analyzing their impacts from a national tax policy perspective.

§9.04 BEPS AND "INTERNATIONAL TAX IMPERIALISM"

The BEPS Project reflects the concerns mentioned above. Under the banner of multilateralism, "International Tax Regime" may be being reshaped in favor of developed countries. The paragraphs below comment on some areas where developing countries should be particularly careful with the obvious solutions presented by the OECD in its BEPS reports.

[A] Arbitration

The debates about using arbitration to settle international tax disputes – or about creating an international tax court for the same purpose – are not new in international taxation.[41] However, after the inclusion of Article 25(5) in the 2008 update to the OECD Model Convention, this topic became even more pressing.

---

41. Sergio André Rocha, *Interpretation of Double Taxation Conventions: General Theory and Brazilian Perspective* (Kluwer, 2009) pp. 188–194.

The final report on Action 14 of the BEPS Project encouraged countries to adopt mandatory binding arbitration in their treaties as an instrument to resolve controversies regarding the application of tax treaties. According to this report:

> The business community and a number of countries consider that mandatory binding arbitration is the best way of ensuring that tax treaty disputes are effectively resolved through MAP. Whilst there is no consensus among all OECD and G20 countries on the adoption of arbitration as a mechanism to ensure the resolution of MAP cases, a group of countries has committed to adopt and implement mandatory binding arbitration as a way to resolve disputes that otherwise prevent the resolution of cases through the mutual agreement procedure. The countries that have expressed interest in doing so include Australia, Austria, Belgium, Canada, France, Germany, Ireland, Italy, Japan, Luxembourg, the Netherlands, New Zealand, Norway, Poland, Slovenia, Spain, Sweden, Switzerland, the United Kingdom and the United States; this represents a major step forward as together these countries are involved in more than 90 percent of outstanding MAP cases at the end of 2013, as reported to the OECD.[42]

Double tax conventions signed by developing countries do not always follow the so-called "International Tax Regime" or "OECD Standards." For instance, as noted by Luís Eduardo Schoueri, Brazil is an example of a country that has been successful in developing a tax treaty policy of its own,[43] that departs from the OECD Model and is closer to the UN Model Convention.[44]

One of the most disregarded features of legal interpretation is that it is not merely declaratory but also has a relevant creative aspect. As this author pointed out in another study:

> "Marco Aurélio Greco is absolutely correct when he states that 'the interpreter has a duty of fidelity to the text, but this does not mean that the result of the interpretation is something merely mathematical or deductive logic'."

> "It cannot be denied, therefore, that within the linguistic limits of the normative text the interpreter exercises a creative function, consisting of determining which of the possible meanings of the text will form part of the individual and concrete norm."

> "The recognition that interpretation comprises a creative function does not mean that the interpreter creates the norm from nothing, *ex nihilo*. According to Eros Roberto Grau, 'the product of the interpretation is the norm expressed as such. But it (the norm) partially preexists, potentially, in the cover of the text, the cover of the statement'."

> "Accordingly, the interpreter creates, but does not create from nothing, nor does his task cease to be circumscribed by limits contained in the text interpreted, in the values and interests at stake, which eliminate any decision making."[45]

---

42. OECD, *Making Dispute Resolution Mechanisms More Effective* (OECD, 2015) p. 41.
43. Luís Eduardo Schoueri, "Contribuição à História dos Acordos de Bitributação: a Experiência Brasileira" (2002) 22 *Revista Direito Tributário Atual*, p. 280.
44. Sergio André Rocha, "El Proyecto BEPS de la OCDE y el Derecho Fiscal Internacional en Brasil" (2016) 35 *Revista Direito Tributário Atual*, pp. 388–389.
45. Sergio André Rocha, *Interpretation of Double Taxation Conventions: General Theory and Brazilian Perspective* (Kluwer, 2009) pp. 66–67.

If treaties signed by developing countries depart many times from what is the "OECD Standard," and if the interpretation of legal texts and international treaties alike is definitely a creative endeavor, it is certainly dangerous for countries that have been able to put in place their own international treaty policy, to subject themselves to international binding arbitration, which could become an instrument of "International Tax Imperialism."

Not even the fact that there would be arbitrators from developing countries participating in the arbitration procedure reduces this concern. In fact, as noted in the previous topic, "Theoretical International Tax Imperialism" knows no borders. Therefore, in this author's view, subscribing to the use of international binding arbitration as a mechanism to settle disputes could be the same as being exposed to an interpretative override of a country's treaty policy.

In November 2016, the OECD published the Multilateral Convention to Implement Tax Treaty Related Measures to Prevent Base Erosion and Profit Shifting (the "Multilateral Convention"). Part VI of the Multilateral Convention established rules regarding arbitration. Its Article 19 deals with Mandatory Binding Arbitration.

In light of previous comments, it is this author's opinion that developing countries should not adhere to the Mandatory Binding Arbitration provision of the Multilateral Convention. This would avoid the risk of having their treaty policy overridden by international binding arbitration.

[B] Transfer Pricing

Perhaps an interesting starting point for this topic is to question whether the BEPS work on transfer pricing highlights a shift in the focus of transfer pricing rules, as is argued by Luís Eduardo Schoueri.

Per Schoueri's lesson, "While originally conceived as an anti-avoidance mechanism, transfer pricing and the related debates have gradually moved towards a consideration of the taxation of the 'fair share' on profits derived by multinational enterprises (MNEs), irrespective of any concern based on the actual income derived from an activity subject to a state's jurisdiction."[46]

In his view, transfer-pricing rules were not initially meant to deal with the sharing of tax revenues between countries, but to deal with "the need for equality between related and unrelated firms."[47]

If this is the case – even though nothing in the BEPS Project clearly indicates that one of its goals is to change existing rules for taxing rights allocation – a combination of Actions 8, 9, and 10 with Action 13 could set the stage for debates regarding the rightful – or fair – allocation of taxing rights between states, which could harm developing countries.

---

46. Luís Eduardo Schoueri, Arm's Length: Beyond the Guidelines of the OECD (2015) 69 (12) *Bulletin for International Taxation*, p. 690.
47. Luís Eduardo Schoueri, Arm's Length: Beyond the Guidelines of the OECD (2015) 69 (12) *Bulletin for International Taxation*, p. 695.

Chapter 9: The Other Side of BEPS §9.04[C]

In fact, in the whole discussion about risks and functions, there is one outsider that is incredibly relevant for developing countries: the consumer market, which is usually the contribution of such countries to the international flow of goods, services, and intangibles.

Using Brazil as an example, the country's transfer pricing rules are based on an adjusted version of the arm's length principle. The focus of Brazil's rules is simplicity.[48] It is to allow a more direct application of the rules by tax authorities and taxpayers. The country has already stated that it does not intend to change its transfer pricing because of BEPS[49] – and it is right in doing so.

Indeed, developing economies should not be rushing to adopt OECD recommendations. They need to consider whether they are actually necessary given their own economic reality and whether the OECD proposed model is the best taking into account its circumstances. As noted by Gemma Patón Garcia, "The adoption of the recommendations of the BEPS Plan must be the result of a meditated process by each state, considering the Plan's evolution on the international scene. However, it is not less certain that national initiatives must be adjusted to the social and economic reality of each country. Moreover, such initiatives should avoid conflicts with the tax administration of other countries with which it has commercial relations, in view of the possibility of such relationships being affected in its competitiveness."[50]

[C] Hybrid Mismatches

Hybrid mismatch arrangements are a direct consequence of the regular exercise of each country's tax sovereignty in the design of their own tax systems. Such design creates opportunities that can be used by multinationals to enjoy an overall reduced tax burden on their transactions.

One might say that there is nothing wrong with what multinationals do when they explore such hybrid mismatches. Per Reinout de Boers and Otto Marres, "A cynical take might be that only two universal principles apply in international tax: the first principle being that states will take what tax revenue they can get (where possible and at the expense of other states through tax competition); the second principle being that taxpayers will pay as little tax as they can (legally) get away (where possible using aggressive tax planning."[51]

Notwithstanding, at the core of the problem of hybrid mismatches is a crucial discussion regarding which country is entitled to tax revenue. Referring again to the article of Reinout de Boers and Otto Marres, "The very nature of hybrid mismatch

---

48. *See* Marcos Aurélio Pereira Valadão, "Brazil Country Practices," United Nations, *United Nations Practical Manual on Transfer Pricing for Developing Countries* (United Nations, 2013) pp. 370–371.
49. OECD. *Aligning Transfer Pricing Outcomes with Value Creation* (Paris: OECD, 2015) p. 185.
50. Gemma Patón Garcia, Análisis de las Medidas Españolas Alineadas con el Plan de Acción BEPS: Desafíos en la Implementación e Incidencia en Latinoamérica, ILADT, *Memorias de las XXVII Jornadas Latinoamericanas de Derecho Tributario* (ILADT: Mexico, 2015) p. 189.
51. Reinout de Boers and Otto Marres, "BEPS Action 2: Neutralizing the Effects on Hybrid Mismatches Arrangements" (2015) 43 (1) *Intertax*, p. 14.

arrangements – which benefit from at least two tax systems and which operate fully within the scope of each such system – renders it impossible to identify the loser state that should repair the mismatch."[52]

This is an area of concern for developing countries. At the heart of the discussions about the tax treatment of hybrids, there is a debate about the allocation of taxing rights. This topic was disciplined by Part II of the Multilateral Convention. In addition to these rules, the OECD has expressed opinions about some regimes established domestically by countries. For instance, in the case of Brazil, the OECD manifested its opinion against the country's dividend exemption and interest on net equity deduction.

The impact of "aggressive tax planning" on the overall tax collection of developing countries should not be highly relevant. Such countries should weigh the pros and cons of OECD's recommendations in this area before adopting them – or changing their own domestic regulations.

[D]   Digital Economy

The outcomes of BEPS Action 1 are disappointing. This is one of the few Actions where a shift of taxing rights could actually take place. Is this a signal that developed nations are pushing back on changes that might result in a loss of tax revenues? This might be the case. This is the opinion of Eva Escribano López, according to whom "The brave, out-of-the-box reform promised by the BEPS report, has been watered down by an Action Plan which, at one stroke, left out of the debate two of the main pillars that sustain the tax system (separate entity approach and standards on the allocation of taxing rights). And what is worse, the most disruptive of the actions, number 1, seems doomed to failure given the predictable internal resistances within the OECD forum. Hence, the outcome we could expect from BEPS will not be the promised comprehensive reform but rather a combination of measures aimed at restoring the effectiveness of current principles."[53]

Developing countries should push towards the development of new permanent establishment rules for the digital economy or reinforce their domestic tax withholding rules. The latter option has been working for Brazil, due to provisions in its tax treaties allowing taxation of technical services at source. However, it has its shortcomings when it comes to the taxation of commerce of goods from digital platforms.

[E]   Improper Use of Tax Treaties

There is a lot of debate regarding treaty shopping or, as the report on BEPS Action 6 calls it, the "granting of treaty benefits in inappropriate circumstances." It raises interesting and at the same time difficult questions. In fact, to ascertain what "inappropriate circumstances" are, one must determine what "appropriate

---

52. Reinout de Boers and Otto Marres, "BEPS Action 2: Neutralizing the Effects on Hybrid Mismatches Arrangements" (2015) 43 (1) *Intertax*, p. 14.
53. Eva Escribano López, "An Opportunistic, and yet Appropriate, Revision of the Source Threshold for Twenty-First Century Tax Treaties" (2015) 43 (1) *Intertax*, p. 13.

Chapter 9: The Other Side of BEPS §9.04[E]

circumstances" are. This task leads to determining what functions are served by a tax treaty, which may vary between the perspectives of a developed country and a developing country.

Indeed, as noted by Paulo Ayres Barreto and Caio Augusto Takano, some argue that in the case of developing countries' tax policies, treaty shopping as an instrument to attract of foreign investments can be considered one of the goals of a treaty. In their words:

> "Accordingly, it seems that the effective attraction of technology and foreign investment to a country which grants the benefits of a tax treaty to a person that (i) is not entitled to such benefits and (ii) indirectly obtains such benefits through the use of a genuine and productive entity (which would otherwise qualify as a resident of one of the contracting states), is not contrary to the objectives and purposes of income tax treaties and thus should not be regarded as an abuse ('improper use') of the particular treaty. If the existence of a legitimate business structure is verified and so enhances investment levels and foreign capital in the country, there is no reason to condemn the behaviour of both the taxpayer (tax avoidance) and that state (tolerating treaty shopping arrangements)."

> "In this sense, the decision of the Supreme Court of India in the Azadi Bachao Andolan case is paradigmatic. Although a comprehensive analysis of the case is beyond the scope of this article 25 a brief overview offers a valuable contribution to the discussion. In this case, the possibility to use the tax treaty between Mauritius and India to attract foreign investment and capital was expressly recognized by the Indian authorities, even though treaty benefits were indirectly granted to residents in third countries that had used structures crafted with the sole purpose of obtaining the benefits of the India-Mauritius treaty."

> "The decision of the Supreme Court of India has the merit of acknowledging that, without a specific limitation-on-benefits rule in the India-Mauritius treaty, its benefits should be granted to parties which, from a formal perspective, may be considered as residents of one of the contracting states and thus are entitled to the benefits of the treaty. [...]."[54]

These comments by Barreto and Takano bring a different perspective to debates regarding the so-called "improper use of tax treaties" from a developing country's perspective. This same position was defended by Luís Eduardo Schoueri. According to him:

> "Regarding treaty shopping, the abuse threshold is more complex, considering that it is not clear whether the fact of a third person using the benefits of the double tax convention can be considered abusive. In fact, if a double tax treaty is seen only as an instrument for mutual concessions to avoid double taxation, then it is clear that the balance initially envisaged by the parties will be undone if the concessions of one state surpasses those of the other, based on reciprocity."

> "However, if this assumption can be accepted in the case of conventions between countries with the same development level, this reasoning must be divergent when considering a relation between a developing and a developed country. In this case, as stated above, the flow of capital and income is unilateral. To the concessions

---

54. Paulo Ayres Barreto and Caio Augusto, "The Prevention of Tax Treaty Abuse in the BEPS Action 6: A Brazilian Perspective" (2015) 43 (12) *Intertax*, p. 828.

made by one of the contracting states (the source state) investment must follow. Hence, equal concessions by both states are not expected. Therefore, it does not seem to be an immediate conclusion that the use of a treaty by a resident of a third State would be considered abusive, as long as that investment resulted on an increment of investment in that state granting the benefits."[55]

Considering these comments, it seems that developing countries should not be too eager in lining up to fight treaty shopping. Most such countries do not have large treaty networks. For instance, Brazil, with its thirty-two double tax conventions, leads Latin America's countries in the number of treaties in force. Therefore, from a developing country's perspective, sometimes treaty shopping is a way of enlarging its treaty network without having to negotiate and sign dozens of new treaties.

The Multilateral Convention established several rules against treaty abuse in its Part III (Articles 6–11). Before adhering to these provisions, developing countries should be conscious about their own treaty policy – which is not always the case. If the country considers treaty shopping to be an integral part of its international tax policy, as a means for channeling foreign direct investment, they should think twice before subscribing to these articles of the Multilateral Convention.

§9.05 IN THE DEFENSE OF A "DEVELOPING COUNTRIES' INTERNATIONAL TAX REGIME"

Given the prior comments, it seems clear that there is not a single "International Tax Regime" – a set of principles that guide a group of countries' positions in defining taxation for cross-border transactions. There is at least one regime that applies to developed countries and another applicable to developing countries. It is likely that even among developing countries there is more than one "International Tax Regime."

It is this author's view that the heart of a "Developing Countries' International Tax Regime" would be the elimination of Article 7 as it stands today. It would be replaced with a provision that would allocate taxing rights to the source country, even without the presence of a permanent establishment.

Not even the League of Nations Model (approved in the Mexico meeting of 1943) had such a bold provision guaranteeing source country taxation rights. Its business profits article had the following wording:

> Article IV
> 1. Income from any industrial, commercial or agricultural business and from any other gainful activity shall be taxable only in the State where the business or activity is carried out.
> 2. If an enterprise or an individual in one of the Contracting States extends its or his activities to the other State, through isolated or occasional transactions, without possessing in that State a permanent establishment, the income derived from such activities shall be taxable only in the first State.

---

55. Luís Eduardo Schoueri, "Tributação e Cooperação Internacional" (2004) 18 *Revista Direito Tributário Atual*, p. 62.

3. If an enterprise has a permanent establishment in each of the Contracting States, each State shall tax that part of the income which is produced in its territory.
4. As regards agricultural and mining raw material and other natural materials and products, the income which results from prices prevailing between independent persons or conforming to world market quotations shall be regarded as realized in the State in which such materials or products have been produced.[56]

The end of Article 7 as it stands today would be the death certificate for various controversies generated by the concept of permanent establishment and the application of Article 5, putting an end to "aggressive tax planning" involving permanent establishments.

Another integral part of a "Developing Countries' International Tax Regime" would be reasonable source taxation on "passive income." Such taxation on dividend and interest payments should be as high as 15%. Moreover, there is no argument to justify non-taxation of royalties at source.[57] Therefore, all developing countries should follow Articles 10, 11, and 12 of UN Model, instead of their counterparts in the OECD Model. The same goes for taxation of "other income," which should be shared between source and residence countries, as established in Article 21(3) of the UN Model.

As pointed out in section §9.03[A] above, another concern of developing counties should be the mechanisms to settle disputes. Given that there is a creative aspect to interpretation,[58] "International Tax Imperialism" requires developing countries to be extra careful before subscribing to mandatory binding arbitration as a mechanism to settle disputes.

Consider, for instance, the case of Brazil, a country with its own treaty policy and one not aligned with OECD standards. Here there is a clear risk of its being overridden by international arbitration. The country's treaties usually employ Article 7, by: (a) establishing that technical services should be taxed as royalties; (b) including the lease of scientific, industrial, and commercial equipment in the concept of royalties; and (c) including insurance and re-insurance in the scope of Article 5 – as provided for in the UN Model Convention.

The taxation of technical services as royalties in Brazil's treaties – which is absent only in the treaties signed with Austria, Finland, France, Japan, and Sweden – is very controversial, and it could trigger a mutual agreement procedure followed by international arbitration.

Would it be favorable to the country to subject itself to international arbitration in this case? It seems that the answer is no.

---

56. Available at Roy Rohatgi, *Basic International Taxation*, 2nd Ed. (Richmond, 2005) p. 416.
57. In his review of reports from thirty-seven countries, Pasquale Pistone says, "Bilateral treaties around the world undoubtedly show that the influence of the OECD Model royalties clause is more the exception than the rule. The UN royalties clause is instead the main point of reference for bilateral tax treaty clauses on royalties, which are often accompanied by additional dedicated provisions." (Pasquale Pistone, "General Report," Michael Lang, Pasquale Pistone, Josef Schuch, and Claus Staringer (eds.), *The Impact of OECD and UN Model Conventions on Bilateral Tax Treaties* (Cambridge University Press, 2012) p. 21).
58. *See* footnote 44.

Therefore, it is this author's view that the "Developing Countries' International Tax Regime" should not include the use of arbitration to settle disputes pertaining to the interpretation of tax treaties. This position would lead to developing countries non-adherence to Articles 18 through 26 of the Multilateral Convention.

§9.06   TAX SOVEREIGNTY IN POST-BEPS TIMES

One of the most identifiable trends in International Taxation in the twenty-first century is standardization and multilateralism. This is the age that social science scholars refer to as risk-society.

According to Ulrich Beck, "In the sense of a social theory and a diagnosis of culture, the concept of risk society designated a stage of modernity in which the threats produced so far on the path of industrial society begin to predominate. This raises the issue of the self-limitation of that development as well as the task of re-determining the standards (of responsibility, safety, monitoring, damage limitation, and distribution of the consequences of damage) attained so far with attention to the potential threats."[59]

Anthony Giddens is another scholar who has studied risk-society at length. In his opinion, "Modernity also has a sombre side, which has become very apparent in the present [20 th] century."[60]

Giddens further argues that "A skeptic might ask, is there anything new here? Hasn't human life always been marked by contingency? Hasn't the future always been open and problematic? The answer is 'yes' to each of these questions. It is not that our life-circumstances today have become less predictable than they used to be; rather the origins of unpredictability have changed. Many uncertainties which face us today have been created by the very growth of human knowledge."[61]

In the industrial age, there was an assumption that passing a new law could solve any social problem. Even though laws were post-factum, they would be able to deal with the new problems created by social interaction.

Risk-society puts this notion in check. One of the major characteristics of risk-society is that there are problems that require a solution that cannot be obtained through any isolated intervention of a single country's legislator.[62] We are referring to problems such as: terrorism; international economic crises; international trafficking of drugs, weapons, and even persons; and degradation of the environment, etc. In the international tax area, the best examples are international tax evasion and aggressive tax planning as well as the budgetary deleterious effects of economic and fiscal crises.

---

59. Ulrich Beck, "The Reinvention of Politics," Ulrich Beck, Anthony Giddens, and Scott Lash (eds.), *Reflexive Modernization: Politics, Tradition and Aesthetics in the Modern Social Order* (Stanford University Press, 1994) p. 6.
60. Anthony Giddens, *The Consequences of Modernity* (Stanford University Press, 1990) p. 7.
61. Anthony Giddens, "Risk, trust, reflexivity," Ulrich Beck, Anthony Giddens, and Scott Lash (eds.), *Reflexive Modernization: Politics, Tradition and Aesthetics in the Modern Social Order* (Stanford University Press, 1994) p. 185.
62. See André-Jean Arnaud, *O Direito Traído pela Filosofia* (Sergio Antonio Fabris Editor, 1991) p. 246.

Brazilian Professor Ricardo Lobo Torres has dedicated part of his research to the analysis of the legal effects of risk-society. In his words, "Risk-society is characterized by some relevant features: ambivalence, insecurity, the search for new principles, and the redrafting of the interactions between States' institutions and society."[63]

Typical risk-society problems require a combined effort from countries and international institutions in pursuing a solution. In other words, such a solution will usually be a multilateral endeavor rather than an isolated effort.

Globalization, the emergence of the digital economy, harmful tax competition among countries, and the new role of services and intangibles have all created potential environment for tax evasion and aggressive tax planning.[64]

One of the features of this international context is that it introduces several paradoxes. For instance, we are witnessing the emergence of a cooperative international tax regime, which, on the other hand, co-exists with international tax competition. In other words, the same countries that cooperate also compete for tax revenues – and this competition is at the source of the problems that require greater cooperation. The same is valid for tax sovereignty.

To some extent, countries' tax sovereignty in the design of their domestic tax systems is intrinsically related to harmful tax competition. In turn, this is intrinsically related to aggressive tax planning – which triggered the BEPS Project, which requires multilateralism and some degree of reduced tax sovereignty. Hence, the paradox: too much tax sovereignty leads to less tax sovereignty.

No doubt, the new international tax environment poses a threat to developing countries' tax sovereignty. The American FATCA provides us with the best example. Because of its economic power, the United States decided that it could – and it actually did – force countries into signing treaties and modifying their domestic regulations whether or not they needed automatic exchange of information of their residents' accounts in the U.S.

This does not imply that developing countries should not engage in the current international tax debates, or that they should reject participating in the BEPS Project as a whole. This author's concern is that multilateralism becomes a mechanism to impose, top down, certain tax positions that are not in favor of developing countries.

Accordingly, it is this author's opinion that the BEPS Project is both an opportunity and a risk for developing countries. Countries that have a sufficiently strong international tax policy can "cherry-pick" what is interesting for them in the Project and discard whatever recommendations seem inappropriate. Thus, the BEPS Project is an opportunity to participate in and engage in a high-level international taxation debate that is happening worldwide. However, for countries that are exposed to pressures from developed countries and do not have a well-formed international tax policy, it seems that the BEPS Project also poses a threat.

---

63. Ricardo Lobo Torres, *Tratado de Direito Constitucional, Financeiro e Tributário: Valores e Princípios Constitucionais Tributários* (Renovar, 2005) p. 177. *See also* Sergio André Rocha, *Tributação Internacional* (QuartierLatin, 2013) pp. 16–49.
64. *See* Victor Uckmar, et.al. *Diritto Tributario Internazionale* (CEDAM, 2012) pp. XXVI–XXXII.

§9.07 FINAL REMARKS

Changes in international taxation that started recently will echo in the years to come. It seems that the focus on collection optimization has eclipsed the discussion regarding the rightful limits of states' taxing powers. On the other hand, one should not forget that debates about the reshaping of the so-called International Tax Regime started with a discussion about precisely what is a country's "fair share of tax."

Current multilateralism was born in the context of struggles for tax revenues. This fact suggests that states engaging in these debates are certainly pursuing an increase in their tax collections. At first glance, it may seem that such tax collection will come from just fighting "aggressive tax planning." However, it is clear that, in some cases, tax collection will result from reshaping the allocation of taxing powers among countries.

Since the dawn of the "International Tax Regime," it is clear that it favors developed countries and reduces the scope of developing countries' taxation powers. However, reviewing the balance between these two groups is not the scope of the BEPS Project or any other international initiative.

It is time for a change. Developing countries should join in the formation of a "Developing Countries' International Tax Regime." Therefore, they should definitely not be too eager to line up in accepting the BEPS Project's recommendations.

CHAPTER 10
Country-by-Country Over-Reporting? National Sovereignty, International Tax Transparency, and the Inclusive Framework on BEPS

Romero J.S. Tavares

§10.01 INTRODUCTION

Dans la nature, rien ne se perd, rien ne se crée, tout se transforme. Lavoisier's widely known eighteenth century expression of this law of nature also resonates in the global tax policy debate of the twenty-first century – particularly in the area of tax transparency, old ideas and solutions have constantly reappeared.[1] In the decade prior to the launch of the Base Erosion and Profit Shifting (BEPS) Project[2] and even earlier, several initiatives concerning different notions of tax transparency have surfaced, morphed and combined into new domestic laws the world over and into new instruments of public international law.[3] In this new era of tax transparency,[4] BEPS Action 13

---

1. See J. Owens, *Embracing Tax Transparency*, Tax Notes International (2013), pp. 1105–1111.
2. See OECD, *Addressing Base Erosion and Profit Shifting*, OECD Publishing (February, 2013) available at http://www.oecd.org/tax/addressing-base-erosion-and-profit-shifting-97892641927 44-en.htm, *Action Plan on Base Erosion and Profit Shifting*, OECD Publishing (May, 2013), available at http://www.oecd.org/tax/action-plan-on-base-erosion-and-profit-shifting-97892642 02719-en.htm.
3. See e.g., *Multilateral Convention on Administrative Assistance in Tax Matters* and *Multilateral Competent Authority Agreement for the Automatic Exchange of Information (MCAEOI or MCAA-CSR)* available at http://www.oecd.org/tax/automatic-exchange/international-framework-for-the-crs/.
4. See M. Lang and P. Haunold, *Transparenz – Eine neue Ära im Steuerrecht*, Linde Verlag (2016).

Deliverables[5] on transfer pricing documentation and their *Country-by-Country Reporting* (hereinafter, CBCR) standard have spurred domestic legislation around the globe: Australia, Canada, Japan, the U.K. and the U.S., all of the European Union (EU), and several other countries initiated the adoption of CBCR,[6] while many more are expected to follow suit.[7]

A fierce debate over whether to make such CBCRs available to the general public still looms in the background[8] and, if unilaterally adopted, might even threaten the global implementation of the new standard or hamper CBCR exchange. Still, rich, poor, high-tax, and low-tax countries alike are all signing into the new international agreements and fully adopting all transparency standards that emerge from Organisation for Economic Co-operation and Development (OECD) initiatives, while taking measures to implement CBCR and all BEPS Action 13 recommendations though domestic legislation, in what may resemble a *stampede effect* – or a *gold rush*. Considering the broader context and dynamics of the tax transparency debate, this global rush towards CBCR raises the question of whether all of the sovereign nations that are endorsing the new standards and adopting CBCR are fully aware of what it entails and what it can realistically achieve in terms of revenues. Most importantly, whether developing countries understand the benefits and burdens to be accrued to their national treasuries stemming from CBCR implementation, in light of the results from BEPS Actions 8–10 in the area of transfer pricing.[9]

---

5. See OECD, *Transfer Pricing Documentation and Country-by-Country Reporting, Action 13 – 2015 Final Report*, OECD/G20 Base Erosion and Profit Shifting Project, OECD Publishing (October, 2015) available at http://dx.doi.org/10.1787/9789264241480-en.
6. See e.g.: J. Scott Wilkie, *Master File, Local File and Country-by-Country Reporting: A Canadian Perspective*, International Transfer Pricing Journal, IBFD (2016), pp. 115–127; S. Rasch, K. Mank, S. Tomson, *Country-by-Country Reporting*, International Transfer Pricing Journal, IBFD (2016), pp. 147–151; A. Casley, K. Norton and M. Krhoda, *The OECD's New Transfer Pricing Documentation Standard: An Overview and Possible UK Implementation*, International Transfer Pricing Journal, IBFD (2015), pp. 3–10.
7. See e.g.: M.A.P. Valadão, *Transfer Pricing in Brazil and Actions 8, 9, 10 and 13 of the OECD Base Erosion and Profit Shifting Initiative*, Bulletin for International Taxation, IBFD (2016); R.J.S. Tavares and J. Owens, *Global Tax Policy Post-BEPS and the Perils of the Silk Road*, 22 Asia Pacific Tax Bulletin 4, IBFD (2016); R.J.S. Tavares and A. Dias, *What Will a Post-BEPS Latin America Look Like?*, Tax Notes International (2016), pp. 551–561; and R.J.S. Tavares and J. Owens, *BEPS Implementation in Eastern Europe and Central Asia: A Status Report*, World Bank Group (forthcoming, 2017).
8. See R. Finley, *German Tax Head Supports Joint Audits, But Not Public CbC Reporting*, Tax Notes International (2016) at 847; R. Finley, *NGOs Urge Treasury, IRS to Make CbC Reports Public*, Tax Notes International (2016), pp. 765–766; M. Herzfeld, *Tax Transparency Is in The Eye of the Beholder*, Tax Notes International (2016), pp. 647–650; R. Finley, Treasury, *NGOs Differ on Purpose of CbC Reporting Data*, Tax Notes International (2016), pp. 384–385; R. Goulder, *NGOs Push G-20 for Country-by-Country Reporting*, Tax Notes International (2011), pp. 451–454.
9. OECD, *Aligning Transfer Pricing Outcomes with Value Creation, Actions 8-10 – 2015 Final Reports*, OECD/G20 Base Erosion and Profit Shifting Project, OECD Publishing, Paris (October 2015) available at http://dx.doi.org/10.1787/9789264241244-en. See also, M.T. Evers, I. Meier and C. Spengel, *Transparency in Financial Reporting: Is Country-by-Country Reporting Suitable To*

Chapter 10: The Inclusive Framework on BEPS §10.01

One cannot help but wonder whether the revenue gains from CBCR are expected to be material and to outweigh implementation costs comparably or proportionately in all countries. Or whether, particularly in developing countries, other resource mobilization options and policy choices would be money better spent, yielding higher returns on the investment of public resources or otherwise producing greater positive effects in-country. Indeed, a question must be raised as to whether a nuanced, *bottom-up* analysis of all outcomes of the BEPS Project and related policy design options would be warranted for developing countries prior to any implementation action.[10] If so, then the so-called *Inclusive Framework* promoted by the OECD and the G20 for implementation of the complete BEPS package as it stands,[11] with an emphasis on CBCR amongst its minimum standards and within the framework of recommendations arising from BEPS Actions 8–10 (and not beyond them), could be viewed as a rushed approach, as it may disproportionately burden developing countries.

Since BEPS Actions 8–10 still did not break away from the Arm's Length Principle (ALP), some tax activists might even view the Inclusive Framework as *marching orders*

Combat International Profit Shifting?, Bulletin for International Taxation, IBFD (2014), pp. 295–303. *See yet again*, R. Finley, *Countering Base Erosion Is Impossible within Current System, Panel Says*, Tax Notes International (2016), pp. 847–848. For a critical view of the shortcomings of the ALP which remain even post-BEPS, *see e.g.*: Y. Brauner, *BEPS: An Interim Evaluation*, 6 World Tax Journal, n. 1 (2014), Journals IBFD; R. Avi-Yonah, *The Rise and Fall of Arm's Length: a study in the Evolution of United States International Taxation*, 15 Virginia Tax Review 89 (1995); Y. Brauner, *Value in the Eye of the Beholder: The Valuation of Intangibles for Transfer Pricing Purposes*, 28 Virginia Tax Review 79 (2008); J. Clifton Fleming, R. Peroni and S. Shay, *Formulary Apportionment in the U.S. International Income Tax System: Putting Lipstick on a Pig?*, 36 Michigan Journal International Law 1 (2015); R. J. Vann, *Taxing International Business Income: Hard-Boiled Wonderland and the End of the World*, World Tax Journal, IBFD (2010), pp. 291–346; M.A. Kane, *Transfer Pricing, Integration and Synergy Intangibles: A Consensus Approach to the Arm's Length Standard*, World Tax Journal, IBFD (2014), pp. 282–314; R.J.S. Tavares, *Multinational Firm Theory and International Tax Law: Seeking Coherence*, 8 World Tax Journal 2, IBFD (2016).

10. *See* M. Durst, *Self-Help and Altruism – Protecting Developing Countries' Tax Revenues*, in T. Pogge and K. Mehta, *Global Tax Fairness* (Eds.), Oxford (2014), pp. 316–338. *See also*, Durst, *Limitations of the BEPS Reforms: Looking Beyond Corporate Taxation for Revenue Gains*, ICTD Working Paper 40 (2015); *and*, M. Durst, *Beyond BEPS: A Tax Policy Agenda for Developing Countries*, ICTD Working Paper 18 (2014).

11. The official position of the OECD is that the BEPS Project "included" over 80 developing countries, and the initiative to support a consistent launch and worldwide implementation of deliverables referred to as the "inclusive framework" already includes over 100 countries. In fact, these countries exerted little to no influence in the technical and political debate, which was very much amongst the G20. *See*, OECD, About BEPS and the inclusive framework, available at http://www.oecd.org/tax/beps/beps-about.htm, which states: *"The inclusive framework brings together over 100 countries and jurisdictions to collaborate on the implementation of the OECD/G20 Base Erosion and Profit Shifting (BEPS) Package. (...) Developing countries have been engaged since the beginning of the BEPS Project. Over 80 developing countries and other non-OECD/non-G20 economies discuss the challenges of BEPS through direct participation in the Committee on Fiscal Affairs, regional meetings in partnership with regional tax organisations, and thematic global fora. Many developing countries are now joining the inclusive framework."*

from the north[12] seeking to prevent the development of alternative transfer pricing standards, under the cloak of an "inclusiveness" misnomer – the ALP with CBCR would be no more than a wolf in sheep's clothes. Many activists might view it instead as a half-win,[13] as a first step towards global formulary apportionment (GFA). This study suggests that it is likely neither.

This chapter explores whether implementing the CBCR standard, without a deeper transfer pricing reform, should be viewed as a priority in every country, and worthy of mobilization of the scarce resources of developing countries. It addresses the question of whether all countries that are contemplating implementation of CBCR are fully aware of its revenue potential, and whether all countries see the implementation of CBCR in the context of a broader debate of transfer pricing standards, as one more episode in the conceptual battle of GFA versus the ALP. The author posits that CBCR might indeed be useful to curb transfer mispricing; however it will not serve to combat tax avoidance achieved through ALP-compliant transfer pricing, which enables non-taxation of substantial intangible-related residual profits within multinational enterprises (MNEs).[14] Furthermore, it may a redundant tool, in light of the new and widespread standards that arise from the *Global Forum on Tax Transparency and Information Exchange* (hereinafter, "the Global Forum").[15]

In this sense, this study acknowledges that CBCR would serve to compare and contrast hypothetical GFA versus ALP results, and thus to stir the debate of transfer pricing reform within the OECD, and amongst developed economies and the G20. Nonetheless, it questions whether the aforementioned transfer pricing debate requires public disclosure of taxpayer-specific CBCR filings, and whether investing now in CBCR and in the ALP versus GFA debate is opportune for developing countries.

---

12. On the relevance of tax activists in the development of global tax policy and tax transparency, see A. Christians, *Tax Activists and the Global Movement for Development Through Transparency*, in Y. Brauner and M. Stewart (Eds.), *Tax Law and Development*, Edward Elgar Publishing Ltd. (2013), pp. 288–315. *See also*, Owens, *supra* n. 1 at 1106, and *infra* n. 49. Since the final deliverables, minimum standards and recommendations arising from BEPS represent the outcome of bargaining between some OECD Member States and the G20 (particularly China and India, and, to a lesser extent, Brazil) wherein the U.S. (the "north") and the EU seems to have prevailed. This bargaining dynamics has not effectively included developing countries, hence the policies that result may be viewed to lack legitimacy. For an overview of the jurisprudential issue of legitimacy as it pertains to international taxation, see e.g., A. Christians, *Sovereignty, Taxation and Social Contract*, 18 Minnesota Journal International Law (2009).
13. *See* R. Goulder (2011), *supra* n. 8, at 453: *"So what do the NGOs want? Formulary apportionment might be their ultimate objective, but they'd settle for a half-step. They're calling on G-20 leaders to urge the International Accounting Standards Board to implement mandatory CBCR."*
14. *See* Tavares & Owens, *Human Capital in Value Creation and Post-BEPS Tax Policy: An Outlook*, 69 Bulletin International Taxation 10, IBFD (2015). *See also* Tavares & Owens (2016), *supra* n. 7. *See yet again*, Tavares (2016), *supra* n. 9.
15. *See*, OECD Website at http://www.oecd.org/tax/transparency/about-the-global-forum/.

§10.02 THE PRE-BEPS TAX TRANSPARENCY GAME:[16] COMPETITION OR REFORM?

[A] Defining Tax Transparency

In order for countries to understand their rules of engagement on international tax transparency, and what is at stake for their national treasuries, first it is necessary to define what tax transparency means.[17] Different meanings stem from different relationships and interactions between the persons from whom information disclosure is required, and by whom information will be used. The object and purpose of rules governing these different situations is varied. Tax transparency can mean the disclosure of taxpayer information to tax authorities, the transparency of tax authorities to taxpayers or to other tax authorities, or the transparency of taxpayers and tax authorities to the general public. Nonetheless, these different dimensions of tax transparency are also interrelated and, thus, are often intertwined in legislation.

The first and most intuitive notion is that taxpayer information must be disclosed to government authorities, i.e., taxpayers must be transparent to the taxing authorities governing them.[18] Taxpayers' rights would be safeguarded by the rule of law, including

---

16. Over the years, a significant trend of interdisciplinary research emerged bringing mathematics, economics and social relations together, whereby "cooperative game theory" (rooted on J. Nash), and bargaining theory (developed by O. Hart), has been widely applied in the study of economic relations and international taxation. This trend has crossed over into the field of international trade law and international tax law. *See* e.g., T. Dagan, *The Tax Treaties Myth*, 32 N.Y.U. Journal of International Law and Politics 939 (2000), who draws on game theory to argue that an unfair transfer of wealth from poorer to richer countries results from tax treaties. *See also*, R. Chisik and R.B. Davies, *Asymmetric FDI and tax-treaty bargaining: theory and evidence*, Journal of Public Economics 88 (2004), pp. 1119–1148; and *Gradualism in Tax Treaties with Irreversible Foreign Direct Investment*, International Economic Review 45, pp. 113–139; *see yet again*, R.B. Davies, *The OECD Model Tax Treaty: Tax Competition and Two-Way Capital Flows*, International Economic Review 44, pp. 725–753; *and*, R.B. Davies, *Tax Treaties, Renegotiations, and Foreign Direct Investment*, Economic Analysis and Policy 33, pp. 251–273. Christians (2009), *supra* n. 12, at 102, also finds relevance in such alternative streams of research, stating: *"The approach of this article is by no means the only analytical framework for examining the OECD as an institution and its influence on national law in the U.S. and elsewhere. The same issues could also be analyzed from a law and economics, utilitarian, game theoretic or international relations approach, among others. See Allison Christians, Steven Dean, Diane Ring & Adam H. Rosenzweig, Taxation as a Global Socio-Legal Phenomenon, 14 ILSA J. INT'L & COMP. L. 303, 306 (2008) (arguing that more analysis of tax policy from these various lines of inquiry would help clarify the role of law in regulating global economic activity)."*
17. *See* Owens, *supra* n. 1 at 1105.
18. *Id.*, at 1105: *"The OECD has for several years been focused on transparency, particularly in its initiatives to counter offshore noncompliance, by requiring and seeking new tools for tax authorities to know the full position of taxpayers, including the ultimate ownership of relevant income and assets. This transparency concept includes the tax authorities knowing all the entities within a country that are controlled by a taxpayer. This form of transparency has broadened in recent years as tax authorities realized that they do not understand fully the profile of the MNE across its global activities, especially when they involve overseas entities affiliated with their domestic taxpayer that are located in low-tax countries. This type of transparency has been enhanced by new initiatives such as more focused reporting requirements related to aggressive tax planning and uncertain tax issues. So the tax authorities are seeking more information about taxpayers' affairs by their greater willingness to challenge more risky issues, those with greater*

a fundamental right to due process, and in most countries a right to tax confidentiality which safeguards the freedom of enterprise.[19] A second notion is a mirror image of the first, and it is grounded on economic psychology studies on tax compliance:[20] governments should be transparent to taxpayers, both in their rule-making processes as well as in the prevention and resolution of disputes.[21] A third perspective coherently

---

potential for tax controversy. This involves initiatives such as Australia's pilot on reportable tax positions, the U.K.'s reporting of aggressive tax 'schemes,' and the U.S.'s disclosures of uncertain tax positions."

19. The fundamental freedom to conduct a business derives from the human rights to ownership, privacy, association, and self-determination. See UN General Assembly, *Resolution 2200A (XXI)* of 16 December 1966 (entry into force 23 March 1976), International Covenant on Civil and Political Rights, Article 1, which states: "1. All peoples have the right of self-determination. By virtue of that right they freely determine their political status and freely pursue their economic, social and cultural development. 2. All peoples may, for their own ends, freely dispose of their natural wealth and resources without prejudice to any obligations arising out of international economic co-operation, based upon the principle of mutual benefit, and international law. In no case may a people be deprived of its own means of subsistence. 3. The States Parties to the present Covenant, including those having responsibility for the administration of Non-Self-Governing and Trust Territories, shall promote the realization of the right of self-determination, and shall respect that right, in conformity with the provisions of the Charter of the United Nations." See also, EU Charter of Fundamental Rights, Article 16: "The freedom to conduct a business in accordance with Community law and national laws and practices is recognised" and Commentary: "This Article is based on Court of Justice case-law which has recognised freedom to exercise an economic or commercial activity (see judgments of 14 May 1974, Case 4/73 Nold [1974] ECR 491, paragraph 14 of the grounds, and of 27 September 1979, Case 230-78 SpA Eridiana and others [1979] ECR 2749, paragraphs 20 and 31 of the grounds) and freedom of contract (see inter alia Sukkerfabriken Nykøbing judgment, Case 151/78 [1979] ECR 1, paragraph 19 of the grounds, and judgment of 5 October 1999, C-240/97 Spain v. Commission [1999] ECR I-6571, paragraph 99 of the grounds) and Article 119(1) and (3) of the Treaty on the Functioning of the European Union, which recognises free competition. Of course, this right is to be exercised with respect for Union law and national legislation. It may be subject to the limitations provided for in Article 52(1) of the Charter."

20. Economic psychology studies grounded on Kirschler, Hoezl & Wahl (2008) support that increasing taxpayer morale not only has a state-building feature but also increases tax compliance and revenues, and that a balance must be struck between enforced and voluntary compliance (the so-called slippery slope framework). This theory and approach motivated the widespread adoption of "cooperative compliance"-type programs throughout the world (e.g., horizontal monitoring in the Netherlands, enhanced relations in the U.K., compliance assurance process in the U.S.) and other "service"-driven initiatives within tax administrations worldwide (e.g., U.S. taxpayers's advocate, small-business or large taxpayer offices, etc.). See, E. Kirchler, E. Hoelzl and I. Wahl, *Enforced Versus Voluntary Tax Compliance: The "Slippery Slope" Framework*, 29 Journal of Economic Psychology 2 (2008), pp. 210–225; E. Kirchler, S. Muehlbacher, B. Kastlunger and I. Wahl, *Why Pay Taxes? A Review of Tax Compliance Decisions*, in J. Alm, J. Martinez-Vazquez, and B. Torgler (Eds.), *Developing Alternative Frameworks for Explaining Tax Compliance*, Oxon: Routledge (2010), pp. 15–31; S. Muehlbacher, E. Kirchler and H. Schwarzenberger, *Voluntary Versus Enforced Tax Compliance: Empirical Evidence for the "Slippery Slope" Framework*, 32 European Journal of Law and Economics 1, (2011), pp. 89–97 available at https://doi.org/10.1007/s10657-011-9236-9; J. Alm, E. Kirchler and S. Muehlbacher, *Combining Psychology and Economics in the Analysis of Compliance: From Enforcement to Cooperation*, 42 Economic Analysis & Policy 2, (2012), pp. 133–151. The fairness debate fits into this utilitarian view of taxpayer morale (i.e., increased compliance) whilst it also fits into a broader state-building framework, of enhanced democracy, individual liberties, and national sovereignty.

21. Transparency in rule making and in the resolution of disputes (i.e., due process) are fundamental features of the democratic rule of law. These characteristics of a nation and tax system are telling of the quality of human rights in any given country, as much as of its investment climate.

binds the first two together in a global economy: tax authorities must be transparent with one another, share information, and cooperate, and thus collectively uphold the rule of law. The normative construct of this third notion imposes that governments should be transparent to other governments concerning taxation, thus not only enabling tax enforcement but curbing *harmful tax competition*.

[B] Tax Transparency and Tax Competition: Harm as a Matter of Law

Some economic debate exists as to whether the so-called race to the bottom and erosion of the corporate tax associated with the use of "tax havens" would lead to inequality and the collapse of states or whether it would be conducive to economic growth and global welfare.[22] Irrespective of such matter of fact, jurisprudential thought would posit

---

See J. Owens, *Tax Policy in the 21st Century: New Concepts for Old Problems*, European University Institute., Issue 2013/05 – Global Governance Program, Robert Schuman Ctr Advanced Stud. (2013). *See also*, J. Owens, *The Role of Tax Administrators in the Current Political Climate*, 67 Bulletin for International Taxation 3, IBFD (2013), at p. 160, stating that: *"[t]oday, tax administrations and taxpayers increasingly recognize that they have a shared interest in minimizing and quickly resolving tax disputes and a recognition that this requires focussing not just on one particular issue, but on the whole process by which they can avoid disputes. This requires engaging taxpayers in the process of policy formulation and implementation. It requires identifying and discussing issues before they become problems. It requires pre-filing resolutions, the type of programmes that we see in the United States (the compliance assurance program (CAP)) or the Netherlands' horizontal monitoring programmes. It also requires a greater use of informal mediation, particularly in the area of establishing the facts in transfer pricing cases. And it requires a wider use of advance pricing agreement (APA) type of programmes and mandatory arbitration. All of this will require a new type of commitment from tax administrations and a willingness to devote scarce and highly trained officials to resolve tax disputes."* See yet again OECD, *Co-operative Compliance: A Framework: From Enhanced Relationship to Co-operative Compliance* (OECD 2013) [hereinafter the "Cooperative Compliance Report (2013)." The tax compliance framework of "TCF," as illustrated in Cooperative Compliance Report (2013), *supra*, at pp. 57–63 provides an adequate approach through which to pursue such goals. The TCF is based on the "OECD Guidelines for Multinational Enterprises," first adopted in 1976 and reviewed five times through to 2011 as part of the OECD, *Declaration and Decisions on International Investment and Multinational Enterprises* (OECD 2011) and is coherent with the *OECD Declaration on Propriety, Integrity and Transparency in the Conduct of International Business and Finance* (OECD 2010). Only if all these statements and reports by the OECD are taken as a coherent whole, interpreted and applied systematically and used as a *context* within which any international tax rules, any guidelines or commentaries by the OECD are used, would the international tax system promoted by the OECD make sense. It would be grounded on "cooperation and ethics," rather than "competition and harm" – hence coherent with the object and purpose of the OECD itself, as per its Charter. *See*, *Convention on the Organisation of Economic Co-operation and Development* (Paris, 1960), Articles 1, 2 and 3, *available at* http://www.oecd.org/general/conventionontheorganisationforeconomicco-operationanddevelopment.htm; the OECD Convention replaced the 1948 Charter of the *Organisation for European Economic Co-operation* (OEEC) developed under the Marshall Plan.

22. K. Vogel, *Worldwide vs. Source Taxation of Income – A Review and Re-evaluation of Arguments (Part I)*, Intertax 8-9, pp. 216–219 (1988) at 216 et seq., references the long-standing U.S. tradition under which the international allocation of taxing rights should favor residence countries, and sees it to be rooted in the theories famously developed by U.S. economists Richard P. Musgrave and Peggy Richman (Peggy Musgrave). Vogel cites to the Musgraves' very influential publications of 1960, 1963, 1965, 1969, 1972 and 1974. Other U.S. economists continued to develop and support the same theory which favors residence countries and the low-taxation of capital. *See* e.g., J.R. Hines, E.M. Rice, *Fiscal Paradise: Foreign Tax Havens and*

that certain modes of tax competition might be defined as unlawful delicts under international law. Unsanctioned delicts would subvert the rule of law and would therefore be "inherently harmful" as a matter of law.

From a tax policy perspective, this critical issue has been debated *ad nauseam*. The 1998 OECD Report on Harmful Tax Competition[23] acknowledged and exposed the factual problem, motivating the inception of the *Global Forum* in 2000, which remains as one of the most successful initiatives ever carried out under the auspices of the OECD.[24] Tax competition would be defined as "harmful," and thus unlawful, only when countries are uncooperative, secretive, *and* when their regimes are designed to distort investment and/or trade flows between other countries. The difficulty here is that "one nation's harmful tax regime is another state's competitive tax policy"[25] – as such, where should international law draw the line? To illustrate the factual problem addressed by the Global Forum, and to apply a framework of analysis grounded on jurisprudential thought, let us use a hypothetical example:

American Business, Quarterly Journal of Economics 109 (1), (1994), pp. 149–182; J.R. Hines, *Altered States: Taxes and the Location of Foreign Direct Investment in America*, American Economic Review 86 (5) (1996), pp. 1076–1094; J.R. Hines, *Tax Policy and the Activities of Multinational Corporations* in A.J. Auerbach (Ed.), *Fiscal Policy: Lessons from Economic Research*, MIT Press, Cambridge, (1997), pp. 401–445; J.R. Hines, *Lessons from Behavioral Responses to International Taxation*, National Tax Journal 52 (2), (1999), pp. 305–322; M.A. Desai, C. Fritz Foley, and J. Hines Jr., *Domestic Effects of the Foreign Activities of US Multinationals*, American Economic Journal: Economic Policy, 1:1 (2009), at pp. 181–203. Unsurprisingly, many U.S. tax legal scholars will tend to follow to the rationale developed in this string of economic literature. See D.N. Shaviro, *Fixing U.S. International Taxation*, Oxford University Press (2014). *See also* e.g., Fleming, Peroni & Shay, *Getting Serious About Curtailing Deferral of U.S. Tax on Foreign Source Income*, SMU Law Review 455 (1999), *Fairness in International Taxation: The Ability-to-Pay Case for Taxing Worldwide Income*, 5 Florida Tax Review 4 (2001), *Designing a U.S. Exemption System for Foreign Income When the Treasury is Empty*, 13 Florida Tax Review 8 (2012). Across the Atlantic, proponents of a consumption-based corporate income tax, or of a so-called optimum corporate tax (which could exempt capital and the financial services sector that flourishes in London and Luxembourg) follow a similar efficiency-seeking rationale. *See* e.g., R.A. Mooij, and M.P. Devereux, *Alternative Systems of Business Tax in Europe: An Applied Analysis of ACE and CBIT Reforms*, Taxud Taxation Papers, European Union (2009).

23. *See*, OECD, *Harmful Tax Competition – An Emerging Global Issue* Paris (1998), available at https://www.oecd.org/tax/transparency/44430243.pdf.
24. *See*, OECD *supra* n. 15.
25. *See* Owens, *supra* n. 1 at 1106: "*Preferential harmful tax regimes have been on both the EU and OECD agendas for some time. This is a complex area. One nation's harmful tax regime is another state's competitive tax policy. (…) The European Commission has become very active in this area. It's going to be hard for either the European Commission or the OECD to shift this debate beyond clear cases of harmful tax practices. BEPS action 5 suggests there is little political will to extend the definition of harmful. It can be expected that work in this area will focus on transparency and information exchange. The action plan, for example, calls for more transparency and the spontaneous exchange of information on rulings related to preferential tax regimes. The EU meanwhile links harmful tax practice identification and its code of conduct to issues of tax rate, substance, and nondiscrimination. Whether an OECD consensus on the definition of harmful tax practices could extend as far as the EU code of conduct remains to be seen. However, the BEPS report does call for a focus on substance requirements for any preferential tax regime (something already foreseen in the 1998 report on harmful tax competition), and it seems likely that the conditions of the EU code of conduct will inform the debate.*"

Suppose a resident of Home State A intends to invest in Host State B, and that a bilateral tax treaty between Country A and Country B limits withholding tax rates on interest and on royalties at 5%. Suppose Country B has entered into a bilateral tax treaty with Country C, under which no withholding taxes can be imposed, and that a similar treaty exists between A and C. Further, suppose Home Country A does not have effective "controlled foreign company" (hereinafter CFC) rules, and that the A-B, B-C, and A-C tax treaties do not have any form of anti-abuse rule [i.e., no limitation on benefits (LOB) clause, no principal purpose test (PPT)]. Suppose these treaties are old and were entered into at a time predating advances in information and communication technologies (ICT) that now enable MNEs to vertically integrate operations and treasuries.[26] This scenario could be observed in many if not most of the more than 3,000 tax treaties that exist today.

Now, suppose that many years after the A-B, B-C and A-C tax treaties come into force, and whether or not through legislation, regulations, or private rulings, Country C starts to grant ring-fenced tax incentives, exempting from corporate income tax and from withholding tax certain categories of income (e.g., interest, royalties) and even active trade and business income earned from foreign sources, or from exports. Non-taxation at Country C could also materialize, for instance, if income is earned through an entity incorporated therein but managed and controlled abroad. From Country C's perspective, the tax exemptions would be permanent if untaxed earnings are distributed to owners that are not residents of Country C.

The unilateral actions of Country C, therefore, would interfere with investments flowing from Country A to Country B, yet without placing Country C in direct competition against Country B as a final Host State. Rather, investors from Home State A would be tempted to simply *route investments through* a legal entity incorporated in Country C, and *not* to invest in Country C *instead of* Host State B. By positioning itself as an intermediary and not as a substitute, Country C would be *deliberately intervening* in the economic relations of Countries A and B, availing a triangular legal structure for investors to execute what essentially remains a bilateral capital flow from Home State A into Host State B. And it can be said that Country C's intervention would adversely affect or harm[27] the national treasuries of A and B.

To better demonstrate the problem, suppose the investment climate in Country C is no better than the investment climate in Countries A and B (i.e., sovereign risk, institutional risks, rule of law, currency issues are all equivalent in A, B, and C), and that there are no other non-tax reasons to justify the aforementioned triangular structure. Country C would position itself as an "investment platform" or "hub" seeking to intermediate investment and trade flows that would otherwise be distributed between A and B only, and that remain originating in A and destined to B. Thus,

---

26. *See supra* n. 14.
27. For an enlightened discussion of the "duty not to harm," *see* R.A. Rodrigues, *Inter-Nation Equity as a Limit for Tax Policy* (forthcoming, 2017).

from a jurisprudential perspective it can be said that Country C's positioning would subvert the bilateral context of tax treaties by undermining the A-B bilateral tax treaty and enabling the multilateral use of A-C and B-C bilateral tax treaties. Home State A taxation would be deferred through this scheme (while earnings are accumulated by a legal entity incorporated in Country C and not distributed as dividends); whereas Host State B taxation would be reduced by the interposition of Country C between A and B and application of the B-C tax treaty.

Moreover, the structure would be *self-serving* as it would result in cash accumulation at Country C, including residual income from intra-group trade,[28] inflated by the amounts of A and B taxes formally avoided, while such accumulation of cash at Country C would require some minimum level of activity to be carried on at Country C. Note, any and all tax revenues collected to the treasury of Country C (irrespective of any exemptions granted by C), would be inherently incremental to Country C, and be diverted from Countries A and B – meaning that no tax subsidies or financial aid would burden the treasury of Country C.[29] The accumulation of capital in Country C, along with the performance of activities resulting from the interposition of C between A and B, would produce indicators of "legal substance"[30] (cash, activities diverted from countries A and B, capital assets including the legal ownership of intangible property), which would in turn allegedly justify the structure.[31] This diversion of activities, intangibles, and cash could also have real distortionary effects,[32] i.e., it could lead to economic inefficiencies detrimental to the welfare of the conjunction of countries A, B, and C. Adding insult to injury, suppose the competent authorities of Country C do not respond to information requests from A or B, do not disclose any information pertaining to the legal entity located in C which earns interest and royalty income from B, or any details concerning the operation of its ring-fenced tax incentives.

Building on the notions established in the 1998 Report and through the Global Forum, countries have effectively *outlawed* the aforementioned mode of tax competition, by defining it as "harmful." From a legitimacy perspective, it should be noted that the Global Forum is a particularly remarkable institution as it congregates states that

---

28. *See supra* n. 9.
29. If Country C were an EU Member State, the fact that this hypothesized "harmful tax competition" scheme would not represent any real onus to the treasury of Country C, but only to the treasuries of Countries A and B and in spite of the apparent "incentive" granted by C, would possibly represent an infraction by Country C to the EU Code of Conduct, but not configure the concession of "State Aid" by Country C. *See*, R.J.S. Tavares, B.N. Bogenschneider and M. Pankiv, *The Intersection of EU State Aid and U.S. Tax Deferral: A Spectacle of Fireworks, Smoke, and Mirrors*, 19 Florida Tax Review 3 (2016).
30. *See* Tavares (2016), *supra* n. 9. *See also*, Tavares, *The "Active Trade or Business" Exception of the Limitation on Benefits Clause*, in M. Lang et al. (Eds.), *Base Erosion and Profit Shifting: The Proposals to Revise the OECD Model Convention*, Linde Verlag (2016).
31. *Id.*
32. Even though some academic and political debate still exists as to whether the tax avoidance effects of such triangular structures are indeed damaging to global economic welfare, to Home State A, or to Host State B. *See supra* n. 22.

are not members of the OECD along with OECD Members "on an equal footing"[33] and under a common cause. It enables the global coordination of key aspects of national tax policies, and it establishes the circumstances in which one country's policy can be deemed harmful against other countries, reaching far beyond the jurisdictions of OECD Members. As such, the success of the Global Forum can also be explained from a jurisprudential perspective.[34]

Opaque and distortive tax policies adopted by one state that are designed to interfere with investment and trade flows between two other states, formally forcing upon such states a set of legal rules which would limit their taxing jurisdictions, carried on under the cloak of secrecy by uncooperative states, may be viewed as not only contrary to the legal principle of good-faith but also as an *unlawful intervention* under general international law (*jus cogens*).[35] The state that engages in such mode of unlawful tax competition would infringe upon the sovereign rights of the states that have their national treasuries harmed by the improper use of bilateral tax treaties and/or by the aiding and abetting of tax evaders.[36] Accordingly, the international community would be justified to react, and to *impose sanctions* on states which perpetrate such unlawful intervention.

The institution of the Global Forum and its *Multilateral Convention on the Mutual Administrative Assistance in Tax Matters* (hereinafter "the Multilateral Convention") and related instruments which tackle uncooperative jurisdictions,[37] function as a

---

33. *See*, OECD *supra* n. 15 which states that *"[t]he Global Forum currently has 137 members participating on an equal footing, together with 15 international organisations participating as observers."*
34. Christians (2009), *supra* n. 12, analyzed this issue not by referencing international law, but instead through political philosophy and Anglo-American jurisprudence. Christians contrasting a Rawlsian "social contract" view of fiscal sovereignty with "rights-based" analysis under Nussbaum's cosmopolitanism. Christians acknowledges, however, that a jurisprudential analysis grounded on international law can be feasible to understand and interpret this matter. Her review of Anglo-American jurisprudential theories leading to cosmopolitanism seems to further reinforce that even in the Anglo-American juridical tradition there would be a sociological context or rights-based imperative which would justify and requires the enforcement of international law. International legal scholars would reach a similar conclusion, yet using a sanctions-based approach. *See e.g.*, H. Kelsen, *Pure Theory of Law*, translation from the second (revised and enlarged) German edition by Max Knight, University of California Press (1989), pp. 279–347.
35. *See supra* n. 19. *See also* Kelsen, *supra* n. 34.
36. Be it through transfer mispricing and tax avoidance, or through tax evasion, money laundering and the sheltering of other illicit activities. This is at the core of Panama Papers and LuxLeaks scandals – nonetheless illicit activities are but one facet of the problem. A much wider equation would encompass aggressive tax planning and avoidance which is still deemed to be legitimate.
37. *See supra* n. 3: *"the Convention on Mutual Administrative Assistance in Tax Matters ('the Convention') was developed jointly by the OECD and the Council of Europe in 1988 and amended by Protocol in 2010. The Convention is the most comprehensive multilateral instrument available for all forms of tax co-operation to tackle tax evasion and avoidance, a top priority for all countries. The Convention was amended to respond to the call of the G20 at its 2009 London Summit to align it to the international standard on exchange of information on request and to open it to all countries, in particular to ensure that developing countries could benefit from the new more transparent environment. The amended Convention was opened for signature on 1 June 2011. Since 2009, the G20 has consistently encouraged countries to sign the Convention including most recently at the meeting of the G20 Finance Ministers and Central Bank Governors Meeting in February 2016 where the communique stated 'We reiterate our call for all countries to*

formal expression of such legal dynamics and of the prevailing force of international law. By setting standards and monitoring states through *peer reviews*, the Global Forum formally recognizes the conditions in which sanctions against noncompliant states are legitimized.

Using our earlier example, the unilateral actions of Country C may not only be deemed to breach the B-C and A-C tax treaties (which in good-faith were meant to be bilateral and to serve as instruments of mutual assistance). Country C's unilateral policies, secrecy, and uncooperative stance, could be viewed as an unlawful economic intervention which harms the national treasuries of A and B, and, as such, acts of aggression against nations A and B. Any tax revenues collected by Country C would be incremental to C and could be viewed as the spoils of *raids* by C against the treasuries of A and B. Through this reasoning, C's tax policies would be an infringement to the sovereign rights of self-determination of A and B, under general norms international law.

If unsanctioned, these so-defined *harmful* tax policies adopted by uncooperative states would subvert the rule of international law, by undermining the sovereign rights of the offended states. Accordingly, countries that reject the Global Forum and the Multilateral Convention, or that fail to demonstrate *through peer reviews* that their unilateral tax policies are not harmful, would not only become pariahs in the international concert of nations; proportionate retaliatory measures adopted against these rogue states would be viewed as *lawful sanctions* from the viewpoint of international law jurisprudence.

Lawful sanctions could take the form of unilateral or multilateral measures, ranging from higher withholding tax rates, special excise taxes or countervailing duties on transactions involving the offending country,[38] or even the termination of treaties and the cessation of financial aid. If materialized, these sanctions could cause significant hardship to the country that adopts a unilateral policy that is deemed harmful to others. From a jurisprudential perspective, the threat of such sanctions would not only discourage *but effectively coerce* all countries to cooperate, forcing all states not to harm one another through predatory tax policies, and thus to abide by general rules of international law.[39]

Therefore, it is no wonder that no less than 137 countries have joined the Global Forum and 107 countries signed the Multilateral Convention and committed to *Exchange of Information upon Request* (EOIR) and to *Spontaneous Exchange of*

---

join the Multilateral Convention on Mutual Administrative Assistance in Tax Matters [...]' 107 jurisdictions currently participate in the Convention, including 15 jurisdictions covered by territorial extension. This represents a wide range of countries including all G20 countries, all BRIICS, all OECD countries, major financial centres and an increasing number of developing countries."

38. Unilateral measures are often adopted and perceived as legitimate under international law. The listing of tax haven that are subject to such defensive measures is a common practice, and have been widely adopted throughout Europe, and Latin America, for example.

39. See Kelsen, *supra* n. 34.

Information (SEOI), while 87 have committed to *Automatic Exchange of Information* (AEOI)[40] under the Multilateral Competent Authority Agreement (MCAA) through the Common Reporting Standard (CSR). And these numbers keep growing. By 2018 all signatory countries will be fully engaged and operating EOIR and/or AEOI, subject to *peer reviews* under the monitoring of the Global Forum.

[C] Tax Transparency and the General Public

Another dimension of tax transparency concerns the right of the general public to have access to information pertaining to the relationship between taxpayers and governments. Here, the goal would be twofold: (a) to prevent the unlawful conduct of government officials (e.g., corruption, granting of illegal subsidies, etc.);[41] and (b) to inform the general public about complex aspects of the tax laws of their countries, enabling the engagement of the public in the debate of legislative reform.[42]

Well-educated and well-informed citizens, with freedom of speech and with other civil liberties such as freedom of association, freedom of enterprise, and a free press, are the cornerstones of any democracy. Individual freedoms and civil liberties, nonetheless, are only guaranteed in any state if subjected to the rule of law, which is operated through the constituted governments of any such democratic state. In jurisprudential theory, it is the democratic rule of law that guarantees both individual liberties and national sovereignty, as both are recognized and safeguarded by international law.[43] Any legislative debate or institutional reform conducted under this framework would be state-building, leading to the full exercise of civil liberties and national sovereignty. The tax transparency debate must also be conducted without

---

40. *See*, OECD *supra* n. 15 which states that *"All member jurisdictions have committed to implementing the international standard on EOIR. The Global Forum conducts rigorous assessments of compliance with this standard, according to the elements set out in its Terms of Reference. In addition, more than 90 countries and jurisdictions have committed to implementing the new standard on AEOI. Work is currently underway to implement this Standard, with the first exchanges occurring on a very ambitious timeline of 2017 and 2018. The implementation of these international standards significantly contributes to the fight against tax evasion, as well as achieving greater international co-operation and enhanced transparency of corporate bodies, arrangements and financial information."*
41. *See* Owens, *supra* n. 1 at 1106: *"There has been growing awareness in many developing countries that the taxes and charges paid by MNEs have in part been taken by politicians and other intermediaries for their private and political purposes. This led to the development of the Extractive Industries Transparency Initiative (EITI), which involves MNEs making public disclosures of their operations in various countries, including payments made to foreign governments. These disclosures enhance the probity and governance of countries in which the MNEs operate."*
42. *Id.*, at 1105, noting the use of public disclosure within the European Union (in respect to extractives and forestry), and beyond: *"Not all developments in this area have been multilateral; some have been purely national. In Australia, for example, the Taxation Office is required to publicly disclose, in relation to companies and corporate tax entities generating more than AUD 100 million in gross income per year, taxpayers' gross income, taxable income, and taxes paid. Australia and Denmark are the only countries to require such widespread public disclosure by all companies."*
43. *See* Kelsen, *supra* n. 34.

resort to anarchy, and within this framework of statehood under the democratic rule of law.

Accordingly, well-educated and well-informed citizens with freedom of speech have formed nongovernmental organizations (NGOs) to fight against corruption, a state-destroying crime perpetrated where the rule of law is subverted by the rule of man. A crime that is particularly devastating to many developing countries that have their natural resources exploited, nations that are poached for their riches by the collusion of corrupt government officials and corrupt enterprises. Enterprises that may be headquartered in developed countries, perhaps MNEs whose securities would be traded and wealth accumulated in nations far away from those wherein natural resources are extracted.

In the 1990s, academic literature highlighted such "resource curse" (well beyond the so-called Dutch disease) detailing how the potential benefits from oil, gas and mining were not being realized while increased poverty, conflict and corruption plagued many natural resource-rich nations.[44] Still in the 1990s, civil society in the developed world embraced the cause for transparency of governments and enterprises in extractive economies.[45]

The *Publish What You Pay* (PWYP) campaign spearheaded since 1999 by *Global Witness* (based on their report "A Crude Awakening" which exposed the opaque mismanagement of the oil industry in Angola)[46] caught on, reinforced by *Human Rights Watch*, *Oxfam Americas*, and many other NGOs and academics, and earned significant and well-deserved media attention. There, the issue was the inequity caused by the unlawful conduct of corrupt governments which colluded with and/or extorted large corporations. By willingly publishing all revenues that they pay to developing country governments, MNEs in the extractive sector that do not engage in corrupt practices would demonstrate the positive impact they may have to the developing economies in which they operate. Any disguised bribes, kickbacks, or other direct or indirect payments ultimately directed to governments or government officials would have to be accounted for and disclosed. All licit payments, i.e., mining royalties, consumption-based taxes, duties and excises, payroll-related taxes, as well as payments for drilling and any other business licenses would be duly accounted for and summed up, so as to inform society how much wealth was paid to a particular country in exchange for the wealth extracted from it in the form of natural resources. This would diminish the ability of opaque governments to underreport such revenues and

---

44. *See* Extractive Industries Transparency Initiative (EITI) website, *Beginnings*, *available at* https://eiti.org/.
45. For a perspective on the U.K. government's role in the inception of the EITI, *see* U.K. National Archives, *available at* http://webarchive.nationalarchives.gov.uk/ + /http:/www.dfid.gov.uk/pubs/files/eitidraftreportstatement.pdf.
46. *See supra* n. 44.

to transfer such wealth to corrupt government agents.⁴⁷ Unsurprisingly, it was often the governments of developing countries who would oppose PWYP.⁴⁸

This movement culminated in the creation of the Extractives Industries Transparency Initiative (EITI) in 2003. As noted on their charter: *"the EITI is a global coalition of governments (16 currently), companies, and civil society working together to improve openness and transparency in the extractive sector. Countries implement the EITI standard to ensure full disclosure of taxes and other payments made by oil, gas, and mining companies. These payments are disclosed in an annual EITI report, which allows citizens to see for themselves how much their government is receiving from the exploitation of their country's natural resources. Those adopting the EITI standard are required to report payments made to both national and local governments, including profit taxes paid."*⁴⁹ The G8 drive⁵⁰ in support of the EITI distinguishes it, and it is

---

47. Note, U.S. multinationals are subject to the Foreign Corrupt Practices Act (FCPA) of 1977; however, several MNEs in the extractive sector do not have securities traded in the U.S. market or are otherwise not owned, managed and controlled by U.S. persons and are thus not subject to the FCPA and its sanctions. Given the FCPA, it would serve the competitive interests of U.S. MNEs if other countries also had rules that would discourage, if not sanction, foreign corrupt practices. Naturally, the U.K.-led G8 response to PWYP and EITI launch was supported by the U.S., as were similar requirements promoted within the European Union. Furthermore, President Obama included the EITI standard in the public disclosures required under the Dodd-Frank Act. *See* Owens, *Supra.* n. 1. Owens (2013) states that these public disclosures can represent a threat or an opportunity for MNEs: *"the tax relationships of the past typically involved taxpayers interacting with tax authorities in relation to their tax affairs behind closed doors, with public awareness of those affairs usually limited to disclosures in the annual accounts or resulting from litigation. In the 21st century, businesses' and even wealthy individuals' tax payments have become the subject of public debate. This affects not only a company's relationships with tax authorities but also its public profile, its relationships with consumers and its employees, and its brand, reputation, and potentially its earnings per share."*
48. *See* EITI, *supra* n. 44, citing Lord John Browne's memoir "Beyond Business" and the negative reaction from the Angolan government to the unilateral disclosure by BP of a "signature bonus": *"[I]t was with great surprise, and some disbelief, that we found out through the press that your company has been disclosing information about oil-related activities in Angola". The backlash and threats from the Angola government, led Lord Browne to conclude "clearly a unilateral approach, where one company or one country was under pressure to 'publish what you pay' was not workable". The oil companies argued for a shift away from company reporting, as sought by PWYP and others, to reporting by governments, in order to reduce conflict with host governments and put contracts at risk. If company reporting was to be required they wanted a global effort to level the playing field that required all companies in a country to disclose." See also* Owens, *supra* n. 1 at 1106: *"Many developing countries continue to oppose the EITI and do not allow the publication of their agreements with individual companies."*
49. Id.
50. Ibid. restating the role of the U.K. and the G8 in the EITI launch: *"[t]he EITI is often thought to have been launched in 2002. It is true that the then UK Prime Minister, Tony Blair, outlined the idea of the EITI in a speech intended for the World Summit on Sustainable Development in Johannesburg in September 2002. (...) At a conference in London in June 2003, a Statement of Principles to increase transparency of payments and revenues in the extractive sector was agreed. These 12 EITI Principles centred on the need for transparent management of natural resources. They affirmed a belief that 'a workable approach to the disclosure of payments and revenues is required, which is simple to undertake and use'. (...) Transparency in natural resource development was championed at a series of G8 Summits. The G8 subsequently, called on the International Monetary Fund and the World Bank to provide technical support to governments wishing to adopt transparency policies. (...)".*

justified by the distinct humanitarian problems underlying the activities of extractive industries in developing countries.

This is a far cry from the CBCR movement initiated in 2003 by those who advocate against the ALP and in favor of GFA and unitary taxation of MNEs.[51] Yet, somehow, the EITI object and purpose of state-building tax transparency and sovereignty in the fight against corruption, have been hijacked by those who are engaged in the narrower ALP versus GFA debate. Using CBCR as a critical component of GFA implementation, and even claiming authorship[52] of the country-by-country (CbC) tax transparency solution (thus ignoring or downplaying the relevance of PWYP and EITI), tax activists engaged in the GFA versus ALP debate have framed it with an EITI spiel. They have purported it as a matter of equity and fairness[53] wherein the hypothetical interests of developing countries would be primarily at stake.

From a jurisprudential perspective, it should be rather clear that the object and purpose of PWYP as embodied in the EITI and in the U.S. Dodds-Frank Act[54] cannot at all be misconstrued and misused in the GFA versus ALP debate. Combating foreign corruption (particularly in extractives) and debating lawful transfer pricing methods (GFA versus the ALP) are utterly not comparable problems. Corruption in the extractive industry is an unquestionable harm undermining the democratic rule of law (and it is contrary to national and international laws), which required a public transparency solution. Whereas the GFA versus ALP debate investigates whether or

---

51. *See*, R. Murphy, *Country-By-Country Reporting*, in T. Pogge and K. Mehta, *Global Tax Fairness*, Oxford (2016), pp. 96–112. *See also*, R. Murphy (on behalf of the Association for Accountancy and Business Affairs), *A Proposed International Accounting Standard Reporting Turnover and Tax by Location* (2003), available at http://visar.csustan.edu/aaba/ProposedAccstd.pdf; R. Murphy, *Country-by-Country Reporting: Accounting for Globalization Locally*, Tax Justice Network (2012), available at http://taxresearch.org.uk/Documents/CBC2012.pdf. *See yet again*, S. Picciotto, *International Taxation and Economic Substance*, Bulletin for International Taxation, IBFD (2016), pp. 752-759.
52. *Id.*
53. *See* Owens, *supra* n. 1 at 1106: *"Media and commentators – including the new breed of tax 'activists' – have questioned the basis for the spending reductions, asking why the relevant programs could not be funded by extracting higher tax revenues from business and the well-off. Although corporate taxes account for only 8 percent of tax revenues in an average OECD country, media and commentators have focused on MNEs and their perceived contribution to tax revenues. At the same time, emerging countries (notably Brazil, China, and India) have questioned whether they are getting their fair share of the tax base generated by MNEs. This scrutiny of the activities of MNEs has been influenced by two related developments that have kept tax planning in the spotlight. (...) But the concept of MNEs disclosing more tax information has been picked up in the broader tax fairness debate. (...) the huge volume of disclosures in recent years of tax evasion by private wealthy individuals and opaque entities, including the use of low-tax countries and tax secrecy jurisdictions, has increased the focus on the use of these countries by MNEs. This public consciousness has led to a greater public discussion about taxes paid by MNEs by politicians, whether in governments or opposition parties. The discussions have included reviews by governments and inquiries by parliaments in numerous countries. It has led to a reexamination of businesses' tax payments, especially those of MNEs, by nongovernmental organizations interested in the welfare of developing countries. The focus on perceived tax fairness, or lack thereof, by politicians and commentators was heightened by the recognition that MNEs paying low taxes due to planning were probably acting in accordance with the letter (although perhaps not the spirit) of the tax law. Public confidence in the fairness of a tax system is critical if countries are to receive most of their revenues without active intervention from the tax authorities."*
54. *Id. See also supra* n. 43.

not a problem exists[55] and, if so, whether GFA would solve it;[56] and it remains unclear which countries would be most benefited by GFA and to what extent. Clearly tax havens would lose tax jurisdiction under GFA – which is indeed a positive feature. But a pragmatic and often overriding question affecting the debate is what countries would win the most taxing powers through the *débâcle* of the ALP and triumph of GFA? Would it be China, India, Brazil, would it be Europe or the United States (U.S.)? Developing countries, it would seem, are not the ones at the forefront of this fight.

The inescapable fact is that the ALP versus GFA battle is a fight between economic behemoths – it is a battle of the G20, to be fought within the OECD. The GFA battle is not theoretical or academic; a fierce political dispute surfaces concerning which formula or which factor-weights to use, and this is where most often consensus cannot be reached, which undermines the feasibility of the GFA approach. What is ultimately at stake here is the allocation of the right to tax residual income earned within MNEs,[57] income which is often driven by intangibles that are not created or maintained in developing countries but within the G20. This residual right, no matter if GFA or the ALP is used, is biased in favor of the world's largest and wealthiest consumer markets (i.e., the U.S., Europe, China and Japan), in favor of economies where sovereign risks are relatively low as compared to developing countries, and in favor of the world's most largest and most sophisticated labor markets (i.e., the OECD, China, India, and other G20 countries). GFA would reshuffle the tax bases within these economies most predominantly, and not redistribute the tax base out of the OECD and the G20 and into poorer, developing countries. That is, different factor-formulas could materially redistribute the U.S., Chinese and European tax bases, but the tax base would materially remain within these countries.

Whether or not the ALP versus GFA is, theoretically, a *just battle* for these countries to fight, does not affect this observation – the biggest winners or losers in this battle will be found amongst the G20, and these countries will determine whether the ALP will ever be materially changed or even abandoned in favor of GFA. So from a conceptual perspective it is utterly *unfair* for this uncertain G20 battle to be prioritized as a national policy to be funded by the treasuries of developing countries through the CBCR experiment.

It is inherently given that MNEs in the extractive sector explore natural resources from source countries, which is equivalent to extracting the endowment of land as a factor of production from these nations, while raising unique sustainability issues and environmental concerns in developing countries. Corruption and conflict plagued many such resource-rich countries, and ample research indicated that the business of MNE extractives fueled such corruption, conflicts, and poverty, and undermined the democratic rule of law within such nations. Accordingly, a broad public view of all economic impacts with transparency over all payments made by MNEs in relation to

---

55. A "second-best" pragmatism favoring the continuing development of the ALP, a "Churchillian" approach to transfer pricing, is evidenced in the research of some influential tax scholars. *See* e.g., W. Schön, *International Tax Coordination for a Second-Best World (Part III)*, 2 World Tax J. 227 (2010); Kane (2014) and Tavares (2016), *supra* n. 9.
56. *See* Tavares (2016), *supra* n. 9.
57. *See supra* n. 55; *see also*, Vann (2010) *supra* n. 9.

extractive activities in each of these countries has been identified by PWYP as an adequate response, and such broad CBCR solution has been embraced by the G8, resisted by some developing countries,[58] embraced by others, and promoted through the EITI.

Cherry-picking the tax transparency feature of the PWYP-EITI solution, and limiting it to corporate income taxes only, as opposed to total taxes and total payments made to each government by each MNE, would only produce a partial view of the impact of such MNE in each country. Furthermore, publishing CBCRs, especially for countries that are not tax havens, can expose non-tax features of MNE business models which now private, non-tax information that does not represent a tax risk, but that may be sensitive to the enterprise in question and affect its bargaining position vis-à-vis suppliers or its competitive stance in the market.[59] Revealing in detail the footprint of asset ownership and workforce employment of an MNE may expose its capital expenditure and financing structure (e.g., buy versus lease), as well as its use of outsourcing models (e.g., buy versus make, hire employees versus contractors), to competitors and suppliers, hence jeopardizing its position and business strategy. This interference may not only be distortive from an economic perspective, but a potential offense to taxpayers' rights tantamount to a violation of fundamental, human rights.

As such, CBCR for corporate income taxes only would represent a threat to taxpayers' rights whilst providing an incomplete set of PWYP data and, therefore, would be inadequate metric to form public opinion. It could enable biased analyses and misleading assertions, and foment a naming and shaming industry of factoids. Any conclusions derived from such biased analyses would not support the state-building object and purpose otherwise justifying the publicity of CbC tax payments made by MNEs.

Tax activists and proponents of GFA understand that applying the century-old *Massachusetts factor-formula* to Action 13 CBCR "indicators" that would be made public, could be taken as a *gospel of truth* for the sourcing of business profits.[60] It would serve as a reliable benchmark of fairness in the allocation taxing rights, which could be used to challenge the validity of any transfer pricing results (no matter how refined) under the ALP. This assertion cannot be proven and is theoretically unsound.

Alleging that any differences between GFA and ALP would mean tax abuse, tax evasion or BEPS, would not only be a conceptual stretch; it would be an irresponsible leap, which could yield distortionary results that are possibly unfavorable to most developing countries. Rallying against MNEs because the ALP remains as a lawful standard is not only incoherent, it is dangerous.[61] Embarking on this frenzy can lead developing countries to engage in unnecessary audits, in spending resources and losing battles in unsound controversy that could unduly harm them.

---

58. *See supra* n. 44.
59. *See supra* n. 19. *See also*, Tavares & Owens (2015), *supra* n. 14.
60. *See* Murphy, *supra* n. 51. *See also*, S. Picciotto, *Towards Unitary Taxation of Transnational Corporations*, Tax Justice Network (2012); *and* S. Picciotto, *Is the International Tax System Fit for Purpose, Especially for Developing Countries?*, ICTD Working Paper 13 (2013).
61. *See* Tavares & Owens (2016), *supra* n. 7.

Chapter 10: The Inclusive Framework on BEPS §10.03[A]

Furthermore, the ALP versus GFA *fairness debate*[62] does not account for differences in tax systems, or for taxes other than the corporate income tax imposed on intercompany profits. A serious and rigorous debate of the economic and social impact of MNEs' vertically-integrated supply chains in developing economies, and should consider not only all tax paid to developing countries' governments in connection with such value chains, but all corresponding spillover effects. Similar work has been done quite extensively in the tax incentives literature, and by international organizations such as the World Bank and the International Monetary Fund (IMF). In these studies, what has been detected as the main tax problem concerning the activities of MNEs in developing countries is the excessive use of tax holidays and of other inadequate and redundant tax incentives which reduce income taxes that would otherwise be legitimately imposed on business profits over which, contrary to the intuition of GFA proponents, taxing rights are actually and lawfully allocated to developing countries under the ALP.

§10.03 PROJECT BEPS, THE GLOBAL FORUM AND TRANSFER PRICING

[A] Redundancies in Tax Transparency Initiatives

The political and social environment of the G20 (and particularly amongst the G8) post-2008, which triggered the inception of the BEPS Project, also gave a renewed impetus to the Global Forum.[63] The accession of 107 countries to the Multilateral Convention, of the 137 countries that participate in the Global Forum, was undoubtedly a remarkable achievement that can be partly credited to the G20 BEPS momentum. The BEPS political momentum would not have occurred if not for the vigilance of tax activists. Nonetheless, the astounding success of the MCAA-AEOI (hereinafter referred to also as MCAA-CSR), now signed by 87 countries,[64] was clearly enabled not only by

---

62. *See* Owens, *supra* n. 1 at 1106: *"NGOs and other commentators have pushed for all companies to disclose more comprehensively the income they generate in every country through their subsidiary entities, and the taxes paid in every country, with a view to enabling a greater public debate about their 'tax fairness.' This debate has also been associated with whether the arm's-length principle can handle highly integrated global MNEs. Developments in this area have occurred at both the multilateral and national levels."*
63. *See* OECD Press Release, *Global Forum on tax transparency pushes forward international co-operation against tax evasion* (October 30, 2015) available at http://www.oecd.org/newsroom/global-forum-on-tax-transparency-pushes-forward-international-co-operation-against-tax-evasion.htm.
64. As of November 2, 2016. 1. Albania; 2. Andorra; 3. Anguilla; 4. Antigua and Barbuda; 5. Argentina; 6. Aruba; 7. Australia; 8. Austria; 9. Barbados; 10. Belgium; 11. Belize; 12. Bermuda; 13. Brazil; 14. British Virgin Islands; 15. Bulgaria; 16. Canada; 17. Cayman Islands; 18. Chile; 19. China (People's Republic of); 20. Colombia; 21. Cook Islands; 22. Costa Rica; 23. Croatia; 24. Curaçao; 25. Cyprus; 26. Czech Republic; 27. Denmark; 28. Estonia; 29. Faroe Islands; 30. Finland; 31. France; 32. Germany; 33. Ghana; 34. Gibraltar; 35. Greece; 36. Greenland; 37. Grenada; 38. Guernsey; 39. Hungary; 40. Iceland; 41. India; 42. Indonesia; 43. Ireland; 44. Israel; 45. Isle of Man; 46. Italy; 47. Japan; 48. Jersey; 49. Korea; 50. Kuwait; 51. Latvia; 52. Liechtenstein; 53. Lithuania; 54. Luxembourg; 55. Malaysia; 56. Malta; 57. Marshall Islands; 58. Mauritius; 59. Mexico; 60. Monaco; 61. Montserrat; 62. Nauru; 63. Netherlands; 64. New Zealand; 65. Niue; 66. Norway; 67. Poland; 68. Portugal; 69. Romania; 70. Russian Federation;

the political momentum but also by the ultimate technical results, standards and recommendations emerging from Project BEPS. This was evidenced by the January 2016 accession of no less than 31 countries to the MCAA for the Exchange of CBCRs (MCAA-CBCR),[65] which now stands with forty signatory states.[66]

Amongst the signatories of the MCAA-CSR, are some of the jurisdictions that in the past were most opaque and secretive, countries that may have engaged in harmful tax competition, and that can be described as tax havens or that, at least, have been perceived by other countries as investor-friendly, low-tax jurisdictions. Some examples are Bermuda, the British Virgin Islands, the Cayman Islands, Curaçao, Cyprus, Gibraltar, Guernsey, Isle of Man, Jersey, Liechtenstein, Malta, Mauritius, and Monaco. Other examples of MCAA-CRS signatories that were secretive in the past and/or that may have specific features in their tax systems which may be deemed to facilitate international tax avoidance are Austria, Belgium, Estonia, Hungary, Ireland, Luxembourg, Malaysia, the Netherlands, Switzerland, the United Kingdom (U.K.) and Uruguay. And yet, many of the same signatories of the MCAA-CSR have also signed into the MCAA-CBCR. For instance, Bermuda, Curaçao, Cyprus, Guernsey, Isle of Man, Jersey, Liechtenstein, Luxembourg, and Switzerland. Not to mention Austria, Belgium, Estonia, Malaysia, the Netherlands, the U.K., and Uruguay. It is highly unlikely that these MCAA-CBCR signatories would have agreed to the automatic exchange of CBCRs if such exchange were not ultimately redundant in light of the Multilateral Convention and MCAA-CSR, and if such exchanges would lead to a material transfer of taxing rights and of tax base away from their national treasuries.

That is, the Global Forum's Multilateral Convention, EOIR and MCAA-AEOI *have become* the international norm. As such, transfer *mispricing* risks can be effectively detected through these mechanisms. Therefore, the MCAA-CBCR and related risk assessment is but an additional tool which is unlikely to lead to material tax assessments beyond what could be achieved through EOIR and AEOI. Still useful – particularly for G20 countries that wish to compare and contrast the operation of the ALP versus the hypothetical functioning of GFA, such as countries within the EU that are contemplating Common Consolidated Corporate Tax Base (CCCTB), or such as China

---

71. Saint Kitts and Nevis; 72. Saint Lucia; 73. Saint Vincent and the Grenadines; 74. Samoa; 75. San Marino; 76. Saudi Arabia; 77. Seychelles; 78. Saint Maarten; 79. Slovak Republic; 80. Slovenia; 81. South Africa; 82. Spain; 83. Sweden; 84. Switzerland; 85. Turks & Caicos Islands; 86. United Kingdom; 87. Uruguay. More information: www.oecd.org/tax/automatic-exchange/international-framework-for-the-crs/.

65. *See* OECD Press Release, *A Boost to Transparency in International Tax Matters: 31 Countries Sign Tax Co-operation Agreement to Enable Automatic Sharing of Country by Country Information* (27 Jan. 2016) available at http://www.oecd.org/newsroom/a-boost-to-transparency-in-international-tax-matters-31-countries-sign-tax-co-operation-agreement.htm.

66. Status as of 7 December 2016: 1. Argentina 2. Australia 3. Austria 4. Belgium 5. Bermuda 6. Brazil 7. Canada 8. Chile 9. Costa Rica 10. Curaçao 11. Cyprus 12. Czech Republic 13. Denmark 14. Estonia 15. Finland 16. France 17. Georgia 18. Germany 19. Greece 20. Guernsey 21. Iceland 22. India 23. Ireland 24. Isle of Man 25. Israel 26. Italy 27. Japan 28. Jersey 29. Korea 30. Latvia 31. Liechtenstein 32. Luxembourg 33. Malaysia 34. Mexico 35. Netherlands 36. New Zealand 37. Nigeria 38. Norway 39. People's Republic of China 40. Poland 41. Portugal 42. Senegal 43. Slovak Republic 44. Slovenia 45. South Africa 46. Spain 47. Sweden 48. Switzerland 49. United Kingdom 50. Uruguay. www.oecd.org/tax/beps/country-by-country-reporting.htm.

Chapter 10: The Inclusive Framework on BEPS §10.03[A]

which is contemplating the use of its own sixth method.[67] Or for countries that wish to use the enactment of CBCR as *propaganda*[68] in the fairness debate. If the G20 never agree on the adoption of GFA, however, then the implementation of CBCR could possibly translate into redundant incremental costs with negligible incremental revenue for most if not all countries that adopt it.

Budgetary data from Australia and from the U.K. concerning CBCR implementation seems to confirm this realistic and disillusioned approach. The forecasts disclosed by their treasury authorities indicates what CBCR implementation costs can be in nominal terms, whereas incremental revenues seem to be negligible in relative terms. Australia budgeted CBCR implementation costs of nearly USD 9 million, of which about USD 3.5 million would be associated with capital expenditures (i.e., ICT infrastructure, software).[69] This is a useful benchmark for any country. If, on the one hand, Australia's economy is large and open, the Australian Tax Office (ATO) is a sophisticated and efficient agency with robust capacity, and which operates on pre-existing ICT infrastructure upon which CBCR tools would be built. Larger or smaller economies may incur comparable or even higher capital expenditure costs (ICT-related), as transaction volumes and pre-existing infrastructure might be more determinative of ICT expenditure needs than transaction values. That is, the *volume of CBCRs* collected, stored, transmitted and received, and not the values of revenues, assets, taxes collected, payroll and other data reported within each CBCR, would determine ICT infrastructure needs.

The volume of CBCRs collected, stored and exchanged would be determined by the number of MNEs affected by the new standard and the number of countries where they operate, more so than by the degree of openness or by the size of each economy.[70] And considering the universe of companies for which CBCRs would be collected and exchanged (no more than two to three thousand MNEs),[71] this volume should be

---

67. See Tavares & Owens (2016), *supra* n. 7. *See also* J. Yuesheng, *Value Creation Theory of the BEPS Report and China's Reasonable Share in Global Value Allocation*, IBFD International Transfer Pricing Journal (2015), pp. 223–229, Journals IBFD; *and* J. Li, *China and BEPS: From Norm-Taker to Norm-Shaker*, 69 IBFD Bulletin International Taxation 6 and 7, (2015), pp. 355–370, Journals IBFD.
68. *See supra* n. 43 and 49.
69. *See* Australian Government, *Budget Paper N. 2 – Budget Measures, Combating multinational tax avoidance – new transfer pricing documentation standard* (2015–2016), *available* at http://www.budget.gov.au/2015-16/content/bp2/html/bp2_revenue-07.htm. In Australian Dollars, the budget estimates A$11.3 million of expenditures, of which A$ 4.4 million would amount to capital expenditures (CAPEX) presumed by the author to be related to ICT-software and hardware infrastructure. This approximates USD 8.6 million in total and USD 3.3 million of CAPEX, rounded up to USD 9 million and USD 3.5 million here.
70. MNEs operate in closed economies as well as in open economies. In closed economies, MNEs would operate with relatively less intra-group trade, that is, with a lesser degree of vertical integration. Transfer pricing risks in closed economies would, therefore, be less relevant in merchandise or service trade, and more relevant in capital transactions (i.e., valuation of royalties and interest flows).
71. *See* Forbes, *Global Fortune* listing available at http://www.forbes.com/lists/2010/18/global-2000-10_The-Global-2000_Rank.html. Roughly 1,900 companies would have global revenues of Euro 750 million or more. If there are 2,000 firms that meet this threshold, and if each of these large MNEs operates in 100 countries, there would be nearly 200,000 CBCRs accessible and exchanged between 100 countries around the globe. If 1,900 firms operate in 40 countries on

comparable for most if not every country that implements Action 13 and that engages in the MCAA-CBCR. As such, Australia's benchmark should be meaningful everywhere. Nonetheless, less-equipped tax administrations (irrespective of the total amount of tax revenues they collect), might incur even higher total costs as compared to those disclosed by the ATO, if their legacy ICT infrastructure and institutional processes needed to collect, audit, protect, and transmit confidential CBCR data, lags behind Australia's.

This illustrates the relevance of questions raised by the author before (Tavares & Owens, 2016):[72] *"if the core of transfer pricing rules remains unchanged under the ALP, what are countries to do with the abundant information and CbCRs, which they will receive? Will the granular information on GVCs of MNEs reveal material BEPS risks, and lead to legitimate assessments which could not have occurred in the past? Or will the scrutiny of massive MNE data simply reveal the complex, controversial but still legitimate operation of the ALP of transfer pricing under the functionally separate legal entity approach?"* It is more realistic to believe in the latter.

The U.K. budgeted incremental revenues *from CBCR* worth GBP 5 to GBP 10 million[73] by 2020. This has to assume that CBCR would reveal transfer-pricing adjustments under the ALP and in accordance with the OECD Guidelines, favoring the U.K. tax base, and not discoverable without CBCR. Note, the U.K. is a large consumer market, with a skilled workforce, operating in a robust capital market capable of funding risk-taking activities and wherein risks are often monitored, and where intangibles are often developed, enhanced, maintained, protected and/or exploited (DEMPE).[74] Therefore, a transfer pricing adjustment under the ALP in the post-BEPS world could indeed reasonably lead to incremental U.K. revenues, possibly recapturing tax base and profits unduly shifted to low-tax countries. Still, such instances of *transfer mispricing* that would be detected by Her Majesty's Revenue and Customs (HMRC) *thanks to CBCR* are forecasted to amount to no more than GBP 5 to GBP 10 million per year, which is advertised in the U.K. Budget as a measure which increases the *fairness*[75] of the U.K. tax system. That is 0.001% of the U.K.'s 2015–2016 public sector receipts of GBP 667 billion, or 0.012% of U.K. corporate tax receipts of GBP 42 billion.[76] To demonstrate how negligible the CBCR revenue impact is to the U.K. Budget, let us compare it with the Diverted Profits Tax (DPT), which is forecasted to raise GBP 25

---

average, there would be 76,000 CBCRs. The volume might be situated between these two estimates, perhaps in the 130,000 to 150,000 range. The ICT infrastructure and administrative capacity (human resources) needed to support the exchange of up to 200,000 CBCRs between up to 100 countries, with the necessary level of data protection for the safeguard of taxpayers' rights, is not negligible, and it can be very material for developing countries.

72. *See* Tavares & Owens (2016), *supra* n. 7. *See also,* Durst (ICDT Working Paper, 2014), *supra* n. 10, noting that it is often not the lack of information but the excess of information that makes transfer pricing audits often impregnable for less sophisticated tax administrations.

73. *See in general* H.M. Treasury, *2015 Budget* (hereinafter "the U.K. Budget"); *and* at p. 4, "Fairness," at p. 60 "Ensuring a Fair Contribution to the Tax System," at p. 66: "Table 2.2. Measures announced at Autumn Statement 2014 or earlier which will take effect from April 2015 or later, line 'r'," and at p. 90 "Tax Avoidance and Evasion."

74. *See* OECD, BEPS Actions 8-10 *supra* n. 9.

75. *See* U.K. Budget, *supra* n. 73. *See also supra* n. 50.

76. *Id.*

Chapter 10: The Inclusive Framework on BEPS §10.03[B]

million in 2017 and to reach GBP 360 million[77] by 2020 – still a fraction of total corporate tax revenues, but expected DPT revenues would be no less than thirty-six times greater than CBCR-related revenues in the U.K.. Both U.K. measures serve as meaningful examples of the post-BEPS tax policy options and choices, among others that are available for developing countries to consider.

[B] Tax Transparency and Transfer Pricing Post-BEPS: Enforcement or Policy Debate?

As the author has noted in the past (Tavares & Owens, 2016),[78] *"unprecedented transparency concerning the footprint of large MNEs and their GVCs, through the exchange of CbCR (authorized not only by domestic laws but also under the MCAA), is one of the main outcomes of the BEPS Project. Tax administrations throughout the world are now asking what to do with all this information and data. Whether the global sharing of such information will alter the international allocation of taxing rights between residence and source countries, however, remains highly uncertain."*

Spending USD 9 to USD 10 million on CBCR in order to earn a GBP 5 to GBP 10 million annuity from CBCR might seem to be a worthy investment that can be replicated in many countries – this assumption, however, is quite uncertain. The Australian cost benchmark of USD 10 million is indeed a reliable figure, which can be expected to materialize in other countries, large and small (although it could be even higher for less sophisticated or less-equipped tax administrations), as discussed above. However, the U.K. revenue stream of GBP 5 to 10 million is not as easily replicated in other countries, and it is quite uncertain. Here the values of transactions subject to the ALP would matter, and the value of U.K. imports and exports of goods, services, as well as the value of transactions involving intangibles, are much higher for the U.K. than for all developing countries, and are amongst the highest within the OECD and the G20. Furthermore, if the depth and breadth of functions, assets, and risks attributable to the U.K. operations of the average MNE are proportionately more significant than those attributable to each developing country that implements CBCR (which is also a reasonable assumption), transfer mispricing assessments enabled by CBCR audits within each such country would be a fraction of what is expected from CBCR-triggered audits in the U.K.. Additionally, the transfer pricing audit capacity of the HMRC is also greater than what can be observed in many developing countries, and hence developing countries may be less efficient or less effective than the U.K. in detecting instances of transfer mispricing through CBCRs.[79] Therefore, if the U.K. Budget data is reliable at all, the revenue potential of CBCR under the ALP should be immaterial in most

---

77. *Ibid.*, at p. 66: "Table 2.2. Measures announced at Autumn Statement 2014 or earlier which will take effect from April 2015 or later, line 'p'." The U.K. DPT is arguably also negligible in relative terms, at 0.857% of corporate tax receipts, and 0.54% of total public sector receipts. It may thus have been designed to serve as a behavioral tool, rather than a revenue-raiser.
78. *See* Tavares & Owens (2016), *supra* n. 7.
79. This assumes, of course, that the HMRC would comply with and enforce U.K. law.

countries, and possibly not a priority worthy of a USD 10 million expenditure in developing countries.

As such, it is reasonable to deduce that, rather than a revenue-raiser, CBCR is an experiment or an exercise of the G20, an investment in a broader and arguably healthy transfer pricing debate, through which the ALP and GFA would be compared and contrasted by and between those the countries with the most revenue at stake. It might also serve as an investment in public relations[80] particularly in countries such as the U.K. and for institutions such as the EU Commission, as the *fairness* advertisement appeases public opinion, and might induce greater compliance by individual taxpayers and local businesses.[81] Indeed, CBCR has been portrayed by Her Majesty's Treasury and the HMRC as an enhancement to fairness in the U.K. tax system,[82] rather than as a significant revenue-raising measure in itself. And while the EU Commissions' discourse and renewed CCCTB impetus[83] do make the ALP versus GFA debate relevant within the EU, it views the CCCTB-GFA as a matter of fairness and administrative efficiency within Europe, as it seeks to harmonize corporate income taxation in the *Internal Market* and thus to curb intra-EU tax competition.

However, CBCR has been presented to legislatures around the world as a revenue-raiser transfer-pricing tool that is unique and significant in the combat against BEPS.[84] This is unfortunate and concerning, as it may mislead the sovereign decisions on BEPS implementation that are being made by many countries. These decisions determine the use of public budgets, dictate fiscal priorities, and the use of tax

---

80. *See* Owens, *supra* n. 1 at 1105: "*Modern tax systems work only if 90 percent of taxpayers, for 90 percent of the time, voluntarily comply. The current global debate about whether MNEs are paying their fair share of tax and the technical and policy issues of BEPS may initially undermine that confidence, but in the long run could lead to a more transparent approach that could help restore trust in the tax system. Greater transparency between taxpayer and tax authority is a good thing as it will lead to fewer disputes, greater mutual understanding, and a relationship based on cooperative compliance. However, it's very important that confidentiality is maintained as transparency has to be built on greater mutual trust. The fear that commercially sensitive information could be released could undermine that trust. It is important that fear is not used as an excuse to halt the move toward better transparency.*"
81. *See supra* n. 20.
82. *See* U.K. Budget, *supra* n. 73.
83. *See* European Commission, *Communications* of 2001 [COM(2001) 582], 2003 [COM(2003) 726], and *Non-Paper to informal Ecofin Council* of 2004, *A Common Consolidated EU Corporate Tax Base*; *see also* European Commission, *Communication* of 2007 *Implementing the Community Programme for improved growth and employment and the enhanced competitiveness of EU business: Further Progress during 2006 and next steps towards a proposal on the Common Consolidated Corporate Tax Base (CCCTB)* (COM/2007/223), and Working Paper, CCCTB: possible elements of a technical outline (CCCTB/WP/057); all *available* online at http://ec.europa.eu/taxation_customs/taxation/company_tax/common_tax_base/index_en.htm. The initiative has been relaunched in 2015 as part of the "Action Plan" to promote a "fair and efficient" corporate tax system in Europe. *See* Communication from the Commission to the European Parliament and the Council, *A Fair and Efficient Corporate Tax System in the European Union: 5 Key Areas for Action* Brussels, 17.6.2015 COM(2015) 302 final. Accordingly, a public consultation has been undertaken wherein "the European Commission seeks the views of all interested parties on how the current rules of the CCCTB Proposal for a Directive can be revised to better reflect the current policy priorities in international taxation," *available at* http://ec.europa.eu/taxation_customs/common/consultations/tax/relaunch_ccctb_en.htm.
84. *See supra* ns. 6 and 7.

administration resources. The opportunity costs here can be immense. Particularly where state resources for capacity building are most scarce and revenue needs are greatest, such as in developing countries, which could build capacity to pursue other more worthy policies and measures.[85]

Furthermore, the likelihood of the G20 and the OECD ever agreeing on GFA appears to be remote. As such, betting on CBCR to achieve GFA (which seems to be the stance of many tax activists) would be a gamble with stakes that might be too high for poorer countries. Countries that will not realistically influence the outcome of this global debate. So the conceptual framing of such gamble as a *fairness* imperative safeguarding the interests of developing countries, sometimes used by tax activists, is rather weak – and remains unproven. Investing in a CBCR gamble seeking to foster the GFA debate would be, in the least, a questionable use of the scarce resources of developing countries.

[C] Tax Transparency and Transfer Pricing Enforcement Post-BEPS: Use of Master Files and Foreign UTP Disclosures

The global adoption of CBCR as a *tentative half-step* towards GFA, while CBCR remains bound to the ALP, might make CBCR less than a priority for developing countries. Accordingly, the sovereign debate of this matter within each developing country in the context of the Inclusive Framework, as different policy choices arise, must be better informed than it has typically been. Other BEPS Actions may provide risk assessment tools that are more cost-efficient for developing countries to combat BEPS, while the developed world and the G20 fight over GFA and the ALP. There are better tax transparency tools arising from the cooperative framework of the Global Forum.

The outcome of BEPS Action 12 – a best practices report – was rather disappointing. It would have been preferable to see a global minimum standard emerging from Action 12, one that would be coherent with Actions 5,[86] 8–10[87] and 13. Note, the tax authorities of G8 residence states, particularly those that have sophisticated CFC rules, would typically collect detailed CbC information from their respective multinationals. U.S. MNEs, for example, provide substantial CbC information to the U.S. Internal Revenue Service (IRS); several forms comprised in the U.S. tax returns[88] provide in

---

85. *See* Durst *supra* n. 10.
86. *See* OECD, *Countering Harmful Tax Practices More Effectively, Taking into Account Transparency and Substance, Action 5 – 2015 Final Report*, OECD/G20 Base Erosion and Profit Shifting Project, OECD Publishing, Paris (2015).
87. *See* OECD, BEPS Actions 8-10 *supra* n. 9.
88. *See* e.g., U.S. IRS website: Form 5471, Information Return of U.S. Persons With Respect to Certain Foreign Corporations, *available at* https://www.irs.gov/uac/form-5471-information-return-of-u-s-persons-with-respect-to-certain-foreign-corporations; Form 8858, Information Return of U.S. Persons With Respect to Foreign Disregarded Entities, *available at* https://www.irs.gov/uac/form-8858-information-return-of-u-s-persons-with-respect-to-foreign-disregarded-entities and Schedule M, Transactions Between Foreign Disregarded Entity of a Foreign Tax Owner and the Filer or Other Related Entities; Form 8832, Entity Classification Election, commonly referred to as "Check-the-Box" Election, available at https://www.irs.gov/uac/form-8832-entity-classification-election; and Form 8865, Return of U.S. Persons With Respect to

great detail most (if not all) of the foreign country information that is now to be collected through CBCR. Whether or not such CFC rules are properly enforced, residence countries should have sufficient information on file to ascertain where BEPS risks could harm, if not their own, the treasuries of foreign countries that are also to the Global Forum's Multilateral Convention.

It is unfortunate that spontaneous exchanges of information under the Multilateral Convention have not been sufficiently used to date (although it is relevant amongst some OECD Members). Still, there would be no excuse for Home States to deny EOIRs that aim to curb BEPS in the context of transfer pricing amongst Host States and intermediary hubs. Such EOIRs could be triggered by MCAA-CRS disclosures or by other risk assessment activities conducted by other signatories to the Multilateral Convention. EOIR responses from Home States could also be expected simply as an expression of the commitment to cooperate under Article 25 of bilateral tax treaties[89] and as a general rule of international law.

Rather than receiving, storing, and running through risk assessment tools thousands of CBCRs[90] with information on countries where no tax avoidance takes place, it would be more useful for all countries to focus on receiving from residence states the Master File referenced in Action 13 for each MNE that operates within their borders. That would complement the transfer pricing Local File, and it could trigger further EOIR or even the start of joint audits.

An improved Master File could contain not only a proper description of an MNE's value chain, but a standard disclosure report highlighting transactions (or business models) that are deemed risky for transfer pricing purposes. Such mandatory reporting would be produced within the spirit of Action 12. This would only be a new exercise for MNEs that are not subject to the disclosure of uncertain tax positions affecting their Home State treasuries, or concerning Host jurisdictions; U.S. MNEs, for instance, are typically required to disclose such information to their shareholders and/or to the U.S. IRS.[91]

In the spirit of transparency that informs BEPS Actions 12 and 13, MNEs should be required to disclose in their Master File any "business restructurings" they undertake, or any "principal-entrepreneur" models they operate whereby entrepreneurial functions, assets and/or risks and intra-group profits are centralized within certain legal entities (typically the low-tax intermediary hubs that were historically less than cooperative), particularly when such entities are not their global headquarters. Such improved Master File should also highlight the operation of any "coordination centers" (i.e., for intellectual property development, treasury, or management functions) or intermediary "hubs" which affect their global transfer pricing. This form of reporting

---

Certain Foreign Partnerships, *available at* https://www.irs.gov/uac/form-8865-return-of-u-s-persons-with-respect-to-certain-foreign-partnerships.
89. M. Lang, *Introduction to the Law of Double Taxation Conventions*, Linde (2014).
90. *See supra* n. 71, estimating a universe of 100.000 to 200.000 CBCRs to be exchanged among up to 100 countries.
91. No news for U.S. corps – FIN 48, Schedule UTP, CAP – just more transparency and cooperation between U.S. IRS and foreign tax authorities.

would also capture any and all "box"-type regimes, adding to the purpose of the minimum standards that emerge from Action 5.[92]

All this could be done in one report per MNE, subject to EOIR (and to spontaneous exchange) – the Master File. Each Local File and transfer pricing study around the world would necessarily reference the global Master File, and thus there would be no need to overburden MNEs and tax administrations with the over-reporting of transactions that do not raise BEPS concerns – which will make up the vast majority of the thousands of CBCRs that will be filed, stored and exchanged across the world. The ICT infrastructure and human resources needed to collect, to store and especially to audit and exchange upon request just one Master File for each MNE, as opposed to thousands CBCRs for all MNEs, would require less capital expenditures from firms and from tax administrations around the world. It would enable transfer pricing risk assessments that are more focused, hence not only more efficient but most likely more effective.[93]

That is, high-tax jurisdictions that are source countries which do not raise BEPS risks would not have to collect and automatically exchange CBCRs, and would simply exchange information as-needed, in the context of audits that could be triggered by an effective risk assessment process that uses this Master File with an Action 12 *twist*. These jurisdictions would request Master Files (improved with an Action 12 disclosure) from residence states in order to assess their transfer pricing risks. This approach would also diminish the risk of unlawful leakage of trade secrets or other strategic information concerning the operations of MNEs in high-tax countries, a concern legitimately raised by multinationals in the context of BEPS,[94] and a risk whose mitigation requires increased capital expenditures in developing countries.

These thoughts serve to demonstrate that developing countries might be well advised not to rush towards CBCR implementation, CBCR exchange and CBCR auditing. Instead, EOIR focused on obtaining Master Files from residence states following Action 13, might represent a better use of their public resources rather than CBCR collection, storage, exchange and audits. As would EOIR targeting transfer

---

92. *See supra* n. 86.
93. Durst, *supra* n. 10, is emphatic: the problem is often too much (useless and complex) documentation, and not too little.
94. Christians (2013), *supra* n. 12, notes the role of the Business and Industry Advisory Committee to the OECD (BIAC) with concern. The positions defended by that organization would seem to be contrary to public interest and only safeguard large multinationals, whereas public officials represented at the OECD would be subject to an undue influence by such "tax-technical lobbyists." The lives of many would be determined by a group of bureaucrats behind closed doors in Paris, along with big business. A dire prospect. However, these public officials are representative of the democratic states that are OECD Members. No policies designed there can be approved without support by the Presidency and Legislative Bodies of Member Countries. Therefore, the solution does not seem to be the replacement of each national government and each national legislature by a public representation at the OECD – much less if such representation is assigned to non-elected persons, representatives of NGOs or Academia, etc. Perhaps an Advisory Committee similar to BIAC could congregate representatives of civil society; however, in its public consultations, the OECD has been more and more open and transparent to receiving and publishing all input received from any interested party. Therefore, if the system remains broken, or if OECD positions crafted by public officials seem inadequate, the governments of each Member State are to blame.

pricing-related disclosures of uncertain tax positions already filed at residence states as reported under Action 12, or the operation of low-tax hubs that can be detected through the MCAA-CRS.

§10.04 CBCR AND THE POST-BEPS WORLD OF TRANSFER PRICING: WINNERS, LOSERS AND GAMBLERS

The G20 BEPS Mandate to redesign what came to be perceived as a broken international tax system, with BRICS and other non-OECD countries "on equal footing" along with OECD Members, was also fueled by BRICS intentions to reform the ALP, and to approximate it to GFA. The BRICS wanted a fundamental reform of the international tax legal system that would increase their taxing rights or legitimize their unilateral policies, while a public response against corporate tax abuse was demanded by voters in OECD countries. The final report delivered under BEPS Actions 8–10,[95] however, does not alter Article 9 of the Model Conventions,[96] and it does not create minimum standard to be enforced by international law – it takes the form of "recommendations" and amends the OECD Guidelines,[97] to be implemented as-needed under national laws where such laws lack refinement – thus, reinforcing the OECD Guidelines and the ALP.

Ultimately, all minimum standards and recommendations tackle what has been defined as "BEPS" through negotiated consensus.[98] As such, the broader framework of residence versus source country taxing rights has not been altered, and the G20-OECD coalition has not substantially reformed the ALP.[99] In fact, the final BEPS report on transfer pricing has fallen short of the expectations raised by many commentators,[100] tax activists, and by countries[101] such as China and India. The new G20/OECD consensus that emerged from the BEPS Project aims to shut down wholly artificial "box" regimes and establish (bare) minimum standards of tax competition, reinforcing and building upon the work Global Forum. As the author has posited in the past (Tavares & Owens 2016), "instead of ending MNE tax avoidance, the OECD and the

---

95. See OECD, supra n. 11.
96. OECD, *Model Tax Convention on Income and on Capital*, OECD (22 July 2010), Models IBFD (the OECD Model Convention).
97. OECD *Transfer Pricing Guidelines for Multinational Enterprises and Tax Administrations*, OECD (2010), International Organizations' Documentation IBFD (the OECD TP Guidelines).
98. See supra n. 16.
99. OECD TP Guidelines, supra n. 97, pp. 37-41. Global formulary apportionment is rejected by the OECD, supra n. 97, pp. 159-167, whilst the use of "safe harbours" (if inconsistent with the ALP) is also discouraged; nonetheless, the Guidelines permit the use of "other methods" which satisfy the ALP, p. 61
100. See e.g., supra n. 9 and 10.
101. See n. 7 and 67. See also, P. Prakash, *Emerging Transfer Pricing and International Tax Issues*, International Transfer Pricing Journal, (2013), pp. 374–378, Journals IBFD, S. Gill, *Intangibles and Transfer Pricing: The Perils Faced by Multinationals in India*, International Transfer Pricing Journal, (2011), pp. 47–56, Journals IBFD *and* S. Wagh, *Transfer Pricing Aspects of Marketing Intangibles: An Indian Perspective*, 69 Bulletin International Taxation 9, (2015), pp. 520–530, Journals IBFD.

G20 have agreed to a 'new normal' for tax competition with new ground rules for corporate tax avoidance."[102]

As such, the U.S., the U.K., and several OECD and EU/EEA Member Countries seem to have been the winners of the transfer pricing battle fought under Project BEPS. These are countries with solid capital markets, and/or with endowments of human capital needed to meet post-BEPS substance standards (i.e., TP-DEMPE, LOB, modified nexus). Aside from the U.S. and the U.K., the Netherlands, Switzerland, Luxembourg, Ireland, Hong Kong, and Singapore, for example, stand to attract transit-FDI and human capital in the era post-BEPS.[103]

The world seems to be now closer to India's traditional stance on the determinative worth of human capital in value creation.[104] This new trend which may have started with the recognition of *significant people functions* under the Authorized OECD Approach (AOA) for Attribution of Profits to Permanent Establishments (APPE)[105] has fallen short of recognizing an intangible asset in relation to assembled workforce; yet it has paved the way for further characterizations of "unique and valuable contributions" made by skilled labor located in India and elsewhere, opening avenues for further application of the profit split method,[106] separate and apart from a forceful view of comparability factors. Brazil's formulary methods remain exotic and insulating – therefore still harmful for Brazil[107] most of all. Brazil remains as an example of what not to do alone. China's drive towards the recognition of market intangibles was not successful; yet it may still overrate its market-related location specific advantages (LSAs)[108] and overplay them as comparability factors in order to pursue a unilateral approach to profit splits or its own sixth method – which would be harmful for China. Another example not to be followed unilaterally. BEPS Actions 8–10, therefore, clearly demonstrate the ALP as a winner – and reforms were kept to a bare minimum. Note, France, Spain, Italy and other countries in Continental Europe might have favored a Chinese approach to the recognition of market intangibles or a broader reform of the ALP; one that would possibly increase their taxing rights over transit-FDI "hubs" such as the U.K., the Netherlands, Ireland, and Luxembourg, and ultimately over U.S.

---

102. See Tavares & Owens (2015), *supra* n. 14. See also, R.J.S. Tavares and B.N. Bogenschneider, *The New de minimis Anti-Abuse Rule in the Parent Subsidiary Directive: Validating EU Tax Competition and Corporate Tax Avoidance?* 43 *Intertax*, Issue 8/9 (2015), pp. 484–494.
103. Id.
104. Ibid.
105. See OECD, *Report on the Attribution of Profits to Permanent Establishments* (OECD 2008), International Organizations' Documentation IBFD, and OECD, *Report on the Attribution of Profits to Permanent Establishments* (OECD 2010), International Organizations' Documentation IBFD. See also OECD, *Commentary on Article 7 Concerning the Taxation of Business Profits*, in *Commentaries on the Model Tax Convention 2010* (Full Version), OECD Publishing (2012); in particular pars 4-9 referencing the *OECD Reports* of 2008 and 2010. The 2008 and 2010 Reports and related OECD Commentary under Article 7(2), effectively establish the Authorized OECD Approach or AOA for the attribution of profits to permanent establishments (APPE).
106. See OECD Guidelines, *supra* n. 97, on "Profit Splits."
107. See Tavares & Dias (2016), *supra* n. 7.
108. See Tavares & Owens (2015, 2016), *supra* n. 7 and 14.

MNEs.[109] In the context of Project BEPS, however, that battle was lost – CCCTB is now their next bet, while State Aid disputes are the ongoing gamble.[110]

The biggest winners arising from Project BEPS, nonetheless, are the transparency instruments of the Global Forum. In fact, CBCR reporting became no more than one additional instrument of government-to-government tax transparency under the auspices of the Global Forum. It may indeed represent an additional obligation for taxpayers, leading to increased taxpayer-to-government tax transparency in non-headquarter jurisdictions; yet, generally, it should not add much to the disclosure of information already required of MNEs at their Home State. Information which could be exchanged through other means, also under the auspices of the Global Forum, as discussed here. CBCR in this sense would not only be redundant as a risk assessment tool, but it would serve as an instrument of propaganda to appease public opinion, particularly in G8 countries such as the U.K.. Viewing it as a half-win towards GFA, therefore, might be no more than wishful thinking – tax activists who take this view, as if it were their win, whether knowingly or not will be serving the public relations strategy of tax administrations of the G8.

It should be noted that government-to-taxpayer transparency has not emerged from the BEPS Project as a winner. Action 14 could have enabled greater transparency if MAP proceedings had been reformed to permit greater taxpayer involvement.[111] Pistone and Baker (2015)[112] would rightly state that the G20/OECD Project missed one "action," which should have been dedicated to establishing minimum standards for the protection of taxpayers' rights that would include greater transparency of governments.

Notwithstanding, and irrespective of whether CBCR increased or facilitated taxpayer-to-government transparency around the world, it should be clear that Actions 3, 5, 8–10 and 12 have not significantly changed the tax competition playing field. Reinforcing CFC rules and effectively creating minimum standards that would close notorious loopholes (such as those arising from U.S. "check-the-box" elections), would increase not only residence-country taxation but, perhaps predominantly, source-country taxation.[113] That would have been a true *game-changer*. If the G20 were to enhance CFC standards, all source countries (including developing economies) throughout the world should gain revenues, while all tax havens should lose. As noted

---

109. *See* Tavares, Bogenschneider & Pankiv (2016), *supra* n. 29.
110. *Id.*
111. OECD, *Making Dispute Resolution Mechanisms More Effective, Action 14 – 2015 Final Report, OECD/G20 Base Erosion and Profit Shifting Project,* OECD Publishing, Paris (October, 2015) available at http://dx.doi.org/10.1787/9789264241633-en. *See* also M. Lang and J. Owens, *International Arbitration in Tax Matters,* IBFD (2016); and Working Papers from the WU Global Tax Policy Center, *International Arbitration in Tax Matters: The Lead-up to the G20 and UN Meetings (Vienna, October 12-13, 2015), in particular,* J. Owens & L. Turcan, *Proposal for New Institutional Framework for Mandatory Dispute Resolution,* and Jasmine Kollmann, *The new OECD Proposal to Making Dispute Resolution more Effective: BEPS Action 14: A Comparison between the December 2014 Draft and the Final 5 October 2015 Recommendations.*
112. *See,* P. Pistone and P. Baker, *General Report – The Practical Protection of Taxpayers' Fundamental Rights,* International Fiscal Association 2015 Basel Congress, IBFD (2015).
113. *See* Durst, *supra* n. 10.

by Durst (2015),[114] strong CFC regimes would likely benefit source countries even more than residence countries, and hence would be truly "altruistic" policies, hence the resistance of home countries in adopting and enforcing such rules. Unfortunately, the CFC battle was lost in the context of BEPS – not only because of competitive issues that could affect U.S. MNEs, but also because of their inherent conflict with EU law.[115]

This is also why not having a global standard emerging from Action 12, and linked to Global Forum instruments, is disappointing. Without effective CFC rules, and without substantially reforming the ALP, it is evident that tax competition – and the "race to the bottom" – will continue. In fact, tax competition has been, once again, legitimized.[116] Now with more taxpayer-to-government and government-to-government transparency, and now using entities and regimes that are not wholly artificial, letterbox schemes.[117]

The definition of BEPS that emerges from the G20/OECD Project, therefore, is limited to *transfer mispricing* (i.e., that disrespects the ALP as interpreted through the OECD Guidelines), as well as to conflicts of legal qualification leading to non-taxation (i.e., cross-border "mismatches" – hybrid entities or hybrid instruments). Both forms of BEPS often arise in the context of wholly artificial structures and letterbox schemes. *A contrario*, legal structures that meet all minimum standards, and that all observe the recommendations emerging from the final G20/OECD Project BEPS deliverables, should escape the "BEPS" qualification, and hence should not be viewed as "abusive."[118]

Perhaps this relatively narrow definition of BEPS explains the relatively low quantification of "BEPS" revenue losses that was put forth under Action 11.[119] Undoubtedly, 4% to 10% of global corporate income tax revenues is a relevant figure: USD 100 billion to USD 240 billion is not at all negligible. This figure is to be monitored and reported to the general public by the OECD, thus reinforcing its definitional framework – and it is large enough to make the headline news. It has been used to herald that the G20 and the OECD found what the problem is, and where the international tax system is broken, and that the BEPS Project is solving it.[120] A noticeable response to the political climate that triggered the inception of the Project in the first place.

---

114. *Id.* Christians (2009) would explain this with *Cosmopolitanism*.
115. *See* Tavares & Bogenschneider (2015), *supra* n. 102.
116. *Id. See also*, Tavares (2016), *supra* n. 30.
117. *Ibid.*
118. Arguably, if the standards arising from Action 7 on the improper use of tax treaties are adopted to their fullest extent (i.e., LOB, PPT, and change of title and preamble), then the use of treaties to enable tax avoidance structures that are not "wholly artificial" could also be deemed improper. Action 7, however, does not establish all of its anti-abuse standards as one single "minimum standard." Instead, a significant degree of optionality will remain, and hence treaty shopping in many tax-avoidance structures can remain lawful. *See* Tavares & Bogenschneider (2015), *supra* n. 102. *See also*, Tavares (2016), *supra* n. 30.
119. *See*, OECD, *Measuring and Monitoring BEPS, Action 11 – 2015 Final Report*, OECD/G20 Base Erosion and Profit Shifting Project, OECD Publishing, Paris (2015), *available at http://dx.doi.org/10.1787/9789264241343-en*.
120. *See* P. Saint-Amans and R. Russo, *The BEPS Package: Promise Kept*, Bulletin for International Taxation (2016), pp. 236–241.

However, if it is intuitive to consider that the tax system works whenever "90% of taxpayers comply 90% of the time,"[121] then no less than 19% of the tax base is always exposed to all forms of noncompliance, including error, evasion, and abuse. Considering the relevance of MNEs in the global corporate tax base, and considering their inherent opportunity to perpetrate what has been defined as "BEPS," attributing 4%–10% out of the 19% noncompliance latitude to this form of abuse so-defined as "BEPS," seems quite reasonable. The figure is anything but surprising.[122] That is, again, because the definition of "BEPS" has been made to fit under the notion of *noncompliance*.

Indeed, it can be said that companies that used wholly artificial, letterbox schemes have not complied with the spirit of the tax laws they allegedly circumvented. From a deeper jurisprudential perspective, this noncompliance should have been deemed unlawful even prior to the BEPS Project – as it might have been in many countries. Some would characterize such mispricing schemes as "tax evasion," others would view it as a misinterpretation of the law in the context of aggressive tax planning and intended tax avoidance ultimately defeated. For these countries, the BEPS Project has not significantly reformed pre-existing international or domestic rules. Rather, it reaffirmed and reinforced them.

Other countries, however, may have been more formalistic or superficial in their interpretation of treaty law and of transfer pricing standards, and may have misinterpreted instances of transfer mispricing or other abusive schemes not as "tax evasion" but as legitimate "tax avoidance" – which should no longer occur post-BEPS. Hence, even though the Project BEPS does not significantly reform pre-existing international standards, it may help countries interpret such rules more appropriately, by reaffirming and reinforcing such standards rather than reforming them.

If, instead, the BEPS Project scope had been broader, encompassing a true *reform* of international tax standards, as opposed to merely curbing *noncompliance*, the deliverables would have been different, and the revenue at stake quantified under Action 11 would have been much higher. For instance, if Actions 3 and 12 had created minimum standards to reinforce CFC rules, along with mandatory disclosures covering host-country tax avoidance in such home-state disclosures (subjecting such disclosures to automatic exchange), and if Actions 8–10 had reformed the ALP more deeply, the amount of revenue studied under Action 11 would not be a fraction of the 19% attributed to noncompliance. It would instead be a significant portion of the 81% of the tax base that now abides by the current letter and by the current spirit of the law.

---

121. See Owens, *supra* n. 1. Owens' reference to a Paretto-optimal compliance environment and 80:20 rule, is confirmed by studies that are cited in the OECD/G20 BEPS Action 11 Report, noting that 22% of firms engage in BEPS-related "avoidance" (whereas 78% do not).
122. *See supra* n. 119. The OECD references that other organizations (such as UNCTAD and the IMF) also came up with revenue loss estimates at roughly USD 100 billion. This obviously would vary according to the definition of BEPS (mispricing, wholly artificial transactions versus aggressive pricing heavily structured transactions with legal substance yet disproportionate or incoherent economic results).

If we assume, merely for illustration purposes, that 80%[123] of such 81% would remain unaltered by deeper reforms (i.e., if 80% of 81% is corporate tax base not affected by MNE tax avoidance currently deemed lawful), the potential revenue at stake in such *quasi*-BEPS MNE structures could reach 15.2% of global corporate income tax revenues, or USD 365 billion. That would be in addition to the noncompliance revenue loss of up to USD 240 billion, hence taking the total BEPS-related tax revenues at stake each year from 4%–10% to 19.2%–25.2%[124] of the global corporate tax revenues. That is, up USD 605 billion yearly. The G20 and the OECD, nonetheless, have not defined this hypothetical incremental revenue as BEPS-related, in spite of the academic studies that may have hinted to such higher figures. And given the outcome of Actions 3, 5 and 8–10 this broader definition and econometrics exercise will not be done, and hence this hypothetical revenue loss will not be recognized or monitored at all by the OECD under Action 11. It is only a rudimentary illustration in this study, even though it reinforces the deeper academic analyses done by reputable econometrists.[125] Those seeking a deeper reform of the international tax system, therefore, have also lost a definitional battle.

Now, if countries attempt to unilaterally pursue the USD 100–240 billion of BEPS mispricing and abuse, a tsunami of tax litigation with highly uncertain outcome would proliferate across the world, engulfing taxpayers and tax administrations.[126] Hence the critical importance of Action 14, which should have created stricter minimum standards concerning MAP, and unfortunately did not enlist countries beyond the "coalition of the willing" that will embrace MAP Arbitration.[127] Even worse, if countries attempt to pursue tax revenues that are "saved" by MNEs through lawful post-BEPS tax avoidance (illustrated here as USD 365 billion per year), not only uncertain litigation will ensue, but significant changes to the competitive stance of countries will create harmful economic distortions.

The under-enforcement or over-implementation of anti-abuse standards is now part of the post-BEPS tax competition game.[128] In this game, under-enforcement would be punished one way or another by the threat of sanctions which would be imposed by the international community. Such under-enforcement might, for instance, be viewed a form of harmful tax competition possibly exposed through the Global Forum, or as a

---

123. *Id.*
124. *Ibid.* The Action 11 Report cites numerous academic studies that would support a broader definition of BEPS-related tax avoidance with estimates ranging from 19% to 30% of CIT revenues, for the corresponding sample of firms (and/or countries) covered within the established parameters of each study – hence validating the rudimentary illustration of 19-25% presented here. *See* RIEDEL, Clausing, others. Yet the narrower definitional parameters used in Action 11 reinforce the lowest ranges of estimates (e.g., UNCTAD, IMF), and disseminates the message that the BEPS problem amounts to no more than 4-10% of CIT revenues. It is reasonable to assume that such higher figures would include revenues that would have shifted amongst the G20 if GFA were to be adopted – yet it is possible that the GFA revenue shift would affect even greater revenues (beyond transfer pricing "planning" under the ALP).
125. *See supra* n. 119.
126. *See* Tavares & Owens (2015, 2016), *supra* n. 7 and 14.
127. *Id.*
128. *Ibid.*

breach to the EU Code of Conduct.[129] Conversely, over-implementation would not be sanctioned under international law, as it would primarily harm those countries that unilaterally opt to do it[130] rather than the international community – that is, to the extent such over-implementation does not disguise a *raid* against the treasuries of other countries.[131] Nonetheless, unilateral actions of any kind, whether to increase or decrease a nation's investment climate through tax policy, would tend to be economically distortive – hence detrimental to global welfare. Global cooperation and uniform BEPS implementation, therefore, would be conducive to global welfare. This notion would justify the *Inclusive Framework* on BEPS Implementation, and frame it within the principle of good faith.[132]

§10.05 SOCIAL RESPONSIBILITY IN TAX ACTIVISM

The role of tax activists in raising public awareness over inequities embedded in tax systems throughout the world is indeed commendable. It is conducive to state-building, and to the democratic rule of law. The BEPS Project would not have started and it would not have accomplished anything without the public pressure and political momentum fueled by the NGOs, and general media. Tax activism, however, must be responsible and well-informed, just as any other activity of great social interest.

Individuals and nations do have a fundamental right to information, which enables the full exercise of individual liberties and national sovereignty. The right of nation-states to self-determination is a fundamental pillar, and a defining feature of sovereignty, and the exercise of such right requires information. States however cannot be ignored. Democracies function through representation – legitimate governments fulfill a mandate. If governments are not corrupt or illegitimate, overruling such mandate would represent anarchy, it would undermine the rule of law and it would be destructive of the state. Tax activists therefore must remain engaged with their representatives in national governments, with their national legislatures, and with their heads of government and heads of state, and exert pressure over their national governments, to ensure their authorities do have access to all information needed to fulfill their democratic mandate. This would be more effective to the cause of fairness and equality in taxation than the criticism of nameless institutions such as the

---

129. *See* Tavares, Bogenschneider & Pankiv (2016), *supra* n. 29.
130. *See* Tavares & Owens (2015, 2016), *supra* n. 7 and 14.
131. *See* Tavares, Bogenschneider & Pankiv (2016), *supra* n. 29. EU over-implementation might be viewed as a raid against the U.S. treasury, caused by the U.S. treasury's enablement of foreign tax savings by U.S. MNEs coupled with the non-enforcement of U.S. tax jurisdiction, which itself may be viewed as under-implementation of anti-abuse standards representing a raid by the U.S. treasury against EU countries. This would be an instance of harm against harm, a treasury war. Both actions could be viewed as unlawful.
132. *See* Lang (2014) *supra* n. 89. *See also, The Vienna Convention on the Law of Treaties* (VCLT) Article 26. The VCLT was concluded in 1969 and became effective in 1980, and has been ratified by 114 countries. It is often viewed as an expression of *customary international law* and as such the principles contained it its terms would be binding to nations before and after the VCLT signing (i.e., reaching non-signatories). This is for instance the express view of the United States, a non-signatory that considers the terms of the VCLT to be but a codification of pre-existing customary law.

OECD – the OECD in this sense is but a reflection of the governments that cooperate and that bargain within it, and controlling it. Pressuring the G8 and the G20, therefore, and in particular pressuring the U.S. concerning the blatant non-taxation of its multinationals, should be more effective.

Taxpayer-to-government transparency, government-to-taxpayer transparency, and government-to-government transparency concerning tax matters, should be priorities not only for tax activists but also for all citizens and all taxpayers. These dimensions of transparency have indeed improved thanks to tax activism. Taxpayer-to-taxpayer transparency (wherein taxpayer-to-activists disclosure of CBCRs would fit), however, should not be viewed as a tax transparency rule or imperative, but rather as an exception to be used in extreme and well-informed cases, such as what has occurred with PWYP and the anti-corruption movement in the extractive sector.

Tax activists are not government officials and are not fulfilling a democratic mandate. As such, they, as other participants in civil society (including owners of capital and managers of business enterprises), do not have the same right to access *taxpayer-specific* information that is afforded to their elected officials and tax authorities (except an overriding circumstance such as corruption and wars surrounding the extractive sector). Where the democratic rule of law is not subverted and the government is not corrupt, human and social rights and freedoms require this distinction between the state agents and the general public. Disrespecting such individual rights and freedoms would undermine the rule of law, and not only be contrary to social interest, but socially irresponsible, and ultimately detrimental to welfare. Public disclosure of taxpayer-specific CBCRs is not a feasible approach to address fairness concerns, it would be merely a tool for misinformed naming, shaming, and lynching. Other instruments can be used by civil society and tax activists that would be more conducive to a well-informed fairness debate.

Access to *aggregate taxpayer data*, for instance, which preserves the name, the rights and freedoms of specific taxpayers, can be viewed as a matter of social interest. Therefore, not only tax activists, but academics and other members of civil society should indeed pressure their governments to ensure adequate laws are in place to enable the access to such aggregate data. This permits the debate of tax policy, be it from an efficiency perspective or from the viewpoint of fairness and equality. An *aggregate CBCR report for all MNEs* would demonstrate their global footprint and enable a quick (albeit superficial) comparison of how GFA could, hypothetically, reshuffle the distribution of the global corporate tax base of MNEs across countries, could be useful to foster the debate of GFA versus ALP. If CBCRs are available, and for the countries that make it available, this exercise could be done and even published by the OECD without harming taxpayers' rights. However, it is doubtful that the G20 would agree on a global formula – hence the prospects of this study being done or being useful are slim.

Tax activists could therefore make a more socially responsible use of their time and of the donations they collect by engaging in more pragmatic efforts that are more likely to bear fruit, and to benefit developing countries. For example, the work of the Global Forum could be greatly reinforced by the engagement of civil society, and this could be pursued by tax activists in a constructive manner. The OECD CFA is expected to monitor BEPS as per Action 11, and to somehow disclose aggregate BEPS information publicly; and it will remain engaged not only with its OECD Members but with other countries that participated in the BEPS Project, as it will keep monitoring and measuring the results of the BEPS Project. Through tax activism and public engagement, the scope of Action 11 and the work of the Global Forum could be expanded and enhanced. The monitoring and quantification of the BEPS problem under Action 11 could be expanded so as to include and build upon Action 12 disclosures that already occur the world over. This could be a mandate from the Global Forum, as an enhancement to Action 11.

Uncertain tax positions concerning transfer pricing or other BEPS-related matters that are reported to each OECD Member could reported in aggregate form, and disclosed to the general public through the Global Forum. This would enable not only the identification of patterns of tax avoidance, but also of areas where the legislation might require improvement. The Global Forum could also monitor and report on tax competition that relies on multilateral structures, that is, on the type of lawful *treaty shopping* that is expected to continue post-BEPS. For example, the use of "box"-type entities (e.g., "knowledge" or "innovation" boxes)[133] that are compliant with the modified nexus approach, as well as their harmful pre-BEPS regimes variants that are being phased out but still function, could be tracked and publicly reported in aggregate form (i.e., per country, and not per MNE).

Any public debate, any naming and shaming, therefore, and any pressure exerted by activists, by academics and other commentators, and by the media, would target countries that engage in tax competition. And would target the laws that have loopholes or other defects, pressuring legislatures that allow such laws to remain in force. The representatives of the people, who should protect public interests, would be exposed and the issues would be properly debated – whether tax competition policies are justified or beneficial to each country would be discussed in the open.

This would take the limelight away from the names, facts and figures of specific MNEs that comply with valid national and international laws. Targeting MNEs or wealthy individuals in order to gather public interest, and not focusing on the countries and officials that attract or sponsor them, can be viewed simply as a deflection or a distraction. And distractions of this sort can undermine and defeat the social cause that propels the debate, which would be socially irresponsible.

MNEs are not supranational authorities. What U.S. MNEs do is a reflection of U.S. laws and U.S. policies, and of the nature of tax competition fostered or sponsored by the U.S. as a nation-state. What MNEs do within the EU, and what some European countries do to attract MNEs, is also a reflection of EU law and of the multilateralism inherent to the present constitution of the Internal Market, which is still affected by the remaining fiscal sovereignty retained by Member States. Whether these laws and policies are conducive to national or global welfare or not, is what must be discussed transparently.

---

133. *See* Tavares & Owens (2015, 2016), *supra* n. 7 and 14.

Focusing media attention and tax activism on MNE operations, attempting to name and shame them for using the laws of the U.S. and the EU, may be appealing to gather public attention. But it can be quite distracting from the real issue underlying tax competition: it is an internal legal matter of sovereign nations which clash, and which shape international law. Highlighting the tax affairs of MNEs, naming and shaming them as the "immoral" culprits, and not agents working within the letter and the spirit of laws that are dated or defective, does make the news, sells newspapers, and has general public appeal. It may enlist more donors, and lead to more funding to tax activism. But it also saves the face of the same legislators and authorities that fail to reform the laws – it takes some of the heat off of governments, deflecting public attention from the legislature to the executive branch and the tax administration, or from the states to the taxpayers. Tax activists that embark on this naming and shaming journey against MNEs and wealthy individuals are not fighting the real battle that must be fought – even though they are selling newspapers and tabloids.

§10.06 WHERE DO DEVELOPING COUNTRIES FIT IN?

National legislatures around the world are examining legislative proposals and receiving signed treaties for ratification concerning tax transparency actions. The usefulness of instruments seems to be clouded by misinformation, and could lead to sovereign decisions that are not representative of the best resource mobilization priorities in developing countries. As discussed, the BEPS Project has not significantly reformed the ALP or materially changed the OECD Guidelines. The recommendations may strengthen transfer pricing regulations in countries that interpreted the ALP in a more formal or superficial manner. That is, instances of transfer mispricing and artificial schemes that should have been viewed as unlawful pre-BEPS, have been reaffirmed as unlawful post-BEPS. This *non-reform* was the result of both cooperative gaming amongst OECD countries and bargaining amongst the G20. Developing countries were not included or represented, and as such are not responsible for this normative outcome.

Developing countries can, however, benefit from the reinforced and clarified guidance that emerges from BEPS Actions 8–10. The redrafted OECD Guidelines can be useful, and serve to frame risk assessments and transfer pricing audits that are more robust. Using CBCRs for such risk assessments, however, can be misleading.

Undoubtedly, CBCRs would demonstrate where high-income is accumulated in low-tax jurisdictions, and this can facilitate the detection of transfer mispricing. This information, however, can be obtained through other methods that may be more cost-efficient, such as the exchange instruments of the Global Forum [i.e., the Multilateral Convention (EOIR) and MCAA-CRS (AEOI)]. Bilateral exchanges under tax treaties and or TIEAs could also serve that purpose. Note, data points other than taxable income and corporate tax payments (such as payroll costs and asset ownership) that are disclosed in the CBCR might be misleading, and steer authorities away from the Functional and Factual Analysis of the OECD Guidelines. That is, if these other data points are used in framing risk assessments, they could raise red flags and trigger transfer pricing audits in numerous structures that do not involve transfer mispricing at all. In this sense, resources that could be focused on higher risks would be diverted to audits that would not yield any revenues. This distraction and diversion of resources might actually facilitate and cover instances of noncompliance. That is, if countries are inundated by CBCRs the excess of information could be a hindrance to their audit capacity.

Information from the Master Files, however, can be more useful and allow a more efficient and effective risk assessment model for developing countries. Such information can guide EOIRs and the monitoring of MCAA-CRS filings, and trigger justified transfer pricing audits. Historically, the information contained in Master Files would often not be included in local transfer pricing documentation. Each country would typically have separate and uncoordinated local transfer pricing files, requiring the reporting of relevant transactions involving only their specific taxpayers and the application of a one-sided transfer pricing method. Exceptionally, taxpayers would disclose further information concerning foreign transactions or entities in ruling requests or submissions for Advance Pricing Agreements (APAs), or when the application of a two-sided method was warranted. An overall view of the MNE group, nonetheless, was often limited to their countries of residence.

As such, only when such limited information base would allow the detection of a transfer mispricing risks, source countries could obtain further information regarding non-resident entities or foreign transactions, through audits and properly motivated EOIR. Intermediary countries used to host box-type entities, however, would often remain secretive and (often legitimately) apply high standards for the justification of information requests issued by foreign tax authorities (thereby not cooperating with so-called fishing expeditions). Given the asymmetry of information between source countries, intermediary hubs, and residence countries, transfer pricing audits initiated by source countries could well be misguided, and information requests in that scenario could be precarious. In practice, this would mean that only residence states would truly have "the full picture" and understand where the "residual profits" of their MNEs would lie, and why.

By auditing Master Files that will be filed by MNEs in their Home States as per Action 13, and by using the exchange instruments of the Multilateral Convention and Global Forum to obtain information concerning the operation of MNEs in low-tax jurisdictions, developing countries could develop efficient risk assessment tools and filters that would allow them to trigger transfer pricing audits where risks of transfer mispricing do exist. It is doubtful whether CBCRs would add much to this; as discussed above, information that is both significant and useful might be redundant, and auditing other data contained in CBCRs (as well as CBCRs from high-tax countries) might be distracting and cost-inefficient.

Requiring developing countries to spend resources and fund the CBCR experiment as a tentative half-win towards GFA, by leading them to believe that CBCR would be itself a significant revenue-raiser, is not *fair*. It would be incoherent for the advocates of tax fairness to make that suggestion. Making that claim would be akin to defending that developing nations should fund the CCCTB debate in Europe, or the interests of the G20. As long as the ALP and the OECD Guidelines remain as they are,

CBCR is unlikely to yield material revenues to developing countries – not beyond what they can collect using the information exchange mechanisms available through the Global Forum, including the audit of Master Files.

Obviously, if GFA was ever adopted, CBCRs would be essential. In fact, the design of CBCRs and their underlying risk assessment rationale are both informed by a GFA theoretical framework (hence their inefficiency for risk assessments under the ALP). The disclosure and exchange of foreign information under such GFA framework, however, beyond triggering unsuccessful audits, may induce source countries to place greater weight on CBCR "substance indicators" that would lead to the broadening of their taxing rights. That is, source countries may become more aggressive in their interpretation of the ALP (following in the footsteps of China's sixth method), and adopt unilateral stances that could lead to undue claims of taxing jurisdiction. Other countries may be induced seek the re-characterization or disregard of foreign entities or foreign transactions using general anti-abuse rules (GAARs) if they use CBCRs to ascertain that such foreign entities are functionally thin, or foreign transactions are tax-motivated. In short, under the cloak of a CBCR-based transfer pricing risk assessment, source countries may seek to reassess their tax claims not based on the actual transactions and entities that are situated within their territories and that produce income within their territories in compliance with the ALP, but based on their perception of whether the overall (residual) profits of an MNE group are fully taxed each year at a high-enough rate. CBCR could lead source countries to operate with a "GFA agenda" or "GFA mindset," and to increase in aggressiveness if residence countries do not fully and immediately exercise their residual right to tax global profits. This is not too distant from the stance adopted by the European Commission in its controversial State Aid claims.[134]

This tension between the ALP and GFA, and constant menace of unilateral measures that stretch transfer pricing risk assessments beyond the arm's length standard, threatens the stability of the international tax system. It was present throughout the discussions of the BEPS Project, and it remains quite relevant, particularly within Europe in the midst of State Aid claims and CCCTB discussions, and in transactions involving China. Developing countries should be wary of this environment which is plagued by uncertainty and thus dampens FDI.

Other areas of risk that are more relevant for developing countries involve the abuse of tax treaties (which unduly reduce withholding taxes or prevents the characterization of permanent establishments), and the lack of transfer pricing rules or equivalent safe harbors (i.e., interest and royalty barriers). Not to mention tax evasion and fraud, beyond corporate income taxation, and in the areas of VAT and excise taxes. These and other[135] policy issues should be viewed as resource mobilization priorities for developing countries, over and above the luxury of a GFA versus ALP debate.

---

134. *See* Tavares, Bogenschneider & Pankiv (2016), *supra* n. 29.
135. *See* Durst, *supra* n. 10.

§10.07 CONCLUSION

In global tax policy, and in the tax transparency debate, *nothing comes from nothing*.[136] Tax transparency and CbC reports were not invented in 2003, although the meaning, object and purpose of different rules has changed in the decade preceding the BEPS Project. Something will come from the global rush towards CBCR. Whether that something is incremental revenue not otherwise attainable by treasuries around the globe, particularly in developing countries, is rather doubtful.

Home State governments typically know their MNEs. Many typically sponsor and support the tax competition that occurs outside of their borders, and will protect their Home tax base but not those of Host states. Intermediary countries that serve as investment or trade platforms for transit FDI, also engage in such tax competition and have a broad view of MNE operations, and of where foreign taxes are lawfully avoided around the world. Such Home States and intermediary hubs foster tax competition and fuel the so-called race to the bottom, which occurs not only through transfer mispricing and hybrid mismatches, but especially through the non-taxation of residual income earned within MNEs. Such state-sponsored MNE activities, therefore, are not caused by tax havens or by MNEs, but primarily by the clash between Home States. It is a battle of the G20.

International economic relations can be understood sociologically as a cooperative game, wherein bargaining also takes place. The dynamics of such cooperation and bargaining are framed by and also shape international law, which forbids certain modes of tax competition whilst enabling others, while shaping national laws that crystallize such tax competition. Tax competition, therefore, also materializes through tax avoidance that is known, deemed lawful and hence permitted. The engagement of civil society in this game can alter the shaping of domestic and international laws. Therefore, civil society can change the rules of the game, reframing it, and limiting the extent of the international bargaining that can be viewed as lawful. Tax activism has a significant role to play in this regard and within each country. This is a dynamics of legitimacy, through which the democratic rule of law functions and frames international taxation. The outcome of the G20/OECD BEPS Project will, therefore, be legitimized through its implementation.

Developing countries were not engaged in the dynamics that shaped the international tax standards and recommendations emerging from the BEPS Project. By fully adhering to the Inclusive Framework and implementing the entire package of minimum standards and recommendations, however, developing countries would legitimize the outcome of the Project. Avoiding the unilateral adoption of incoherent anti-BEPS rules and standards would indeed be recommendable – as such the

---

136. A concept known in Greek philosophy (Empedocles, circa 490-430 BC) long before its development in modern science. *See* G.S. Kirk and J.E. Raven, *The Presocratic Philosophers – A Critical History with a Selection of Texts*, Cambridge (1957), at 323: "*414. Fools -for they have no far-reaching thoughts who fancy that that which formerly was not can come into being or that anything can perish and be utterly destroyed. For coming into being from that which in no way is is inconceivable, and it is impossible and unheard-of that that which is should be destroyed. For it will ever be there wherever one may keep pushing it*".

implementation of consistent standards and recommendations that have emerged from the BEPS Project is, in principle, advisable.

However, given the dynamics of bargaining and cooperation in which developing countries were not included, some of the standards and recommendations arising from the final BEPS deliverables might not represent the best interests (or the highest priorities) of developing countries. Particularly where implementation of such standards would consume the scarce resources of developing countries that could be put to better use in the development or implementation of other tax policies, devoting resources to the full implementation of the BEPS Inclusive Framework package, might be less than ideal for many developing countries.

CBCR implementation is one of these standards. CBCR would be very useful if the ALP had been abandoned in favor of GFA, or if it had been deeply reformed – which has not occurred. The success of the Global Forum and prospects of greater government-to-government transparency and cooperation (materialized in the broad adoption of EOIR and AEOI through the MCAA-CRS), would make the risk assessment tools that can be developed through CBCRs rather redundant. On the other hand, information concerning the global operations of MNEs will be produced in Master Files, and are subject to EOIR along with other informational returns filed at Home States (e.g., concerning foreign entities operations and uncertain tax positions). As such, developing countries may develop more cost-efficient risk monitoring tools for transfer pricing without resorting to CBCR implementation.

Some tax activists and commentators that favor GFA still believe that CBCR might be relevant for developing countries. This chapter demonstrated that this is not likely the case. Furthermore, if China, India and Brazil have tried, one way or another, to defend GFA in the context of Project BEPS and failed, and if no consensus on GFA (through CCCTB) could be reached even within the EU, it is highly unrealistic to expect that CBCR – whether or not public – would be decisive to enable GFA adoption in the foreseeable future. Therefore, any investments in CBCR made by any country should be justified by the transfer mispricing assessments under the ALP that could be successfully defended and that can be attributed to CBCR risk assessment tools. Such assessments are likely immaterial, as discussed here, but the CBCR investment may still pay off in developed countries and larger economies – even if only as a public relations, and trust-building propaganda. Not in developing countries.

The sovereign decision concerning BEPS implementation that will be made by countries around the globe must look through the platitudes of public relations statements concerning the alleged success of the BEPS Project, and through the vested interests of those that determined the outcome of the BEPS Project (i.e., the G8, the G20, the EU, and the OECD). Developing countries should not be rallied to fight against the ALP or the OECD, hasted to adopt harsher and unilateral anti-BEPS measures, or pressured to join the Inclusive Framework and blindly fund the adoption of all standards and recommendations that emerge from the BEPS Project. These sovereign nations should set their own priorities. And they should be wary of the capricious libels that are put forth by commentators and tax activist from the U.S. and the U.K., who purport to defend the interests of developing countries by defending GFA (and CBCR implementation as a step towards it), without knowing what developing countries would stand to gain from such reform in terms of revenues, or from CBCR implementation as it stands, under the ALP.

The realities of developing countries cannot be compared with those of Great Britain, Brussels, Paris or Washington D.C. Other resource mobilization priorities must be considered. Implementation and enforcement of transfer pricing as per the OECD Guidelines (where many developing countries still lack any such rules), the development of bilateral tax treaty networks that are duly protected by the highest anti-abuse clauses emerging from BEPS Action 6, the development of a proper withholding tax policy which enables the development of a robust treaty network, and the use of safe harbors (such as interest or royalty barriers) that are coherent with transfer pricing, as well as reforms and enforcement of VAT and excise taxes, should all be higher priorities. In light of these priorities, CBCR and the GFA debate would either be redundant and/or superfluous.

Developed countries, on the other hand, should focus on enhancements to the ALP beyond what has been achieved through the BEPS Project – broadening ALP reforms would be a realistic and sustainable policy stance to be adopted by the G8 and the OECD. The ALP versus GFA debate survives in academic circles and is passionately fielded by tax activists (and by some of the G20), and thus should be fully acknowledged by the U.S., by the EU and by the OECD, and not deflected. If CBCR is a reality in a high-enough number of countries, the OECD should produce a study which aggregates CBCR information and simulates the base shifting effect that could result from GFA adoption. This exercise should demonstrate that the G20 would not agree on a single GFA formula that would significantly reshuffle their taxing jurisdictions, and that GFA would not likely yield greater revenues to poorer, developing countries. In light of this G20 impasse over a GFA formula – which could be felt in the beginning of Project BEPS and breathed in CCCTB discussions in Brussels, but which was not sufficiently transparent to the general public – the OECD could commit to deeper ALP reforms. Such reforms should be broader than those accomplished through Project BEPS, and would therefore discourage incoherent or unilateral GFA measures, such as what underlies EU State Aid claims or the Chinese Sixth Method. Additionally, if the U.S. and the G8 should strengthen CFC rules and empower the OECD to develop a minimum CFC standards – this would increase both Home and Host State taxing rights, leading to an international allocation of taxing rights that would be far more equitable.

CHAPTER 11

How Are We Doing with BEPS Recommendations in the EU?

Tomas Balco & Xeniya Yeroshenko

§11.01 INTRODUCTION

Most of the twenty-eight EU member countries are also members of the Organisation for Economic Co-operation and Development (OECD).[1] As such, we could therefore say that most of the member countries of the European Union (EU) are also leading participants of the OECD Base Erosion and Profit Shifting (BEPS) project. This is perhaps also the reason, why the EU is making significant progress on regional implementation of BEPS project recommendations compared to other regions around the world. This progress, which is further analysed in this chapter can be compared and contrasted with little or no coordinated regional progress on BEPS-related issues in the regional economic unions – such as Eurasian Economic Union,[2] East-African Community[3] and CARICOM.[4]

For some of the EU Member States the BEPS practices posed a drain on the public budgets in form of lower tax collections due to diverted profits and eroded tax base.[5] It

---

1. Out of thirty-five OECD Member States, twenty-two are EU Member States. Only six EU Member States are not represented in the OECD: Bulgaria, Croatia, Cyprus, Lithuania, Malta, Romania. List of OECD Member States available at: http://www.oecd.org/about/membersandpartners/list-oecd-member-countries.htm.
2. Member countries: Armenia, Belarus, Kazakhstan. Kyrgyzstan and Russia.
3. Member countries are Burundi, Kenya, Rwanda, Tanzania and Uganda.
4. Stands for Caribbean Community and comprises fifteen countries: Antigua and Barbuda, Bahamas, Barbados, Belize, Dominica, Grenada, Guyana, Haiti, Jamaica, Montserrat, Saint Lucia, St Kitts and Nevis, St Vincent and the Grenadines, Suriname, Trinidad and Tobago.
5. The European Parliamentary Research Service estimates that around EUR 50–EUR 70 billion a year are lost by the EU due to corporate tax avoidance through profit shifting. The Parliamentary Research Services also notes that is to assume no base from sources other than profit shifting, the estimation of revenue losses for the EU due to corporate tax avoidance would amount to around

might have been also a reason for part of the budget deficits and cause of significant financial pressure on some of the governments, which could have been coupled with excessive public spending.[6] Therefore, for some EU Member States – actions aimed at stopping and preventing BEPS practices has been a matter of national tax policy priority.

On the other hand, we must be equally fair in acknowledging that BEPS practices and facilitation of such practices by intermediaries and service providers has been an important part of certain Member States service industry. The location of certain types of companies and the servicing of these companies has lead to direct and indirect employment in these EU Member States, especially in the white-collar sector. For these Member States, the legitimate concern was the impact of the OECD BEPS project and its possible implementation within EU on the employment generated from such practices.[7]

It can be now clearly understood, that implementation of OECD BEPS project within EU is not a smooth and tensionless process. Quite to the contrary, the BEPS implementation within EU is accompanied with significant policy discussion as well as comments and reactions of stakeholders, which include both the business representatives and NGO's. The Member States interest may not be fully aligned – in fact, they can be conflicting, which can bring further tension to the EU BEPS implementation efforts.

In this regard, the role of the EU Commission[8] must be highlighted as it certainly played an instrumental role in the process both as an institution present at the OECD BEPS project deliberations, but also as the sole institution with the legislative initiative within EU.[9] The Commission also correctly acknowledged that it is essentially important for the EU to follow the OECD recommendations in a coordinated way to assure that Single Market economy is not hampered by the uncoordinated and diverse

---

EUR 160–EUR 190 billion. This would encompass special tax arrangements, inefficiencies in collection and other practices. Retrieved from http://www.europarl.europa.eu/RegData/etudes/STUD/2015/558773/EPRS_STU(2015)558773_EN.pdf p. 7.

6. Budget deficit in excess of 3% tolerable limit established by the EU law is experienced currently by several Member States: Croatia, Portugal, France, Greece, Spain and UK. For more details *see* http://ec.europa.eu/economy_finance/economic_governance/sgp/corrective_arm/index_en.htm In 2015, seven Member States had deficits equal to or higher than 3% of GDP: Greece (-7.2%), Spain (-5.1%), Portugal and the United Kingdom (-4.4% each), France (-3.5%), Croatia (-3.2%) and Slovakia (-3.0%). Retrieved from http://ec.europa.eu/eurostat/documents/2995521/7235991/2-21042016-AP-EN.pdf.
7. *See* study on analysing effects of Dutch corporate tax policy on developing countries, available at: https://www.government.nl/documents/reports/2013/11/14/iob-study-evaluation-issues-in-financing-for-development-analysing-effects-of-dutch-corporate-tax-policy-on-developing-countries For report on Irish spillover effects on developing countries *see* http://budget.gov.ie/Budgets/2016/Documents/IBFD_Irish_Spillover_Analysis_Report_pub.pdf.
8. The EU Commission is one of the EU institutions acting as an executive body of the Union and promotes its general interests. It proposes new legislation to the European Parliament and the Council of the European Union, and it ensures that EU law is correctly applied by member countries. To read more about the Commission refer to http://ec.europa.eu/atwork/index_en.htm. For more information about the Commission's work in tax sphere refer to http://ec.europa.eu/taxation_customs/common/about/welcome/index_en.htm.
9. *See* about the work of Commission in brief at: http://ec.europa.eu/atwork/index_en.htm.

interpretation of the newly proposed standards.[10] The different approaches that could be adopted by different Member States in the process of implementation of BEPS recommendations on unilateral basis could indeed lead to double taxation or also to new opportunities for double non-taxation.

The drive for swift and effective implementation of BEPS project is being balanced by repeated calls by some Member States as well as business associations, which caution about the implications from BEPS implementation on the attractiveness of the EU or certain Member States for business.[11] The BEPS recommendations are gradually being implemented by means of both hard-law measures (mainly through the Directives of EU Council) and soft-law measures (mainly through Council Conclusions).

One of the challenges of the EU is that while the Commission is a relatively stable and persistent element in respect of the tax policy debate, the Presidency of the EU Council is rotating on a six- month basis.[12] In other words, every six months, there is a different EU Member State with different priorities behind the EU Tax policy steering wheel. The Commission is an important stakeholder in the EU Tax Policy process, because as mentioned, it is the only institution with the right of legislative initiative in the EU Tax matters.[13] On the other hand, the Council is the only institution, which can adopt the EU Tax legislation, because taxation remained as a part of the EU Member States national sovereignty within the sole domain of the Council, which adopts the tax legislation in unanimity approval process, compared to other types of legislation, which is being adopted in co-decision with the EU Parliament and where qualified majority may be sufficient. Any EU tax legislation proposal can be blocked by any single EU Member State. This is the additional reason, why implementation of BEPS within EU is a very sensitive and a very tensed diplomatic process.

To keep the focus and continuity, at the level of the Council, the work on the BEPS implementation within EU is brought forward on the basis of concrete road maps, which are developed and approved semi-annually by the Member States in charge of

---

10. *See* The Commission's staff working document, p. 5, available at: http://ec.europa.eu/taxation_customs/resources/documents/taxation/company_tax/anti_tax_avoidance/swd_2016_6_en.pdf.
11. *See* for instance note by the Invest Europe at http://www.investeurope.eu/policy/key-topics/taxation-issues/tax-fairness/ Impact on the Dutch tax system and its potential risks on cross-border transactions available at http://subscriber.e-mark.nl/online.php?db = 812V189&mailing = 13V482692652&user = 2833V1486729606 BusinessEurope makes concern that EU ATAD goes beyond the OECD agreement and by raising effective corporate tax rates and deviating from international agreements will put the EU at a competitive disadvantage in attracting global investment. *See* https://www.businesseurope.eu/sites/buseur/files/media/position_papers/ecofin/2016-03-07_anti_tax_avoidance_package.pdf AmCham of the European Union is in particular concerned that public CbC may potentially negative impact on EU competitiveness and attractiveness as an investment destination, *see* http://www.amchameu.eu/media-centre/press-releases/european-commission-proposal-country-country-reporting.
12. The presidency of the Council rotates among the EU Member States every six months. During this six-month period, the presidency chairs meetings at every level in the Council, helping to ensure the continuity of the EU's work in the Council. For more *see* http://www.consilium.europa.eu/en/council-eu/presidency-council-eu/.
13. Other institutions may, however, propose Commission the ideas for legislative proposals, and if the Commission refuses it should justify it.

the EU presidency. It started with an Italian presidency in 2014, which has started with the idea of the development of an EU/BEPS work programme (EU/BEPS Roadmap) with the initial focus on international and BEPS-related aspects of the Common Consolidated Corporate Tax Base (CCCTB) proposal. The follow-up road maps on implementation of the BEPS project recommendations were prepared and implemented by:

- Italian presidency at the end of 2014.[14]
- Latvian presidency in early 2015.[15]
- Luxembourg presidency in the beginning of July 2015.[16]
- Dutch presidency in February 2016 and.[17]
- Slovakian presidency in the middle of July 2016.[18]

Each such road map sets out the number of actions for the short and medium-term periods, as well as clearly indicates the preliminary delivery timing. The current presidency is led by the Slovak Republic. Its roadmap, for instance, provides for the follow-up work on, among others, amendments of the interest-royalty Directive (IRD), transparency initiatives and hybrid mismatches as to the short-term priorities. Among the medium-term priorities Slovak presidency identified the work on patent boxes, proposal for Improvement of Dispute Resolution Mechanism within the EU, as well as the proposal for a renewed Common (Consolidated) Corporate Tax Base (CCCTB) and other points, that will be further discussed in more details in this chapter.

As noted already, the EU Commission has been playing a crucial role in *'pursuing an ambitious campaign for a coordinated EU approach against tax avoidance, following the global standards developed by the OECD'*.[19]

These initiatives of the EU Commission date back to OECD pre-BEPS times. Already in 2012 the EU Commission set the fight against corporate tax avoidance as its main priority.[20] In its Action Plan of 2012 it set out concrete steps to enhance administrative cooperation and to support the development of the existing good governance policy, the wider issues of interaction with tax havens and of tackling aggressive tax planning (ATP) and other aspects, including tax-related crimes. Later in June 2015, t*he Commission issued updated Action Plan to fight corporate tax avoidance*

---

14. The Italian Presidency presented only the draft roadmap in the Working Party on Tax Questions (WPTQ) on 5 December 2014 setting out a number of priorities for actions in the short, mid and long term. The Latvian Presidency undertook to continue work on the basis of this draft roadmap, and circulated a final version of its Presidency roadmap. Retrieved from http://data.consilium.europa.eu/doc/document/ST-6039-2016-INIT/en/pdf p. 2.
15. *See* Doc. 5968/15 FISC 15.
16. *See* Doc. 10649/15 FISC 93.
17. *See* Doc. 6039/16 FISC 20.
18. *See* Doc. 11071/16 FISC 121.
19. Retrieved from http://europa.eu/rapid/press-release_MEMO-16-2265_en.htm.
20. *See* Communication from the Commission to the European parliament and the council, 'An Action Plan to strengthen the fight against tax fraud and tax evasion', available at: http://ec.europa.eu/taxation_customs/resources/documents/taxation/tax_fraud_evasion/com_2012_722_en.pdf.

and ensure fair and efficient taxation.[21] The Anti-Tax Avoidance Package[22] is the latest step in delivering on this agenda. Presented in January 2016, it contains a series of initiatives for a stronger and more coordinated EU stance against corporate tax abuse – within the Single Market and beyond. It rests on three key pillars:

- Effective taxation whereby all companies pay taxes where they make their profits.
- Tax transparency so that Member States have the information needed to ensure fair taxation.
- Addressing the risk of double taxation so that companies which pay their fair share of taxes are not penalised for making use of the EU's internal market.

The Package contains a number of legislative and non-legislative initiatives to help Member States protect their tax bases, create a fair and stable environment for businesses and preserve EU competitiveness vis-à-vis third countries. The Package also contains a Chapeau Communication and Staff Working Document, which explain the political and economic rationale behind the individual measures. The table 11.1 below illustrates the measures proposed under this package, while further details and relation of measures to the BEPS project outcomes are discussed further in this chapter.

Table 11.1

Chapeau Communication outlining the key policy messages of the Commission.			
Anti Tax Avoidance Directive	Recommendation on Tax Treaties	Revised Administrative Cooperation Directive	Communication on External Strategy
Legally binding anti-avoidance measures	Advice on how to revise tax treaties against abuse	Country-by-Country reporting between tax authorities	Measures to promote tax good governance internationally
Staff Working Document elaborating on some of the technical aspects of proposals.			

Further in this chapter, the authors will elaborate on BEPS recommendations and analyse the respective EU actions taken both at the level of the Council and Commission in more details.

---

21. *See* COM(2015) 302 final, Communication from the Commission to the European parliament and the Council, 'A Fair and Efficient Corporate Tax System in the European Union: 5 Key Areas for Action', available at: https://ec.europa.eu/priorities/sites/beta-political/files/com_2015_302_en.pdf.
22. http://ec.europa.eu/taxation_customs/taxation/company_tax/anti_tax_avoidance/index_en.htm.

§11.02 OVERVIEW OF THE BEPS ACTION PLANS AS ADDRESSED BY THE EU

[A] Action 1 Addressing the Tax Challenges of the Digital Economy

The tax aspects Digital economy presents both opportunities for certain jurisdictions in the EU, but also challenges for the other jurisdictions. Something similar was acknowledged at the OECD, where no consensus was reached on the solutions in the direct tax area, rather several policy options were identified, while in the indirect tax a common direction was identified, which was also implemented in the EU and further work is under way.

[1] Direct Taxes: Lack of Action

No particular direct tax measures were yet taken at the EU level to address the challenges of the digital economy. The Council was not presented any specific proposals by the European Commission, which does not seem to support the idea of introducing special types of taxes on the digital economy considering such measure as a temporary and impractical decision, which will undermine the tax neutrality principle.[23] The European Commission has decided not to invoke at this stage any special action at the EU level, but to monitor the situation to see if the general anti-avoidance measures may be enough to address digital risks.[24]

In a meanwhile, it is believed that the BEPS problem caused by the digitalisation of the economy is being gradually addressed through implementation of OECD recommendations, particularly on actions 5, 6, 7, 8–10 that will be discussed later in this chapter. Additionally, the Commission has launched the state aid investigations on tax rulings issued to digital tech giant companies by the governments of the Netherlands, Luxembourg, Ireland and Belgium.[25] The tax rulings allowing tax planning and facilitating tax avoidance are potentially considered as illegal state aid, which is prohibited under Article 107 of the TFEU, since it may *'lead to a competitive disadvantage for companies, which lack the opportunity to engage in sophisticated planning schemes because of their size, their geographic focus or their business model'*.[26] Should the national measures found to be illegal and incompatible with the single market, they will have to abolished by the Member States and compensated by the companies. This

---

23. *See* report of the EU Parliament on Tax challenges in the Digital economy, Doc IP/A/TAXE2/2016-04 available at: http://www.europarl.europa.eu/RegData/etudes/STUD/2016/579002/IPOL_STU(2016)579002_EN.pdf.
24. *See* European Commission (2016) Fact Sheet The Anti-Avoidance Package-Questions and Answers, available at: http://europa.eu/rapid/press-release_MEMO-16-160_en.htm.
25. For the list of investigation processes refer to report of the EU Parliament on Tax challenges in the Digital economy, at p. 21.
26. *See* report of the EU Parliament on Tax challenges in the Digital economy p. 19.

has already been decided in some of the cases – i.e., Apple,[27] Fiat,[28] Starbucks,[29] case on Belgian 'Excess Profit' tax scheme[30] and several more investigation cases by the Commission are still pending – i.e., Amazon,[31] McDonalds.[32] However, these state aid investigations by the Commission do not address future policy issues, but rather past administrative practices of certain Member States. The decisions may be a sort of precedent for future argumentation of the Commission and also a message to the Member States that special tax rulings may violate the EU State Aid rules. These proceedings will however not lead to creation of special rules addressing digital economy companies, since each decision targets only specific situations and it will take long time to adjudicate these cases by the European Court of Justice as most countries seem to be appealing the decisions of the Commission.[33]

Back in 2014,[34] the Commission's High Level Expert Group on Taxation of digital economy prepared a special report on taxation of digital economy, where it expressed an independent view on how the EU should pose itself and its coordinated tax system to manage the tax challenges of digital economy and also to take the respective economic benefits the digitalisation may bring.

Thus, the Group believes that the EU should support the functioning of digital (innovative) companies, including the small and medium enterprises (SMEs), who are considered as drivers of digital economy. In view of the Group it is advisable to simplify the tax measures and in general to reduce the complexity of tax compliance across the

---

27. *See* press release on Commission decision, where it concluded that Ireland had granted illegal state aid to Apple worth up to EUR 13 billion (30 August 2016), available at: http://europa.eu/rapid/press-release_IP-16-2923_en.htm *See also* for updates Alleged state aid to Apple, case SA.38373 at http://ec.europa.eu/competition/elojade/isef/case_details.cfm?proc_code=3_SA_38373.
28. Commission concluded that Luxembourg had granted illegal state aid to Fiat, *see* official decision SA.38375 (21 October 2015) at: http://ec.europa.eu/competition/elojade/isef/case_details.cfm?proc_code=3_SA_38375.
29. Commission concluded that the Netherlands had granted illegal state aid to Starbucks, *see* official decision SA.38374 (21 October, 2015) at http://ec.europa.eu/competition/elojade/isef/case_details.cfm?proc_code=3_SA_38374.
30. The European Commission has concluded that selective tax advantages granted by Belgium under its 'excess profit' tax scheme are illegal under EU state aid rules. The scheme has benefitted at least thirty-five multinationals mainly from the EU, who must now return unpaid taxes to Belgium in total at around EUR 700 million. *See* Excess Profit exemption in Belgium, Commission Decision SA.37667 (11 January 2016), 2016 O.J.C. L/260/2016 available at: http://ec.europa.eu/competition/elojade/isef/case_details.cfm?proc_code=3_SA_37667.
31. *See* Alleged aid to Amazon, Commission Decision COMP/SA.38944, 2015 O.J. C 44/15, available at: http://ec.europa.eu/competition/elojade/isef/index.cfm?fuseaction=dsp_result.
32. *See* Alleged aid to Mc Donald's – Luxembourg, SA.38945, current status at http://ec.europa.eu/competition/elojade/isef/case_details.cfm?proc_code=3_SA_38945.
33. *See* for instance *Netherlands v. Commission*, Case T-760/15, 2016 O.J. C 59/50 (action brought on 23 December 2015 by the Netherlands seeking to annul Starbucks Decision), *see also Luxembourg v. Commission*, Case T-755/15, 2016 O.J. C 59/48 (action brought on 30 December 2015 by Luxembourg seeking to annul Fiat Decision); *Fiat Chrysler Finance Europe v. Commission*, Case T-759/15, 2016 O.J. C 59/49 (action brought on 29 December 2015 by Fiat Chrysler Finance seeking to annul Fiat Decision). *See also* overview on *The European Commission's recent state aid investigations of transfer pricing rulings* prepared by the U.S. Department of the Treasury dated 24 August 2016, available at: https://www.treasury.gov/resource-center/tax-policy/treaties/Documents/White-Paper-State-Aid.pdf.
34. Report of the Commission Expert Group on Taxation of the Digital Economy, dated 28 May 2016.

EU. This, in view of the Group should facilitate the growth and profitability of the SMEs. The group has considered an option to introduce special R&D incentives, special exemption from capital gains and employees stock option to promote the investments into digital companies, however, although it finds such measures as able to increase the attractiveness of the tax climate in Europe, especially for the digital start-ups with future potential, it has not make any specific recommendations, concluding that such measures will bring the EU tax regimes away from the tax neutrality and fairness principles.

In a long run, the Group supports the measures proposed by the OECD BEPS project, however, it believes that more fundamental and systematic review of fundamental international tax law principles is required in order to address the existing challenges. For instance, the Group invites the EU Member States to assess the appropriateness of the new transfer pricing profit-split methods for the EU, taken that the CCCTB proposal follows formulary apportionment method, and the new OECD proposed rules may be costly. The Group calls EU Member States to examine the extent to which *'new international standards and in particular a possible movement towards transfer pricing profit split methods would justify additional simplification within the EU, particularly if the new rules generate significant costs'*. The Group proposes that this could be done on the level of Council in the context of work on CCCTB and also *'on the appropriate allocation of the common base where businesses operate in more than one Member State e.g. via consolidation and formula apportionment.'*[35]

[2] Indirect Taxes: Single Registration Point Implemented and VAT Package Expected

What concerns indirect taxation, since 1 January 2015 the new place of supply rule for Value added Tax (VAT) purposes applies in the EU with respect to the telecommunications, broadcasting and electronic services. It became compulsory for the VAT payers to charge VAT on these services upon their supply to individuals and non-taxable business customers within the EU[36] in accordance with the rules and amounts due in the country where the customer belongs to irrespective whether the provider of services is business registered within or outside the EU.

This change is the modification of the rules on the place of supply of services in the EU VAT system that were adopted in 2008 as part of the 'VAT Package' and became effective on 1 January 2010.[37]

To comply with the new rule, the EU and non-EU businesses will first need to distinguish whether the customer is a taxable or a non-taxable person, and second, the

---

35. For more on this consult the Report of the Commission Expert Group on Taxation of the Digital Economy, at p. 49 and further. *See also* M. Petutschnig *'Sharing the Benefits of the EU's Common Consolidated Corporate Tax Base within Corporate Groups'*, World Tax Journal, 2015, Vol. 7, No. 2.
36. *See* Council Implementing Regulation (EU) No. 1042/2013 of 7 October 2013.
37. *See* Council Directive 2008/8/EC of 12 February 2008 amending Directive 2006/112/EC as regards the place of supply of services (OJ L 44, 20.2.2008, p. 11).

country where the customer belongs to.[38] Up to 1 January 2015, the place of supply upon provision of these services in B2C transactions was the country of the supplier. In fact, it meant that suppliers established in the countries with lower VAT rates had a competitive advantage over businesses established in other Member States due to the different rates the suppliers could charge on the same or similar products.[39] This has led to tax planning for VAT purposes and competitive positioning of certain jurisdictions as hubs for e-commerce services. Now the new place of supply rule should assure a better level playing field and also ensure that the VAT receipts accrue to the Member State of consumption and not to the state of service provider.[40]

To assure that the above principle works in practice the Mini One Stop Shop (MOSS) mechanism was introduced. It allows taxpayers supplying telecommunication services, broadcasting and other electronically supplied services[41] to non-taxable persons in the EU Member States in which they do not have an establishment to account for VAT due on those supplies via a web-portal in the Member State in which they are identified. This scheme is not compulsory, however, it significantly simplifies the fulfilment of VAT obligations with the new rule of supply, by allowing the service suppliers to avoid registering in each Member State of consumption, but instead register only in the one of the EU states. The MOSS mirrors the scheme applicable for supplies of electronically supplied services to non-taxable persons by suppliers not established in the EU up to 2015.

In practice, under the scheme, a VAT payer registers for MOSS in only one Member States, where it electronically submits MOSS VAT returns detailing supplies of telecommunications, broadcasting and electronically supplied services to non-taxable persons in other Member States (Member States of consumption) and transfers the collected VAT due. These returns, along with the VAT paid, are then transmitted by the Member State of Identification[42] to the corresponding Member States of consumption.[43]

Table 11.2 below illustrates the new place of supply rule for electronic, telecommunication and broadcasting services.[44]

---

38. *See* the European Commission Explanatory notes on the EU VAT changes to the place of supply of telecommunications, broadcasting and electronic services that enter into force in 2015 (Explanatory notes on the EU VAT changes), dated 3 April 2014, p. 10.
39. *Ibid*. Explanatory notes on the EU VAT changes, p. 10.
40. *Ibid*. Explanatory notes on the EU VAT changes, p. 10.
41. Note, that electronic services for which the new place of supply rule is introduced does not include all supplies of goods or services carried out over electronic systems such as the Internet. As such, for example, the following activities are not covered by these changes: (1) the supply of goods (including distance selling) where use is made of electronic systems only to place the order; and (2) the supply of services other than telecommunications, broadcasting and electronic services. *See* Explanatory notes on the EU VAT changes, p. 11.
42. This is the term used to refer to the Member State, where the taxable person is registered for the mini One Stop Shop. *See* European Commission Guide to the VAT mini One Stop Shop dated 23 October 2013.
43. For more details concerning registration, deregistration, VAT returns, payments and other issues *see* the European Commission Guide to the VAT mini One Stop Shop.
44. Table is prepared by authors on the basis of information available at: http://ec.europa.eu/taxation_customs/taxation/vat/how_vat_works/telecom/index_en.htm.

Table 11.2

Supplier / Consumer	EU Businesses Supplying To:	Non-EU Businesses Supplying To:
VAT payers in another EU country	No VAT charged. Reverse-charge mechanism should apply.	No VAT charged. Reverse-charge mechanism should apply.
Consumer (individual or non-taxable business) in another EU country	Must charge VAT in the EU country where the customer belongs[45]	Must charge VAT in the EU country where the customer belongs
Business or consumer outside the EU	No EU VAT charged.	Not covered

[B] Actions 2, 3 and 4: Focus on Domestic Law Provisions and Adoption of ATAD

Actions 2, 3 and 4 are aimed at strengthening the domestic law provisions. As such recommendations enshrined in these actions were an ideal candidate on harmonised legislative action within EU. This has happened as a part of January 2016 'anti-tax-avoidance package', which contained several items, one of which was the Anti-Tax Avoidance Directive also referred to as 'ATAD'.

Being proposed as a draft Directive by the Commission on 28 January 2016, it was approved in record time, when the political consensus on general approach took place in June and on 12 July 2016 the Council formally adopted this ATAD.[46] Even though the ATAD Directive lays down the rules against tax avoidance practices that directly affect the functioning of the internal market (GAAR provision and Exit Tax Rule), it simultaneously should address implementation of several action recommendations in the context of the initiative against BEPS namely the above-mentioned three BEPS actions:

- Action 2 Neutralise the effect of hybrid mismatch arrangement.
- Action 3 Strengthen the CFC rules.
- Action 4 Address BEPS through limitation of interest deduction and other financial payments.

Below we elaborate on each of the action.[47]

---

45. The term 'belongs' in the Explanatory note refers to 'the place (country) where the customer is established, has his permanent address or usually resides', see p. 12.
46. See Directive 2016/1164 dated 12 July 2016 laying down rules against tax avoidance practices that directly affect the functioning of the internal market, available at: http://eur-lex.europa.eu/legal-content/EN/ALL/?uri=CELEX:32016L1164.
47. For preliminary analysis of the draft Directive and EU law, see A. Navarro, L. Parada & P. Schwarz, 'The Proposal for an EU Anti-avoidance Directive: Some Preliminary Thoughts', EC Tax Law Review, 2016, Vol. 3.

[1] Action 2: 'Somewhat' Neutralising the Effect of Hybrid Mismatch Arrangement Within the EU

With respect to hybrid mismatches, the Directive provides for a principal-based guidance, so we see here the hundreds pages of BEPS Action 2 being condensed into two sentences. Article 9 of the Directive prescribes that should the hybrid mismatch result in a double deduction, the deduction shall be given only in the Member State where such payment has its source. Second, the article provides that should the hybrid mismatch result in a deduction without inclusion, the Member State of the payer shall deny the deduction of such payment. Thus, it will be up to the Member States to decide how to best implement these principles in the national tax provision or instrument to achieve the aim of the Directive.[48]

Several Member States may have been uneasy that such principles may render their tax system, which were carefully designed to facilitate international double non-taxation ineffective. Therefore, recital 13 of the preamble to the Directive emphasises that the above rule to tackle hybrid mismatch situations shall apply only in the cases when the mismatch occurs due to differences in the legal characterisation of a financial instrument or entity by the states and shall not affect the general features of the tax system of a Member State. Those Member States, which do not effectively address this issue at the implementation stage, may remain exposed to intra-EU tax BEPS based on these mismatches which arise from features, which were carefully crafted as general features of the tax systems of some Member States.

As also explained in the Directive, the ambition was not to fix the problem of hybrid mismatches in its entirety, but to make it look like this has been done and making at least the first step in this direction. Some of the Member States were concerned that by fully addressing the hybrid mismatches rule, their jurisdictions will stop being attractive in the arena of international tax avoidance. This is evidenced by the fact that the scope of the rules is currently limited only to intra-EU situations. The third countries having transactions with the EU therefore remain fully exposed to the hybrid mismatches jurisdictions, so the BEPS problem remains in the EU-third country situations as well as on some of the intra-EU situations.

It is also surprising that despite the fact that the Member States have spent several years debating the hybrid mismatches and have also agreed guidance, within the framework of the Group of the Code of Conduct on Business Taxation on the tax treatment of hybrid entities and hybrid permanent establishments within the Union as well as on the tax treatment of hybrid entities in relations with third countries[49] the Directive did not address most of these other principles already agreed at Group of Code of Conduct. Instead, they were omitted. Directive outlines in recital 13 of the

---

48. On compatibility of the linking rules with the EU law, see analysis by Alexander Rust, 'BEPS Action 2: 2014 Deliverable–Neutralising the Effects of Hybrid Mismatch Arrangements and its Compatibility with the Non-discrimination Provisions in the Tax Treaties and the Treaty on the Functioning of the European Union', British Tax Review, 2015.
49. For the Guidance, see the Report of the Code of Conduct Group Doc. 14302/15 dated 23 November 2015, FISC. 159 ECOFIN 883, available at: http://data.consilium.europa.eu/doc/document/ST-14302-2015-INIT/en/pdf.

preamble that it is 'critical that further work is undertaken on hybrid mismatches between member states and third countries, as well as on other hybrid mismatches such as those involving permanent establishments'.[50]

[2] Action 3: Did Somebody Say There Was a Need for Designing 'Effective CFC Rules'?

The objective of BEPS Action 3 was to provide policy recommendations introducing or making the existing CFC rules effective. This recommendation has been now implemented in Articles 7 and 8 of ATAD, which contain the rules and principles for the minimum standard of the CFC rules to be incorporated in the Member States' national tax systems. Below we will briefly discuss the main elements of the rules. Finding the common agreement on CFC rules was another challenge, requiring significant compromises and even softening the original rule as suggested in the original draft Directive by the Commission.

Definition of control – the foreign entity will be considered as controlled if it itself, or the taxpayer itself, or together with associated companies holds a direct or indirect participation of more than 50% of the voting rights, or owns directly or indirectly more than 50% of capital or is entitled to receive more than 50% of the profits of the foreign entity. Since the Directive establishes a minimum standard, the Member States can go stricter by reducing the control threshold.[51]

Definition of foreign-controlled entity – the definition of CFC will include foreign entity or the permanent establishment the profits of which are otherwise exempted, if the corporate tax paid by such entity or permanent establishment is lower than the difference between the corporate tax that would have been charged on the entity or permanent establishment under the applicable corporate tax system in the Member State of the taxpayer and the actual corporate tax paid on its profits by the entity or permanent establishment in the foreign jurisdiction. This very strange provision is supposed to establish the tax rate trigger of the foreign jurisdiction. However, the tax rate being a very sensitive subject in the EU, it is not mentioned in the wording and instead it is carefully crafted as a result of this verbal formula. Effectively the outcome of this formula means that if the tax rate paid by the foreign entity or permanent establishment is less than 50% of the domestic rate, the tax rate trigger of CFC rules is activated. The Directive makes it clear that the Member State may establish a stronger tax rate threshold.[52] In addition, the Directive also mentions the option that the Member States may use administrative practice using different types of lists of jurisdictions (white, grey or black list).[53] The effect of CFC rules is weakened by the escape clause, where the foreign entity may be excluded from the scope of CFC rule, if two-thirds or more of its income is derived from active type of business, but not in a form of passive investment income or income from sales, where the foreign entity

---

50. *Ibid.* para. 13.
51. Paragraph 12 of the Recitals to the ATAD.
52. Paragraph 12 of the Recitals to the ATAD.
53. Paragraph 12 of the Recitals to the ATAD.

added little or no economic value. The safe harbour provides opportunity to Member States for the option to exclude such entities from the scope of the rule.

Inclusion of income into tax base – the CFC rules in ATAD have the effect that the non-distributed income shall be included into the taxable base. The Member States may choose to include the entire income of the low-taxed subsidiary or only specific categories of income (tainted income) or to limit the rules to income which has been artificially diverted to the subsidiary. The Directive provides for a specific list of tainted income, which is mainly passive income, such as: interest generated from financial assets, royalties and other income from intellectual property, dividends and income from disposal of shares, income from financial leasing, but also insurance, banking and other financial activities. Additionally, the list of tainted income that is to be included into taxable base shall include income from sales and services, where the foreign entity acts as intermediary between associated companies – purchases goods and services from and sells such goods and services to associated persons and adds little or no economic value. At this point, there is another safe harbour where the Member States may not include into taxable base the income of foreign entities, which carry on a substantive economic activity supported by staff, equipment, assets and premises, as evidenced by relevant facts and circumstances. Finally, the list of tainted income, which is to be included into the tax base, includes the income arising from non-genuine arrangements, which have been put in place for the essential purpose of obtaining a tax advantage. ATAD provides here that an arrangement or a series thereof are regarded as non-genuine to the extent that the foreign entity would not own the assets or would not have undertaken the risks which generate all, or part of, its income if it were not controlled by a company of a Member State where the significant people functions, which are relevant to those assets and risks, are carried out and are instrumental in generating the controlled company's income.

Since the rule should apply to both intra-EU and to EU third-country situations, for the rule to comply with the EU fundamental freedoms, the national law implementing the CFC rules should allow for a substance carve-out aimed to limit, within the Union, the impact of the rules to cases where the CFC does not carry on a substantive economic activity.[54] *Computation of taxable income* – the determination of taxable income shall be carried out in accordance with the national rules of the Member State. Herewith, the Directive establishes that losses of the foreign entity or permanent establishment shall not be included in the taxable base but may be carried forward, according to national law, and taken into account in subsequent tax periods.

In case of non-genuine arrangements as defined above, the Directive provides for arm's length approach as a guidance to be used to determine the income attributable from such types of arrangements.

Elimination of double taxation – Directive provides for the option to exempt from taxation the distributed income of foreign entity, which was previously taxed under the CFC rule. Similarly, the elimination of double taxation is provided upon sale of foreign entity, its part or elimination of permanent establishment, should any of these proceeds

---

54. Paragraph 12 of the Recitals to the ATAD.

have been taxed earlier. The tax credit is also possible under the Directive with respect to income taxes paid by the foreign entity or permanent establishment.

[3] Action 4: Limitation of Interest Deductibility or Shall We Call it Interest Deferral Rule?

In implementing the recommendations of Action 4, the Commission did not depart much from the BEPS Action 4 recommendations. The rule as envisaged by the OECD introduces the Earnings Before Interest, Taxes, Depreciation and Amortization (EBITDA)limit on deductibility of interest on any debt – irrespective of whether this debt originates from related or independent party. The harshness of the rule is then being mitigated by a high safe-harbour threshold as well as other escape clauses – such as group ratio rule and the carry forward rules, which may allow the carry forward of both – disallowed interest deduction and also the unutilised EBITDA limit. Result of this controversial recommendation is that interest will not be actually disallowed but deferred to a later period – assuming the company will have sufficiently high EBITDA one day.[55]

The Directive implements this recommendation in its Article 4 – so BEPS action 4 is the only Action, which also has identical number Article in the ATAD Directive. As noted above, the rule establishes a limit for deductibility of interest in the current year based on the EBIDTA (taxpayer's earnings before interest, tax, depreciation and amortisation).[56] This means that the taxpayer is eligible to deduct net[57] exceeding borrowing costs for up to 30% of EBIDTA. At the same time, as recital 6 of the preamble to the Directive explains, the Member States could 'decrease this ratio' to ensure a higher level of protection. This reflects the idea that ATAD merely provides for a minimum standard and the Member States are free to reduce the EBITDA limitation below the given 30%. Such a move would need to be logically combined by softening the negative effects but using the allowed safe harbours and longer carry forward periods, otherwise the law would be excessively harsh taken that it applies also to potentially legitimate loan financing from third parties.

The Directive provides that EBIDTA must include any tax-adjusted amounts for exceeding borrowing costs as well as the tax-adjusted amounts for depreciation and amortisation. Tax exempt income shall be excluded from the EBIDTA of a taxpayer. Along with that, taken that the Directive sets only the minimum standard of the rule, it remains possible for the Member States 'to adopt an alternative measure referring to

---

55. For detailed analysis of the EBITDA rule in the ATAD, its functioning and compatibility with the EU principle of proportionality and the previously decided CJEU cases, see Pieter van Os, 'Interest Limitation under the Adopted Anti-Tax Avoidance Directive and Proportionality', EC Tax Law Review, 2016, No. 4, pp. 184–198. The author comes to preliminary conclusion that the rule adopted under the ATAD may potentially be considered as incompatible with the principle of proportionality.
56. For the rule refer to Art. 4 of the ATAD.
57. Interest expenses exceeding the interest receipts.

a taxpayer's earnings before interest and tax (EBIT) and fixed in a way that it is equivalent to the EBITDA-based ratio'.[58]

Herewith, the Member States could in addition to the interest limitation rule provided by the Directive also use other 'targeted rules against intra-group debt financing, in particular thin capitalisation rules'.[59]

As noted above, the Directive provides for the option to introduce the safe-harbour rules. For example, the safe-harbour rule may apply to the stand alone companies,[60] which may be allowed to deduct the full amount of exceeding borrowing costs. As clarified in the Directive, since the BEPS practice in principle takes place through excessive interest payments among entities which are associated enterprises, the stand alone companies should not pose significant BEPS risk of tax avoidance.

Another safe-harbour rule is up to EUR 3 million net annual interest expense threshold – which Member States can use to allow deductibility of any interest – irrespective of whether this is paid to related party or to unrelated party. This threshold can be reduced to a lower amount or not to be introduced at all. For companies that form a group in a Member State – this threshold applies at the group level, so it can be further increased or multiplied if applied at entity level.

The Directive in paragraph 5 also provides for further safe harbours in form of group ratios and this is namely:

– The group equity to asset ratio.
– The group EBITDA ratio.

Where the company can demonstrate that the entity equity to asset ratio is higher than the group equity to asset ratio, the interest can be fully deductible. Alternatively, the Member States can allow the companies to deduct a higher amount of interest calculated by reference to the group EBITDA ratio. Finally, an important outcome of the political negotiation in the Council was the safe harbour in reference to the loans concluded prior to 17 June 2016 – the interest on such loans can be excluded from such EBITDA limitation and thus fully deductible. In addition, the interest incurred on loans used to finance long-term public infrastructure projects can be also excluded from the application of this rule.[61]

Furthermore, the Directive preserves the right of the Member State to allow some of the options for carry back and forward the excess amount of exceeding borrowing costs and unutilised EBITDA capacity,[62] which cannot be utilised in the current tax period. The financial undertakings are excluded from the scope of the rule due to specific nature of the rule and need for a more customised approach required to prevent BEPS in a form of interest deduction by financial undertakings. The ongoing work of OECD in this regard may be important and the question is whether at any time in the future EU will manage to agree for interest limitation rule for financial undertakings.

---

58. *See* recital 6 of the Preamble to ATAD.
59. *See* recital 6 of the Preamble to the ATAD.
60. Companies, which are not part of corporate groups.
61. Both of these safe harbours are provided for in Art. 4, para. 4 of ATAD.
62. Article 4 para. 6 of ATAD – choice of 3 options is available a)-c).

[4] Other Measures Introduced by ATAD Directive

Additionally, the Directive includes measures on exit taxation and a general anti-abuse rule. There was also the sixth measure, which as a part of political compromise did not make it to the final version of the Directive – switch-over clause. We will give the brief overviews of these measures below.

[a] Exit Tax

The objective of exit taxes is to allow taxation of gain on assets prior to their transfer from one jurisdiction to another. The exit tax rules differ from traditional capital gain tax rules in the aspect that the exit tax rule provide for a deemed disposal, where the actual sale (change of legal ownership) did not take place, but the asset has moved from one jurisdiction to another, which has impact of the ability to exercise the right to tax. The exit tax rules in the ATAD Directive have "the function of ensuring that where a taxpayer moves assets or its tax residence out of the tax jurisdiction of a State, that State taxes the economic value of any capital gain accrued in its territory even though that gain has not yet been realised at the time of the exit'.[63]

The Directive provides for the cases, when the taxpayer shall be subject to exit tax rules. In particular, the exit tax is due upon:

- Transfer of assets from its head office to its permanent establishment (or vice versa) in another Member State or in a third country in so far as the Member State of the head office no longer has the right to tax the transferred assets due to the transfer.
- Transfer of tax residency to another Member State or to a third country, except for cases when assets which remain effectively connected with a permanent establishment in the first Member State.
- Transfer of the business carried on by its permanent establishment from a Member State to another Member State or to a third country in so far as the Member State of the permanent establishment no longer has the right to tax the transferred assets due to the transfer.[64]

The tax applies at an amount equal to the market value of the transferred assets, at the time of exit of the assets, less their value for tax purposes.[65] The payment of exit tax may be deferred by paying it in instalments over five years, but only in cases when the assets or tax residence are transferred to another Member States or third state, which a party to EEA Agreement and has concluded an agreement with the Member State of the taxpayer or with the Union on the mutual assistance for the recovery of tax claims, equivalent to the mutual assistance provided for in Council Directive

---

63. *See* para. 10 of the Preamble to the Directive.
64. *See* Art. 5 para. 1 of the ATAD Directive.
65. *Ibid*.

2010/24/EU.[66] The Directive thus provides for different treatment of intra-EU/EEU and third countries transfers by not allowing deferred payment of exit taxes in case the transfer is done to the third states other than those referred above.[67]

The receiving state shall accept the value established by the Member State of the taxpayer or of the permanent establishment as the starting value of the assets for tax purposes, unless this does not reflect the market value. Should the later case happen, the preamble to the Directive emphasizes that the receiving State should have the right to dispute the value of the transferred assets by referring to the existing dispute resolution mechanisms.[68]

The introduction of the Exit Tax Rule in the ATAD Directive is an important milestone in the evolution of the European Tax Law. The Exit Tax, which has been already in place by some Member States has been subject to scrutiny by the Court of Justice of the EU, which has initially ruled that applying the exit tax might be contrary to the fundamental freedoms if it discriminates cross-border transactions in comparison to domestics ones, requires immediate payment of exit tax without possibility to defer or imposes special disproportionate conditions on deferral.[69] In 2006 the European Commission has issued Communication calling for coordinated approach with respect to imposition of exit taxes in order to eliminate cases of double taxation, inadvertent non-taxation and preventing abuse and tax base erosion,[70] however, without proposing any particular measures. The Commission in this Communication noted that in its view the exit taxes should be permitted if it is provided that they 'do not give rise to an immediate charge to tax and that there are no conditions attached to the deferral'.

It has been a source of frustration to some Member States that the CJEU has ruled that states may not levy exit taxes when a company moves its tax residence to another EU or EEA country.[71] In 2011, however, the CJEU takes important decision on exit taxation, which is different from the previously decided cases and gives some freedom to Member States.[72] In particular, the CJEU decided that Member States should be eligible to apply exit taxes, provided that there is a possibility to defer the payment.

[b]   General Anti-avoidance Rule

In addition to the above, the Directive has introduced the General Anti-Avoidance Rule (GAAR). The GAAR shall apply to arrangements, which have been put into place for

---

66. Council Directive 2010/24/EU of 16 March 2010 concerning mutual assistance for the recovery of claims relating to taxes, duties and other measures (OJ L 84, 31.3.2010, p. 1).
67. For more on the same *see* A. Navarro, L. Parada & P. Schwarz, *'The Proposal for an EU Anti-avoidance Directive: Some Preliminary Thoughts'*. EC Tax Law Review, 2016, Vol. 3, p. 120.
68. *See* recital 10 of the Preamble to the ATAD Directive.
69. *See* for instance Lasteyrie du Saicase C-9/02, N case C-470/04. The cases concerned the changes of residency by an individual.
70. *See* Commission communication COM(2006)825 on exit taxation and the need for coordination of Member States' tax policies, available at: http://eur-lex.europa.eu/legal-content/EN/TXT/?uri=URISERV%3Al31060.
71. *See* report of the EU Parliament on Tax challenges in the Digital economy, at p. 53.
72. *See* National Grid Indus, C-371-10. This was also the first case, which specifically considered exit taxes applicable to corporate taxpayers.

the main purpose or one of the main purposes of obtaining a tax advantage that defeats the object or purpose of the applicable tax law and are non-genuine. As Preamble clarifies the rule should apply *'to arrangements that are not genuine; otherwise, the taxpayer should have the right to choose the most tax efficient structure for its commercial affairs'*.[73] As non-genuine are defined the arrangements, which were not put into place for valid commercial reasons which reflect economic reality. The Preamble also clarifies that GAAR should equally cover domestic and cross-border situations, including situations with third countries.[74]

[c] Switch-Over Clause

As mentioned above, the sixth measure proposed in the original Directive, which did not make it into the final version of ATAD was the switch-over rule.[75]

This rule was intended to complement the CFC rules – where the CFC rules do apply to non-distributed profits from low tax jurisdictions and the switch-over rule was supposed to apply to distributed profits, but also to capital gains and profits of foreign permanent establishments, which would be normally subject to exemption under domestic rules or tax treaty provisions in many EU Member States. The unintended negative effect of exemption approach is that it may encourage untaxed or low-taxed income to enter the internal market and then, circulate – in many cases, untaxed – within the Union, making use of available instruments within the Union law.[76]

This rule would prevent circumventing the CFC rules by the actual distribution of profits earned in the current year by the Foreign Controlled Company. If such company would not retain, but actually distribute the earned profits in the current year, the CFC rules do not apply by definition as they apply only to non-distributed profits. The rule was intended to apply not only to distributions from controlled companies, but also from portfolio-owned companies, where the shareholder owns less then the controlling percentage of shares or voting rights.

Some Member States however strongly resisted the idea of introducing the switch-over clause and as a result, this measure was removed from the ATAD Directive.[77]

The element of profits earned by foreign permanent establishments was however addressed and this element was transferred into the CFC rule as was also suggested by Action 3 of BEPS project.[78] At the same time, elimination of switch-over rule from ATAD, in combination with the design of the CFC rule and absence of taxation of

---

73. *See* recital 11 of the Preamble to the Directive.
74. *See* recital 11 of the Preamble to the ATAD Directive.
75. *See* EC COM (2016)26 dated 28 January 2016 with the initial proposal for ATAD Directive. In particular, for more on switch-over clause, *see* Part 5 of Explanatory memorandum in the Directive.
76. *Ibid.*
77. *See* Isabella de Groot, *'The Switch-Over Provision in the Proposal for an Anti-tax Avoidance Directive and Its Compatibility with the EU Treaty Freedoms'*, EC Tax Law Review, 2016-3.
78. *See* Art. 3 para. 1 of the ATAD Directive.

dividends and capital gains creates a major loophole in the system, which creates opportunities for tax planning and tax avoidance.

[C] Action 5 Countering Harmful Tax Practices

The OECD recommendations on BEPS Action 5 included two levels of measures – one set of measures establishing a strengthened requirement of substance for the special tax regimes and the second set of measures aimed at improving transparency, especially in respect of special regimes resulting from administrative practices – such as different types of rulings.

At the EU level, the recommendations on Action 5 are currently implemented through two set of measures as well:

- The Code of Conduct agreement on Patent Box – Modified Nexus Approach.
- Directive on Administrative Assistance 3 ('DAC 3') on automatic exchange of tax rulings.

We elaborate on both measures below, where we however need to highlight that the first one is only a soft-law measure and this only implies political (gentlemen) commitments, while the second is actually a hard-law measure, which means that the Member States must implement it into their domestic law measures. This distinction is already proving and showing relevance in the current days.

[1] Code of Conduct: Agreement on Patent Box – Modified Nexus

The fight against harmful tax competition has started long ago in the EU with adoption in 1998 of the Code of Conduct on Business Taxation ('Code of Conduct').[79] It is not a legally binding instrument, but rather a source of soft law, which serves as a politically binding instrument within the EU.[80] By adopting the Code of Conduct, the Member States agreed to change the national tax regimes, which were considered as harmful, and also committed to abstain from introduction of new ones. The Code of Conduct identifies certain criteria for determination whether the national tax regime is harmful, where the gateway criterion is currently the principle that:

> the effective level of taxation which is significantly lower, including zero taxation, than the general level of taxation in the country concerned is a risk indicator, which should trigger further review of the addition criteria of harmfulness of the tax regimes.

The remaining five criterions, which confirm whether the regime is indeed harmful are the following:

---

79. Resolution of the Council 98/C 2/01.
80. For more about the Code of Conduct on Business taxation see H. Gribnau, 'The Code of Conduct for Business Taxation: An Evaluation of an EU Soft-Law Instrument', in Dennis Weber (ed.), Traditional and Alternative Routes to European Tax Integration, 2010.

- tax benefits are reserved to non-residents or transactions carried with non-residents;
- tax incentives apply mainly for activities which are isolated from the domestic economy and therefore have no impact on the national tax base (ring-fencing);
- granting of tax advantages even in the absence of any real economic activity (substance) and substantial economic presence within the Member State offering the advantage;
- the basis of profit determination for companies in a multinational group departs from internationally accepted rules, in particular those approved by the OECD;
- lack of transparency of tax measures, including where legal provisions are relaxed at administrative level in a non-transparent way.[81]

Over the time, hundreds of national cases were examined by the Code of Conduct Group and around 100 were found harmful, where the Member States have agreed to modify or abolish the regimes. During 2014, based on the mandate of the Council, the Group has examined the IP box regimes existing in several EU Member States against the background of OECD/BEPS developments.[82] By the end of 2014, the Group has presented its report, where all of the regimes were found harmful and not compatible with the modified nexus approach developed under the BEPS project,[83] and consequently endorsed by the Code of Conduct Group[84] and the Council's Conclusions.[85] The Group agreed that the existing and potential future regimes similar to patent or IP box regimes shall be amended to comply with the OECD/G20 'modified nexus approach'.[86] As a result of this agreement, the Member States had to amend the existing regimes by the end of June 2016 and thus preventing the entry into such harmful regimes to any taxpayers wishing to do so, but under the grandfather rule, the taxpayers who entered into such regimes prior to June 2016 can benefit from the existing patent box regimes but no longer than June 2021, when all the existing modified nexus non-compliant patent boxes are due to expire. The Group of Code of Conduct was invited by the Council to monitor the further work on respective legislative processes.

As of the latest information, most of the EU Member States, which have the IP Box or Patent box regimes have complied with the modified nexus approach, either by modifying their existing rules or by closing the possibility of entry into these regimes by

---

81. See Resolution of the Council 98/C 2/01, paragraph B.
82. See para. 9 Report on the Code of Conduct dated 9 December 2014, Doc 16553/114 REV 1 FISC 225 ECOFIN 1166, available at: http://data.consilium.europa.eu/doc/document/ST-16553-2014-REV-1/en/pdf.
83. See para. 12, Ibid.
84. See the Report of the Code of Conduct dated 9 December 2014.
85. See Council Conclusions 16846/14, FISC 233, dated 11 December 2014, available at: http://data.consilium.europa.eu/doc/document/ST-16846-2014-INIT/en/pdf.
86. See OECD/G20 Agreement on Modified Nexus Approach for IP Regimes, available at: http://www.oecd.org/ctp/beps-action-5-agreement-on-modified-nexus-approach-for-ip-regimes.pdf.

new entrants. France, is however, the only Member State, which refused to comply[87] with these commitments and the question is what will be the implications for it as well as future of such political commitments, which do not get complied with.

The issue of compatibility of the modified nexus approach with EU law and especially with the freedom of establishment and freedom to provide services has been actively discussed in the EU.[88] With this respect, the Code of Conduct group and the Council Legal Service believe that there is indeed a risk that the modified nexus approach may be found incompatible with the EU Treaty freedoms in the future, since once incorporated into national law, it may in certain cases restrict the right of companies to decide where to carry out their R&D. However, in their view, it will all depend on a particular legal and factual circumstances of the case, and it not an absolute outcome in all cases.[89]

[2]   DAC 3: Automatic Exchange of Rulings

The need for improved transparency of special regimes based on administrative practices was strongly underlined with the above mentioned State Aid cases[90] as well the so-called Lux Leaks,[91] where hundreds of private rulings issued by the Luxemburg authorities to around 370 companies were leaked and made publicly available.[92] Today, this database of leaked rulings in publicly accessible on the website of International Consortium of investigative journalists (ICIJ).[93]

The Lux Leaks indeed accelerated the process for improvement of transparency of these rulings, which in many cases lead to tax avoidance resulting from the information asymmetry and absence of transparency, where one jurisdiction in the EU would experience tax base erosion, while the other jurisdiction would grant a generous tax exemption by making a downward tax base adjustment based on transfer pricing exemption. On 15 March 2015, the Commission has presented the draft proposal of Council Directive on extending further the automatic exchange of information (AEoI)

---

87. France believes that current patent box regime introduced therein is not harmful. *See* the official response of the Commission, available at: http://www.europarl.europa.eu/sides/getAllAn swers.do?reference = P-2016-005395&language = EN.
88. *See* for instance C.HJI Panayi, 'The *Compatibility of the OECD/G20 Base Erosion and Profit Shifting Proposals with EU Law*', Bulletin for International Taxation, Issue: January/February 2016, pp. 102–104.
89. *See* para. 9, Report on the Code of Conduct dated 9 December 2014 referred above.
90. *See* section §11.02[A] of this Chapter for information regarding EU state aid cases – i.e., Apple, Fiat, Starbucks, case on Belgian 'Excess Profit' tax scheme.
91. The first set of documents on Luxembourg tax deals was published on 5 November 2014 by the ICIJ (International Consortium of investigative journalists) and its media partners.
92. Most of these companies are international giants, audited and consulted by the Big4 companies. For more information and specific stories, consult the webpage of ICIJ available at: https://www.icij.org/project/luxembourg-leaks.
93. Available at: https://www.icij.org/project/luxembourg-leaks/explore-documents-luxembourg-leaks-database.

to rulings and advance pricing arrangements[94]- so-called DAC 3. This Directive amends the existing Directive 2011/16/EU on administrative cooperation in the field of taxation, which sets out the foundations for exchange information and other practical aspects of administrative cooperation between the Member States.

Already on 8 December 2015, the last ECOFIN meeting of the Presidency of Luxemburg, this Directive was adopted by the Council.[95] The Directive requires the Member States to exchange information on cross-border rulings automatically and also to provide further information upon request where appropriate.

To facilitate the exchange and use of information, the Commission will be responsible for development of secure central directory, where the exchanged rulings and agreements will be stored. This directory will be made available for all Member States, but only to the extent it is required for correct implementation of the Directive. The exchange of rulings will become obligatory from 1 January 2017.[96]

Under the rules of the Directive, the competent authorities of the states will need to exchange rulings and agreements issued or concluded (but also renewed or amended) dated from January 2012 and later. Exceptionally, states may be exempt from obligation to exchange ruling or agreement if it was issued before 31 December 2013 and was not valid by 1 January 2014. One more exemption may apply to rulings and agreements concluded with companies, whose group annual net turnover is less than EUR 40 million This exemption however applies only in cases, where such ruling or agreement was issued, amended or reviewed before 1 April 2016.[97] All other agreements and rulings shall be exchanged with no exceptions.

[D] Actions 6 and 7

The measures to address the challenges discussed by the BEPS project under Actions 6 and 7 on prevention of tax treaty abuse and artificial avoidance of PE status respectively, require mainly changes at the level of tax treaties, however even some aspects of these recommendations can also involve domestic law provisions. These would involve especially special or GAARs in domestic law as also acknowledged by Action 6.

In this respect, the EU Commission has limited its actions to recommendations to encourage the Member States to implement the principle purpose test as the key solution. The Limitation of Benefits (LoB) Clause does not seem as the right solution by the Commission in view of the previous CJEU decisions, which considered that LoB clauses might be incompatible with the freedom of establishment and the principle for

---

94. See Commission Communication COM (2015) 135 final, available at: http://ec.europa.eu/taxation_customs/sites/taxation/files/resources/documents/taxation/company_tax/transparency/com_2015_135_en.pdf.
95. See Press Release available at: http://www.consilium.europa.eu/en/press/press-releases/2015/12/08-ecofin-cross-broder-tax-ruling/ For the text of the Directive see Directive EU 2015/2376, available at: http://eur-lex.europa.eu/legal-content/EN/TXT/?uri=CELEX:32015L2376.
96. See Art. 2 of the Directive EU 2015/2376.
97. See Art. 8a in the updated Directive 2011/16/EU on administrative cooperation in the field of taxation.

Chapter 11: How Are We Doing with BEPS Recommendations in the EU? §11.02[D]

the free movement of capital.[98] The Commission actually recently has started an infringement procedure against the Netherlands, where it challenges the compliance of the LoB clause with the EU law.[99] The EU implementation of the recommendations of the Actions 6 and 7[100] is currently limited to political recommendations and commitments enshrined in Council Conclusions dated 26 May 2016.[101]

Thus, Council noted that Recommendation from the Commission to ensure implementation of the OECD BEPS recommendations on Actions 6 and 7[102] is compliant with the EU law.[103] It welcomes the proposed anti-abuse provisions in a form of principal purpose test (PPT) and amendments to the permanent establishment definition as proposed by the OECD to be included into bilateral tax treaties agreed by the Member States.

The Commission also encourages Member States to insert in the tax treaties the PPT based anti-avoidance rules in accordance with the wording provided the OECD Model Tax Convention but in the following modification:

> Notwithstanding the other provisions of this Convention, a benefit under this Convention shall not be granted in respect of an item of income or capital if it is reasonable to conclude, having regard to all relevant facts and circumstances, that obtaining that benefit was one of the principal purposes of any arrangement or transaction that resulted directly or indirectly in that benefit, unless it is established that *it reflects a genuine economic activity or that* granting that benefit in these circumstances would be in accordance with the object and purpose of the relevant provisions of this Convention.[104]

The Commission noted that to ensure compliance with EU law, '*the general anti-abuse rule based on a principal purpose test as suggested in the final report on Action 6 needs to be aligned with the case law of the Court of Justice of the European Union as regards the abuse of law*'.[105]

---

98. See Gottardo C-55/00 and Open Skies C-466/98. See also C. HJI Panayi, 'Open Skies for EC Tax?', British Tax Review, 2003, No. 3; G.W. Kofler, 'European Taxation Under an "Open Sky": LoB Clauses in Tax Treaties Between the U.S. and the EU Member States', Tax Notes International, 5 July 2004, p. 45.
99. See EC Memo 15-6006 dated 19 November 2015. The Commission believes that the LoB wording in particular treaty of the Netherlands with Japan restricts the freedom of establishment, since it limits the treaty benefits only to entities, held by Dutch shareholders or entities, which are traded on certain stock exchanges, the list of which, however, does not include all EU Member States.
100. See the Commission recommendations EU 2016/136 dated 28 January 2016 on the implementation of measures against tax treaty abuse, available at: http://eur-lex.europa.eu/legal-content/EN/TXT/PDF/?uri=CELEX:32016H0136&from=EN.
101. Council conclusions on an external taxation strategy and measures against tax treaty abuse, 281/16, dated 25 May 2016, available at: http://www.consilium.europa.eu/en/press/press-releases/2016/05/25-conclusions-tax-treaty-abuse/.
102. See the Commission recommendations EU 2016/136 dated 28 January 2016.
103. For more analysis of the OECD conclusions on Action 6 and also its compatibility with the EU law see E. Pinetz, 'Final Report on Action 6 of the OECD/G20 Base Erosion and Profit Shifting Initiative: Prevention of Treaty Abuse', Bulletin for International Taxation, Issue: January/February 2016, pp. 117–119.
104. See the Commission recommendations EU 2016/136 dated 28 January 2016, p. 2, Art. 2.
105. See recital 7 of the preamble to the Commission recommendations EU 2016/136 dated 28 January 2016.

In addition to that, the Council acknowledges that bilateral tax treaties remain the competence of the Member States and that other measures elaborated in the context of OECD BEPS Action 6 may be also helpful, such as limitation on benefits clauses.[106]

[E] Actions 8-10: Aligning Transfer Pricing Outcomes with Value Creation in the EU?

The recommendations from Actions 8-10 are being reflected in the draft new Chapters of OECD Transfer Pricing Guidelines. Since most EU Member States are OECD members, these changes to the Transfer Pricing Guidelines would be effected in most EU countries automatically.

There are however several Member States who are not OECD members (Bulgaria, Croatia, Cyprus, Lithuania, Malta, Romania). While there may be no need for specific additional measures in the EU - the issue may be that not all the EU Member States may automatically subscribe to the recommended approaches of BEPS Actions 8-10. This may lead to situations that outcomes foreseen in Actions 8-10 will not be fully achieved within EU. For this purpose, it would be useful that the principles of Actions 8-10 are officially endorsed by the Council - perhaps in the form of Council Conclusions.

Furthermore, specific guidance for implementing the conclusions of the OECD report on Actions 8-9-10 and 13 may be expected at the EU level. So far, the Code of Conduct Group was invited by the Council to assess the opportunity, in light of the fourth criterion, of developing such guidance with the support of the Commission and its advisory bodies, notably the EU Joint Transfer Pricing Forum (JTPF).[107] Work and efforts aimed in this direction are under way during the Slovak presidency as indicated in the EU BEPS roadmap.

Other possible measures could include updated recommendations of JTPF in the areas, where JTPF has previously formulated recommendations. This is especially in the area of intra-group services[108] and in the area of transfer pricing documentation.[109]

---

106. See para. 19 of the Council conclusions on an external taxation strategy and measures against tax treaty abuse.
107. See para. 24, Council conclusions on corporate taxation - base erosion and profit shifting, available at: http://www.consilium.europa.eu/en/press/press-releases/2015/12/08-ecofin-conclusions-corporate-taxation/ For the work plan of JTPF for the years 2015-2019 see DOC: JTPF/005/FINAL/2015/EN, available at: http://ec.europa.eu/taxation_customs/resources/documents/taxation/company_tax/transfer_pricing/forum/jtpf0052015programmeofwork.pdf.
108. See EC DOC: JTPF/008/FINAL/2012/EN on Report on Cost Contribution Arrangements on Services not creating Intangible Property (IP), available at: http://ec.europa.eu/taxation_customs/sites/taxation/files/resources/documents/taxation/company_tax/transfer_pricing/forum/jtpf/2012/jtpf_cca_report_en.pdf and COM(2011) 16 dated 25 January 2011 on the work of the EU Joint Transfer Pricing Forum in the period April 2009 to June 2010 and related proposals (1) Guidelines on low value adding intra-group services; and (2) Potential approaches to non-EU triangular cases.
109. See Resolution of the Council and of the representatives of the governments of the Member States, meeting within the Council, of 27 June 2006 on a code of conduct on transfer pricing documentation for associated enterprises in the European Union (EU TPD) (2006/C 176/01), available at: http://eur-lex.europa.eu/legal-content/EN/TXT/?uri=uriserv:OJ.C_.2006.176.01.0001.01.ENG&toc=OJ:C:2006:176:TOC.

[F] Action 11: Measuring and Monitoring BEPS in the EU?

Action 11 recommendations are aimed at establishing analytical and measurement procedures to measure and monitor BEPS practices with a view to assess the impact, but also improvements after introduction of other measures. There is an expectation for a special EU study on assessment of impact various types of ATP on the Member States' effective tax rates.[110]

One study with the review of the EU Member States national tax systems was recently published by the European Commission.[111] In the study, the group of researchers worked on identification of model ATP structures and defined indicators of ATP, which as such facilitate or allow ATP, consequently the group reviewed the corporate income tax systems of the EU Member States by means of the ATP indicators, in order to identify those tax rules and practices (or lack thereof) that result in Member States being vulnerable to ATP.[112] The Group formulated seven ATP models and thirty-three ATP indicators. As ATP indicators were considered provisions of national legislations, case law and also absence of such legislation. The assessment of national systems indicated that minimum four and maximum seventeen ATP indicators are present in the Member States' systems. Among other observations, the study provides interesting statistics: for instance, (1) half of the Member States (fourteen) do not have CFC rules, (2) thirteen Member States did not apply any beneficial-owner test when accepting a claim for a reduction or exemption of withholding tax, (3) with the exception of Denmark, Spain and (partly) Hungary, no Member State has rules to counter the mismatching tax qualification of a local partnership or company by another state.

[G] Action 12: Possible Mandatory Disclosure Rules

As outlined in the Slovak Council Presidency roadmap on future work in the Council with respect to BEPS,[113] there has been significant improvements with respect to transparency enhancement at the EU level. Thus, by amending the Directive on Administrative Cooperation was gradually implemented the common reporting standard, the automatic exchange of rulings and Country by Country (CbC) reporting. *'The last remaining element of disclosure and transparency that has not been addressed by the EU is in the area of mandatory disclosure rules (MDR)'*. In its conclusions adopted on 8 December 2015, the Council invited the Code of Conduct Group 'to assess the opportunity of developing EU guidance for implementing OECD BEPS conclusions on

---

110. *See* Press Release dated 21 June 2016, available at: http://europa.eu/rapid/press-release_MEMO-16-2265_en.htm.
111. *See* EC Study 'Study on Structures of Aggressive Tax Planning and Indicators', Working Paper N. 61 – 2015, ISSN 1725-7565 (PDF), available at: http://ec.europa.eu/taxation_customs/sites/taxation/files/resources/documents/taxation/gen_info/economic_analysis/tax_papers/taxation_paper_61.pdf.
112. *See* executive summary to the EC Study 'Study on Structures of Aggressive Tax Planning and Indicators'.
113. Available at: http://data.consilium.europa.eu/doc/document/ST-11071-2016-INIT/en/pdf.

Action 12 (disclosure of aggressive tax planning), notably with a view to facilitate exchange of such information between tax authorities'.[114]

Herewith, the issue was also discussed during the Council meeting in April 2016, where in its Conclusion presented on 25 May 2016, the Council invites 'Commission to consider legislative initiatives on Mandatory Disclosure Rules inspired by Action 12 of the OECD BEPS project with a view to introducing more effective disincentives for intermediaries who assist in tax evasion or avoidance schemes'.[115]

In its statements the Council calls for different bodies to assist with the work on implementation of the OECD Action 12 recommendations – the Group of Code of Conduct experts and the Commission, whereas instruments that could be developed respectively would have different legal force. While one of the options that could be considered was *'to adopt guidance in the Code of Conduct Group on mandatory disclosure rules targeting specific offshore tax evasion schemes'*, and gradually prepare for the possible future EU legislative initiatives, the Commission has already indicated its intention to prepare a legislative proposal in its Commission Communication on further measures to enhance transparency and the fight against tax evasion and avoidance.[116] In this respect, the Slovak presidency has initiated Council conclusions that acknowledge *'the need to increase oversight of enablers and promoters of aggressive tax planning and to introduce more effective disincentives for such activities'*, welcome *'the intention of the Commission to launch in autumn 2016 a public consultation to gather feedback on the most appropriate approach to achieve greater transparency on the activities of intermediaries who assist in tax evasion or avoidance schemes'* and take note of *'the intention of the Commission to explore possibilities for Mandatory Disclosure Rules inspired by Action 12 of the OECD BEPS project, drawing on the experiences in this area of some EU Member States, and to possibly come forward with a legislative proposal in 2017'* and further more encourage *'the Commission to start reflecting on the possibility for future exchange of such information between tax administrations in the EU'*.[117] It thus expected that the Commission will launch soon a public consultation process, which should lead to a legislative proposal expected during 2017.

[H] Action 13: Revising Requirements Fort Transfer Pricing Documentation

The key recommendations on the transfer pricing documentation in Action 13 relate to recommendations on structure of transfer pricing documentation – namely concept of Master File and Local File and also a new type of documentation – CbC Report.

---

114. Doc. 15150/15, para. 25, available at: http://www.consilium.europa.eu/en/press/press-releases/2015/12/08-ecofin-conclusions-corporate-taxation/.
115. Doc. 281/16, para. 12, available at: http://www.consilium.europa.eu/en/press/press-releases/2016/05/25-conclusions-tax-treaty-abuse/.
116. *See* COM(2016) 451 final, available at: https://ec.europa.eu/taxation_customs/sites/taxation/files/docs/body/com_2016_451_en.pdf.
117. *See* Council Conclusion dated 11 October 2016, available at: http://www.consilium.europa.eu/en/press/press-releases/2016/10/11-ecofin-conclusions-tax-transparency/.

Chapter 11: How Are We Doing with BEPS Recommendations in the EU? §11.02[H]

It is interesting to point out that in respect of Master File and Local File, the EU has already undertaken a similar initiative within the recommendation of JTPF which was adopted by the Resolution of the Council and is known as the Code of Conduct on transfer pricing documentation for associated enterprises in the European Union (EU TPD).[118] This Code introduced the concept of Master File and Local file in EU already since 2006. The Code thus provided for '*a way for MNE Groups in the Union to provide tax authorities with information on global business operations and transfer-pricing policies ("the Master file") and information on the concrete transactions of the local entity ("the local file")*'.[119] However, the Code itself is not a binding instrument and it was up to the MNE groups to decide whether to opt for the EU TPD requirements or not. Additionally, the EU TPD does not provide for a mechanism for provision and exchange of the CbC reports. The Action 13 has thus partially embraced the earlier JTPF recommendations and perhaps even enhanced it in a few aspects. It will be now again on JTPF to reflect on these advancements and to see how the EU guidance can either adopt the OECD recommendations or further enhance them as well.

The CbC Report is however a new concept, which needed a specific legislative action, unless the EU Member States will only await a gradual and perhaps slow adoption of CbC report requirements by different Member States. To avoid the risk that OECD recommendations are implemented differently taken also the fact that not all Member States are members of the OECD, it was desired to introduce the Directive and prevent the loopholes in the EU transparency network.

This in fact happened and the Commission has issued the legislative proposal on 12 April 2016[120] which was aimed at implementing the CbC Reporting requirement as recommended by Action 13 through an amendment to the Directive on Administrative Cooperation.

This proposal was successfully adopted on 25 May 2016 as Council Directive 2016/881 (DAC4) amending Directive 2011/16/EU as regards mandatory AEoI in the field of taxation.[121] The Directive provides for the introduction of binding measures for submission by MNEs and exchange between the Member States of the CbC reports as prescribed under the BEPS project framework. As noted by the Commission[122] it was deemed important for the EU to have coordinated and legally binding approach to CbC, although most of the Member States have committed to introduce CbC under the BEPS framework.

The Directive now establishes an obligation for each Member State to introduce measures requiring MNEs located or operating in the EU to submit annual country-by-country reporting. Currently, only the MNEs with annual total consolidated revenue,

---

118. The text of the Code is available at: http://eur-lex.europa.eu/legal-content/EN/TXT/?uri= uriserv:OJ.C_.2006.176.01.0001.01.ENG&toc=OJ:C:2006:176:TOC.
119. *See* recital 5 of the Preamble to the Directive 2016/881 (DAC4).
120. *See* COM/2016/0198 on proposal for amending Directive 2013/34/EU as regards disclosure of income tax information by certain undertakings and branches, available at: http://eur-lex. europa.eu/legal-content/EN/TXT/?uri=CELEX:52016PC0198.
121. Text of the Directive available at: http://eur-lex.europa.eu/legal-content/EN/TXT/?uri= CELEX%3A32016L0881.
122. *See* http://europa.eu/rapid/press-release_MEMO-16-160_en.htm.

which equals or is higher than EUR 750 million will be covered by new measures. The report shall be filled by the ultimate parent company, or other company selected by the MNE in its state of residence to the tax authorities of its country of residence. The OECD projects that only 10%-15% of the MNE groups will be covered by the new rules, while this portion of companies exactly represents the approximate 90% of corporate revenues.[123]

The CbC report shall include information on each country, where the Group has operations. In particular – amount of revenue, the profit or loss before income tax, the income tax paid and accrued, the number of employees, the stated capital, the accumulated earnings and the tangible assets other than cash and cash equivalence of each company in the group. In general, the template for CbC reporting established under the final report on Action 13 should be prescribed as a model by the Member States. There are no major departures from the OECD Action 13 model. The CbC reports submitted to the tax authorities will be then exchanged between the competent authorities of the Member States, where the MNE group will have taxable presence either due to tax residency or PE status.[124] The national measures shall require exchange of CbC reports on annual basis starting from 2017, which means that the first CbC reports will have to be submitted by MNEs for the fiscal year 2016. MNEs will have twelve months to submit the report since the last day of the reporting fiscal year.

The information received by competent authorities by means of communication may be used not only for assessment of transfer pricing risks, but also for assessment of other BEPS risks. However, the Directive precludes the use of information for immediate transfer pricing adjustments and instead encourages Member States to use CbC reports as indications of transfer pricing risks and to request MNEs for further information.[125]

[I] Action 14: Dispute Resolution – Enhancing the Current Arbitration Mechanism in the EU?

Action 14 of BEPS project calls for an effective resolution of cross-border tax disputes especially through improving the Mutual Agreement Procedure mechanism. While OECD has already introduced the Arbitration provision into the OECD Model Tax Convention, the Action 14 does not call for Arbitration as the 'must do' recommendation. This is possibly because many countries may be hesitant about accepting the binding arbitration mechanism.

In the EU, the arbitration is binding already since 1990 as a result of Multilateral Convention of EU Council on the elimination of double taxation in connection with the

---

123. Proposal for a Council Directive amending Directive 2011/16/EU as regards mandatory automatic exchange of information in the field of taxation, p. 3 available at: http://eur-lex.europa.eu/resource.html?uri=cellar:89937d6d-c5a8-11e5-a4b5-01aa75ed71a1.0014.02/DOC_1&format=PDF.
124. *See* Art. 8aa of the updated Directive 2011/16.
125. *See* Art. 16 para. 6 of the updated Directive 2011/16.

adjustment of profits of associated enterprises.[126] The convention provides for a combined mechanism of mutual agreement procedure and arbitration. The mechanism allows for taxpayers to initial access the Mutual Agreement Procedure, which would be leading to a binding arbitration if the dispute is not resolved by two years.

There are however weaknesses of this mechanism and the major limitation is the fact that the scope of the convention only applies to double taxation resulting from transfer pricing or attribution of profits to permanent establishment. All other situations of double taxation in the EU are left potentially unresolved and the taxpayers can only access the Mutual Agreement Procedures if the bilateral tax treaties between the relevant Member States provide for this mechanism.

In early 2016, the Commission has initiated public consultation to address the dispute resolution issues and it is now expected that in late autumn of 2016 the Commission will propose a legislative measure as foreseen in the Commissions June 2015 Action Plan for fair and efficient corporate taxation in the EU.[127]

[J] Action 15: Multilateral Instrument (MLI)

Action 15 foresees a multilateral convention, which would allow implementation of recommendations identified in Actions 6 and 7 by changing several thousand tax treaties with one single multilateral instrument.

There is currently no specific action envisaged at the EU level with respect to the OECD Multilateral Instrument. The Commission did issue however warning to the Member States that upon joining the MLI they should take into consideration the practice of the CJEU and align the provision of the PPT rule with the EU principles.[128] For this purpose, the Commission has offered the slightly modified wording of the PPT provision, which was presented above in the paper in section §11.02[D].

Taken that the Multilateral instrument is likely to be concluded in 2017, we can foresee possible political statements or official endorsement by the Council in 2017.

§11.03 OTHER EU BEPS ISSUES: PROGRESS AND DEVELOPMENTS

[A] Changes to Parent Subsidiary Directive

The parent-subsidiary Directive[129] is intended to eliminate double taxation with respect to corporate profits distributions made by cross-border groups and align treatment of

---

126. *See* Convention 90/436/EEC: Convention on the elimination of double taxation in connection with the adjustment of profits of associated enterprises, available at: http://eur-lex.europa.eu /LexUriServ/LexUriServ.do?uri=CELEX:41990A0436:en:HTML.
127. *See* Commission Communication, available at: http://ec.europa.eu/taxation_customs/reso urces/documents/taxation/company_tax/fairer_corporate_taxation/com_2015_302_en.pdf.
128. *See* EU Commissions' Recommendation dated 28 January 2016 on the implementation of measures against tax treaty abuse, available at: http://ec.europa.eu/taxation_customs/resour ces/documents/taxation/company_tax/anti_tax_avoidance/c_2016_271_en.pdf.
129. *See* Directive 2011/96/EU dated 30 November 2011 on the common system of taxation applicable in the case of parent companies and subsidiaries of different Member States. This Directives replaced an earlier Council Directive on the same 90/435/EEC.

purely domestic dividends with cross-border ones. This is achieved either through application of double exemption – where the Directive requires both Member States (paying and receiving) to exempt from taxation qualified profit distributions received by parent companies from their subsidiaries in other Member States, or alternatively provide an underlying tax credit with respect to corporate income tax paid abroad, should the respective foreign dividends be taxable in the hands of the parent company. Equally, Directive prevents the Member States where subsidiaries are located from imposition of withholding taxes on inter-community profit distributions.

This legislative measure has been however also abused in practice and therefore the EU Commission proposed to amend Directive with the twofold objective – tackle hybrid loan mismatches and introduce GAAR provision therein. The proposal was presented by the Commission in November 2013 and by the end of 2014 both amendments were agreed at the Council level.[130]

The first amendment was agreed in July 2014 and addressed the hybrid mismatch situation, where the income from certain financial instruments is differently characterised – for example interest on profit participating loan can be treated as deductible expense in one country and exempted in the other country. The change introduced into the Directive was in form of particular linking rule, as was discussed under the Action 2 of the BEPS project to tackle the problem of double non-taxation of dividends caused by hybrid loan arrangements.[131] Under the new rule, the Member State of the parent company will refrain from taxing profits from the subsidiary only to the extent that such profits are not tax deductible for the subsidiary.[132]

The second change into the Directive was the binding targeted anti-abuse clause, which was introduced with the second amendment to the Directive in January 2015,[133] is a '*de minimis*' rule, which requires governments to refrain from granting the benefits of the parent-subsidiary Directive to an arrangement, or series of arrangements, that are not 'genuine' and have been put in place to obtain a tax advantage, while not reflecting economic reality. The introduction of the anti-abuse clause in the Directive should ensure greater consistency in its application by different Member States. Member States were supposed to transpose the anti-abuse rule into national legislation by the end of 2015.[134]

---

130. See press release ST 15103/14 dated 9 December 2014, available at: http://www.consilium.europa.eu/en/workarea/downloadasset.aspx?id=40802190601.
131. See Council Directive (EU) 2014/86 of 8 July 2014 amending Directive 2011/96/EU on the common system of taxation applicable in the case of parent companies and subsidiaries of different Member States.
132. Ibid.
133. See Council Directive (EU) 2015/121 of 27 January 2015 amending Directive 2011/96/EU on the common system of taxation applicable in the case of parent companies and subsidiaries of different Member States.
134. Ibid.

[B] Changes to Interest Royalty Directive: Pending

IRD[135] provides for common system of taxation application to inter-community payments of interest and royalties done between the associated enterprises. The Directive requires the source Member State to exempt from any taxes interest and royalties paid to the company or permanent establishment in another Member State provided that the recipient is a beneficial owner. This Directive therefore achieves a similar effect as Article 12 of OECD Model Tax Convention does – where country of source loses the taxing right, which is granted exclusively to the country of residence. This feature may be very attractive for tax planning and tax avoidance purposes and similarly to the Parent-Subsidiary Directive, the IRD is often abused by taxpayers, who explore the loopholes between the national tax systems of Member States and manage to avoid taxation completely: this is possible due to elimination of withholding taxes in source state and preferential or zero taxation in the residence state or paying the interest or royalty from the receiving state, where it is deducted against the received payment in back-to-back fashion – out to a third jurisdiction. Thus, in 2011 the Commission proposed to amend the Directive and introduce the 'effectively subject to tax criteria'.[136] 'Effectively subject to tax requirement' should ensure that the benefits of the Directive are only granted when the income derived from the payment is effectively subject to tax in the Member State of the receiving company or in the Member State where the recipient permanent establishment is situated.[137]

The effectively subject to tax requirement has gradually transformed into discussion of Minimum effective tax rate discussion, which is becoming difficult and controversial issue to reach consensus. Some Member States would like that the interest or royalty paid from one Member State to another should be subject to minimum rate of tax in the hands of the receiving company. Other Member States strongly oppose this suggested requirement.

The discussion of this rule together with the rule similar to the anti-avoidance clause adopted for the Parent-Subsidiary Directive is currently held at the Council level.[138] However, the Member States cannot reach the consensus – some Member States deem it sufficient to include an anti-avoidance rule as introduced into the Parent-Subsidiary Directive, while others believe a more robust anti-avoidance measures are needed. This leads to a deadlock situation where no progress was made during the several preceding presidencies.

---

135. *See* Council Directive 2003/49/EC, available at: http://eur-lex.europa.eu/LexUriServ/LexUriServ.do?uri = CELEX:32003L0049:en:HTML.
136. *See* EC communication, COM(2011) 714 final, available at: http://eur-lex.europa.eu/legal-content/EN/TXT/?uri = COM:2011:0714:FIN.
137. *See Ibid.* p. 11.
138. *See* Slovak presidency road map, p. 3, available at: http://data.consilium.europa.eu/doc/document/ST-11071-2016-INIT/en/pdf.

[C] Other: Code of Conduct Activities

Reform of the Code – mission (im)possible?

Besides the work on Action 1 and Action 5 undertaken by the Code of Conduct Group and discussed earlier in this chapter, the work on enhancement of the Code of Conduct mandate and changes to the current model of functioning of its group are currently taking place.

In December 2015, the Council has adopted the conclusion on the future of the Code of Conduct on business taxation (doc. 15148/15). The Council agreed that the Code of Conduct should be reinforced for the better use of its existing mandate; along with that the future work should focus on 'examining the possibilities and modalities to extend the mandate and to update the criteria and on the possible need to adjust the governance of the Code accordingly'.[139]

There is again desire of certain Member States to amend the mandate of Code of Conduct in such a way that the taxation lower than certain given % will indicate a possible harmfulness of the regime, irrespective of the relation of the special tax rate to the main tax rate – whether it is significantly lower or not than the main tax rate. This idea is again facing a significant resistance of other Member States who believe that the rate of tax is a sacred issue related to their sovereignty.

The Code of Conduct group has been also criticised for its lack of transparency – taken that after twenty years of its work, there are significant issues reported on harmful tax practices of different Member States – often through media and leaks, rather than as a result of the work of the Code of Conduct and it is being argued that the work of the Group should be more transparent. The EU Parliament would wish that it should regularly report on its progress and also give access to the EU Parliament to its internal discussion documents and meetings' briefs. The Council has been very hesitant to change the mode of operation of Code of Conduct and the Council conclusion dated December 2015, strives to strike the diplomatic balance between transparency needs and confidentiality needs of this group to work efficiently by stressing: '*the necessity to increase the transparency of the group on past and ongoing work, whilst stressing the importance to ensure that result-orientated cooperation within the Code of Conduct Group can continue in a confidential manner*'. It then merely invited 'the Group to explore initiatives to further inform the public on the results of its meetings and to report back to ECOFIN on this issue by June 2017'.

[D] Common EU Blacklist: Is That Feasible?

As a part of the anti-avoidance package the Commission has issued Communication on an external strategy for effective taxation to deal with tax good governance matters with third countries in a coordinated manner.[140] This Communication provides for an

---

139. *See* Council Conclusions, Doc. 15148/15, Dated 8 December 2015, para. 6, available at: http://data.consilium.europa.eu/doc/document/ST-15148-2015-INIT/en/pdf.
140. *See* Commission communication COM/2016/024, available at: http://eur-lex.europa.eu/legal-content/EN/TXT/?qid=1454056581340&uri=COM:2016:24:FIN.

Chapter 11: How Are We Doing with BEPS Recommendations in the EU? §11.03[D]

update of good governance standards that were previously proposed by the Commission as recommendations and endorsed by the Council in 2013.[141]

As good governance standards are considered the minimum principles and rules that third countries should follow to cooperate in the fight against harmful tax competition and prevention of BEPS. The Recommendation encouraged Member States to use transparency, information exchange and fair tax competition as the three criteria for assessing third countries' tax regimes and, where necessary, to apply common counter measures.[142]

However, the initial recommendation was not very effective: Member States either failed to apply the measures or did it inconsistently – so, no expected result was achieved. Therefore, taken the inefficiency of the initial recommendation, fundamental changes in the global tax environment and outcome of the BEPS project it was decided to update the EU's good governance criteria. The proposed criteria are the following:[143]

(1) Transparency and exchange of information on request – at EU level, the assessment of third countries' compliance with the transparency and exchange of information on request standards will take into account the compliance ratings published by the Global Forum.
(2) AEoI of financial account information – for the EU, the assessment of third countries' compliance with the AEoI standard will take into account the compliance ratings published by the Global Forum as a result of its peer reviews.
(3) Fair tax competition, which means that a third country should not operate harmful tax measures in the area of business taxation. The assessment of whether the particular measures are harmful the account should be taken of the criteria as provided for in the Code of Conduct on Business Taxation endorsed by the Council.
(4) G20/OECD BEPS standards – it is expected that third countries will as minimum follow the minimum standards developed under the BEPS project.
(5) Financial Action Task Force (FATF)[144] international standards on Combating Money Laundering and the Financing of Terrorism and Proliferation. The FATF recommendations (as updated in October 2015) comprise forty specific recommendations to tackle money laundering, including Recommendations 24 and 25 regarding the identification of beneficial owners.

---

141. *See* Commission Recommendation, C(2012) 8805, available at: https://ec.europa.eu/taxation_customs/sites/taxation/files/docs/body/c_2012_8805_en.pdf.
142. *See*. Commission communication COM/2016/024.
143. *See* annexes to the Commission Communication COM/2016/024.
144. The Financial Action Task Force (FATF) is an inter-governmental body established in 1989 to set standards and promote effective implementation of measures to combat money laundering, terrorist financing and other related threats to the international financial system. http://www.fatf-gafi.org/home/.

Member States are encouraged to promote good governance standards and transparency by use of any means, including bilateral and multilateral regional trade agreements that may contain a special clause on good governance. Very recently, the Commission started to work towards development of common EU list of third-countries' jurisdictions who fail to follow good-governance standards (kind of black list) and to whom common counter measures will be applied by the Member States.

[E] Access to Beneficial Ownership Information

The EU adopted regulations on money laundering (Anti-Money Laundering Directive – AMLD) in 2015 to increase transparency and to address the problems posed by shell companies, foundations and trusts. Accordingly, companies in EU Member States are expected to declare the real owner of such entities but countries differ in their level of ambition when it comes to its implementation. At the same time, only persons having a 'legitimate interest' are granted access to the registers of real owners and it is not clearly defined who these real owners are.[145] Therefore, as a part of July 'Transparency' package, it was proposed by the Commission to amend the Directive on Administrative Cooperation by an amendment, which would become 'DAC5' if approved, see doc. 10978/16).[146] The purpose of this amendment will be to allow tax authorities to access to the information on beneficial ownership as well as to the relevant mechanisms, procedures, documents and information of the AMLD. The work at the level of the Council is currently being carried out with this respect.

§11.04 SUMMARY AND CONCLUSIONS

As can be seen from the above overview, a lot has been done in the EU to progress the fight against tax avoidance and tax evasion. This has been to a large extent inspired by the G20/OECD BEPS project, where EU has been striving to act on the implementations formulated in this project.

Many of the BEPS Actions have been implemented within the EU, some in more and some in less robust way. Action 1 has been partially disappointment at least from the perspective of direct tax, but in the area of Value Added Tax, some important steps have been taken, which lead to improvement of the situation. More work may need to be done in the area of direct taxation, but little ambition has been demonstrated by the Commission in this area.

Some of the other Actions have become part of the hard law, obliging the EU Member States to implement it into their domestic law. This has been especially the case with Actions 2, 3 and 4 in the form of anti-tax avoidance (ATAD) Directive. While it can be argued that many of the measures in ATAD are rather weak, it is still an important step in the history of writing and legislating for EU Direct Tax Law measures,

---

145. See Eurodad (2015) Fifty Shades of Tax Dodging: The EU's role in supporting an unjust global tax system, p. 26) See Doc IP/A/TAXE2/2016-04, Tax challenges in the digital economy, Study of the European Parliament, 2016, p. 12.
146. Available at: http://data.consilium.europa.eu/doc/document/ST-10978-2016-INIT/en/pdf.

where it usually took decades to adopt any direct tax Directive. The authors believe that more can be done on the domestic level in the process of implementation of ATAD into the domestic law and the EU Commission could formulate such guidance to allow strengthening their domestic law measures on unilateral basis.

Important progress was also achieved on Action 5, where the automatic exchange of rulings within the EU has been achieved through DAC 3 – an amendment to Directive on Administrative Cooperation. However, even here compromises were needed and the timing and size of business exemptions from exchange of rulings could hide some important information, which the Member States may seek to obtain on the basis of targeted request for exchange of information.

The remaining part of Action 5 – substance requirement for special tax regimes has been achieved only partially as a political commitment – which also as shown on the example of French patent box – is lacking its enforceability. This can be also an argument, which could suggest that further hard-law action may be needed in this area. One option would be to address the aspect of Patent box regimes in the IRD, by formulating the modified nexus requirement as pre-condition for application of IRD. This will however address the substance requirement only in respect of one regime and further work may need to be done at the level of Code of Conduct – to extrapolate the substance requirement also for other regimes.

Actions 6 and 7 call for strengthening of the tax treaty network. Here the EU Commission has provided only limited and confused guidance – confused on the one hand by initiating an infringement procedure against the Netherlands on the basis of the LoB clause and further by basically disregarding the LoB clause and scaring the Member States from using it. In this respect, the Council conclusions have been a bit more ambitious and in fact endorsing also the use of LoB clause.

Actions 8–10 (Aligning results of Transfer Pricing) have attracted so far little action and attention by the EU Commission, but the authors believe that explicit endorsement of these actions by the EU would be useful – taken that not all EU Member States are the OECD members and also perhaps updating the past guidance of the EU in this area – especially by the JTPF, which were also endorsed by the Council, could bring some value.

Action 11 (Measuring Impact of BEPS) has not been attracting much attention, while it could actually provide some important analytical intelligence on where further actions may be needed, but little attention and focus seems to be allocated to this area by the EU Commission and also by the Member States.

Action 12 (Mandatory Disclosure Rules) is waiting for its legislative action, which has been indicated to arrive in 2017. In the meantime – the public consultation is coming up soon. Significant debate and resistance from tax advisors and taxpayers may be expected in the process of bringing this action into life in the EU.

Action 13 (Transfer Pricing Documentation) has been successfully implemented through DAC 4 – an amendment to the Directive on Administrative Cooperation. The CbC Report has thus become an obligatory part of the documentation of large MNE's in the EU, including the AEoI.

Action 14 (Dispute Resolution) may soon be debated in the Council, where the Commission has already completed the public consultation and at the time of writing, the authors were awaiting of the legislative proposal to be published. The actual implementation of Action 14 may be more robust, if it will build on existing binding mechanisms, which already exist within EU.

Action 15 (Multilateral Instrument) will require little of specific attention of EU Commission taken that this is initiative fully in the hands of the OECD. We may therefore expect political endorsements of the process and perhaps coordination on the positions among EU Member States.

Some other EU measures have been also amended in light of BEPS recommendations – e.g., Parent Subsidiary Directive – to bring forward a quick implementation of Action 2 recommendations and preventing some of the hybrid mismatches.

Other EU instruments are being held hostage to the contradictory expectations of EU Member States and little or no progress is being done – e.g., IRD, which continues to be abused for BEPS practices, while the Member States debate the contradictory requirement of Minimum Effective Tax rate.

Additional progress in the area of transparency and access of tax authorities to the Beneficial ownership information may be seen soon through DAC 5, which is currently pending and if adopted – it would be another amendment to the Directive on Administrative Cooperation.

The EU Member States are currently indeed in the process of mutual coordination in respect of the third countries and the most important demonstration of this process is the initiative leading to creation of a Common EU list of non-cooperative jurisdictions. Should the Member States succeed in setting ambitious criteria and full-heartedly and constructively act on the common responses to such jurisdictions, this would indeed mean that we have reached another era of development of EU Tax Law.

This does not necessarily mean that the tax competition within EU will disappear and that the tax base will suddenly stop disappearing within the EU, but the progress made in the last several years, which was largely inspired by BEPS has been unprecedented.

CHAPTER 12
U.S. Tax Sovereignty and the BEPS Project
*Tracy A. Kaye**

§12.01 INTRODUCTION

Under international law, each sovereign nation has the right to regulate conduct based on a nexus of the conduct to the territory of the nation (territoriality) or to a natural or juridical person (nationality) whose status links the person to the nation.[1] Most nations' income tax systems are premised on these two bases of jurisdiction, which are commonly known as source or residence jurisdiction.[2] Over the past fifty-seven years, the Organisation for Economic Co-operation and Development (OECD) has developed normative tax principles aimed at resolving conflicting claims of tax jurisdiction that arise with respect to cross-border income.[3] These principles, primarily developed for the relief of double taxation, can be found in the provisions of the OECD Model Tax Convention on Income and on Capital (OECD Model Treaty).[4]

The global financial crisis highlighted the perceived increase in base erosion and profit shifting (BEPS) resulting from the cross-border activities of multinational corporations (MNCs). Various studies, hearings, and news reports underscored the

---

* I would like to gratefully acknowledge the research assistance of Wesley Buirkle and the financial support provided by the Seton Hall University School of Law Dean's Research Fellowship program.
1. Restatement (Third) of Foreign Relations Law of the United States, §§ 402, 403 (1987).
2. Joint Committee on Taxation (JCT), Background, Summary, and Implications of the OECD/G20 Base Erosion and Profit Shifting Project 6, JCX-139-15 (November 30, 2015), [hereinafter Summary of BEPS].
3. *Ibid* at 2–7. The OECD is a fifty-seven year old influential forum where over thirty governments, including the U.S., come together to discuss economic and tax policy, among other topics, and set international standards. OECD website, at http://www.oecd.org/about/membersandpartners.
4. OECD, Model Tax Convention on Income and on Capital: Condensed Version 2014, http://dx.doi.org/10.1787/mtc_cond-2014-en (July 15, 2014).

difficulty of taxing corporations with multijurisdictional operations.[5] At the G20 Leaders' Summit in June 2012, world leaders declared that BEPS must be prevented and voiced support for the OECD's efforts with respect to this issue.[6] Governments have expressed concerns over the potential double taxation that might "arise if governments acted unilaterally to protect their respective corporate tax revenue bases, and resulting uncertainty for taxpayers with cross-border operations."[7]

The G20/OECD's BEPS project, discussed in Part II, was intended to provide an internationally coordinated approach to the base erosion issue. An important goal of the BEPS project was "to provide governments with more efficient tools to ensure the effectiveness of their sovereign tax policies."[8] Effective sovereignty has been described as the "ability to achieve policy goals by means of legislation."[9] However, the BEPS project has also raised concerns about a State's potential loss of tax sovereignty. Some members of the United States (U.S.) Senate Finance Committee and the House of Representatives Ways and Means Tax Policy Subcommittee have expressed concerns about the impact of the BEPS recommendations on U.S. multinationals and their loss of input into the process.[10] In Part III, I focus on the negotiations surrounding two of the final BEPS reports, Action 6: Preventing the Granting of Treaty Benefits in Inappropriate Circumstances and Action 13: Transfer Pricing Documentation and Country-by-Country Reporting, to demonstrate that U.S. tax sovereignty was enhanced through the G20/OECD BEPS project.

§12.02 OECD BEPS PROJECT

The OECD issued a report on BEPS in February 2013. This BEPS report reviewed various data and studies and found an increased separation between the locations of the actual business activities and the reporting of profits for tax purposes.[11] The OECD followed up this report in July 2013 with an Action Plan of fifteen steps to address profit shifting by multinational corporations and move toward international coherence in corporate income taxation.[12] The OECD BEPS Action Plan targeted harmful tax practices by establishing a working party on aggressive tax planning and by requiring

---

5. OECD, *Addressing Base Erosion and Profit Shifting*, 13–14, http://dx.doi.org/10.1787/9789264 192744-en (February 12, 2013) [hereinafter *Addressing Base Erosion and Profit Shifting*].
6. G20, *G20 Leaders' Declaration*, 9, para. 48, http://www.g20.org/English/Documents/Past Presidency/201512/P020151225642876170923.pdf (June 19, 2012).
    The members of the G20 are Argentina, Australia, Brazil, Canada, China, France, the European Union, Germany, India, Indonesia, Italy, Japan, the Republic of Korea, Mexico, Russia, Saudi Arabia, South Africa, Turkey, U.K. and U.S.
7. *Summary of BEPS*, supra note 2, at 8.
8. OECD, OECD/G20 Base Erosion and Profit Shifting Project: Explanatory Statement, 4, http://www.oecd.org/ctp/beps-explanatory-statement-2015.pdf (2015), [hereinafter *Explanatory Statement*].
9. Laurens van Apeldoorn, *BEPS, Tax Sovereignty and Global Justice*, Critical Review of Social and Political Philosophy 1, 2, (forthcoming 2017).
10. *See infra* notes 47–50 and accompanying text.
11. Addressing Base Erosion and Profit Shifting, *supra* note 5, at 15.
12. OECD, *Action Plan on Base Erosion and Profit Shifting*, http://dx.doi.org/10.1787/9789264202 719-en (July 19, 2013), [hereinafter *BEPS Action Plan*].

§12.02

disclosure of aggressive tax planning arrangements as well as the global allocation among countries of the income, economic activity, and taxes paid to the relevant tax administrations (known as country-by-country (CbC) reporting).[13] The OECD BEPS Action Plan sought to realign taxation with the relevant economic substance and ensure that taxable profits cannot be artificially shifted.[14]

The G20 finance ministers unanimously endorsed the OECD BEPS Action Plan in 2013 at their July 20th meeting in Moscow,[15] as did the G20 Leaders on September 6th stating:

> We fully endorse the ambitious and comprehensive Action Plan – originated in the OECD – aimed at addressing base erosion and profit shifting ... We welcome the establishment of the G20/OECD BEPS project and we encourage all interested countries to participate. Profits should be taxed where economic activities deriving the profits are performed and where value is created.[16]

Note that the G20 includes countries such as China, India, Saudi Arabia, Russia, Brazil, Indonesia, South Africa, and Argentina that are not members of the OECD but may participate in this project as Associates "on an equal footing with OECD members."[17]

In October of 2015, OECD's Committee on Fiscal Affairs released thirteen final BEPS reports covering the tax issues surrounding the digital economy, hybrid entities and instruments, and treaty abuse as well as transfer pricing guidelines for intangibles.[18] The G20 leaders endorsed these reports at the Antayla Summit, stating:

> To reach a globally fair and modern international tax system, we endorse the package of measures developed under the ambitious G20/OECD Base Erosion and Profit Shifting (BEPS) project. Widespread and consistent implementation will be critical in the effectiveness of the project.... We, therefore, strongly urge the timely implementation of the project and encourage all countries and jurisdictions, including developing ones, to participate.[19]

The OECD made recommendations for revisions to domestic tax laws, the OECD Model Tax Convention, the Commentary to the OECD Model Tax Convention, and the OECD Transfer Pricing Guidelines as well as the development of a multilateral

---

13. *See ibid.*, Action 5, at 18; Actions 11–12, at 21–22. Actions 8–10 focus on various transfer pricing issues, including those with respect to intangibles, so as to "[a]ssure that transfer pricing outcomes are in line with value creation." *Ibid.* Actions 8–10, at 20.
14. *Ibid.*, at 13–14.
15. Kevin A. Bell, *G-20 Finance Ministers Meeting in Moscow Unanimously Back Anti-Evasion Action Plan*, Int'l Tax Monitor (2013).
16. G20, G20 Leaders' Declaration, 12, para. 50, http://www.g20.org/English/Documents/Past Presidency/201512/P020151225709417239707.pdf (September 6, 2013).
17. BEPS Action Plan, *supra* note 12, at 25.
18. *See* OECD, *BEPS 2015 Final Reports*, http://www.oecd.org/ctp/beps-2015-final-reports.htm (2015); *see also Explanatory Statement*, *supra* note 8, at 5.
19. *See* G20, *G20 Leaders' Communiqué, Antayla Summit*, para. 15, http://www.consilium.europa.eu/en/press/press-releases/2015/11/16-g20-summit-antalya-communique/ (November 15–16, 2015).

instrument to facilitate implementation of these recommendations.[20] All OECD and G20 countries have pledged to adhere to minimum standards with respect to preventing treaty abuse, requiring CbC reporting, and fighting harmful tax practices.[21] The explanatory statement accompanying the BEPS Project's final reports includes the following statement:

> With the adoption of the BEPS package, OECD and G20 countries, as well as all developing countries that have participated in its development, will lay the foundations of a modern international tax framework under which profits are taxed where economic activity and value creation occurs.[22]

This chapter focuses on two of the final BEPS reports Action 6: Preventing the Granting of Treaty Benefits in Inappropriate Circumstances and Action 13: Transfer Pricing Documentation and Country-by-Country Reporting.

[A] Action 6: Preventing the Granting of Treaty Benefits in Inappropriate Circumstances

Action 6 identifies treaty abuse through treaty shopping as one of the most significant BEPS problems.[23] Treaty shopping involves strategies by which a nonresident of a country that is party to a specific bilateral income tax treaty, attempts to obtain the benefits of that treaty, which are only meant to be available for residents of that treaty country.[24] The OECD report recommends a three-pronged approach to counter treaty abuse: (1) treaty countries should include an express statement in their treaties that tax evasion, avoidance, or treaty shopping is not condoned;[25] (2) use of limitation-on-benefits (LOB) clauses, a specific anti-abuse rule that limits the availability of treaty benefits to entities satisfying certain objective tests,[26] should be considered; and (3) use of the principal purposes test (PPT), a general anti-abuse rule based on the principal purposes of transactions, should be considered in order to address situations not caught under the LOB rule.[27] LOB clauses and the PPT will be included in the OECD Model tax treaty but the OECD acknowledges that "each of the LOB and PPT rules has

---

20. OECD, *OECD Presents Outputs of OECD/G20 BEPS Project for Discussion at G20 Finance Ministers Meeting*, http://www.oecd.org/tax/oecd-presents-outputs-of-oecd-g20-beps-project-for-discussion-at-g20-finance-ministers-meeting.htm (October 5, 2015).
21. *Explanatory Statement*, supra note 8, at 6.
22. *Ibid.*, at 9.
23. OECD, OECD/G20 Base Erosion and Profit Shifting Project: Preventing the Granting of Treaty Benefits in Inappropriate Circumstances, Action 6: 2015 Final Report, http://dx.doi.org/10.1787/9789264241695-en (2015), [hereinafter Action 6: 2015 Final Report].
24. Summary of BEPS, *supra* note 2, at 21.
25. *Action 6: 2015 Final Report*, supra note 23, at 91.
26. *Ibid.*, at 9; *see also* Summary of BEPS, *supra* note 2, at 21. ("The LOB conditions, which are generally based upon the legal nature, ownership in, and activities of the entity, seek to ensure that there is a sufficient connection between the entity and the country of residence.")
27. *Action 6: 2015 Final Report*, supra note 23, at 9. The report also recommends targeted rules for inclusion in tax treaties to address other forms of treaty abuse such as "certain dividend transfer transactions, real property transactions, dual-resident companies, and structures intended to arbitrage varying definitions of what constitutes a permanent establishment." *Summary of BEPS*, supra note 2, at 22.

strengths and weaknesses."[28] Furthermore, combining the two rules may not be appropriate for all countries given the domestic law of some countries.[29]

[B] Action 13: Transfer Pricing Documentation and Country-by-Country Reporting

The Final Action 13 report rewrites Chapter V of the OECD transfer pricing guidelines, addressing documentation, in order to ensure that taxpayers consider the appropriate transfer pricing requirements when establishing prices for transactions between related entities and reporting the respective income on their tax returns.[30] The idea is to give tax administrations a global picture of where the taxes, profits, and economic activities of MNCs are being reported. The new documentation rules should provide tax administrations with the information necessary to conduct transfer pricing risk assessments and thorough audits of the transfer pricing practices of the entities subject to tax in their jurisdictions.[31]

The Action 13 report develops rules for transfer pricing documentation including a common template to be used by the MNCs to provide relevant "information on their global allocation of the income, economic activity, and taxes paid among countries."[32] The OECD recommends three documents (a master file,[33] a local file,[34] and a CbC report[35]) that will "require taxpayers to articulate consistent transfer pricing positions."[36]

The master file will give an overview of the MNC's global business operations whereas the "local file provides detailed information relating to specific intercompany

---

28. *Action 6: 2015 Final Report, supra* note 23, at 10.
29. *Ibid.; see also Summary of BEPS, supra* note 2, at 22. ("The report describes changes to the OECD Model treaty aimed at ensuring that treaties do not inadvertently prevent the application of domestic anti-abuse rules as well as a clear statement that the countries intend to deny treaty benefits in circumstances involving abusive transactions.")
30. OECD, OECD/G20 Base Erosion and Profit Shifting Project: Transfer Pricing Documentation and Country-by-Country Reporting, Action 13: 2015 Final Report 14, http://dx.doi.org/10.1787/9789264241480-en (2015), [hereinafter Action 13: 2015 Final Report].
31. *Ibid.*
32. *Ibid.*, at 9.
33. *Ibid.*, at 14–15; *see also Summary of BEPS, supra* note 2, at 30. The master file "is intended to provide tax administrations with high-level information regarding the global business operations and transfer pricing policies of the multinational enterprise group's transfer pricing practices. The master file information ... contains relevant information in five categories: (1) organizational structure; (2) description of the business or businesses; (3) intangibles; (4) intercompany financial activities; and (5) financial and tax positions."
34. *Action 13: 2015 Final Report, supra* note 30, at 15; *see also Summary of BEPS, supra* note 2, at 30. The local file "will identify material related party transactions, the amounts involved in those transactions, and the company's analysis of the transfer pricing determinations made with regard to those transactions."
35. *Action 13: 2015 Final Report, supra* note 30, at 16; *see also Summary of BEPS, supra* note 2, at 30–31. "The country-by-country report requires aggregate tax jurisdiction-wide information relating to the global allocation of the income, the taxes paid, and certain indicators of the location of economic activity among tax jurisdictions in which" the MNC does business.
36. Summary of BEPS, *supra* note 2, at 30.

transactions."[37] The annual CbC report will provide, for each jurisdiction in which the MNC operates, "the amount of revenue, profit before income tax, income tax paid and accrued... their number of employees, stated capital, retained earnings, and tangible assets."[38] It applies only to MNCs with annual consolidated group revenue equal to or exceeding EUR 750 million[39] (or approximately USD 850 million) and requires the MNC to identify each entity within the group doing business in a particular tax jurisdiction and an indication of its business activities. The CbC reporting requirements are effective for fiscal years beginning on or after January 1, 2016.[40]

§12.03 U.S. RESPONSE TO THE BEPS PROJECT

As a member of both the OECD and the G20, the U.S. has actively engaged in the BEPS Project. Concerns had been expressed by a number of U.S. policymakers that aggressive tax planning by some taxpayers has resulted in inappropriate erosion of the U.S. tax base as well as substantial shifting of income to low-tax jurisdictions.[41] The Joint Committee on Taxation (JCT) has determined that the average tax rate of U.S.-controlled foreign corporations has declined from 26% in 1998 to 10.6% in 2012.[42] Professor Clausing has estimated that profit shifting cost the U.S. government between USD 77 and USD 111 billion in 2012, a substantial increase from recent years.[43] The OECD's 2015 report on measuring BEPS found that worldwide annual tax revenue losses from aggressive tax planning range from USD 100 billion to USD 240 billion.[44]

The JCT has stated that with respect to corporate taxation, "both U.S. and foreign MNCs are potentially implicated in engaging in behavior resulting in BEPS."[45] Concern over BEPS is influencing the ongoing discussion on reform of the U.S. international tax system. For example, the Treasury Department's revenue proposals for fiscal years 2015, 2016, and 2017 have each included a number of proposals, such as restricting the use of hybrid entities and securities and the deduction of excessive interest expense, which are broadly consistent with the recommendations of the various BEPS Project action recommendations.[46]

---

37. Ibid.
38. Action 13: 2015 Final Report, supra note 30, at 9.
39. Ibid., at 10; see also OECD, OECD/G20 Base Erosion and Profit Shifting Project: Mandatory Disclosure Rules, Action 12: 2015 Final Report, http://dx.doi.org/10.1787/9789264241442-en (2015).
40. Action 13: 2015 Final Report, supra note 30, at 10. Countries participating in the BEPS Project are to review the implementation of the new standards and to reassess by the end of 2020 whether modifications to the content of the reports should be made to require reporting of additional or different data. Ibid.
41. Summary of BEPS, supra note 2, at 33.
42. Ibid.
43. Kimberly Clausing, The Effect of Profit Shifting on the Corporate Tax Base in the United States and Beyond, 1, (2015) (on file with author).
44. OECD, OECD/G20 Measuring and Monitoring BEPS: Action 11: 2015 Final Report, 104–105, http://dx.doi.org/10.1787/9789264241480-en,??fix (2015).
45. Summary of BEPS, supra note 2, at 33.
46. Ibid., at 41. ("These proposals address hybrid arrangements, the digital economy, manufacturing services arrangements, excessive U.S. interest deductions, and corporate inversions."); see

Chapter 12: U.S. Tax Sovereignty and the BEPS Project §12.03

Members of the U.S. Senate Finance Committee and the U.S. House of Representatives Ways and Means Tax Policy Subcommittee have expressed concerns about the impact of the BEPS recommendations on U.S. multinationals and held hearings on December 1, 2015 with respect to this issue.[47] House Ways and Means Tax Policy Subcommittee Chairman Paul Boustany complained about the limited input accepted from Congress throughout the process stating that "[the] OECD's BEPS project recommendations are...[an] aggressive attempt to impose substantial tax policy changes on the international community under the guise of eliminating so-called 'harmful tax practices'...."[48] Boustany went on to explain that:

> The OECD's BEPS project was intended to target limited, overly aggressive tax planning that resulted in inappropriate tax avoidance...[such as] "cash boxes" – i.e., shell companies with few employees or economic activities and which are subject to no or low taxes. However, the project quickly morphed into a fundamental rewrite of global tax practices, including those of the United States, in an opaque process outside the reach of the U.S. political process.[49]

Chairman Hatch of the Senate Finance Committee also complained that "[w]hile the U.S. was a party to the BEPS negotiations, Congress had neither a seat at the negotiating table nor a meaningful opportunity to weigh in...."[50] However, as U.S. Treasury deputy assistant secretary (international tax affairs) Robert Stack testified before the Senate Finance Committee, "Our active participation is crucial to protecting our own tax base from erosion by multinational companies, much of which occurs as a result of exploiting tax regime differences."[51] Using two BEPS Action Plan examples, I demonstrate below that the tax policy and business interests of the U.S. were extremely well represented in the OECD international tax policy deliberations.

---

also U.S. Department of the Treasury, *General Explanations of the Administration's Fiscal Year 2015 Revenue Proposals*, 61, https://www.treasury.gov/resource-center/tax-policy/Documents/General-Explanations-FY2015.pdf (2014); U.S. Department of the Treasury, *General Explanations of the Administration's Fiscal Year 2016 Revenue Proposals*, 35–36, https://www.treasury.gov/resource-center/tax-policy/Documents/General-Explanations-FY2016.pdf (2015); U.S. Department of the Treasury, *General Explanations of the Administration's Fiscal Year 2017 Revenue Proposals*, 25–26, https://www.treasury.gov/resource-center/tax-policy/Documents/General-Explanations-FY2017.pdf (2016).

47. U.S. Senate Committee on Finance, *International Tax: OECD, BEPS, and EU State Aid*, http://www.finance.senate.gov/hearings/international-tax-oecd-beps-and-eu-state-aid (December 1, 2015); *see also* U.S. House Committee on Ways and Means, *Chairman Boustany Opening Statement: Examining the OECD Base Erosion and Profit Shifting (BEPS) Project*, https://waysandmeans.house.gov/chairman-boustany-opening-statement-examining-the-oecd-base-erosion-and-profit-shifting-beps-project/ (December 1, 2015).
48. *Ibid.*
49. *Ibid.*
50. U.S. Senate Committee on Finance, *Hatch Statement at Finance Hearing on OECD BEPS Reports*, http://www.finance.senate.gov/imo/media/doc/12.1.15%20RELEASE%20Hatch%20Statement%20at%20Finance%20Hearing%20on%20OECD%20BEPS%20Reports.pdf (December 1, 2015).
51. U.S. Senate Committee on Finance, *Testimony of Robert B. Stack, Deputy Assistant Secretary (International Tax Affairs)*, http://www.finance.senate.gov/imo/media/doc/01dec2015Stack.pdf (December 1, 2015).

[A] CbC Reporting

The Internal Revenue Service (IRS) released final regulations on CbC reporting for U.S. MNCs on June 30, 2016.[52] These final regulations are modeled on the OECD recommendations for CbC reporting under Action 13 of the OECD BEPS project.[53] Under the CbC final regulations, the parent of a U.S. MNC group with annual revenue of USD 850 million or more must file Form 8975, "Country-by-Country Report," containing certain information, on a CbC basis, related to the U.S. MNC group's income and taxes paid as well as various indicia of economic activity within the U.S. MNC group.[54] U.S. Treasury deputy assistant secretary Stack reported that between 1,600 and 1,800 U.S. MNCs will meet the revenue threshold and be subject to U.S. CbC reporting rules.[55]

Stack had previously objected to the OECD's draft CbC reporting standards, stating that they required too much information from multinationals.[56] "My own instinct is that the template that came out is probably too many columns for what the risk assessment needs to be," Stack said. He stressed that tax authorities only needed "a few high-level data points, namely income, taxes, and revenues, and maybe the number of employees and the property, plant, and equipment in a particular country."[57] The OECD's discussion draft had called for detailed CbC reporting of financial and tax information for each entity organized in the country.[58] In particular, the draft CbC template had required the following information: (1) place of effective management; (2) important business activity codes; (3) revenues; (4) earnings before income tax; (5) income tax paid on a cash basis (a) to the country of organization; and (b) to all other countries; (6) total withholding tax paid; (7) stated capital and accumulated earnings; (8) number of employees; (9) total employee expense; (10) tangible assets other than cash and cash equivalents; (11) royalties paid between associated entities; (12) interest paid between associated entities; and (13) service fees paid between associated entities.[59]

---

52. Internal Revenue Service; Country-by-Country Reporting; 81 Fed. Reg. 42482 (June 30, 2016) (codified as 26 C.F.R. Pt. 1), [hereinafter CbC Final Regulations]. The Final Regulations apply to the reporting periods of the parent corporations of U.S. MNC groups that begin on or after the first day of the tax year of the parent corporation that begins on or after June 30, 2016.
53. See Action 13: 2015 Final Report, supra note 30.
54. Treas. Reg. section 1.6038-4(a). See also the preamble to CbC Final Regulations at section 14 ("The reporting threshold of $850,000,000 in the proposed regulation was determined by reference to the USD equivalent of €750,000,000 on January 1, 2015, as provided in the Final BEPS Report.")
55. Julie Martin, U.S. Tax Officials Discuss 2016 BEPS Agenda, Country-by-Country Reporting, EU State Aid Controversy, http://mnetax.com/us-tax-officials-beps-state-aid-13068-13068 (January 21, 2016).
56. Deloitte, *U.S. Official Says OECD Reporting Draft Asks for Too Much Specificity*, https://www2.deloitte.com/content/dam/Deloitte/kr/Documents/tax/tax-newsletter/2014/kr_tax_global-tax-alerts_us_01_20140320.pdf (2014).
57. Ibid.
58. OECD, *Discussion Draft on Transfer Pricing Documentation and CbC Reporting*, 5, https://www.oecd.org/tax/transfer-pricing/discussion-draft-transfer-pricing-documentation.pdf (January 30, 2014).
59. Ibid. at 18–20.

Chapter 12: U.S. Tax Sovereignty and the BEPS Project §12.03[A]

U.S. business interests complained about the costs of complying with such burdensome requirements.[60] It is widely understood that the U.S. was instrumental in the resulting reduction in information that was eventually required by the OECD. Stack noted that the OECD will reexamine CbC reporting in 2020 in exchange for the reduction of the number of items on the CbC template stating that "countries that let us get away with fewer items ... said we should come back if it doesn't do enough."[61] The OECD will revisit the guidelines to determine their effectiveness and whether to require the transactional reporting of payments of royalties, interest, and service fees between associated entities as laid out in its initial discussion draft.[62]

Form 8975, patterned after the OECD template, will require the following information with respect to each entity in the U.S. MNC group: (i) the legal name; (ii) the jurisdiction for tax residence purposes; (iii) the tax jurisdiction in which the entity is organized or incorporated; (iv) the tax identification number; and (v) the main business activity or activities of the entity.[63] The return must also include aggregated information on revenues; profit or loss before income tax; total income tax paid on a cash basis or accrued to all tax jurisdictions, and any taxes withheld on payments received by the respective entities; stated capital; total accumulated earnings; total number of employees on a full-time equivalent basis; and the net book value of tangible assets with respect to each tax jurisdiction in which one or more entities of the U.S. MNC group is resident.[64]

The CbC reports will be filed with the IRS and exchanged with the appropriate jurisdictions pursuant to competent authority agreements. The preamble to the final regulations points out in section 1 that this results in the filed return benefiting from all the "confidentiality requirements, data safeguards, and appropriate use restrictions" that are found in the respective competent authority agreement.[65] Furthermore, should a foreign tax jurisdiction fail to meet these requirements, safeguards, and use restrictions, the U.S. will stop exchanges of all reports with that tax jurisdiction.[66] Using competent authority agreements to exchange the CbC reports was also the method of exchange preferred by the US.[67]

---

60. *See* e.g., Deloitte, *supra* note 56.
61. Kristen A. Parillo, *Stack Provides Insights on BEPS Reports*, 144 Tax Notes 1367 (September 22, 2014).
    Robert Stack, U.S. Treasury deputy assistant secretary (international tax affairs) further stated during the Deloitte Tax LLP webcast on BEPS Reports that "we can come back and see if it's working for you, but we want to be able to build in there some kind of accountability for how countries make use of that information."
62. *Action 13: 2015 Final Report*, *supra* note 30, at 10.
63. Treas. Reg. section 1.6038-4(d)(1).
64. Treas. Reg. section 1.6038-4(d)(2). There are also special requirements for permanent establishments. For example, "accumulated earnings of a permanent establishment must be reported by the legal entity of which it is a permanent establishment." Treas. Reg. section 1.6038-4(d)(2)(vii).
65. CbC Final Regulations, *supra* note 52, at Preamble section 1.
66. *Ibid*.
67. *See* e.g., Deloitte, *supra* note 56. ("Speaking at the Tax Council Policy Institute's annual Tax Policy and Practice Symposium in Washington, Stack said the second big issue with the reporting standards is how the information gets transmitted. 'We tend to favour the government-to-government exchange for reasons of confidentiality,' Stack said.")

[B] Treaty Abuse Limitations

For over two decades, U.S. tax treaty policy has required the inclusion of a LOB clause in any negotiated tax treaty.[68] These objective rules are intended to prevent the treaty shopping that occurs when "an investor from a third country routes investment into the United States through a company resident in a treaty partner" without the necessary nexus to the income attempting to benefit from that treaty.[69] These LOB clauses preclude the U.S. from inadvertently negotiating a "treaty with the world."[70] However, the OECD Discussion draft released on March 14, 2014 proposed that countries should not only include in tax treaties a specific anti-abuse rule based on the U.S. style LOB provisions[71] but also a more general anti-abuse rule.[72] This general anti-abuse rule would incorporate a PPT, also known as a main purpose test, into tax treaties.[73]

U.S. practitioners and business representatives had "concerns over the layers of rules" being proposed, believing that they would "add considerable complexity, cost, and uncertainty."[74] Many commentators thought that the OECD Model tax convention "should provide that either a Limitation on Benefits or a General Anti-Avoidance Rule approach should be adopted, and not both."[75] The Association of Global Custodians noted that the concern about the vagueness and subjectivity of the main purpose test is what led the U.S. Senate to reject such a proposed "test in a pending U.S. treaty over 10 years ago and to mandate that no future U.S. treaties contain such a provision."[76]

---

68. U.S. Department of the Treasury, *Preamble to 2016 U.S. Model Income Tax Convention* 4 (February 17, 2016).
69. Ibid.
70. Richard Doernberg, *International Taxation in a Nutshell* 149 (8th ed. West 2009).
71. OECD, *Public Discussion Draft, BEPS Action 6: Preventing the Granting of Treaty Benefits in Inappropriate Circumstances*, 5, https://www.oecd.org/tax/treaties/treaty-abuse-discussion-draft-march-2014.pdf (March 14, 2014 – April 9, 2014) ("Such a specific rule will address a large number of treaty shopping situations based on the legal nature, ownership in, and general activities of, residents of a Contracting State.")
72. Ibid. ("in order to address other forms of treaty abuse, including treaty shopping situations that would not be covered by the specific anti-abuse rule ... (such as certain conduit financing arrangements)").
73. See Ibid. ("That rule will incorporate into tax treaties the principles already reflected in ... the Commentary to Article 1, according to which the benefits of a tax treaty should not be available where one of the main purposes of arrangements or transactions is to secure a benefit under a tax treaty and obtaining that benefit... would be contrary to the object and purpose of the relevant provisions of the tax treaty...").
74. See e.g., The Business Industry and Advisory Committee to the OECD (BIAC), *OECD Discussion Draft on BEPS Action 6: Granting of Treaty Benefits in Inappropriate Circumstances*, 2, http://biac.org/wp-content/uploads/2015/01/2014-04-BIAC-Comments-on-the-OECD-Discussion-Draft-on-BEPS-Action-6-Preventing-the-Granting-of-Tax-Benefits.pdf (April 9, 2014); see also Business Europe, *Business Europe Comments on OECD Discussion Draft "BEPS Action 6: Preventing the Granting of Treaty Benefits in Inappropriate Circumstances" 14 March 2014 – 9 April 2014*, at 3, https://www.businesseurope.eu/sites/buseur/files/media/imported/2014-00497-E.pdf (April 9, 2014).
75. BIAC, *supra* note 74, at 2; *see also* Business Europe, *supra* note 74, at 3.
76. The Association of Global Custodians, *Re: Comments on Discussion Draft on BEPS Action 6: Preventing the Granting of Treaty Benefits in Inappropriate Circumstances*, (April 9, 2014) (on file with The Association of Global Customs at http://www.theagc.com/Ltr.%20to%20Marlies%20de%20Ruiter%20dated%20April%209,%202014%20re%20AGC%20Comment%20Letter%20on%20Tax%20Treaty%20Abuse%20DD%20(2).pdf).

Thus, the U.S. Senate is on record as opposing the main purpose test. The U.S. Treasury Department's position is that main purpose and principle purpose tests are too subjective.[77] The concern is that this subjectivity allows "governments the authority to deny income tax treaty benefits to otherwise legitimate business transactions that were not meant to be covered."[78]

The Treasury Department released proposed changes to the 2006 U.S. Model Income Tax Convention on May 20, 2015.[79] The U.S. Model is Treasury's starting point for its negotiations with the tax treaty partners of the U.S.[80] The timing of this release was intended to affect the OECD discussions on BEPS Action 6: Preventing the Granting of Treaty Benefits in Inappropriate Circumstances as well the negotiations with respect to the new multilateral instrument that would implement these changes.[81] In fact, the OECD noted in the October 2015 Final Report for Action 6 that "additional work will be required in order to fully consider" the LOB proposals released by the U.S. in May 2015 in connection with updating its model treaty.[82]

In February 2016, the U.S. Treasury Department finalized the new 2016 U.S. Model Income Tax Convention ("2016 US Model").[83] One of Treasury's stated purposes for the release of this new U.S. Model, was to incorporate certain policy considerations of the OECD's BEPS initiative.[84] For example, the 2016 U.S. Model incorporates "[a] revised preamble for tax treaties that makes clear the intentions of the treaty partners that the purpose of a tax treaty is the elimination of double taxation with respect to taxes on income without creating opportunities for non-taxation or reduced taxation through tax evasion or avoidance."[85] However, the preamble to the 2016 U.S. Model emphasizes that U.S. tax treaty policy has for over two decades incorporated several of

---

77. Parillo, *supra* note 61, at 2.
78. BASF, Re: Comments on OECD Discussion Draft on BEPS Action 6: Preventing the Granting of Treaty Benefits in Inappropriate Circumstances, (April 9, 2014). ("Our aversions to the proposed subjective main purpose test include a) greater transactional uncertainty, b) reduced treaty reliance, and c) increased competent authority dependence.") (on file with OECD at http://www.oecd.org/tax/treaties/comments-action-6-prevent-treaty-abuse.pdf).
79. U.S. Department of the Treasury, *Treasury Releases Select Draft Provisions for Next U.S. Model Income Tax Treaty*, (May 20, 2015) (on file with the Treasury at https://www.treasury.gov/press-center/press-releases/Pages/jl10057.aspx).
80. *Ibid.*
81. "The Proposed Changes were designed to 'influence the debate at the OECD', according to Henry Louie, a U.S. Treasury Department official." DLA Piper, *Putting the final BEPS reports into perspective: from recommendations to implementation Tax Update* October 14, 2015, https://www.dlapiper.com/en/us/insights/publications/2015/10/putting-the-final-beps-reports-into-perspective/ (accessed January 30, 2017). The OECD adopted the Multilateral Convention to Implement Tax Treaty Related Measures to Prevent Base Erosion and Profit Shifting on November 24, 2016. J.P. Finet, *The OECD Adopts Multilateral Instrument*, 84 Tax Notes Int'l 879, 879 (2016).
82. *Action 6: 2015 Final Report*, *supra* note 23, at 11. *See also Summary of BEPS*, *supra* note 2, at 22.
83. U.S. Department of the Treasury, *Treasury Announces Release of 2016 U.S. Model Income Tax Treaty*, (February 17, 2016) (on file with the Treasury at https://www.treasury.gov/press-center/press-releases/Pages/jl0356.aspx).
84. U.S. Department of the Treasury, *Preamble to 2016 U.S. Model Income Tax Convention* 8-9 (February 17, 2016).
85. *Ibid.*

the key recommendations regarding bilateral tax treaties from the G20/OECD's BEPS initiative such as LOB provisions.[86]

The 2016 U.S. Model revises the LOB article to add a more robust base erosion test that also applies the public subsidiary test.[87] This stricter base erosion test requires that not only less than 50% of the company's gross income but also less than 50% of the tested group's income be paid in the form of deductible payments to non-qualified payees. Thus, the 2016 U.S. Model expands the base erosion test to both the tested entity as well as the entire tested group.[88] The Model also provides for a new derivative benefits test, a new headquarters company test, and a more limited active trade or business test.[89] However, the US' preference for LOB articles is not universal.[90] For example, the Confederation Fiscale Europeenne (CFE) stressed that LOB provisions based on the U.S. Model are "exceedingly complex and very difficult to administer."[91] Furthermore, the CFE doubted that the proposed LOB, as it reflects a specific legal framework, "would be useful in negotiations between countries whose legal systems do not resemble those of the US."[92] Other commentators noted that "the proposed LOB article is lengthy, containing many terms and concepts that may be fairly well understood in certain countries but not so well understood in other countries" given the limited current utilization of LOB clauses (predominately the U.S. and Japan).[93]

Nevertheless, the U.S. delegation insisted that "we do not want to have to agree to change what we do, because we like it."[94] Stack commented that "[t]he working group eventually decided that as long as countries meet a minimum standard...they can use the treaty policies that are most appropriate for them."[95] The U.S. delegation to the BEPS discussions successfully persuaded the OECD to dilute its initial proposal and "convince[d] the BEPS drafters that objective LOB clauses are a viable alternative to subjective treaty abuse clauses."[96] In the final recommendations for Action 6 released in September 16, 2014, the OECD offered its more flexible approach described in Part

---

86. U.S. Department of the Treasury, *Preamble to 2016 U.S. Model Income Tax Convention* 4, 8 (February 17, 2016).
87. U.S. Department of the Treasury, *2016 U.S. Model Income Tax Convention*, Art. 22 (February 17, 2016) [hereinafter 2016 U.S. Model]. The previous base erosion test required that less than 50% of gross income be paid to persons not entitled to treaty benefits. U.S. Department of the Treasury, *2006 U.S. Model Income Tax Convention*, art. 22 (2006).
88. *See e.g.*, 2016 U.S. Model, *supra* note 87, at Art. 22(2)(d)(ii), (2)(f)(ii), 4(b), and 5(f).
89. *Ibid.*, at Art. 22.
90. Parillo, *supra* note 61, at 2. ("The rest of the world thinks it can be under-and overinclusive," Stack said.)
91. Confederation Fiscale Europeenne, Opinion Statement FC 5/2014 of the CFE on the OECD Discussion Draft: Preventing the Granting of Treaty Benefits in Inappropriate Circumstances (BEPS Action 6), para. 5, http://www.cfe-eutax.org/sites/default/files/CFE%20Opinion%20Statement%20FC%205-2014%20on%20Tax%20Treaty%20Abuse%20(BEPS%20Action%206)_1.pdf (April 2014).
92. *Ibid.* at para. 6.
93. The Banking and Finance Company Working Group on BEPS, *Preventing the Granting of Treaty Benefits in Inappropriate Circumstances*, (April 9, 2014) (on file with the OECD at http://www.oecd.org/tax/treaties/comments-action-6-prevent-treaty-abuse.pdf).
94. Parillo, *supra* note 61, at 2.
95. *Ibid.*
96. Kristen A. Parillo, BEPS Action 6 (Treaty Abuse): U.S. Gets Its Way, 2014 WTD 180-3 (2014).

II.[97] The U.S. approach, which combines an LOB provision with domestic anti-abuse rules, satisfies the requisite minimum standard.

The OECD adopted the Multilateral Convention to Implement Tax Treaty Related Measures to Prevent BEPS[98] (the "Convention") on November 24, 2016, with a signing ceremony planned for June 2017. More than 100 jurisdictions including the U.S. and the U.K., were involved in the negotiations although it is unlikely that the U.S. will sign the Convention.[99] The Convention will allow countries to more efficiently implement the BEPS treaty recommendations, designed to curtail tax avoidance by MNCs, into their bilateral tax treaty networks.[100] It is clear that the U.S. tax treaty policy with respect to LOB has influenced the outcome of the BEPS Treaty Abuse work.[101] The Simplified LOB provision that is found at Article 7 of the Convention is based on the U.S. LOB provisions.[102]

§12.04 CONCLUSION

The G20/OECD BEPS Project is an ambitious project whose objective is to end double non-taxation and realign the location of profits to the countries where the actual economic activity is taking place. This has required negotiation and consensus building between the OECD and G20 countries over the last three years. The base erosion profit shifting (BEPS) problem was not going to disappear of its own accord and countries were beginning to enact unilateral solutions to this problem. Although some in the U.S. saw the BEPS Project as a threat to U.S. tax sovereignty, I take the position that this project was necessary in order for the U.S. to effectively wield its tax sovereignty. By examining the negotiations that yielded improvements to the OECD Model Tax Convention with respect to preventing treaty abuse and to the transfer pricing documentation rules, I conclude that U.S. tax sovereignty was enhanced through the G20/OECD BEPS project.

---

97. OECD, OECD/G20 Base Erosion and Profit Shifting Project: Preventing the Granting of Treaty Benefits in Inappropriate Circumstances, Action 6: 2014 Deliverable, 11, http://dx.doi.org/10.1787/9789264219120-en (2014).
98. OECD, *Multilateral Convention to Implement Tax Treaty Related Measures to Prevent Base Erosion and Profit Shifting*, http://www.oecd.org/tax/treaties/multilateral-convention-to-implement-tax-treaty-related-measures-to-prevent-BEPS.pdf (2016) [hereinafter Convention].
99. OECD press release, *Multilateral Convention to Implement Tax Treaty Related Measures to Prevent BEPS*, http://www.oecd.org/tax/treaties/multilateral-convention-to-implement-tax-treaty-related-measures-to-prevent-beps.htm (2016).
100. Kevin Bell, *U.S. Unlikely to Sign Multilateral Tax Treaty*, 231 Daily Tax Report I-3 (2016) (Bloomberg BNA).
101. *See* Jonathon Schwarz, *US Model Treaty 2016: What does it say about the US and BEPS*, http://kluwertaxblog.com/2016/02/21/us-model-treaty-2016-what-does-it-say-about-the-us-and-beps/ (accessed January 1, 2017).
102. Convention, *supra* note 98, at Art. 8.

Index

A

Abuse (avoidance)
   and BEPS mispricing, 233
   common-law principles, 184
   deferral of tax on foreign income, 108
   domestic anti-abuse rules, 83, 291
   form of, 232
   mean tax, 218
   PE definition, 112, 113
   perceived, 126
   tax base erosion, 259
   tax treaties, 239
   threshold, 195
Aggressive tax planning, 116, 182, 187, 193, 194, 197–200, 232, 246, 268, 280, 281, 284, 285
ALP. See Arm's Length Principle (ALP)
Anti-Avoidance Rule approach, 288
Anti-tax avoidance, 90, 247, 252, 276
Argentine Income Tax Law in 2003, 133
Arm's Length Principle (ALP), 102–104, 114, 115, 128, 132, 141, 193, 203, 204, 216–220, 222–225, 228, 229, 231, 232, 235, 237–239, 241, 242
ATAD Directive
   exit tax rules, 258–259
   GAAR, 259–260
   measures, 258
   switch-over clause, 260–261

B

Base erosion and profit shifting (BEPS)
   action plans (see BEPS action plans)
   best practices, 173
   minimum standards, 173
   project (see BEPS project)
   recommendations (see BEPS recommendations in EU)
   sovereignty (see Sovereignty)
   tax power (see Taxing powers and BEPS)
BEPS action plans
   dispute resolution, 270–271
   domestic law provisions and ATAD, 252–261
   harmful tax practices, 261
   limitation of benefits (LoB) clause, 264
   mandatory disclosure rules, 267–268
   measuring and monitoring, 267
   multilateral instrument (MLI), 271
   OECD Model Tax Convention, 265, 270, 273
   prevention, 264–266
   principal purpose test (PPT), 265
   recommendations
      in EU (see BEPS recommendations in EU)
      OECD BEPS, 244–245, 262, 265, 266
   tax challenges, digital economy (see Digital economy)

Index

transfer pricing
  outcomes, 266–267
  requirements, documentation, 268–270
BEPS project
  sovereign tax policies, 280
  U.S. responses
    CbC reporting, 286–287
    treaty abuse limitations, 288–291
BEPS recommendations in EU
  action plans (*see* BEPS action plans)
  aggressive tax planning, 246
  CCCTB proposal, 246
  EU/BEPS work programme, 246
  EU Member States, 243–245, 276–278
  EU tax policy process, 245
  functions, EU Commission, 244–246
  implementation, 243, 244, 246, 276–278
  interest-royalty Directive (IRD), 246
  intermediaries and service providers, 244
  issues
    beneficial ownership information, 276
    code of conduct activities, 274
    governance standards and transparency, 274–276
    Interest Royalty Directive, 273
    Parent-Subsidiary Directive, 271–272
  OECD BEPS project, 244, 250, 268, 276
  stakeholder, 244, 245
  tax legislation, 245
Bilateral tax treaties
  CEN (*see* Capital export neutrality (CEN))
  CIN (*see* Capital import neutrality (CIN))
  CON (*see* Capital ownership neutrality (CON))
Bit tax on digital transactions, 42

Business
  activities, 39–41, 99, 280, 284, 286, 287
  and civil society, 106
  coordinated operations, 103
  customers, 250
  enterprise, 187, 235
  income, 51, 98, 99, 125–130, 137–139, 141, 189, 209
  jurisdictions
  location, 37
  manifestations, 125
  models, 29, 30, 40, 107, 135, 147, 199, 218, 226, 248
  opportunities, 108
  owners, 25
  profits, 16, 38, 39, 57, 129, 189, 196, 218, 219
  purposes, 131
  sagacity, 11
  taxable, 117, 250, 252
  tax rules, 38
  traditional, 40

C

Capital export neutrality (CEN), 52, 119
Capital import neutrality (CIN), 52, 119
Capital ownership neutrality (CON), 56, 119
Collective investment vehicles (CIVs), 112
Committee on Fiscal Affairs (CFA), 144, 281
Common Consolidated Corporate Tax Base (CCCTB), 220, 224, 230, 238, 239, 241, 242, 246, 250
Compliance
  collection, 159
  enforcement, 34
  slippery slope framework, 206
Confederation Fiscale Europeenne (CFE), 290
Consensus
  free market, 58

political, 252
WHT, 34
Consumption taxation, digital goods
  characteristics, 143, 150–152
  definition, 150–151
  design issues and sovereignty
    intra-jurisdictional reach (*see*
      Intra-jurisdictional reach)
    tax collection, 159–161
  sovereignty concept, 155indirect tax
    purposes (*see* Indirect tax)
  intangible goods, 150
  legal framework
    Australia, 148–149
    EU, 145–148
    New Zealand, 149–150
Controlled Foreign Companies (CFC), 91
Controlled foreign corporation
  Brazilian tax law
    abuses of tax deferral, 126
    avoiding double taxation, 128
    BEPS Draft Report, 129
    business income, 125–130
    Código Tributário Nacional (CTN),
      Art. 43, 126
    constitutionality, 128
    double taxation treaties (DTTs), 127
    Economic Administrative Court of
      the Nation (CARF), 127
    foreign subsidiary, 127
    jurisdiction, 125, 127
    legal personality of foreign entities,
      126
    level of taxation, 126, 139
    Medida Provisoria (MP), Art. 74,
      126
    MP 627/13, 129
    non-privileged foreign jurisdiction,
      126
    OECD Model Convention, 126
    Supremo Tribunal Federal (STF),
      128
    taxation, business income,
      125–129, 137–139, 141
    Vale case, 128, 129

rule, 126
Country-by-Country Over-Reporting
  (CBCR). *See also* Sovereignty
  ALP, 203, 204, 223–225, 228, 229,
    231, 232, 237–239, 241, 242
  BEPS Actions, 201–203, 225, 226, 228,
    229, 237, 242
  Developing Countries, 202–204,
    223–225, 227, 237–238
  GFA *vs.* ALP, 204, 239
  implementation, 202–204, 221, 224,
    227, 233, 234, 241–242
  inclusive framework, 203–204
  international agreements, 202
  MNEs, 204, 227, 230, 232, 238, 240,
    241
  requirement, 166–177
  social responsibility (*see* Social
    responsibility in tax activism)
  tax transparency, pre-BEPS (*see*
    Pre-BEPS tax transparency)
  transfer pricing
    and Global Forum (*see* Transfer
      pricing and tax transparency)
    and post-BEPS, 228–234
  reform, 204
  transparency standards, 202
Country by Country (CbC) reporting,
  U.S. MNCs, 281, 287
Court of Justice of the European Union
  (CJEU), 153, 154, 259, 264, 265,
  271

D

Developing countries' international tax
  regime, 196–198, 200
Digital economy
  BEPS, 136, 137
  business models, 135
  and enforcement jurisdiction, 44–46
  equalization levy, 135–138
  erosion and profit-shifting, 135
  gross-basis final withholding tax, 136,
    137

Index

OECD's efforts, 135
and substantive jurisdiction
   bit tax, 42
   consumer market, 42
   e-commerce, 44
   permanent establishment (PE), 38–40
   residence taxation and source taxation, 38
   WHT, 40–42
tax challenges
   direct taxes, 248–250
   indirect taxes, 250–252
   jurisdictions, 248
U.K. DPT, 137, 138
VAT, 138
Digital goods taxation
   Australia, 148–149
   European Union, 145–148
   New Zealand, 149–150
Direct tax, 70, 136, 137, 248–250, 276, 277
Dispute resolution mechanisms, 88–89, 299
Diverged Profit Tax (DPT), UK, 137
Domestic law and ATAD
   adoption, 252
   ATAD Directive, 258–261
   CFC rules, 254–256
   hybrid mismatch effects, 253–254
   interest deferral rule, 256–257
   international double non-taxation, 253
   international tax avoidance, 253
   limitation, interest deductibility, 256–257
   provisions, 252
Double taxation, 6–9, 16, 17, 31, 38, 49, 50, 57, 65, 83, 84, 101, 109, 127, 128, 132, 134, 139, 179, 181, 195, 245, 247, 255, 259, 270, 271, 279, 280, 289
Double Tax Conventions (DTCs), 65, 181, 195, 196
Double tax treaties, 250–252

E

Earnings Before Interest, Taxes, Depreciation and Amortization (EBIDTA)
   Art. 4, ATAD Directive, 256
   capacity, 257
   carry forward rules, 256
   group ratio rule, 256
   limitation, 256, 257
   safe-harbour rules, 257
   tax exempt income, 256–257
   taxpayer's, EBIT, 256, 257
EBIDTA. *See* Earnings Before Interest, Taxes, Depreciation and Amortization (EBIDTA)
EITI. *See* Extractives Industries Transparency Initiative (EITI); Extractives industries transparency initiative (EITI)
Electronically supplied services, 145, 152, 153, 155, 251
Electronic commerce
   business models, 29
   digital economy (*See* Digital economy)
   taxation, 10,
European Union (EU)
   digital supplies/online services, 145
   place-of-supply rules, 146, 152, 156
   reverse charge mechanism, 146, 252
Extractives industries transparency initiative (EITI), 215, 216, 218

F

Finance
   crisis, 37, 66, 81, 97–100, 182, 183, 279
   financial intermediary, 34, 41
   financial transaction, 34
Financial crisis, 37, 66, 81, 97–100, 182, 183, 279
Fiscal state aid, 210
Foreign Account Tax Compliance Act (FATCA), 20–25, 67, 69, 199

Foreign direct investment (FDI), 65, 104, 121, 131, 196, 229, 239, 240
Foreign personal holding company (FPHC) rules, 122
Forum on Harmful Tax Practices (FHTP), 110, 111

G

General Anti-Avoidance Rule (GAAR), 259–260, 288
Global financial crisis, 81, 279
G20/OECD's BEPS project, 230, 231, 240, 276, 280–284, 290, 291

H

Harmful tax practices
  automatic exchange of rulings, 263–264
  code of conduct, 261–263
  OECD recommendations, BEPS Action, 261, 269
Hybrid(s)
  entities, 11, 83, 107, 231, 253, 281, 284
  instruments, 231
  mismatch arrangements, 82–86, 108, 193–194, 252–254

I

Imperial taxation
  aggressive tax planning, 182, 187, 193, 194, 198–200
  financial crisis, 182, 183, 186, 187
  fundamental tax principles, 187
  Global Forum, 186, 188
  "in dire need of tax revenues", 187
  international tax regime, 181, 184, 186, 188–198
  Magna Carta, 184–185
  MNE tax avoidance, 187
  principle of transparency, 185, 186
  "Scarlet Letter", 188
  States' tax collection, 188

taxpayers' rights, 186–188
Inclusive framework
  comprehensive BEPS Package
  developing countries, 202–204, 214–219, 223–225, 227, 235, 237–242
  G20/OECD, 228, 230, 231, 240
  jurisdictions, 211, 217, 220, 226, 227, 230, 237–239, 242
Indirect taxation
  broadcasting services, 251
  capital gains, *Vodafone* and *Sanofi Pasteur* cases, 130–132
  digital publications, 153
  electronic, 152
  electronically supplied services, 152
  EU
    CJEU, 153
    and non-EU businesses, 250–251
    VAT legislation, 252–255
  ISP, 152
  minimum human intervention, 145, 152, 155
  MOSS mechanism, 251
  non-digital services, 152
  OECD, 152
  remote services, 152
  supply rule, 250
  telecommunication, 152, 250
  VAT, 250–252
Inequality, 64, 97–100, 207
Information
  AEoI, 213, 219, 220, 237, 241, 263, 269, 275, 277
  CbC, 87
  CBCR, 111
  exchange, 21, 22, 66–69, 155, 160, 204, 239, 275
  ISP, 152
  VIES, 160
Intangible goods, 150
Interest deferral rule, 256–257
Internal Revenue Service (IRS), 124, 225, 226, 285–287

Index

International allocation of taxing rights
  action plan, 47, 60
  "fair share" payment, 47, 48, 71
  inter-nations equity (*see* Inter-nations equity)
  residence taxation
    bilateralism (*see* bilateral tax treaty)
    double tax treaties, 50–52
    value creation, 58–63
International Tax Imperialism
  arbitration, 190–192
  definition, 188
  digital economy, 194
  hybrid mismatches, 193–194
  improper use of tax treaties, 194–196
  transfer pricing, 192–193
International tax regime
  abusive tax planning, 81
  bilateral tax treaties, 78, 89–90
  CFC rules, 91
  challenges, 80, 81, 91
  competition
    framework, 80
    and harmonization, 79, 80
  competitiveness, 119–120
  conservative tax treaty law, 81
  constructive unilateralism, 123
  corporate
    expatriations, 120
    tax avoidance, 122
  country-by-country reporting, 121
  developing countries, 196–198
  EU-based multinationals, 119, 123
  fiscal devices and polices, 78
  lock-out problem, 123
  lower tax on foreign source income, 123
  multilateral current taxation, 120
  neutrality, 119
  principal, adopters improved, 122
  standardization, 78
  tax competition, FDI, 121
  tax incentives, 108, 111, 121
  US-based MNEs, 122, 123
Inter-nations equity

digital economy, 69–71
DTCs, 65
economic allegiance and neutrality, 66
information exchange, 66–69
multilateralism, 65–66
OECD, 63, 65–67, 69, 70
realistic approach, 64
Internet Service Packages (ISP), 152
Intra-jurisdictional reach
  consumption taxes, 157
  destination-based VAT system, 156–157
  destination principle, 156, 157
  digital goods consumption, 157–159
  legitimate claim, 156
  origin principle, 156
  presumptions, 157–159
  regulatory framework, 158
  tax electronic services, 158
  transaction-based assessments, 159
  VAT
    Directive (2006/112), 158
    explanatory notes, 158
    Implementing Regulation (282/2011), 157
ISP. *See* Internet Service Packages (ISP)

J

Joint Committee on Taxation (JCT), 284
Jurisdiction
  enforcement, 33–34
  hybrid mismatches, 83, 253
  sovereign state, 30–34
  substantive
    tax, 9, 29, 31, 32, 34–38, 40, 42, 43, 46, 48, 49, 61, 81, 82, 122, 125, 128, 129, 131, 134, 137–139, 141, 156, 217, 220, 227, 237, 238, 258, 260, 279, 284, 287

L

Limitation, BEPS Project
  ALP, 102–104

CBCR, 111, 116, 117
CFC rules and transfer pricing, 108
digital economy
    exacerbated BEPS risks, 106
    tax challenges, 136
    TFDE, 107
harmful tax practices, 110–111, 261–264
hybrid mismatch arrangements, 104, 107–108
inclusiveness and multilateralism, 105–106
independent entity principle, 112
informed risk assessment, 116
interest deductibility, 256–257
international tax law, 100–104, 106, 109, 111
MAP, 117
recommendations
    concerning data collection and dissemination, 116
    internal law and bilateral treaties, 107
single tax principle, 101
substance and transparency, 110
systemic tax risks, 116
tax treaty-related BEPS, multilateral instrument, 118
traditional benefit principle, 104
traditional PE definition, 112
transfer pricing
    documentation, 117
    rules, 114
treaty abuse, 288–291
Limitation-on-benefits (LOB) clauses, 264, 266

M

Mini One Stop Shop (MOSS) mechanism, 146, 147, 161, 251
Multinational corporations (MNCs), 279, 283, 284, 286, 291
Multinational enterprises (MNEs), 81, 101–105, 108–110, 112–114, 116, 117, 121–124, 128, 165, 167, 168, 192, 204, 209, 214, 216–219, 221–223, 225–227, 230–233, 235–238, 240, 241, 269, 270
Mutual agreement procedure (MAP), 88, 89, 117, 186, 191, 197, 230, 233, 246, 270, 271,

N

Neutrality
    CEN, 52–55, 57, 62, 71, 119
    CIN, 52, 53, 55, 57, 62, 119
    CON, 55–57, 119
    VAT, 154
New International Tax Framework and Developing Countries
    AOA, 168
    BEPS project, 165–170, 172
    dispute resolution and sovereignty, post-BEPS, 172–174
    double non taxation, 167, 172–174
    global implementation, BEPS, 166
    legitimacy, 166, 169, 171
    multilateralism, 165, 167, 168, 170–173, 175
    OECD and G-20 countries, 165
    principles, standards and regulating bodies, 165
    substantive/formal multilateralism, 170–172
    tax coordination and transparency, 167, 175

O

OECD Model Tax Convention, 78, 112
Offshore
    consultancy and professional services, 149
    low-taxed accumulated earnings, 123
    suppliers, 149, 150
    tax evasion, 23, 268
Organisation for Economic Co-operation and Development (OECD)

Index

BEPS Project
  G20 finance ministers, 281
  realign taxation, 281
  tax practices, 282
  transfer pricing documentation and country-by-country reporting (Action 13), 282–284
  treaty abuse, 281, 282, 289–291
  treaty benefits, inappropriate circumstances (Action 6), 282–283
CFA, 235
G-20 BEPS Project, 182
Organisation for European Economic Co-operation (OEEC), 181
Origin basis, 6, 9

P

Permanent establishment (PE)
  artificial avoidance, 107, 264
  characterization, 239
  construction, 41
  corporate tax paid, 254
  definition, 188, 254
  dependent agent, 41
  digital, 38–40, 194
  foreign entity, 254, 255
  international tax imperialism, 188, 189
  Member States, 80, 91
  OECD BEPS Project, 38–40
  profit allocation, 39
  traditional, 112, 136, 137
Post-BEPS and transfer pricing
  Authorized OECD Approach (AOA), 40, 168, 229
  BRICS and non-OECD countries, 228
  EU/EEA Member Countries, 229
  G20-OECD coalition, 228
  G20/OECD Project, 230, 231
  India, 228, 229, 241
  market-related location specific advantages, 229
  OECD, 222
  tax evasion, 218, 232
  taxpayer-to-government transparency, 230–231
  transparency instruments, 223
  UK, 220
  under-enforcement/over-implementation, anti-abuse standards, 233–234
  US, 217
Pre-BEPS tax transparency
  and general public
    corporate income taxes, 218
    corruption, 213, 214, 216, 217
    EITI, 215, 216, 218
    GFA vs. ALP, 216–217
    individual freedoms and civil liberties, 213
    limitation, 209
    MNEs, 209, 214, 216–219
    NGOs, 214
    taxpayers and governments, 213
  governments concerning tax, 207
  relationships and interactions, 205
  rules of engagement on international tax, 205
  tax authorities, 205, 206, 225, 235, 238
  and tax competition (see Tax competition, harmful)
  taxpayers, 205, 206, 213, 218, 224, 230, 232, 233, 235, 237, 238
Principal purposes test (PPT), 209

R

Reporting
  biased, 87
  CbC (see Country-by-country reporting)
  CBCR (see Country-by-Country Over-Reporting (CBCR))
  idiosyncratic, 87
  standard, 87
Residence
  consumer, 43, 145, 159, 161
  jurisdictions, 49, 99, 104, 122, 239

Index

residence-source dichotomy, 171
source-residence taxation, 170
taxation
   bilateralism (see bilateral tax treaty)
   double tax treaties, 50–52
   value creation, 49
taxpayer, 56, 67

S

Sanofi Pasteur case, 130–132
Social responsibility in tax activism
   aggregate taxpayer data, 235
   democratic rule of law, 234, 235
   donations, 235–236
   fairness and equality, 234, 235
   fundamental right to information, 234
   Global Forum, 235, 236
   MNEs, 235–237
   participation, 235, 236
   public awareness, 234
   public engagement, 236
   States rights, 234, 235
   tax competition, 236, 237
   transparency, 235
Soft law
   dispute resolution and sovereignty, 172–174
   international tax regime, 78
   lack of translations, 174
   measures, 245, 261
   and multilateral cooperation, 90
   primarily, 78
   recommendations, 167
   source, 261
Source
   expertise, 7, 111, 114
   jurisdictions, 9, 49, 99, 100, 104, 108, 119
   and residence, 9–11, 122, 197
   source-based approach, 180
   taxation, 9, 10, 38, 39, 44, 49, 51, 54, 190, 197
Sovereignty
   argument, 80, 85, 86
   Bodin's categorization, 77
   claim and BEPS
      bilateral tax treaties, 89–90
      country-by-country reporting, 86–88
      dispute resolution mechanisms, 88–90
      hybrid mismatch arrangements, 82–86
      multilateral instrument, 89–90
      Post BEPS EU action, 90–92
      transfer pricing documentation, 86–88
   concept of, 30, 33, 64, 76, 90, 145, 155
   and design issues, 155–161
   and digital economy, 29–46
   and dispute resolution, Post-BEPS fiscal action, 77
   and inter-nations equity, 63–71
   national, 30, 34, 64, 89, 201–242, 245
   notion, 75, 76, 78, 88, 92, 93
   responsibility, 75
   superior power, state, 77, 78
   and taxation, 73–93
   treaty law, 77
   US tax, 279–291
Supply/supplies/supply chain, 29, 70, 71, 144–150, 152–162, 219, 250–252

T

Tax collection, 33, 44, 46, 54, 60, 66, 159–161, 185, 188, 194, 200, 243
Tax colonization, 190
Tax competition, harmful
   erosion of corporate tax, 207–208
   Global Forum Report, 1998, 208–211
   international law, 208, 211–213, 216
   Multilateral Convention, 211, 212
   OECD Report, 208
   opaque and distortive tax policies, 211
   sanctions, 211–213
   self-serving, 210

Index

tax policies, 211–212
tax policy perspectives, 208
Tax haven, 207, 217, 218, 220, 230, 240
Taxing powers and BEPS
  control, 3, 19, 21, 24, 25, 27
  convergence theory, 4
  corporate and capital income, 4
  counter-tax evasion, 20–21
  destroy, 25–27
  exercise of power, 23–25
  FATCA, 20–25
  historical and international perspective, 3
  international taxation, 6, 15–17, 20, 21, 27
  learning, 19, 27
  multilateralism, 3, 4, 27
  OECD's initiatives, 23
  policymaking, 4, 5, 19–20
  public reactions, 5
  in 1920s
    autonomous powers, 14
    double taxation, 6, 8, 9
    economic allegiance doctrine, 10
    international diplomatic power, 8
    international tax issues, 7
    jurisdiction, 6, 8, 9, 11, 13
    League of Nations, 6, 8
    multinational corporation, 13
    "myth of ownership", 12
    nation's jurisdiction, 8
    OECD, 6, 10, 14
    right to global income tax base, 7, 10, 12
    sharing, global tax base, 6
    source of expertise, 7
    tax incentives, 10
    technical experts, 7
    trading, 12
  in 2010s
    bilateralism, 26, 27
    corporation 14, 18, 19
    cross-border activities, 16
    determination of nationality, 18
    economic consequences, double taxation, 7, 16
    enforceability, 18
    global tax reform, 15
    jurisdiction, 16–18, 22, 24
    non-taxation of multinationals, 17
    OECD, 15–18
    technical rules, 17
    unilateralism, 20, 26, 27
    U.S. taxpayers, 21
Tax jurisdiction
  customary law, 34–36
  international law
    formal territoriality, 33–34
    material territoriality, 31–33
  OECD, 37
Tax sovereignty
  e-commerce, 29
  jurisdiction (*See* Tax jurisdiction)
  post-BEPS times, 29–46
Tax transparency
  pre-BEPS (*see* Pre-BEPS tax transparency)
  social responsibility in tax activism, 235
  standards, 202
  and tax coordination, 167
  and transfer pricing (*see* Transfer pricing and transparency)
Technology
  economy, 69, 136, 145, 152
  evolution, 143
  information, 29, 40
Transfer pricing
  critiques, 192
  documentation
    and country-by-country reporting, 86–88
    revising requirements, 268–270
  and Global Forum, 219–228
  guidelines, 113, 114, 132, 266, 281, 283
  "imperial taxation" and "international tax imperialism", 179–200

Latin America
   ALP, 132, 133
   Argentine law, 133
   Brazilian system, 134
   commodities, 133, 134, 139
   comparable uncontrolled price method, 132
   cost plus method, 132
   cross border commodity transactions, 133
   double taxation risk, 132, 134
   guidelines, 132–134
   income, commodity exporters, 132–135
   OECD, 132–134
   resale price method, 132
   Sixth Method, 133
   transactional net margin method, 132
   transactional profit split method, 132
  methods, 114, 125, 216, 238
  and tax transparency (*see* Transfer pricing and tax transparency)
  value creation, EU, 266
Transfer pricing and tax transparency
  and post-BEPS
   CBCR, 228–234
   enforcement, 233–234
   GFA, 228, 230
   OECD, 228–231, 233
   UK tax system, 228
  redundancies, 219–223
Treaties
  abuse limitations, 288–291
  tax treaties, 18, 20, 36, 38, 40, 50–52, 61, 65, 70, 78, 83, 89–92, 99, 117, 160, 171, 180, 191, 194–196, 198, 209–212, 226, 237, 239, 247, 264–266, 271, 288–290
  TFEU, 248

U

United Nations Tax Committee, 106
UN Model Convention, 40, 160, 189, 191, 197
2016 U.S. Model Income Tax Convention (2016 US Model), 289

V

Value
  allocation, 281
  creation, 49, 58–63, 71, 82, 98, 100, 107, 113, 115, 165, 168, 170, 229, 266, 282
  and interests, 191
  measurement, 61
Value added tax (VAT)
  Directive (2006/112), 152–153
  Explanatory Notes, 146, 147, 152, 157
  goods and services tax (VAT/GST) guidelines, 144
  Implementing Regulation (282/2011), 146, 147, 152, 157
  VIES, 160
VAT. *See* Value added tax (VAT)
VAT Information Exchange System (VIES), 160
Vodafone case, 35, 131
Voluntary disclosure, 267–268

W

Withholding income tax (WHT), 34, 40–42
World Bank, 167, 168, 219

SERIES ON INTERNATIONAL TAXATION

1. Alberto Xavier, *The Taxation of Foreign Investment in Brazil*, 1980 (ISBN 90-200-0582-0).
2. Hugh J. Ault & Albert J. Rädler, *The German Corporation Tax Law with 1980 Amendments*, 1981 (ISBN 90-200-0642-8).
3. Paul R. McDaniel & Hugh J. Ault, *Introduction to United States International Taxation*, 1981 (ISBN 90-6544-004-6).
4. Albert J. Rädler, *German Transfer Pricing/Prix de Transfer en Allemagne*, 1984 (ISBN 90-6544-143-3).
5. Paul R. McDaniel & Stanley S. Surrey, *International Aspects of Tax Expenditures: A Comparative Study*, 1985 (ISBN 90-654-4163-8).
6. Kees van Raad, *Nondiscrimination in International Tax Law*, 1986 (ISBN 90-6544-266-9).
7. Sijbren Cnossen (ed.), *Tax Coordination in the European Community*, 1987 (ISBN 90-6544-272-3).
8. Ben Terra, *Sales Taxation. The Case of Value Added Tax in the European Community*, 1989 (ISBN 90-6544-381-9).
9. Rutsel S.J. Martha, *The Jurisdiction to Tax in International Law: Theory and Practice of Legislative Fiscal Jurisdiction*, 1989 (ISBN 90-654-4416-5).
10. Paul R. McDaniel & Hugh J. Ault, *Introduction to United States International Taxation* (3rd revised edition), 1989 (ISBN 90-6544-423-8).
11. Manuel Pires, *International Juridicial Double Taxation of Income*, 1989 (ISBN 90-6544-426-2).
12. A.H.M. Daniels, *Issues in International Partnership Taxation*, 1991 (ISBN 90-654-4577-3).
13. Arvid A. Skaar, *Permanent Establishment: Erosion of a Tax Treaty Principle*, 1992 (ISBN 90-6544-594-3).
14. Cyrille David & Geerten M.M. Michielse (eds), *Tax Treatment of Financial Instruments*, 1996 (ISBN 90-654-4666-4).
15. Herbert H. Alpert & Kees van Raad (eds), *Essays on International Taxation*, 1993 (ISBN 90-654-4781-4).
16. Wolfgang Gassner, Michael Lang & Eduard Lechner (eds), *Tax Treaties and EC Law*, 1997 (ISBN 90-411-0680-4).
17. Glória Teixeira, *Taxing Corporate Profits in the EU*, 1997 (ISBN 90-411-0703-7).
18. Michael Lang et al. (eds), *Multilateral Tax Treaties*, 1998 (ISBN 90-411-0704-5).
19. Stef van Weeghel, *The Improper Use of Tax Treaties*, 1998 (ISBN 90-411-0737-1).
20. Klaus Vogel (ed.), *Interpretation of Tax Law and Treaties and Transfer Pricing in Japan and Germany*, 1998 (ISBN 90-411-9655-2).
21. Bertil Wiman (ed.), *International Studies in Taxation: Law and Economics; Liber Amicorum Leif Mutén*, 1999 (ISBN 90-411-9692-7).
22. Alfonso J. Martín Jiménez, *Towards Corporate Tax Harmonization in the European Community*, 1999 (ISBN 90-411-9690-0).

23. Ramon J. Jeffery, *The Impact of State Sovereignty on Global Trade and International Taxation*, 1999 (ISBN 90-411-9703-6).
24. A.J. Easson, *Taxation of Foreign Direct Investment*, 1999 (ISBN 90-411-9741-9).
25. Marjaana Helminen, *The Dividend Concept in International Tax Law: Dividend Payments Between Corporate Entities*, 1999 (ISBN 90-411-9765-6).
26. Paul Kirchhof, Moris Lehner, Kees van Raad, Arndt Raupach & Michael-Rodi (eds), *International and Comparative Taxation: Essays in Honour of Klaus Vogel*, 2002 (ISBN 90-411-9841-5).
27. Krister Andersson, Peter Melz & Christer Silfverberg (eds), *Liber Amicorum Sven-Olof Lodin*, 2001 (ISBN 90-411-9850-4).
28. Juan Martín Jovanovich, *Customs Valuation and Transfer Pricing: Is It Possible to Harmonize Customs and Tax Rules?*, 2002 (ISBN 90-411-9888-1).
29. Stefano Simontacchi, *Taxation of Capital Gains under the OECD Model Convention: With Special Regard to Immovable Property*, 2007 (ISBN 978-90-411-2549-1).
30. Michael Lang, Josef Schuch, & Claus Staringer (eds), *Tax Treaty Law and EC Law*, 2007 (ISBN 978-90-411-2629-0).
31. Duncan Bentley, *Taxpayers' Rights: Theory Origin and Implementation*, 2007 (ISBN 978-90-411-2650-4).
32. Sergio André Rocha, *Interpretation of Double Taxation Conventions: General Theory and Brazilian Perspective*, 2008 (ISBN 978-90-411-2822-5).
33. Robert F. van Brederode, *Systems of General Sales Taxation: Theory, Policy and Practice*, 2009 (ISBN 978-90-411-2832-4).
34. John G. Head & Richard Krever (eds), *Tax Reform in the 21st Century: A Volume in Memory of Richard Musgrave*, 2009 (ISBN 978-90-411-2829-4).
35. Jens Wittendorff, *Transfer Pricing and the Arm's Length Principle in International Tax Law*, 2010 (ISBN 978-90-411-3270-3).
36. Marjaana Helminen, *The International Tax Law Concept of Dividend*, Second Edition, 2017 (ISBN 978-90-411-8394-1).
37. Robert F. van Brederode (ed.), *Immovable Property under VAT: A Comparative Global Analysis*, 2011 (ISBN 978-90-411-3126-3).
38. Dennis Weber & Stef van Weeghel, *The 2010 OECD Updates: Model Tax Convention & Transfer Pricing Guidelines - A Critical Review*, 2011 (ISBN 978-90-411-3812-5).
39. Yariv Brauner & Martin James McMahon, Jr. (eds), *The Proper Tax Base: Structural Fairness from an International and Comparative Perspective— Essays in Honour of Paul McDaniel*, 2012 (ISBN 978-90-411-3286-4).
40. Robert F. van Brederode (ed.), *Science, Technology and Taxation*, 2012 (ISBN 978-90-411-3125-6).
41. Oskar Henkow, *The VAT/GST Treatment of Public Bodies*, 2013 (ISBN 978-90-411-4663-2).
42. Jean Schaffner, *How Fixed Is a Permanent Establishment?*, 2013 (ISBN 978-90-411-4662-5).

43. Miguel Correia, *Taxation of Corporate Groups*, 2013 (ISBN 978-90-411-4841-4).
44. Veronika Daurer, *Tax Treaties and Developing Countries*, 2014 (ISBN 978-90-411-4982-4).
45. Claire Micheau, *State Aid, Subsidy and Tax Incentives under EU and WTO Law*, 2014 (ISBN 978-90-411-4555-0).
46. Robert F. van Brederode & Richard Krever (eds), *Legal Interpretation of Tax Law*, 2014 (ISBN 978-90-411-4945-9).
47. Radhakishan Rawal, *Taxation of Cross-border Services*, 2014 (ISBN 978-90-411-4947-3).
48. João Dácio Rolim, *Proportionality and Fair Taxation*, 2014 (ISBN 978-90-411-5838-3).
49. Paulo Rosenblatt, *General Anti-avoidance Rules for Major Developing Countries*, 2015 (ISBN 978-90-411-5839-0).
50. Gaspar Lopes Dias V.S., *Tax Arbitrage through Cross-Border Financial Engineering*, 2015 (ISBN 978-90-411-5875-8).
51. Geerten M.M. Michielse & Victor Thuronyi (eds), *Tax Design Issues Worldwide*, 2015 (ISBN 978-90-411-5610-5).
52. Oktavia Weidmann, *Taxation of Derivatives*, 2015 (ISBN 978-90-411-5977-9).
53. Chris Evans, Richard Krever & Peter Mellor (eds), *Tax Simplification*, 2015 (ISBN 978-90-411-5976-2).
54. Reuven Avi-Yonah & Joel Slemrod (eds), *Taxation and Migration*, 2015 (ISBN 978-90-411-6136-9).
55. Alexander Bosman, *Other Income under Tax Treaties: An Analysis of Article 21 of the OECD Model Convention*, 2015 (ISBN 978-90-411-6610-4).
56. John Abrahamson, *International Taxation of Manufacturing and Distribution*, 2016 (ISBN 978-90-411-6664-7).
57. Frederik Boulogne, *Shortcomings in the EU Merger Directive*, 2016 (ISBN 978-90-411-6713-2).
58. Angelika Meindl-Ringler, *Beneficial Ownership in International Tax Law*, 2016 (ISBN 978-90-411-6833-7).
59. Andreas Waltrich, *Cross-Border Taxation of Permanent Establishments: An International Comparison*, 2016 (ISBN 978-90-411-6832-0).
60. Sergio André Rocha & Allison Christians (eds), *Tax Sovereignty in the BEPS Era*, 2017 (ISBN 978-90-411-6707-1).